# TWENTIETH-CENTURY GLOBAL CHRISTIANITY

---

## PRAISE FOR THIS SERIES

"The concept of this 'people's history' represents a virtual revolution in the writing of Christian history, a change that means something dynamic, something that should draw the attention of many who do not think of themselves as likers of history. . . . These stories may come up from the basement of church history, but news about their existence deserves to be shouted from the housetops."

**MARTIN E. MARTY,** *University of Chicago Divinity School*

"Hidden for centuries by their anonymity and illiteracy, the people of God—the body of Christ, the church!—are finally having their story told, and by some of today's finest historians of the church. The saints, bishops, and theologians of traditional histories can now be placed against the panoramic and fascinating backdrop of the lived religion of ordinary men and women of faith. Highly recommended."

**MARK U. EDWARDS JR.,** *Harvard Divinity School*

---

# A PEOPLE'S HISTORY OF CHRISTIANITY

## Denis R. Janz
*General Editor*

Volume 1
## CHRISTIAN ORIGINS
Richard Horsley, editor

Volume 2
## LATE ANCIENT CHRISTIANITY
Virginia Burrus, editor

Volume 3
## BYZANTINE CHRISTIANITY
Derek Krueger, editor

Volume 4
## MEDIEVAL CHRISTIANITY
Daniel E. Bornstein, editor

Volume 5
## REFORMATION CHRISTIANITY
Peter Matheson, editor

Volume 6
## MODERN CHRISTIANITY TO 1900
Amanda Porterfield, editor

Volume 7
## TWENTIETH-CENTURY GLOBAL CHRISTIANITY
Mary Farrell Bednarowski, editor

# A PEOPLE'S HISTORY OF CHRISTIANITY

Volume 7

# TWENTIETH-CENTURY GLOBAL CHRISTIANITY

MARY FARRELL BEDNAROWSKI

Editor

FORTRESS PRESS

*Minneapolis*

TWENTIETH-CENTURY GLOBAL CHRISTIANITY
A People's History of Christianity, Volume 7

Cover images: © George Doyle / Getty Images, © Plush Studios / Getty Images, © Carole Gomez / iStockphoto.
Cover design: Laurie Ingram
Book design: James Korsmo

Further materials on this volume and the entire series can be found online at www.peopleshistoryofchristianity.com.

Library of Congress Cataloging-in-Publication Data

Twentieth-century global Christianity / edited by Mary Farrell Bednarowski.
      p. cm. — (A people's history of Christianity ; v. 7)
  Includes bibliographical references and index.
  ISBN 978-0-8006-3417-9 (alk. paper)
  1. Christianity—20th century. I. Bednarowski, Mary Farrell.
  BR479.T84 2008
  270.8'2—dc22

                          2007045636

The paper used in this publication meets the minimum requirements of American National Standard for Information Sciences—Permanence of Paper for Printed Library Materials, ANSI Z329.48-1984.

Manufactured in U.S.A.
  12    11    10    09    08    1    2    3    4    5    6    7    8    9    10

# CONTENTS

# CONTRIBUTORS

**Victoria J. Barnett** is Staff Director of Church Relations at the United States Holocaust Memorial Museum. She is also one of the general editors of the Dietrich Bonhoeffer Works, the English translation series of Bonhoeffer's complete works being published by Fortress Press. She is the author of *For the Soul of the People: Protestant Protest against Hitler* (Oxford University Press, 1992) and *Bystanders: Conscience and Complicity during the Holocaust* (Greenwood, 1999). She is the editor/translator of Wolfgang Gerlach's *And the Witnesses Were Silent: The Confessing Church and the Jews* (University of Nebraska Press, 2000) and the new revised edition of Eberhard Bethge's *Dietrich Bonhoeffer: A Biography* (Fortress Press, 2000).

**Mary Farrell Bednarowski** is Professor Emerita of Religious Studies at United Theological Seminary of the Twin Cities, Minnesota. Her teaching, research, and writing interests have focused on encounters between religion and culture in American religious history with particular interest in theological creativity and innovation in women's religious writings, new religions, literature, and religious autobiography. Her books include *American Religion: A Cultural Perspective* (Prentice-Hall, 1984); *New Religions and the Theological Imagination in America* (Indiana University Press, 1989); and *The Religious Imagination of American Women* (Indiana University Press, 1999).

**Margaret Bendroth** is Executive Director of the American Congregational Association and director of the Congregational Library in Boston, Massachusetts. She is the author of several books, including

*Fundamentalism and Gender, 1875 to the Present* (Yale University Press, 1993) and *Growing Up Protestant: Parents, Children, and Mainline Churches* (Rutgers University Press, 2002). She was co-editor, with Virginia Brereton, of an award-winning book of essays, *Women and Twentieth-Century Protestantism* (University of Illinois Press, 2002).

**Oscar Cole-Arnal** is Professor Emeritus of the History of Christianity, Waterloo Lutheran Seminary, Waterloo, Ontario. He has published five books, including a Canadian liberation theology and *Priests in Working Class Blue* (Paulist, 1986), about the French worker-priests, and over twenty articles, mostly about modern French Catholicism. Currently he is working on two books, one on Quebec Catholicism and the working class and the other a theological book with a colleague Timothy Hegedus on the politically radical side of the Protestant doctrine of justification by grace through faith.

**Valerie DeMarinis** is Professor in Psychology of Religion and Cultural Psychology and chair of the Department of Religion and the Social Sciences at Uppsala University in Uppsala, Sweden. She is the director of the European Union Diploma Program in Psychology of Religion for the Scandinavian countries. Her current research projects include the subject of religiosity and meaning-making as well as cultural psychology, health, and intervention systems, including an interdisciplinary project focused on Afro-Brazilian culture, religiosity, and empowerment in Salvador, Bahia, Brazil.

**Eleazar S. Fernandez**, a native of the Philippines, is currently Professor of Constructive Theology at United Theological Seminary of the Twin Cities, Minnesota. Among his major works are *Reimagining the Human* (Chalice, 2004), *Realizing the America of Our Hearts*, co-edited with Fumitaka Matsuoka (Chalice, 2003), *A Dream Unfinished*, co-edited with Fernando Segovia (Orbis, 2000), and *Toward a Theology of Struggle* (Orbis, 1994).

**Bruce David Forbes** is the Arthur L. Bunch Professor of Religious Studies at Morningside College in Sioux City, Iowa. He is a cofounder of the Religion and Popular Culture program unit within the American Academy of Religion. He is the coeditor of *Religion and Popular Culture in America* (University of California Press, 2000, revised 2005) and *Rapture, Revelation, and the End Times: Exploring the Left Behind Series* (Palgrave Macmillan, 2004), and he is the author of *Christmas: A Candid History* (University of California Press, 2007).

**Patrick Henry** taught in the religion department at Swarthmore College in Pennsylvania (1967–1984) and was executive director of the Collegeville Institute for Ecumenical and Cultural Research in Minnesota (1984–2004). His books include *New Directions in New Testament Study* (Westminster, 1979), *The Ironic Christian's Companion: Finding the Marks of God's Grace in the World* (Riverhead, 1999), and, with Donald Swearer, *For the Sake of the World: The Spirit of Buddhist and Christian Monasticism* (Fortress Press, 1989). He is the editor of *Benedict's Dharma: Buddhists Reflect on the Rule of St. Benedict* (Riverhead, 2001).

**Ada María Isasi-Díaz**, a native of Cuba, is Professor of Ethics and Theology at Drew University, New Jersey. Since the 1970s she has lectured extensively in the USA and abroad and has taught in Cuba, Philippines, and Korea. Her publications include *Hispanic Women: Prophetic Voice in the Church* (University of Scranton Press, 2006), *En la Lucha—A Hispanic Women's Liberation Theology* (Fortress Press, 1993), *Mujerista Theology: A Theology for the 21st Century* (Orbis, 1996), and *La Lucha Continues—Mujerista Theology* (Orbis, 2004). She is currently writing a book on justice as a reconciliatory praxis of care and tenderness.

**Paul Mojzes** is Professor of Religious Studies at Rosemont College, Rosemont, Pennsylvania, and is visiting professor of Holocaust and Genocide Studies at Richard Stockton College of New Jersey. A native of Yugoslavia, Mojzes is the coeditor of the *Journal of Ecumenical Studies* and founder and editor of *Religion in Eastern Europe*. He is the author of five and the editor of several books and has written many articles. Among his recent books are *Religious Liberty in Eastern Europe and the USSR* (1992), *Yugoslavian Inferno: Ethnoreligious Warfare in the Balkans* (Continuum, 1994), and, as editor or coeditor, *Religion and War in Bosnia* (American Academy of Religion, 1998) and *Interreligious Dialogue toward Reconciliation in Macedonia and Bosnia* (*Journal of Ecumenical Studies*, 2002).

**Mark A. Noll** is Francis A. McAnaney Professor of History at the University of Notre Dame. His recent books include *America's God: From Jonathan Edwards to Abraham Lincoln* (Oxford University Press, 2002), *The Civil War as a Theological Crisis* (University of North Carolina, 2006), and *Race, Religion, and American Politics from Nat Turner to George W. Bush: A Short History* (2008). He has also written widely on the history of evangelical Protestantism, including *The Scandal of the Evangelical Mind* (Eerdmans, 1994) and *The Rise of Evangelicalism: The Age of Edwards, Whitefield, and the Wesleys* (InterVarsity, 2004).

**Mercy Amba Oduyoye**, a native of Ghana, has been a high school teacher and a Professor of Religious Studies and served as Deputy General Secretary of the World Council of Churches in Geneva. She is the author of numerous articles and a number of books, among them *Daughters of Anowa: African Women and Patriarchy* (Orbis, 1995), *Introducing African Women's Theology* (Pilgrim, 2001), and *Beads and Strands: Reflections of an African Woman on Christianity in Africa* (Orbis, 2004). Her research interests and publications reflect her concern for the liberation of African women, and she is presently serving as the founding director of the Talitha Qumi Centre, an institute of Women, Religion, and Culture on the campus of Trinity Theological Seminary, Accra, Ghana.

**Ann M. Pederson** is Professor of Religion at Augustana College in Sioux Falls, South Dakota. She is also an adjunct Associate Professor in the Section of Ethics and Humanities at the Sanford School of Medicine at the University of South Dakota. She has authored three books, including *The Music of Creation* (Fortress Press, 2005), which she coauthored with Arthur Peacocke. She is also the author of numerous articles in various journals on topics ranging from feminist thought in religion and science to Lutheran theology. Her current research interests focus on the intersection between theology and medicine.

**Luis N. Rivera-Pagán** is Emeritus Professor of Ecumenics at Princeton Theological Seminary. His publications include *A Violent Evangelism:*

*The Political and Religious Conquest of the Americas* (Westminster John Knox, 1992), *Mito, exilio y demonios: literatura y teología en América Latina* (1996), *Diálogos y polifonías: perspectivas y reseñas* (1999), and *Essays from the Diaspora* (2002). He has edited the official report of the most recent assembly of the World Council of Churches, *God, in Your Grace . . .* (Geneva, 2007). His current area of research focuses on theology and culture in Latin America.

**Rosetta E. Ross** teaches religious studies at Spelman College in Atlanta, Georgia. Her research and writing explore the role of religion in black women's activism. She is author of *Witnessing and Testifying: Black Women, Religion, and Civil Rights*, which examines religion as a source that helped engender and sustain activities of seven black women civil rights leaders. Ross and her partner, Ronald S. Bonner, reside in Atlanta.

**Ethan R. Sanders** is a postgraduate student on the faculty of history at the University of Cambridge. While he has a broad interest in global Christianity during the last two centuries, his main area of study is in the history of modern Africa. He has written a forthcoming article on Christianity in Central Africa, and his current project focuses on the role played by graduates of Universities' Mission to Central Africa schools in the Tanganyika African National Union and the making of Tanzanian nationalism. He is a member of Selwyn College.

**Cristina L. H. Traina** is Associate Professor of Religion at Northwestern University, where she teaches courses in Christian theology and Christian and comparative ethics. She is the author of *Natural Law and Feminist Ethics: The End of the Anathemas* (Georgetown University Press, 1999) and of a number of articles on the ethics of sexuality and assisted reproduction, theology and ethics of childhood, and topics related to trade, immigration, and the environment. She is currently writing a book on the ethics of touch in parent-child relations.

**Jean-Paul Wiest**, founder and former director of the Center for Mission Research and Study at Maryknoll, is presently Research Director of the Beijing Center for Chinese Studies and Distinguished Fellow of the EDS-Steward Chair at the Ricci Institute of the University of

San Francisco. His primary field of research is the history of Christianity in modern and contemporary China with an emphasis on Sino-Western cultural and religious interactions. He has published extensively in French, English, and Chinese. Among other volumes, he is the author, with Thomas Bamat, of *Popular Catholicism in a World Church: Seven Case Histories in Inculturation* (Orbis, 1999).

# ILLUSTRATIONS

Color Plates (following page 204)

# FOREWORD

This seven-volume series breaks new ground by looking at Christianity's past from the vantage point of a people's history. It is church history, yes, but church history with a difference: "church," we insist, is not to be understood first and foremost as the hierarchical-institutional-bureaucratic corporation; rather, above all, it is the laity, the ordinary faithful, the people. Their religious lives, their pious practices, their self-understandings as Christians, and the way all of this grew and changed over the last two millennia—*this* is the unexplored territory in which we are here setting foot.

To be sure, the undertaking known as people's history, as it is applied to secular themes, is hardly a new one among academic historians. Referred to sometimes as history from below, or grassroots history, or popular history, it was born about a century ago, in conscious opposition to the elitism of conventional (some call it Rankean) historical investigation, fixated as this was on the "great" deeds of "great" men, and little else. What had always been left out of the story, of course, was the vast majority of human beings: almost all women, obviously, but then too all those who could be counted among the socially inferior, the economically distressed, the politically marginalized, the educationally deprived, or the culturally unrefined. Had not various elites always despised "the people"? Cicero, in first-century BCE Rome, referred to them as "urban filth and dung"; Edmund Burke, in eighteenth-century London, called them "the swinish multitude"; and in between, this loathing of "the meaner sort" was almost universal among the privileged. When the discipline called "history" was professionalized in the nineteenth century, traditional gentlemen historians perpetuated this contempt, if not by outright vilification, then at least by keeping the masses invisible. Thus when people's history came on the scene, it was not only a means for uncovering an unknown dimension of the past but also in some sense an instrument for righting an injustice. Today its cumulative contribution is enormous, and its home in the academic world is assured.

Only quite recently has the discipline formerly called "church history" and now more often "the history of Christianity" begun to open itself up to this approach. Its agenda over the last two centuries has been dominated by other facets of this religion's past, such as theology, dogma, institutions, and ecclesio-political relations. Each of these has in fact long since evolved into its own subdiscipline. Thus the history of theology has concentrated on the self-understandings of Christian intellectuals. Historians of dogma have examined the way in which church leaders came to formulate teachings that they then pronounced normative for all Christians. Experts on institutional history have researched the formation, growth, and functioning of leadership offices, bureaucratic structures, official decision-making processes, and so forth. And specialists in the history of church-state relations have worked to fathom the complexities of the institution's interface with its sociopolitical context, above all by studying leaders on both sides.

Collectively, these conventional kinds of church history have yielded enough specialized literature to fill a very large library, and those who read in this library will readily testify to its amazing treasures. Erudite as it is, however, the Achilles' heel of this scholarship, taken as a whole, is that it has told the history of Christianity as the story of one small segment of those who have claimed the name "Christian." What has been studied almost exclusively until now is the religion of various elites, whether spiritual elites, or intellectual elites, or power elites. Without a doubt, mystics and theologians, pastors, priests, bishops, and popes are worth studying. But at best they altogether constitute perhaps 5 percent of all Christians over two millennia. What about the rest? Does not a balanced history of Christianity, not to mention our sense of historical justice, require that attention be paid to them?

Around the mid-twentieth century, a handful of scholars began, hesitantly and yet insistently, to press this question on the international guild of church historians. Since that time, the study of the other 95 percent has gained momentum: ever more ambitious research projects have been launched; innovative scholarly methods have been developed, critiqued, and refined; and a growing public interest has greeted the results. Academics and nonacademics alike want to know about this aspect of Christianity's past. Who were these people—the voiceless, the ordinary faithful who wrote no theological treatises, whose statues adorn no basilicas, who negotiated no concordats, whose very names themselves are largely lost to historical memory? What can we know about their religious consciousness, their devotional practice, their understanding of the faith, their values, beliefs, feelings, habits, attitudes, and their deepest fears, hopes, loves, hatreds, and so forth? And what about the troublemakers, the excluded, the heretics, those defined by conventional history as the losers? Can a face be put on any of them?

Today, even after half a century of study, answers are still in short supply. It must be conceded that the field is in its infancy, both methodologically and in terms of what remains to be investigated. Very often historians now find themselves no longer interrogating literary texts but rather artifacts, the remains of material culture, court records, wills, popular art, graffiti, and so forth. What is already clear is that many traditional assumptions, timeworn clichés, and well-loved nuggets of conventional wisdom about Christianity's past will have to be abandoned. When the Christian masses are made the leading protagonists of the story, we begin to glimpse a plot with dramatically new contours. In fact, a rewriting of this history is now getting under way, and this may well be the discipline's larger task for the twenty-first century.

A People's History of Christianity is our contribution to this enterprise. In it we gather up the early harvest of this new approach, showcase the current state of the discipline, and plot a trajectory into the future. Essentially what we offer here is a preliminary attempt at a new and more adequate version of the Christian story—one that features the people. Is it comprehensive? Impossible. Definitive? Hardly. A responsible, suggestive, interesting base to build on? We are confident that it is.

Close to a hundred historians of Christianity have generously applied their various types of expertise to this project, whether as advisers or editors or contributors. They have in common no universally agreed-on methodology, nor do they even concur on how precisely to define problematic terms such as "popular religion." What they do share is a conviction that rescuing the Christian people from their historic anonymity is important, that reworking the story's plot with lay piety as the central narrative will be a contribution of lasting value, and that reversing the condescension, not to say contempt, that all too often has marred elite views of the people is long overdue. If progress is made on these fronts, we believe, the groundwork for a new history of Christianity will have been prepared.

In this seventh and final volume of our People's History, we can begin to gauge how far Christian believers have come since the earliest "Jesus movements" of first-century Galilee. We would be living in a dream-world, however, if we thought that here the loose ends would be neatly tied up in an ultimate denouement, of either triumph or oblivion. Satisfying as that might be on one level, it would be less than honest. History is not over, nor is it transparent. The data dealt with here are ambiguous. Direction is difficult to discern: we are forced to speak not of one but of multiple trajectories. For help in sorting through and making sense of twentieth-century Christianity's various trends, movements, currents and countercurrents, I cannot think of a better guide than the editor of this volume, Mary Farrell Bednarowski. Her intelligence, her careful judgment, her grasp of the big picture, and her warm humanity have made my work with her a happy learning experience at every stage.

As this publication nears completion, I cannot fail to express my appreciation to the many people at Fortress Press who facilitated the project at every stage. It was seven years ago in Denver that Editor-in-Chief Michael West planted the initial idea and asked me to develop it. Since then he has been a constant source of encouragement, wise advice, and good humor. I owe him a large debt of gratitude.

Denis R. Janz, General Editor

# MULTIPLICITY AND AMBIGUITY

## MARY FARRELL BEDNAROWSKI

### CHRISTIAN HISTORY AS STORY

On the eve of *el dia de los muertos* we are gathered in the crypt of the *parrochia*, the parish church, in the center of San Miguel de Allende in the state of Guanajuato, Mexico. Our guide, Cesar del Rio, points to the tomb of his uncle who committed suicide when Cesar was three years old, not long after his uncle had had an encounter with what he experienced as an evil force or spirit in this same crypt where other ancestors are buried. Cesar acknowledges both the impossibility that this event was "real"—he knows a lot about psychology—and his own inability to disbelieve it completely. He tells us that he is typical of many Mexican people born in the 1960s: of *mestizo* (European and indigenous) heritage; a professional person who holds a law degree; a teacher of history; Roman Catholic by heritage and, at least in part, by belief. He is, he tells us, "superstitious." He participates fully and proudly in an annual procession that begins its winding way down from the mountains behind San Miguel at midnight and culminates in the city at sunrise. He occasionally visits the shrine of Our Lady of Guadalupe with his mother and other relatives. As he looks at the shrine's much-venerated painting, he is powerfully moved because of all she means to the people of Mexico and to people of other Latin American countries, but he asks Our Lady, "Are you real? Do you really help us?"[1]

1

\* \* \*

The island of Gotland lies in the Baltic Sea where it borders Latvia, Estonia, and Sweden, to which it has belonged since 1645. A short ferry ride to the north is the island of Faro, site of Ingmar Bergman's home and film studios. Only fifty kilometers wide (population approximately 57,600), Gotland is home to more than ninety medieval churches built between 1100 and 1350. Church-building ceased in 1350 after Gotland's fortunes as a major Hanseatic League port declined. The churches were left "frozen in time" according to a pamphlet, "The Key to the Churches in the Diocese of Visby," published for visitors by the Church of Sweden (Lutheran). Although thousands of stained glass windows, wooden statues, and wall paintings were destroyed during and after the Reformation, the churches themselves were not destroyed, most likely because there were not sufficient funds to demolish and rebuild them, as happened in other parts of Sweden. The churches may be frozen in time architecturally, but they are all still in use today, not merely tourist attractions. Congregations are small, between a hundred and three hundred, and attendance is low at the every-other-Sunday services, sometimes not more than ten or twenty. The churches are "in the midst of life" on Gotland, says the Bishop of Visby, concerned not just with church life but with what happens in the community: "Spiritual and secular interests are interlinked. The church on Gotland has accepted the challenge of forming modern church services in medieval church chambers."[2]

\* \* \*

Marika Cico (pronounced "tsitso"), a ninety-five-year-old Albanian Orthodox Christian when writer Jim Forest met her in the early 1990s, tells the story of the first liturgy celebrated in the town of Korca since the communist government closed all the churches in 1967. "Finally," she said, "the Communist time began to end [in 1990]. We were so happy, but all the churches were closed. In response to our request, the government in Korca decided we could have one church back and that we would be permitted to have the liturgy there. The first service we prepared for was Theophany on the 6th of January in 1991. We had been preparing everything, but needed a bell! Then we found the solu-

tion, a large brass mortar used for grinding garlic. It rang perfectly."
The "time of no churches" was over.[3]

\* \* \*

"When he was in his mid-teens Sadao Watanabe, a well-known
Japanese print artist, first visited a Christian church, introduced by
a neighbor who was a school teacher. He had lost his father when
he was ten years old, and tended to live a closed and isolated life. He
described his first impression of Christianity as follows:

"'In the beginning I had a negative reaction to Christianity. The
atmosphere was full of 'the smell of butter,' so foreign to the ordinary
Japanese.'

"Now in his print work he joyfully depicts the celebration of the
holy communion with *sushi*, pickled fish and rice, a typical Japanese
dish, served on traditional folk art plates. For him rice is a more natural
and a more fitting symbol of daily food than bread which is foreign."[4]

\* \* \*

According to longtime Maryknoll missionaries Joseph Healey and
Donald Sybert, there are many concrete African metaphors for the
church as "the people of God." One is the fireplace or the hearth:

> In Kenya, the Kikuyu word for "fire" is "mwaki." Traditionally, a
> small group or community gathered around the fire, fireplace, or
> hearth. A neighborhood community was called "mwaki" from the
> way that people made a fire and shared that fire. When the fire
> had been lit in one home, all the other homes in the neighborhood
> took their fire from that one place. This sharing of fire helped
> them to identify themselves as one community. "Mwaki" or "fire"
> was symbolic of other types of sharing and forms of communion,
> such as celebrations, performing local ceremonies, and discussing
> and approving important community issues. The fireplace with a
> cooking pot is a symbol in Africa for God blessing the people.[5]

\* \* \*

An eighty-year-old Christian man stands guard at his wife's hospital
bed in Minneapolis, Minnesota. She has been on life support for several

months and is unresponsive. Her doctors are concerned that her body is beginning to deteriorate. Her husband is convinced that he has the moral obligation to keep her alive "until God takes her." Their adult children are divided on how to proceed.

In the neonatal intensive care unit of the same hospital, young parents, members of a social justice–oriented Roman Catholic parish, watch their twin daughters from behind a wall of glass. Born fourteen weeks premature, they are attached to numerous tubes and tiny enough to fit in their father's hand. There is no certainty about what lies ahead for them, physically or mentally. At the very least there will be many surgeries and months in the hospital. The parents have always said to each other that they would never choose—for themselves—to hold on to life at all costs. But what are the most loving, the most Christian decisions to make for their daughters? And what will help them decide? Medical advice? The counsel of clergy? The wisdom of their own hearts?

* * *

The *New Saint Joseph People's Prayer Book*, published by the Catholic Book Publishing Company in 1980 and 1993, is available at any ordinary Roman Catholic religious goods store. Along with "traditional and contemporary prayers for every need and occasion," there is a section of more than eighty pages called "Prayers from Other Religions": Protestant and Orthodox Christians; Jewish religion; religions of the East; and religions of the Americas (Native American prayers). One of the most intriguing prayers, given the history of Christianity's innumerable and often violent disputes over matters of doctrine and ritual, is a "Prayer of Thanksgiving for the Gifts of the Various Christian Churches," with invocations such as the following: "For the *Eastern Orthodox Church*: its secret treasure of mystic experience; its marvelous liturgy; its regard for the collective life and its common will as a source of authority," and "For the power of the *Methodists* to awaken the conscience of Christians to our social evils; and for their emphasis upon the witness of personal experience, and upon the power of the disciplined life."[6] Who would have dreamed in the years before the Second Vatican Council (1962–1965) that such a prayer book, meant for ordinary Catholics, would exist before the end of the twentieth century, if ever?

* * *

So many stories! And such various stories. Religion is story before it is anything else, and it is story after it is everything else. This is the intriguing claim of sociologist, novelist, and Roman Catholic priest Andrew Greeley, one that he has made many times in both scholarly and popular arenas. A people's history of Christianity is, finally, story-history—not analyses of theological abstractions or institutional development and disputes. These are stories about daily life, about emotions and struggles, about transformations and tragedies, about the devotional piety and convictions and doubts, the creation and disruption and re-creation of families, communities, and worldviews. They are not isolated stories, because stories without context and interpretation are merely anecdotes—interesting, often touching or instructive, but not necessarily illuminating about broader issues and patterns. Thus for each of the stories above and for those that will follow in the chapters of this volume, there are back stories, distinctive histories of religious and cultural circumstances.

We find in these twentieth-century stories multiple plotlines that take on powerful significance when we look at them in terms of people's history:

- encounters between intense religious devotion and modern and postmodern consciousness;
- the waning of church membership and attendance and the decline of this institution's cultural relevance—or so it appears at the moment—in many developed countries of the West;
- the repression and then the reemergence of Christianity in the aftermath of totalitarian regimes;
- the several-centuries-long unfolding of religious dynamics related to colonialism, inculturation, and postcolonialism in Africa, Asia, and Latin America;
- the realization that women, while very much present in the church, have been for the most part absent from written history;
- the bewilderment not just of ordinary people but of experts,

both religious and medical, over issues related to the beginning and the end of life;

- the realities associated with increasing religious pluralism and the discovery that "the other," whether Christian or non-Christian, now lives not on another continent or in the neighboring town but next door;
- the discoveries of dimensions of power and wisdom, courage and creativity that figure prominently in the people's stories and that bring new depth to the study of Christianity.

The people's histories of Christianity in the twentieth century differ from continent to continent, country to country, tradition to tradition, and even neighborhood to neighborhood. For that reason the stories and the themes in this last volume of A People's History of Christianity are geographically and culturally, chronologically and methodologically, literally and figuratively all over the map. The chapters cannot attempt to cover global Christianity, from the beginning of the twentieth century to its end. There are other volumes available that take this chronological approach.[7] Instead, this book offers a range of angles on some of the crises, the opportunities, the challenges, the disillusionments, and the hopeful surprises that Christianity has encountered in the twentieth century: global, regional, communal, and individual. A more modest title for this volume might well be *Some Selected Elements of a People's History of Twentieth-Century Global Christianity.*

## CHRISTIANITY ON EVERY CONTINENT

By the end of the twentieth century Christianity had taken root and shape all over the world and in the consciousness of Christians as a global religion. One of the major themes of this volume is the extent to which Christianity has demonstrated its capacity to assume multiple forms and still be recognizable as the religion of Jesus. If the history of the people's Christianity in the twentieth century tells us anything, it lets us know that whatever else it may be—and this it has in common with other world religions—it is a vast arena of human creativity whose symbols, rituals, scriptures, and stories are translatable across multiple cultural and historical boundaries.

The face of Jesus is familiar when it appears in the art of many cultures, no matter how different he looks from the famous and ubiquitous *Head of Christ* by Warner Sallman.[8] The elements of communion are recognizable within the forms of dried fish and rice and in the basic foods of other parts of the world. What is essential, the histories of the people tell us, is the gathering for a meal taken together. The stories of the Bible are translatable, capable of speaking movingly to experiences that cross many kinds of boundaries, although this kind of translating is not merely a process of substituting the words of one language for the words of another. Translation is interpretation is transformation, and the Bible in the "non-biblical world," as Hong Kong scholar Kwok Pui-lan tells us, is not the same "book" that it is in the West.[9] To claim these things is by no means to make the case that the history of the people's Christianity in the twentieth century is a history of triumphalism, one of Christianity's traditional temptations to excess. It is to say that all these things speak of the people's history of Christianity as the history of the people's creativity: taking the "stuff" of Christianity—its scriptures, symbols, rituals, and moral codes—and making it their own in various parts of the world.

Fig. 0.1. *Head of Christ* by Warner Sallman (1892–1968). © 1941 Warner Press, Inc., Anderson, Ind. Used by permission.

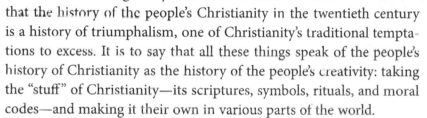

## CHRISTENDOM OR CHRISTIANITIES

As many sources tell us, Christianity at the end of the twentieth century remained the largest of the world's religions, although not by as large a percentage of the world's population as was the case in 1900.[10] Much of the news about Christianity at the end of the twentieth century focused on the extent to which its population centers had moved to the southern hemisphere. Predictions abound about what this means. Will the shift southward bring with it very different forms of Christianity, the likes of which we have not seen before? Or, as some suggest, will it be mostly a premodern Christianity, a supernaturalist Christianity, very familiar to anthropologists and historians of religions?

If the number of Christians is increasing in the southern hemisphere, what is happening in the north? What does the history of Christianity in the West tell us? Is Christianity in the northern hemisphere losing its vitality, its cultural relevance? Is it collapsing into secular culture, becoming so "worldly" that soon its distinctive characteristics will no longer be discernible? Or is it changing its forms in ways that are only barely evident at present, moving away from reliance on church bureaucracies and beginning to revitalize the churches with new forms of community? Some huge urban Roman Catholic parishes in the United States are dividing into "house churches" and at the same time retaining their connection to "the mother church,"

and popular and scholarly religious journals and books in North America and Great Britain are full of articles about "the emerging church," devoted to suggestions about what the church needs to look like and be like in a pluralist, postmodern world.

The nearly two-millennia-long history of Christianity makes it unlikely that any one form of Christianity will prevail in either hemisphere. More and more, historians are discovering that Christianity has been diverse from its very beginnings, much more diverse, as it turns out, than we have imagined. The earlier volumes in this series focus as much on diversity as this one does, in fact, and it seems wise to take a clue from sociologists of religion like Rodney Stark and William Sims Bainbridge, who make the case in *The Future of Religion* that in any religious economy, as they call it, there are always three processes going on at the same time: secularization;

**Fig. 0.2.** *Jesus Christ and close-up* by Kaadaa. Photo © Kaadaa/Stock Illustration Source/Getty Images. Used by permission.

innovation, or the creation of new forms of religion; and revival, which they interpret to mean "restoring vigorous unworldliness to a conventional faith."[11] However true that may be in some contexts, I would argue in addition that at the end of the twentieth century "revival" often meant restoring a *worldly holiness* to conventional faith, bringing it down to earth. Stark and Bainbridge's insight nonetheless helps to make sense of why no one trajectory is adequate to interpret what is going on in the religious history of ordinary people, particularly if we think about global Christianity as the economy with which we are concerned, not just one continent or region. The stories in the chapters of this volume will help make clear not only the extent to which secularization, innovation, and revival are intertwined with each other all over the world but the multiple ways that Christians in different parts of the world are in touch with each other.

Present-day mission history is, in fact, instructive about these realities. Missionaries at mid-century and even more recently have been maligned for bringing colonialism, imperialism, an egregious sense of cultural and religious superiority, and so many kinds of exploitation to Asia, Africa, and Latin America that they undermined any of the goods of education and medical services they brought as well. By the end of the twentieth century, missionaries were coming to be seen as experts about the dynamics of cross-cultural exchange, stressing especially the fact that "it was the missionaries who were converted" to new cultures and new ways of being Christian and that mission work is an experience in reciprocity, not of merely "bringing to." Speaking in particular to the widespread assumption that "Christian Britain has died," Kenneth R. Ross, general secretary of the Church of Scotland's Board of World Mission, speaks of "God's spiral of renewal" and wonders whether the "new Christendom" of the southern hemisphere, once the mission territory of the Church of Scotland, may become the vehicle for its own spiritual renewal.[12] It may well be that the people's history of twentieth-century Christianity has been teaching us to speak not of "Christendom" and where its center has been or will be found at a given moment in history, but of "Christianities," whose overlapping circles will have different kinds of centers visible to each other across the globe.

## NEW QUESTIONS

Looking for and learning to tell the people's histories requires a kind of metanoia on the part of historians, a turning around, an academic conversion experience. We know that church historians are only recently finding their way to the realities and the significance of people's history, because that history, however interesting to anthropologists, sociologists, psychologists, and social historians, has not appeared to reveal where the real action was taking place in the church. The people's ordinary lives, we assumed, were focused on matters not weighty enough to survive the filtering process of histories concerned with philosophical or theological claims that in an earlier time—not so long ago!—were assumed to embody the truest, highest aspects of the church irrespective of historical or cultural context. This is a bit of a caricature, of course, but even though each of us has our own individual histories, it has taken us a long time as scholars to discover the obvious: the historical and religious significance of the daily life that surrounds us in particular places, *lo cotidiano*, as Ada María Isasi-Díaz calls it.

In a book that has become very popular among North American Protestants and Catholics, *Memories of God: Theological Reflections on a Life*,[13] Roberta Bondi expressed the astonishment she felt upon discovering at an ecumenical consultation that the particularities of her own life story not only could be shared but took on theological and historical significance when placed in the context of the broader community. They were not merely personal or cloyingly trivial in the greater scheme of things. In the stories of those broader "gathered" communities, the people's history takes on new life and gives new life in return. In her study of religious congregations in the United States, *Pillars of Faith: American Congregations and Their Partners*, religious sociologist Nancy Ammerman points to a gap in the study of religion: "People studying religion either wrote about the great theological and cultural trends of the day or asked individuals what they believed."[14] People's history helps to fill that gap.

Writing history in new ways requires asking new questions and demands new geometric configurations. It is not enough to invert the traditional triangle of hierarchy on top and the faithful on the bottom and declare, "Now we will write about 'the people.'" People's history is about new kinds of relationships and finding new ways to assess the value of the people's history for understanding the nature of the church. We have only recently learned to ask questions like the following: Whose voices have we simply never heard in histories of Christianity? What stories do we need to unearth about the church and about Christianity that will reveal to us why there are so few names of women in standard religious histories when women have outnumbered men in church membership for centuries? How much of the history of Christianity have we missed by failing to take note of the experiences of half of all Christians and to record them? Mission historian Dana Robert makes a powerful case that world Christianity is a women's movement and that its contours and its details have been subsumed within larger narratives about global history. Robert asks what the study of Christianity would be like if women's stories were put in the center of research with an emphasis on the complex and diverse reasons that motivate women to convert to Christianity.[15]

There is no end to the questions. What realities in the lives of ordinary people in Latin America have moved so many to embrace Pentecostalism? What symbols and rituals will people in the countries of northern Europe draw from as they encounter the need for spiritual depth while the influence of state churches appears to be waning? By what strategies do ordinary people keep Christianity alive at times and in places where displaying any attachment to Christian practice, even giving your child a "Christian" name, is to court censure, unemployment, imprisonment, and even death? What is it about Christianity and its stories, scriptures, and rituals that have spoken to the lives of growing numbers of people in Africa and Asia, far from the Christian heartlands of the West? To what extent and in what ways is the church involved when the people say "Enough!" about economic injustices and exploitation?

## COMMONALITIES, DISTINCTIONS, PERSPECTIVES

Volume 7 has in common with the other volumes in the series the challenge of exploring how the history of Christianity and Christians changes its contours when we emphasize the people's history rather than the institution's history. Like the others, this volume takes for granted that no single definition of "the people" is adequate for the stories that follow, particularly not those traditional polarities by which we have tried to decide who is ordinary and who is not and in spite of the fact that there is some truth in all of them: laity rather than clergy; more likely to be female than male; uneducated rather than educated; poor rather than affluent; nonprofessional rather than professional (meaning those who have devoted their lives to the church); and, more recently, southern rather than northern. These either-or configurations mask the complexities of interaction that make up the lives of Christians. There are just too many kinds of cross-pollination among categories for this on-the-one-hand, on-the-other-hand typology to work.

A major purpose of the whole series is to open up multiple meanings of "people's history," even some that appear contradictory. Are there circumstances in which theologians or priests, bishops or nuns might be considered "people" too? Priests and nuns in many parts of the world live the life of the people they serve, suffering with them the deprivations of poverty and the lack of even modest political power. Theologians, some of them famous, undergo crises of faith that are not resolved by knowledge of sophisticated theological formulations, and their existential angst cannot be separated from that of any other Christian. One can turn that question around the other way, too, of course, and ask whether there aren't contexts in which "the people" become the experts, for example, the Latina women about whom Ada María Isasi-Díaz writes—they put together rituals based on their knowledge of traditional Roman Catholic devotions and the experiences of their own lives. The task is not to find the single best definition but to demonstrate what a lively, fruitful, and provocative concept "ordinary people's history" can be—to say nothing of subversive. We are, really, just getting started.

"Ordinary," we discover, is itself a relative term that varies not only from culture to culture but even from body to body. In many cultures, as will become clear in the chapters to follow, most Christians are always hungry. It is a basic reality of their daily lives. Some very astute observations about what it means to live an "ordinary" life are emerging from the writings of people with physical disabilities who speak in terms of learning how to live their "difficult but ordinary" lives.[16]

There are also issues particular to this volume. Volume 7 focuses on a one-hundred-year period of time rather than on a discernible era in church history like the Reformation. In his *History of Christianity in the United States and Canada,* Mark Noll reminds us, "It is a sloppy intellectual habit to think that the dynamics of lived human experience can be neatly packaged into discrete decades."[17] No doubt this is even more true of the arbitrary demarcation of one hundred years. It is striking and very much a part of the people's history that the twentieth century has seen so much scientific, medical, and technological progress and so little movement in the realm of "human" progress. The century started with the Second Boer War (1899–1902), and World War I—the Great War, the "war to end all wars"—was only the beginning rather than the end of the century's endless warfare. Further, there are no obvious demarcations of the kind that neatly delineate eras of intellectual history. Many of the chapters in this volume demonstrate that the premodern, the modern, and the postmodern do not constitute eras that follow one another but rather are entangled with each other right to the end of the century in any given culture or congregation or even individual life. Cesar del Rio's autobiographical account at the beginning makes this point.

The most obvious challenge of this volume is to select compelling, representative, evocative, and multifaceted examples of the people's histories from endless possibilities. As religious studies scholar David Chidester has said of his own global history of Christianity,[18] readers will find their own favorite omissions—an exercise, it is hoped, that will be stimulating rather than frustrating. In contrast with most earlier eras of Christian history, the twentieth century offers too many sources from which to choose, rather than hardly any.

There is the additional matter of perspective: not only the certainty that we are often "blinded to the recent past," to use Catholic

Fig. 0.3. *Jesus of the People* by Janet McKenzie, who comments about her painting: "Jesus stands holding his robes, one hand near his heart, and looks at us—and to us. He is flanked by three symbols. The yin-yang symbol represents perfect harmony, the halo conveys Jesus' holiness, and the feather symbolizes transcendent knowledge. The feather also refers to the Native American and the Great Spirit. The feminine aspect is served by the fact that although Jesus was designed as a man with a masculine presence, the model was a woman. The essence of the work is simply that Jesus is all of us." © 1999 Janet McKenzie, www.janetmckenzie.com.

writer Hilaire Belloc's (1870–1953) phrase, but the fact that many of the authors of these chapters have lived or are presently living the histories about which they write. This is true of their subjects as well. This dual reality does not render historians incapable of writing good history. If there is anything we have learned in these last generations of history writing and have come to confess with at least qualified enthusiasm rather than ruefulness, it is this: that there is no such thing as objective history, that is, history that does not include the biases—personal, religious, academic, economic, gender, racial, psychological, political—of the authors. But the question arises then: Who should write the people's history? Insofar as possible, the authors of these chapters let the people tell their own stories. They work to let the people about whom they write speak through them rather than speaking for them. In *Learning about Theology from the Third World*, evangelical scholar William A. Dyrness reminds his readers, in implicit sympathy with Andrew Greeley, that we have moved away from nineteenth-century understandings of history as a transcript of things as they actually were: "History is rather a people telling their story." It makes a difference, Dyrness says, that Latin American history has been told up to now by people who held power over the region. "What if this same history," he asks, "is told by the people who have suffered under the hardships?"[19] Dyrness's question applies to multiple contexts in global Christianity. People's history lets the people speak. Because we are closer to the sources of people's history in the twentieth century than are historians concerned with previous centuries, there is a great deal in the chapters of this volume not just about what people have done but about what they have had to say.

Then there is the matter of tone: how to tell the people's history without romanticizing it or being condescending toward it or being fearful of its influence. No family of the Christian tradition seems to be without some acknowledgement that the people, "the faithful," have a significant role to play, one that is more than just obedient support for the leadership. Examples include the Roman Catholic concept of the *sensus fidelium*, the belief that the people of God, empowered by the Holy Spirit, share among themselves a wisdom about what is true, right, and good; the Reformation passion for the priesthood of all believers; in Russian Orthodoxy the "gathered" (*sobranie* or *sobor*), without whose consent doctrine cannot be affirmed. Both leaders and laity often assume implicitly that the faithful's role should be more passive than active in terms of contributing to the "deposit of faith," however much contemporary historians and theologians see this concept as connoting a living rather than a static entity. The people can make the leaders, even in very low-church traditions, very nervous, and many institutional safeguards ensure against giving too much credence to the *sensus fidelium*, especially if it feels to church leaders more like mere popular opinion. The doctrine of the primacy of individual conscience in Roman Catholicism teaches that when members of the church feel deeply that the church is wrong, they have a moral obligation to act or refuse to act in accord with their own consciences. The assumption is nonetheless that the individual's conscience has been formed by the tradition to begin with.

Taking very seriously the practices and beliefs, various forms of resistance and persistence, faithfulness and rebellion of ordinary Christians calls into question—and this is the purpose of the entire series—what we have long assumed to be the proper subject matters of church history or, as we have called it more recently, Christian history: theology, church as institution, clergy and hierarchy, doctrinal disputes. None of these elements is missing from a people's history, but they assume the background rather than the foreground of the chapters in this volume.

We witness in the telling of these stories a transvaluation of values: that is, they turn upside down and all around the aspects of Christianity that historians have considered important enough to record. When Ada María Isasi-Díaz writes about Latina women in Spanish Harlem telling Roman Catholic bishops in a dispute over the closing of a parish church, "We are the church, the people of God," we recognize that they are drawing from the deepest wells of the Catholic tradition as well as from the changes brought about in Catholicism by the Second Vatican Council.[20] They are also calling on the authority of their life experiences and, ironically, in some cases, the church's own rhetoric of egalitarianism. Eleazar Fernandez, who grew up in the Philippines, says of the piety of Filipino taxi drivers, farmers, and fisherfolk that "humility or knowing how to bow down to the religious intuitions of those who are not bred by the academy may be an expression of wisdom." When statistics show that self-identified Roman Catholics practice birth control and seek abortions about as often as others in the population in spite of official church prohibitions against both, we become aware that there is a serious disjuncture between church teaching and the practices of those who nonetheless consider themselves faithful. When we learn that *babushkas* (grandmothers) were major contributors to the survival of Orthodox Christianity in Eastern Europe during the communist era, we get a powerful sense that "hierarchy," even in an intensely hierarchical part of the Christian tradition, must take its place as part of the church, not all of the church, not even the "top" of the church—that the ostensibly powerless in both church and society have their own kind of power. One of the major purposes of a people's history of Christianity is to stir things up rather than to settle them down.

Finally, a people's history of Christianity in the twentieth century published only a few years after its ending has one foot in the future. This is particularly true of subjects like biomedical ethics or speculations about the future of Western European Christianity in relation to increasing numbers of Christians in the southern hemisphere. Is it the task of the historian, generally the purveyor of the past, to resist the temptation to predict, however cautiously, what recent history suggests for the future of Christianity in many different forms and all over the world? Or is this an obligation that the historian is expected to fulfill?

## WE CAN'T STEP INTO THE SAME RIVER TWICE

In terms of major cultural themes in the people's history of Christianity in the twentieth century, there doesn't seem to be much new under the sun. At many levels it is a history of the repetition of disillusionments: endless warfare; the relentlessness of global poverty and the disparity between rich and poor; the rapidity with which Christians turn on one another in various parts of the world; the failures of the churches to protect the innocents of the world—their own and those of "others"; the terrifying extent to which Christianity and its leaders could be co-opted by totalitarian governments in places like Nazi Germany, the countries of the former USSR, various African one-party systems, and China (the government-approved part of the Catholic Church), as well as, many would say, by the conservative wing of the Republican Party in the United States.

But those are not the only stories. There were also manifestations of hope and courage, just as there have been in previous eras: the Barmen Declaration of 1934 written by German theologians to resist the Nazis' use of Christian beliefs to further their cause; the many, many "righteous Gentiles" who are memorialized at the Yad Veshem Holocaust memorial in Israel for helping to save Jews from the Holocaust; the churches' roles in the civil rights movement in the United States and in the end of apartheid in South Africa; the women's movement as a catalyst for recognizing both the immense contributions of women to Christianity and the extent of women's exclusion from centers of power and from historical accounts; the ongoing work of church social agencies in response to multiple natural and human-made disasters; the emergence of liberation theologies related to gender, race, class, and sexual orientation; the beginnings of Christian response to ecological degradation.

Besides the stories of disillusionment, hope, and courage, the history of Christianity in the twentieth century is full of the unexpected. There have been surprising events that are still unfolding, like the Second Vatican Council and the astonishing fact that a huge part of the Christian tradition (Roman Catholics constitute half the Christians in the world) can undergo a cataclysmic change that no one anticipated. There is the ecumenical movement that at the end of the twentieth century some experts considered to be moribund, but its ongoing influence appears to be moving Christianity into a post-denominational world. There is the transformed nature of mission work and the Christianizing of sub-Saharan Africa. Historians would have been likely to predict none of this at the beginning of the twentieth century. Many consider the World Missionary Conference in Edinburgh in 1910 the start of the ecumenical movement, for example, but no African delegates were present because of the assumption that the most important mission fields lay in Asia. We might even count as a surprise the fact that the secularization thesis—at its most fundamental the assumption that religion would eventually disappear because it was no longer needed by a thoroughly enlightened humanity—has been disproved at this most basic level of interpretation and has evolved in more sophisticated forms.[21] While there are always secularizing processes at work, as Stark and Bainbridge and many others have pointed out, Christianity as an arena of human creativity is no more likely to disappear than art or politics or economics.

From the vantage point of people's history, we return to the "human-ness" of Christianity as a major and paradoxical discovery of religious and church historians during the twentieth century. At one level and in the parlance of theology, this refers to its fallibility, its sinfulness, its brokenness. But at another level we have come to understand the churches' human-ness as a mark of its creativity. What Christians once assumed (and, of course, many still do) was "God-given" in a very direct way—scriptures, doctrines, rituals and the "rightness" of traditionally prescribed rites—we have come to see through the people's history as the fruits of the Christian imagination, that is, the capacity of ordinary Christians to question and to respond in new ways when they are confronted by experiences that do not find resolution in already-existing structures or assumptions about "the way things are and should be" in either church or society.

We now have overwhelming evidence that the Christian church in all its varieties, and however it ultimately participates in the transcendent, is a human institution for good and for ill. Although this seems to be a discovery of the obvious, it has nonetheless been a long time in coming. For some it has been a frightening thing to admit. But in some interesting ways, focusing on the people's history has had the effect of freeing church historians from the need to defend the church. Not to put too fine a point on the matter, the church is a mixed bag. In every era, its history calls for both rejoicing and repenting. The complexities of the people's history can make it difficult even to discern virtues from vices: persistence from submission or apathetic endurance; conservatism from rigidity: innovation from loss-of-moorings. We don't know which are which until we hear the stories, know the context, and discover who is making the assessment.

## TELLING THE STORIES

However much the stories in the chapters that follow are all over the map, they have in common an emphasis on the voices, the agency, the emotions, and the daily dilemmas and joys of ordinary Christian people. There are, on the other hand, major contrasts in culture and context and in how under drastically differing circumstances, Christians interact with culture and negotiate its enticements and its injustices. The authors of these chapters pay careful attention to the creativity of response that twentieth-century Christians in different parts of the world brought to their circumstances, whether it be a creativity related to survival or protest, acculturation or resistance to culture, or recognition of new realities in science, medicine, and technology.

Precisely because one volume cannot begin to take into account more than a fraction of what the term "global Christianity" suggests that it should, many of the chapters do double and triple duty. The chapters by Rosetta Ross and Ada María Isasi-Díaz inform us about two specific communities of women in the United States, but they give us intimations as well about the dynamics and historical consequences of "diaspora" from Africa and Latin America. A little reading between the lines of Mercy Amba Oduyoye's history of the Circle of Concerned African Women Theologians reveals a history of the trajectory of colonialism, mission history, and the postcolonial efforts of Africans to construct an authentic African Christianity—something new that also recognizes the needs of women

Fig. 0.4. *Head of Christ,* Elimo P. Njau (Tanzania). Courtesy National Archives (Contemporary African Art Select List collection, #146).

and their contributions to this enterprise. Eleazar Fernandez's chapter on Filipino popular Christianity is not at first glance about ecology, but in his focus on people who depend on the land and the ocean for their living, there are lessons about natural resources and sustainable

**Fig. 0.5.** With an image of Jesus watching over them, street vendors carry goods at a bus station in Port au Prince, Haiti, during the 1990s. Photo © Richard Bickel /Corbis.

living. There is no one chapter about emotion in this volume, but emotions are very much at the forefront of a people's history of Christianity, and not just traditional religious emotions (praise, joy, repentance, and so forth). Taken together, these chapters offer an immense compendium of feelings: resistance, persistence, anger, sorrow, defiance, pride, disgust, ruefulness, celebration, delight, fear, skepticism. The emotional history of twentieth-century Christianity is also all over the map.

The four chapters of part 1, the Authority of New Voices, opens up the lives of those whose presence has been mostly absent from the history of Christianity, at least until very recently. Or, to put that a little differently, the authority of their voices and their experiences has been absent. When they have appeared at all, it is generally because others are telling their stories and interpreting the significance of those stories. In the chapters that follow, we gain knowledge of how the history of Christianity expands and takes on new dimensions when historians and theologians ask people, "What do you know about Christianity that comes out of the realities of your own lives?" and "How have you been moved to take action in light of the convictions that have become clear to you?"

In his portrayal of Filipino people's religiosity, Eleazar Fernandez writes about the eclectic piety, the daily lives, and the economic struggles of ordinary Filipinos. Unlike the rest of Asia, the Philippines is 85 percent Catholic, and issues of colonization continue to abound on its many islands. Filipino piety crosses institutional boundaries between Catholicism, Protestantism, and practices from folk and nature religion. Fernandez describes popular Christianity as a "creative interweaving of worldviews" that also derives wisdom from living close to nature. He draws on the folk wisdom of the people to be found in popular sayings and argues that "popular spirituality calls for a spiritual practice that is not isolated in certain places and moments considered spiritual." He interprets the role of major aspects of the Christian tradition—Jesus, Eucharist, devotion to the saints—in the popular piety of Filipinos with critical empathy. Fernandez's willingness to learn from this piety, not just to teach official Christianity in the same old ways as a corrective to it, offers evidence of the reciprocal energies that theologians and historians are experiencing from a focus on the people's Christianity.

Rosetta Ross's chapter on rural, evangelical black women in the mid-twentieth-century South describes the details of daily life for women who were poor sharecroppers denigrated for reasons of race. Some of these women, like Victoria Way DeLee (b. 1925) and Fannie Lou Townsend Hamer (1917–1977), found in evangelical Christianity the courage and the community support to take on exploitative agricultural labor practices, white supremacy, and the violence of the civil rights era. Ross analyzes how both black and white rural Bible belt evangelical Christianity shaped the upbringing and identities of DeLee and Hamer positively and negatively and contributed powerfully to their success. Both women became famous for their civil rights work, particularly Hamer, but in a poignant concluding statement, Ross tells us, "Neither DeLee nor Hamer ever fully escaped poverty" or completely realized "the benefits of their activism."

Mercy Amba Oduyoye incorporates references to a history of colonialism and Western Christianity in a chapter that recounts the history of the Circle of Concerned African Women Theologians, of which she is the primary founder. She offers the opportunity to listen to voices heretofore unheard in public, those of African women. Her story combines elements of theology, strategy, cultural analysis, and deep practicality in the construction of a women's institute that will bring together and serve women, men, and the church all over Africa. The numerous "communities of accountability" that the Circle claims—churches, seminaries, academic women, church workers, women who cannot read, women and men with AIDS—give us a good idea of the complexities of Christian life in Africa today. The goals of the Circle range from the traditionally academic (Oduyoye and many other members of the Circle have been theologically educated in the West) to the meeting of the most basic needs of Africans. For Oduyoye, the Circle's work also requires the constructing of an African theology that is new: two-winged (that is, both female and male) and dependent upon neither the static worldview of traditional African religion nor the traditional forms of Western Christianity.

Ada María Isasi-Díaz writes about Latinas in Spanish Harlem, women who are the heart of their parish church and who embody the life of its community. They are very much aware of themselves as church, in opposition to the dictates and the indifference of the clergy and the hierarchy. They convene retreats and conduct services and exhibit their own ritual expertise, educated and empowered by the liturgies they have attended all their lives. They are theologically reflective, deeply convinced that they are indeed the people of God, and unafraid to confront bishops. They have strong opinions about God, about relationships, and about the way the universe operates. A large percentage (now more than one-third) of Catholics in the U.S.A. are Hispanic, and Hispanic women and their form of Christianity are bound to have an increasing influence in the years to come.

The chapters in part 2, Traditions and Transformations, focus on some of the variety of contexts all over the globe that not only foster change but compel it in response to political and economic realities and calamities, as well as issues of cultural influence. In keeping with an emphasis on people's history, these chapters play up not just broad trends but the daily realities of ordinary Christians from very different parts of the Christian tradition. Each essay emphasizes the dynamic relationship—sometimes stimulating, sometimes frustrating or distorting or dangerous—between Christianity and the distinctive cultures in which it dwells.

In "Orthodoxy under Communism," Paul Mojzes turns us in the direction of a very different kind of Christian people's experience, that of Eastern Europeans during the years of communist rule. Mojzes provides us with sufficient background on the worldview and ecclesial structure of Orthodox Christianity to help us understand the sufferings of Christians under a regime that deprived them not only of the devotional comforts of everyday life but of access to the liturgy, the center of Orthodoxy. Mojzes elaborates on the realities of life for Orthodox Christians in the Soviet Union—the place of the laity within the framework of the church; their modes of survival when not only employment but sometimes life itself was at stake if one were detected engaging in outward practices of piety. He describes an intriguing inversion of power that is often a part of the people's history—that the tradition was preserved by those with the least to lose, the least powerful, and, therefore, ironically empowered in their powerlessness to safeguard the faith and its practices for their children and grandchildren when the time came—as it did—that they could once again be public about their faith. The rapidity with which Orthodox Christianity was resurrected in the countries of the former Soviet Union offers evidence as to how close to the surface it had remained, however invisible to onlookers both outside and inside.

Mark Noll and Ethan Sanders outline a people's history of North American evangelicalism with a focus on prayer, worship (particularly music), and material culture. They demonstrate how pervasive evangelical piety is within North American society, how attuned it is to popular culture, and where it fits within the broader framework of American Protestantism. Evangelicalism is "entrepreneurial," they say, in matters of worship and music and in the growth of "Christian retail," even though ordinary evangelicals have retained and adapted traditional practices of intercessory prayer, reliance on born-again experiences, and the wisdom of the Bible. They predict that the future of North American evangelical worship and piety is tied to "the volatile evangelical dance with American popular culture" and to what is happening in the rest of world evangelicalism—in sub-Saharan Africa, China, Korea, the Pacific Islands. Most pivotal, they predict, is how evangelicals negotiate their "twin but sometimes competing strengths"—connection to the historic tradition and the impulse to adjust the faith to new realities.

Luis Rivera-Pagán grounds his study of the growing attraction of Pentecostalism for Latin Americans in a classic anthropological text by Stanley W. Mintz, *Worker in the Cane: A Puerto Rican Life History* (1960), whose astonishment at Taso Zaya's conversion to Pentecostalism has been ignored by most scholars. Rivera-Pagán places Taso within the context of the brutal life of cane workers to interpret why his conversion is a story of "extraordinary healing, both physical and spiritual" and a transformation of identity, family life, and purpose in the world. Rivera-Pagán does not romanticize Taso's life after his conversion or that of his common-law wife, Elizabeth. Taso and his family never escaped their poverty or a life of unending physical labor, but they experienced new life nonetheless. Rivera-Pagán generalizes from Taso's story to explain why Pentecostalism speaks to so many of the poor of Latin America. "Religion matters in Latin America," says Rivera-Pagán. "And it matters even more in its increasing and astounding variety." He speaks, also, to controversies about whether Pentecostal religion offers a worldly or unworldly religious worldview in Latin America, suggesting a need to redefine what historians and theologians mean by those concepts. Neither one seems adequate on its own to explain what is happening.

Bruce Forbes analyzes how a biblical theme—the Apocalypse and the struggle between good and evil (and, more broadly, American Christianity's apocalyptic expectations)—crosses the boundaries of institutional Christianity and shapes the imagination of popular culture. He focuses on apocalyptic fiction as it is manifested in the immensely popular Left Behind series, cowboy narratives (the traditional "western"), and tales of superheroes in comic books. He argues that if we stop with explorations of traditional Christian theologies of apocalypticism and millennialism, we will never understand the popularity of this theme in the public imagination. "What the general public *really* believes," he says, "often finds expression more in the trends of popular culture than in the statements of elite, formal theologians."

Jean-Paul Wiest's chapter on Catholicism at the end of the twentieth century in China is somewhat more institutionally oriented—the Chinese government and the Vatican—than the other essays in this book. But it points to the complexities of Catholicism's situation in China at the very end of the twentieth century and the beginning of the twenty-first, and the pressures that ordinary Chinese Catholics have to negotiate as a result. Ironies and conflicts abound when, as Wiest explains, increasing numbers of Chinese Catholics belong to the "large gray area" between the Chinese Catholic Patriotic Association (the CCPA) recognized by the government and the underground, or hidden, church. Wiest views the two as one church, however wounded it is by the dichotomy. He points to marks of Chinese Catholic piety that transcend the division and the extent to which priests, sisters, and "ordinary Christians" face risks while working for reconciliation. Wiest's analysis reinforces the people's history discovery that an understanding of Catholicism in China focused only on the struggle between two mammoth institutions will come nowhere near telling the whole story.

In her chapter on existential ritualizing in contemporary Sweden, Valerie DeMarinis speculates that although Christianity appears to be declining in the West, particularly in Western Europe, looking at people's history makes us more inclined to ask not, "Why is religion going away?" but "What new forms is religion taking?" She demonstrates that those who have departed from traditional observance in the state Lutheran church nonetheless have a need for spiritual depth in their lives and for ritual celebration, or at least marking, of significant aspects of their lives. They work to create a vital worldview using components from both religion and nature. Further, says DeMarinis, the process of forced migration is bringing more privatized and secularized cultures such as Sweden into direct contact with a wide variety of cultures and worldviews that raise challenges to an unreflected-upon religious Protestantism and the cultural value assumptions underpinning worldviews, gender construction, tolerance, and religious freedom. The people she studies are all members of nonprofessional groups trying to make existential sense out of unplanned chaos, and in an intriguing cross-pollination of disciplines, it appears to be mental health professionals who are becoming as acutely aware of the need for ritualizing as are those who are part of the church.

The chapters in part 3, Innovation and Authenticity, offer examples of how people's history can illuminate the efforts of twentieth-century Christians to respond to dilemmas and opportunities in their daily lives that require new ways of thinking and acting as Christians: family realities, work, personal identity crises, relationships with other Christians, inevitable and "ordinary" crises of life and death. It is not always, or even often, easy to discern what is both innovative and authentic. And "authentic" here means not clearly "right" (rather than obviously "wrong") but flowing in recognizable ways, however diverse they may be, from the deep wells of Christian scripture, tradition, and history. Such authenticity is, in fact, part of the appeal of people's history. In demonstrating both the multiplicity and the ambiguity of Christianity, it points to the depth and the breadth of the tradition as well.

There are nonetheless tragic moments in a people's history of Christianity in the twentieth century when all emphasis on ambiguity must be cast aside. Victoria Barnett's chapter about ordinary Christians in Nazi Germany before and during the Holocaust depicts the distorted use of theological innovation for the sake of upholding the power of cultural ideology and state power. The result was a drastic failure of authenticity. She analyzes the "cautious accommodation" of institutional Protestantism and Catholicism to the Nazi state that failed to resist anti-Jewish policies. In her focus on ordinary Christians—both bystanders and rescuers—she points to widespread active and passive complicity in the Nazi regime and the reality that help for persecuted Jews often came from Christians on the margins in various ways, many of them women, rather than from church leaders.

Patrick Henry relates how ordinary people, theologians and laypeople alike, have moved ecumenism into the everyday lives of Christians much faster than the official ecumenical agreements and bilateral dialogues of denominations and faith and order commissions. This is a grassroots ecumenism fostered by the issues of daily life—intermarriage, relationships with colleagues and neighbors, and collaboration in social justice work with churches from other denominations in the same neighborhood. The virtues needed for ecumenism, says Henry, are new in one sense and ancient and very everyday in another: courtesy, common sense, listening to each other's stories "with the ear of the heart," as the Benedictines put it, and having a sense of humor. Grassroots ecumenism often gets its start at the kitchen table rather than in official meeting places.

Its insights and accomplishments offer previews of a Christianity that will be postdenominational: more unified but not necessarily lacking the distinctive characteristics of its various branches. Recall the prayers of gratitude for Orthodox Christians and Methodists at the beginning of the chapter. Margaret O'Gara speaks of this phenomenon as "the ecumenical gift exchange," in a book by the same name,[22] a reality that has by no means come totally to fruition but whose spirit can be discerned in the stories Henry tells.

Margaret Bendroth's chapter on gender in twentieth-century Christianity relates issues of gender to the recent scholarly "discovery" of gender as an essential category of analysis for understanding religion and to how assumptions about gender identity affect the daily lives of Christians. As scholars of women's history have been pointing out over the last forty years, we cannot adequately understand a religious worldview or the experiences of people who embrace it without asking, "What is it like to be a woman in this tradition?" and "What is it like to be a man?" Bendroth looks at how gender issues

> ### "Perhaps the World Ends Here" / Joy Harjo
>
> The world begins at a kitchen table. No matter what,
>     we must eat to live.
> The gifts of earth are brought and prepared, set on the
>     table. So it has been since creation, and it will go on.
> We chase chickens or dogs away from it. Babies teethe
>     at the corners. They scrape their knees under it.
> It is here that children are given instructions on what it
>     means to be human. We make men at it, we make
>     women.
> At this table we gossip, recall enemies and the ghosts
>     of lovers.
> Our dreams drink coffee with us as they put their arms
>     around our children. They laugh with us at our poor
>     falling-down selves and as we put ourselves back
>     together once again at the table.
> This table has been a house in the rain, an umbrella in
>     the sun.
> Wars have begun and ended at this table. It is a place
>     to hide in the shadow of terror. A place to celebrate
>     the terrible victory.
> We have given birth on this table, and have prepared
>     our parents for burial here.
> At this table we sing with joy, with sorrow. We pray of
>     suffering and remorse. We give thanks.
> Perhaps the world will end at the kitchen table,
>     while we are laughing and crying, eating of the
>     last sweet bite.
>
> "Perhaps the World Ends Here" from
> *The Woman Who Fell from the Sky* by Joy Harjo.
> Copyright © 1994 by Joy Harjo. Used by permission of
> W. W. Norton & Company, Inc.

have played out in different parts of the world and how the lives of both women and men have been circumscribed by inflexible expectations about what they must do or what they cannot do based on gender. This is one of those issues that forces historians to keep one foot in the past and one in the future. Bendroth places importance in this chapter on the "family claim" as a constantly recurring theme in different eras of Christianity. She concludes by acknowledging that when it comes to gender, "here emerge some of the deepest, most puzzling questions about what it means to be human, to be at once independent and responsive to the needs of others." Those daunting questions—now that scholars and ordinary people have become aware enough to ask them!—can be just as intractable at the kitchen table as they are in boardrooms or the sanctuaries of established religions.

Oscar Cole-Arnal takes on labor and social justice movements in Canada from a comparative perspective: Social Gospel Protestants in western Canada and urban Roman Catholicism in Quebec. His account begins with an angry gathering of farmers in 1901 in what became the province of Saskatchewan. They were protesting the price manipulations by railroad barons, bankers, and international grain exchanges to make more profit by depriving wheat farmers of fair prices for their grain. This is a narrative of agricultural and urban poverty and exploitation and of the activists, both laypeople and clergy, who worked to change those realities that so powerfully affected the daily lives of farmers and factory workers. Interwoven in the details of Cole-Arnal's dual account are politics of the institutional church and people, with radicals and conservatives among clergy and laity, some of them resisting change and some of them fomenting it. It is not a story in which the work of clergy and laity is easily distinguished, but it is a compelling illustration of the complexities of people's history.

Cristina Traina analyzes popular Catholic manuals on sexuality and marriage over three different periods in the twentieth century. She looks into the bases on which Catholic writers, many of them celibate, negotiated popular, cultural understandings of "good" sexuality and its place in marriage, and tried to find ways to make them conform to Catholic teachings. As the century wore on, the insights of psychologists and biologists became more prominent in these conversations, and Traina illustrates how devoted Catholics felt themselves to be at the mercy of not-very-understanding experts in regard to the intimate relationships in their lives. Ordinary people came to be defiant of official prescriptions as they came into conflict with the realities they experienced in the privacy of those lives. Traina's story is about "the evolution of official Roman Catholic teaching on sexuality" over the course of the twentieth century, but "it also reflects just as strongly ethnic Catholic assimilation and coming-of-age in American culture."

Ann Pederson catalogues the dilemmas faced by ordinary people when they encounter the complexities of life's beginnings and endings at the close of the twentieth century when it became clear, because of advances in science and medicine, that these experiences are no longer discernible moments but processes. Their unfoldings are fraught with uncertainly and dissent, both individual and cultural. In many cases the advice of experts, religious or medical, does not suffice. The experts in these two arenas are often bewildered themselves, because their separate realms of expertise have not kept pace with each other in terms of ethical dilemmas and can therefore be very difficult to relate to each other. Pederson's particular setting is the American midwestern state of South Dakota—atypical, or at least distinctive, in some respects, as she points out, but whose citizens are nonetheless beset by dilemmas around beginnings and endings of life that are familiar to most Christians.

## LIVING CHRISTIANITY

Christian history takes on a new vitality when historians embrace the multiple and ongoing stories of people all over the globe for whom Christianity is a living tradition. This new kind of history opens up the everyday realities of Christians that have been concealed by theological abstractions, too-neatly-framed timelines, typologies that suggest stasis rather than dynamism and unquestioned assumptions about what elements of Christian history are significant enough to record. All that said, it is not the aim of people's history to toss out theology, timelines, and working assumptions. It is obvious from the chapters in this book that such a move would not only be unwise; it would be impossible. What the people's histories in this volume demonstrate is the need for many approaches and emphases. We need statistics and maps, like the one on pages 32–33, to keep before us the big picture of how concentrations of Christians in the world have changed between 1900 and 2000. This broad scope motivates the kinds of questions that have dominated both scholarly and popular sources at the end of the twentieth century—not only "whither Christianity" but "Whose Religion Is Christianity?" The latter is the title of a well-known book by Lamin Sanneh, a professor of missions and world Christianity at Yale University, and its specific focus is evident in the subtitle: *The Gospel beyond the West*.[23] His question, though, is applicable in a much more general way and across a variety of national, international, theological, and institutional boundaries. And it is a question that authors of these chapters respond to from many different perspectives.

Writing people's history and reading it, as well, requires a willingness not just to expand our repertoire of historical sources and to be receptive to new questions. It is an enterprise that demands an agility in the entertaining of different, and sometimes competing, angles of vision. The very specific stories that undergird people's history challenge us to see how the local and the global, the universal and the particular, the cosmic and the domestic are inter-twined with each other. In her poem, "Perhaps the World Ends Here," Muscogee Indian poet Joy Harjo evokes just this juxtaposition but also the integration of the cosmic and the domestic, the very local and the vastly global, the living out of daily routines and their much wider significance that are so much a part of the spirit of a people's history of Christianity. "The world begins at a kitchen table," she writes. "No matter what, we must eat to live." Harjo catalogues the whole of human history, people's history, unfolding around the table—bringing gifts, chasing dogs and chickens away, instructing children, giving birth, "preparing our parents for burial." She depicts the kitchen table as the place where wars are begun and ended: "It is a place to hide in the shadow of terror. /A place to celebrate the terrible victory." She concludes with a poignant speculation that combines the ordinary and the apocalyptic but it is an apocalyptic whose arena has been domesticated without being tamed of its powerful meaning: "Perhaps the world will end at the kitchen table, while we are laugh-/ing and crying, eating of the last sweet bite."[24] In the people's histories that follow there are similar striking combinations of the local and the global that promote fresh understandings of the depth and breadth of the recent Christian past and of the fact that it is a living and often surprisingly self-renewing tradition.

## FOR FURTHER READING

Bamat, Tomas, and Jean-Paul Wiest, eds. *Popular Catholicism in a World Church: Seven Case Studies in Inculturation.* Maryknoll, N.Y.: Orbis Books, 1999.

Chidester, David. *Christianity: A Global History.* New York: HarperCollins, 2000.

Healey, Joseph and Donald Sybertz. *Towards an African Narrative Theology.* Maryknoll, N.Y.: Orbis Books, 1996.

Jenkins, Philip. *The New Faces of Christianity: Believing the Bible in the Global South.* New York: Oxford University Press, 2006.

McLeod, Hugh, ed. *World Christianities c.1914–c. 2000.* Cambridge History of Christianity. Cambridge: Cambridge University Press, 2006.

Moore, Rebecca. *Voices of Christianity: A Global Introduction.* Boston: McGraw Hill, 2005.

Thistlethwaite, Susan Brooks, and Mary Potter Engel, eds. *Lift Every Voice: Constructing Christian Theologies from the Underside. Revised and Expanded Edition.* Maryknoll, N.Y.: Orbis Books, 1998.

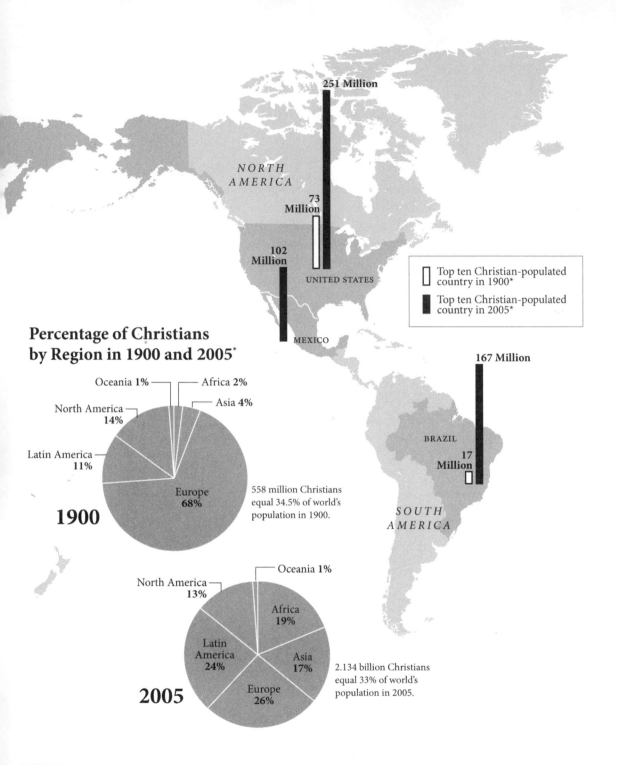

251 Million

*NORTH AMERICA*

73 Million

102 Million

UNITED STATES

Top ten Christian-populated country in 1900*

Top ten Christian-populated country in 2005*

MEXICO

167 Million

BRAZIL

17 Million

*SOUTH AMERICA*

## Percentage of Christians by Region in 1900 and 2005*

Oceania 1% — — Africa 2%

North America 14% — Asia 4%

Latin America 11%

Europe 68%

**1900**

558 million Christians equal 34.5% of world's population in 1900.

Oceania 1%

North America 13%

Latin America 24%

Africa 19%

Asia 17%

Europe 26%

**2005**

2.134 billion Christians equal 33% of world's population in 2005.

SOURCES:

*Christianity in Global Context: Trends and Statistics,* Todd M. Johnson, Ph.D., Director, Center for the Study of Global Christianity, Gordon-Conwell Theological Seminary; Prepared for the Pew Forum on Religion & Public Life; ‡*Christianity, by the Numbers.* Tidings Online, February 4, 2005 by George Weigel, Senior Fellow of the Ethics and Public Policy Center, Washington, D.C.

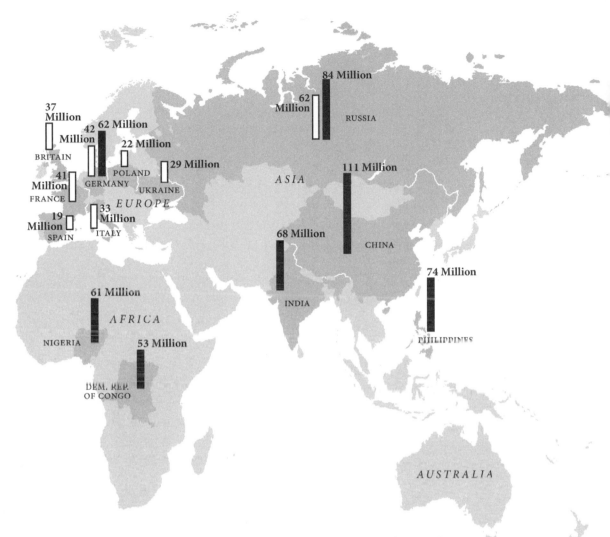

37 Million
BRITAIN

42 Million
GERMANY

62 Million
POLAND

22 Million

29 Million
UKRAINE

62 Million

84 Million
RUSSIA

111 Million
CHINA

74 Million
PHILIPPINES

68 Million
INDIA

41 Million
FRANCE

19 Million
SPAIN

33 Million
ITALY

*EUROPE*

*ASIA*

61 Million
NIGERIA

*AFRICA*

53 Million
DEM. REP.
OF CONGO

*AUSTRALIA*

## Percentage of Christians by Affiliation in 1900 and 2005‡

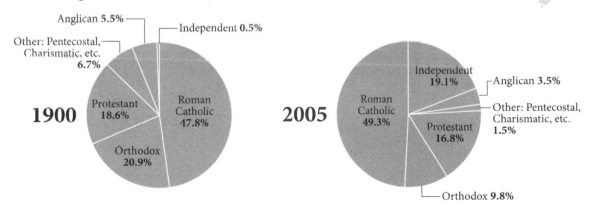

**1900**

Anglican **5.5%**
Independent **0.5%**
Other: Pentecostal, Charismatic, etc. **6.7%**
Protestant **18.6%**
Roman Catholic **47.8%**
Orthodox **20.9%**

**2005**

Independent **19.1%**
Anglican **3.5%**
Other: Pentecostal, Charismatic, etc. **1.5%**
Roman Catholic **49.3%**
Protestant **16.8%**
Orthodox **9.8%**

# THE AUTHORITY
# OF NEW VOICES

# Part 1

# FILIPINO POPULAR CHRISTIANITY

## ELEAZAR S. FERNANDEZ

Miguel de la Cruz, a *jeepney* driver in Metro Manila, sets aside as a *panata* (vow) a portion of his meager daily income to buy a garland of *sumpuguitas* (jasmine) every day to decorate the image of the Black Nazarene that is mounted on the dashboard of his *jeepney*. Also, every Friday Miguel goes to Quiapo Church to light a few candles, recite the rosary, and wipe the feet of the Black Nazarene with his towel, which he wraps around his neck all day. Another towel (also used to wipe the feet of the Black Nazarene) he keeps at his house. The towel, he believes, has received some power from the Black Nazarene that can bring both protection and good luck for him and his family.[1] Miguel's form of religiosity is not uniquely his. He shares this kind of piety with many Filipinos, particularly those classified by Philippine society as the common *tao* (person) or the lowly ones.

As in most sociohistorical accounts, the history of the common people often remains unarticulated. This is particularly true of the religious experience, thoughts, and practices of the vast number of ordinary Christian believers. It is ironic that the day-to-day Christianity that informs the lives of common people does not fall within the orbit of the dominant theological discourse. A clerical and class bias against the religious worldview and practices of the common people seems to persist. By no means does this suggest that this kind of religiosity is totally absent among the upper class. It should not be a surprise if clergy and theological scholars (whether Roman Catholics or Protestants), who were trained mostly under the Enlightenment paradigm, manifest certain distrust toward the more effusive,

**Fig. 1.1.** *Jeepney* is the primary mode of land transportation in the Philippines. It is a Filipino adaptation of the original U.S. military jeep. Photo © Josephine A. Fernandez. Used by permission.

spontaneous, emotional, symbolic, mythic, and cultic practices of the common people. Many liturgical renewal movements continue to reflect this bias against common people's religious expressions. Even those who claim to articulate a people's theology often fail to take into serious account the religious worldview and practices of the common people. Liberation theologians are not exempt from this peculiar bias against popular religious expressions.[2]

What is happening in the larger theological discourse is also true in the Philippines. The general Enlightenment and class bias against the religious expressions of the common people, often labeled as *ignorantes y pobres*, is present. To be sure these religious expressions have been tolerated, if not given blessings, by the church hierarchy, which continues to view them as inferior to official Christianity. They are prevalent in the day-to-day lives of the people, but official Christianity confines them to the periphery. In spite of this marginalization, these expressions have not only continued to exist but also gained vitality. Thus, alongside official church teachings, the religious expressions of the common people exist. Philippine literature calls it "folk Christianity."

I concur with Orlando Espín that popular Christianity can be understood as a vehicle of the people's "faith-full intuitions" or as "cultural expression of the *sensus fidelium*."[3] In other words, popular Christianity is an expression of the common people's religious experience. Underlying popular Christianity is an implicit theology, a concrete expression of a transcendent God that points to a way of understanding as well as doing theology. The last portion of this essay—humility in discerning the theologies of the lowly ones—is my attempt to lift up and give voice to the scattered theological gems of the common people. This should be interpreted not as a wholesale endorsement of every expression of Filipino popular religiosity, but as an invitation to consider it a subject that matters. Regardless of how one views popular religious expressions, they demand our thoughtful engagement.

## COLONIALIZATION AND CHRISTIANIZATION

Wherever there was colonization there was Christian mission. For those steeped in the worldview of the fifteenth and sixteenth centuries, the alliance between colonialism and mission should not be a surprise. No Roman Catholic or Protestant ruler of the period would imagine that in conquering and acquiring other nations he was only advancing his political hegemony. It was taken for granted that the conquered and colonized people must also be missionized. Mission and colonization were inseparable: To colonize was to missionize, and to missionize was to colonize.[4]

This kind of alliance between colonizing powers and Christianity was at work in the Philippines, in the presence of both the Spaniards and the U.S. imperialists. Christianity arrived on the Philippine shores along with Western colonization. With the arrival of Fernando Magallanes (March 16, 1521), Christianity was brought to the Philippine shores. On Easter Sunday of that same year, historical accounts say that Magallanes celebrated the first Mass on the island of Limasawa. Magallanes proceeded to the island of Cebu, where Christianity made its first major advancement. King Humabon of Cebu and his household (including eight hundred subjects) were baptized. As a baptismal gift, one historical account says, the Spaniards gave the queen a wooden statue of the Child Jesus (Santo Niño).[5] The next wave of Spanish conquistadors followed and colonized more areas, planting not only Spanish rule but also Roman Catholic Christianity.

What the Spaniards found when they arrived in the Philippines was a world stabilized by a religious cosmology that provided an overarching framework for the community's social structure. The relationship between social subjects reflected the wider cosmic scheme of relationship. The day-to-day life of the natives revolved around a world inhabited by powerful invisible spirits and their intermediaries. At the top of the cosmic world was the Supreme Being, popularly called *Bathala*, the all-powerful creator (*Puong Maykapal*) whose abode was the sky. The *Bathala* had intermediaries on earth called *anitos* (spirits). There were varieties of *anitos* with specific assignments: fishing and navigation, battlefields, health, nursing mothers, lovers, and so forth. And like their Asian neighbors, the early Filipinos had high regard for their ancestors: They were given *anito* status and were called upon to intercede on the people's behalf with *Bathala*. Performing the religious rituals of the people were priests and priestesses called *katalona* or *babailan* (*babaylan*).

Basic knowledge of this religious cosmology is crucial to understanding why certain popular religious beliefs and practices have evolved into their current forms. In other words, without this basic knowledge we would not be able to recognize the creative process at work in current expressions of popular religiosity.

## THE MAKING OF FILIPINO POPULAR CHRISTIANITY

Filipino popular Christianity is a product of the encounter between Christianity and indigenous Filipino culture and religion. One may view this encounter as an *encontronazo* (clash) between a more powerful force and a less powerful one, but the clash did not result in the total acceptance of everything foreign or in the abdication of everything indigenous.[6] The Filipinos, says historian John Leddy Phelan, were no mere passive recipients of the socioreligious and political package imposed on them by the Spanish colonialists. No doubt Christianity was brought to them, if not imposed on them. But under the circumstances they had considerable freedom in selecting their responses to Hispanization, ranging from acceptance to indifference and even rejection.[7] If there was considerable freedom under the circumstances, then the Filipinos' acceptance of the new and foreign faith suggests openness on their part. Scholar of religion Aloysius Pieris attributes this openness to the prevalence of "cosmic religion" (a form of religion whose main foundation is the cosmic elements or forces of nature, pejoratively referred to as "animism") and the absence of metacosmic soteriologies (for example, notions of salvation or of the highest good—*summum bonum*—such as nirvana) among indigenous Filipinos before the arrival of the Spaniards, except in some places in the south (Mindanao) where Islam had taken earlier and stronger root. This is not the case in other parts of Asia, for example, where non-Christian metacosmic soteriologies constituted the main edifice of the people's worldview as a result of the strong presence of Islam,

Buddhism, and to some extent Taoism.[8] Whatever theoretical framework one uses to take account of this openness, Christianity found general reception among early inhabitants of the Philippines.

It appears from the consensus among scholars that the Christianization of Filipinos was not a one-way imposition but a double process of conversion. The adoption of Christianity by the early Filipinos, contends Steffi San Buenaventura, involved a "conversion process that was more complex than a simple procedure of removal and replacement of faith."[9] James Alexander Robertson argues for a similar point: "The readiness with which the early Filipinos embraced the Faith does not mean that the old forms and beliefs were discarded in their entirety, nor that they have yet altogether disappeared."[10] This complex double process of conversion has given birth to Filipino popular Christianity. Lest it be interpreted as a finished product, popular Christianity continues to develop new forms in response to the contemporary socioeconomic and political challenges. Filipino popular Christianity has even traveled with the Filipino diaspora in this era of heightened globalization.[11]

The Roman Catholic Church has officially recognized and shown growing sensitivity to the religious expressions of the common people, though deep-seated attitudes take time to change. Regardless of the attitude of the church hierarchy, popular Christianity has continued to flourish, such as *Misa de Gallo* (Dawn Masses), *Flores de Mayo* (Flower Festival in May), *santakrusan* (Search for the Cross), *panata* (vow), *sinakulo* (Passion play), *lamay* (wake at home), and fiesta. Popular images have also flourished with a widening number of devotees; these include Santo Niño (Holy Child), Santo Cristo (the Crucified Christ), Santo Entiero (the Holy Corpse), Nazareno (Black Christ), and images of Mary, the mother of Jesus.

Fig. 1.2. *The Suffering Christ*, San Agustin Church, Manila. Photo © Eleazar S. Fernandez. Used by permission.

To be sure, folk Christianity is predominantly a Roman Catholic phenomenon, but it is not totally absent among Protestant Filipinos and other nativistic socioreligious movements.[12] Though they are overshadowed by the Roman Catholic majority, Protestants and other nativistic movements share the same soil (indigenous belief system) that has given birth to Roman Catholic popular Christianity. A study by F. Landa Jocano of Malitbog (Panay Island) reveals the presence of folk Christianity even among Protestants.[13] San Buenaventura's observation is accurate that folk Christianity has been a "convenient conduit that has allowed many Filipinos to cross the institutional boundaries between the two Christian religions [Roman Catholic and Protestant], if not because of dogma, certainly for cultural reasons."[14] Many Protestants, for example, celebrate fiesta (primarily in honor of a patron saint) not because of dogma but because it is part of their social world. Of course, more evangelical forms of Protestant Christianity have strong prophetic pronouncements against fiesta celebration.

> ### Fiesta
>
> Fiesta is a gesture of respect and self-esteem for many Filipinos. It is a time of showing appreciation to the saints for favors or blessings received. It is an occasion for establishing social position and cementing social relations. Also, it is an occasion for paying back debts of gratitude (*utang na loob*).
>
> —Tomas Andres and Pilar Ilada-Andres, *Understanding the Filipino* (Quezon City, Philippines: New Day, 1987), 35.

## SOME EXPRESSIONS OF CREATIVE INTERWEAVING

Filipino popular Christianity demonstrates the people's creative interpretation and appropriation of Christianity, which suggests not only their conversion to the new faith but also the transformation of Christianity. It is a creative localization or contextualization of Christianity by common Filipinos. This is not meant to suggest that this creative interpretation and appropriation process is always liberating, but I venture to say that it must be making sense or that it resonates with the lived experience of the people. When we associate reason only with logical consistency, we may not the see the creative reason of the common people that is attuned to the complex and mysterious. For common Filipinos, mystery is not something to be solved but calls for a posture of wonder and surrender. When logical inconsistency appears, they do not have the same impatience of a Western educated person. The answer they normally give is (in Tagalog) "*Ganyan talaga yan*" (It is really like that, or That is what reality is).[15]

## A WORLD OF SPIRITS

Filipino popular Christianity has evolved into its current expression because it reflects the worldview of the people. Through their faithful intuitions the common people integrated their worldview into their new faith. At home in a cosmology with a hierarchy of supernatural beings and intermediaries, Filipinos arrived at religious beliefs and practices that matched their cosmology: they replaced their *anitos* with images of Christian saints and converted their *magaanito* rituals into veneration of saints. As there were *anitos* for every major human activity, there are now saints for specific human activities or specific favors: a saint for workers, for farmers, for travelers, as well as for sterile mothers who desire to have children and for finding a good husband.[16] With a familial structure reflective of this cosmology, Mary as a way to Jesus is a prominent feature of popular Christianity.[17]

Familiar with a world inhabited by powerful spirits that affect one's life, common Filipinos evolved a form of Christian religiosity that is fully cognizant of their presence. In walking through a forest one has to ask permission from the spirits (*panabitabi*) to be allowed to go through, or one has to ask permission before wading into the lake for fishing. Popular Christianity, in spite of modern challenges, has retained this sense of harmony with nature and the spirits. It may be true that this reverence of the spirits is mixed with fear, but the dominant attitude to the created world is one of harmony with it.

Moreover, common Filipinos are at home in a world that cannot conceive of a space that is not sacred, for there is no separation between the sacred and the secular. As a result, popular Christianity has developed a religiosity encompassing the whole gamut of life while breaking down the wall that separates sacred and secular. The people's religiosity goes with them at all times and places and cannot be confined within church walls or to officially sanctioned church liturgies. This religiosity is not measured in how often one goes to church and participates in its official life. This religiosity is practiced by people who rarely go to church or by those who may go to church only for their own *binyag* (baptism), *kasal* (wedding), and *libing* (funeral). We see this religiosity in gestures that common people make when they perform the sign of the cross when passing by a cemetery or a church, or when they utter their memorized prayers while in a bus or a boat. They say *buyag* (from the Cebuano language—to counter bad luck that an evil spirit may bring) when someone expresses something admirable (for example, "Your baby girl is beautiful!"). From major points in the life cycle to livelihood, relationship with either the living or the dead, constructing an edifice, traveling, inviting good fortunes, and so on, Filipinos have evolved a comprehensive and elaborate set of religious beliefs and practices.

Filipinos' acute awareness of the precariousness of life, whether brought by natural disasters (sometimes not purely natural) or human destructiveness, has given birth to a distinct popular religiosity. Filipino popular Christianity revolves around adapting life to the contingencies of living, especially living in harmony with the forces beyond oneself. A community's significant experience, whether positive or negative (flood, epidemic, bountiful harvest, and so on), gets carved in the collective memory and finds expression in some religious beliefs and observances. One example is the fiesta in honor of San Isidro (May 15), the patron of good harvest. In farming communities where the fiesta celebration includes a procession into the fields, the religious leader or priest blesses the fields, either as an expression of gratitude for a good harvest or as a petition for good harvest through the intercession of San Isidro to God.[18]

## FILIPINO NOTIONS OF DESTINY AND HUMAN AGENCY

If Filipinos' general attitude to the world is one in harmony with forces beyond their full control, how do we discern human agency in this context? There are many elements in popular culture and religion that support the idea of resignation to fate or to God's mysterious purpose. The overall religious climate points to a common belief that everything happens within the purview of God's power and purposes, and within God's own time. Higher power is always involved, giving or withholding blessings as well as punishing. If something is not realized, one may say in Cebuano: "*Wala itugot sa kahitas-an*" (The all-powerful God did not grant it) or "*Dili pa iyang panahon*" (Its time has not yet come). This "time" is more than *chronos*. It is God's providential time. Or rather than being proactive, one may let the circumstances define the outcome. In this case, whatever the outcome must be God's answer. The outcome may be negative, but who would dare to disagree with God?

Two of the popular attitudes toward the world—*gulong ng palad* (wheel of fortune) and *bahala na* (what will be will be)—reinforce an attitude of resignation or fatalism. In the wheel of life there are times when one is up and at other times down. Caught in what appears to be an inevitable fate, common Filipinos can think of life only as *kapalaran* (a life dictated by the lines on the palm of one's hands) or *gulong ng palad*. When this fatalistic worldview is compounded with economic hardships, such as having a family of eight children with only ₱250.00 (U.S. $5) a day salary, what else is there to say but "*bahala na*"?

There are, however, other aspects of Filipino culture and religion that seem to bring balance to fatalism or resignation. Yes, God's will and time set the overall frame, but human effort is also considered crucial: in Tagalog, "*Na sa Dios ang awa, na sa tao ang gawa*" (Mercy comes from God, but labor belongs to humans). Even the term *bahala na* may have a positive spin. It could mean total surrender to God, as in *bahala na ang Dios* (It is up to God whatever the outcome be), which may have been derived from the word *Ba[t]hala* (God).[19] It may be due to the people's belief in *Bathala*'s lavish generosity, according to Jocano, that the dominant risk taking and venturesome trait of Filipinos arose: "*Bathala* will always take care."[20]

The Cebuano compound word *panimpalad* offers a good example of the integration of the Filipino venturesome spirit with the recognition of a power beyond one's control. *Panim* suggests personal agency (effort, determination, and taking risk), while *palad* suggests submission to one's *palad* (the lines on the palms of one's hands) or to a power beyond one's control (God). It is this spirit of *panimpalad* that has propelled Filipinos to leave their familiar village in the provinces and go to the already crowded urban areas of Metro Manila, Cebu City, or Davao City in search of a better life. Likewise, it is this *panimpalad* spirit that has driven Filipinos, in spite of the many stories of maltreatment from their employers, to work in Hong Kong or Singapore as domestic helpers or in the Middle East as contract workers.

## FINDING HUMANITY IN COMMUNITY

Filipino popular religiosity is generally a familial and communal affair: it is tied to the strengthening of communal relation. Fiesta, for example, more than thanksgiving in honor of a patron saint, is for building the social network. It is an expression of social obligation, social status, and a debt of gratitude (*utang na loob*), as well as a gesture of extravagant hospitality. This fiesta hospitality extends not only to friends but also to strangers. Even those who can hardly afford a regular meal go to the extent of borrowing money to prepare for the big fiesta celebration that covers two days or more. Critics of the fiesta celebration point to this negative aspect. A Filipino wisdom saying offers this warning: in Tagalog, "*Ubos-ubos biyaya, pagkatapos nakatunganga*" (Spend lavishly, and you end up with nothing; in a more literal translation, Spend all your blessings, and you end up not only with nothing but also not knowing what to do [*nakatunganga*]).

Baptismal and wedding ceremonies also provide occasions for extending one's social network through the *compadrazco* system. The more sponsors (*ninong* [godfather] and *ninang* [godmother]) one has, the wider one's social network becomes. As extensions of the family, it is assumed that *ninong* and *ninang* provide religious and moral guidance to the child or the newlywed couple. But there is more to this: the sponsors are extensions of the family in times of crisis or when their influence is needed, such as in finding a job or facilitating certain transactions.

The communal dimension of Filipino popular religiosity is likewise visible during the day of the dead (All Saints Day). Filipino communal life extends to both the living and the dead. All Saints Day in the Philippines is like a fiesta, except that the main venue of the celebration is the cemetery, where people stay until late at night. Meals are prepared and brought to the cemetery not only for

---

**On Suffering**

Suffering is a pervasive theme among Filipinos. It is not a surprise that the suffering Jesus has an important place among them. This has served Filipinos in at least two ways: either to make them accept the harsh realities of life or to strengthen them in their struggle for a new humanity. The power wielders no doubt have used the suffering and passive Jesus to continue their control of the status quo. Nevertheless, the suffering but struggling Jesus is not absent. The suffering but struggling Jesus, the inspirer of those who are struggling, is discernible in many instances in the history of the Filipino people.

—Eleazar S. Fernandez, *Toward a Theology of Struggle* (Maryknoll, N.Y.: Orbis Books, 1994), 102–3.

the living (family members and friends) but also for the long dead. Filipinos believe that when their own time comes, they will be together with their departed loved ones, who are waiting in the *kabilang-buhay* (other life/world).

In these religious observances it seems that Filipino popular Christianity provides teaching moments on how to be human. It is not only enough to exist as human (*tao*), but one must know how to be human (*magpakatao*) and to be human-in-relation (*makipagkapwa-tao*). *Makipagkapwa-tao* may be understood in a limited sense as *pakikisama* (being in harmony with others) or in a larger and nobler sense as establishing right relation with fellow human beings. The journey to be truly human is, of course, not an easy one. A well-known Filipino saying (in Tagalog) puts it this way: "*Madaling maging tao, ngunit marihap magpakatao*" (It is easy to be a man/woman, but difficult to make oneself human). Interpretations can take many angles, but they all point to the value of social relations.[21]

## SUFFERING CHRIST, SUFFERING FILIPINOS

In a country where suffering is the lot of the masses, it is not surprising, says Benigno Beltran, that "the image of the Crucified One, head bowed, mouth agape in excruciating agony, provides consolation and an outlet for pent-up emotions of sympathy and tragedy for the ignorant and the heavy-laden." The image of the Crucified God, continues Beltran, "increases the resolve to survive. . . . In the sight of the Cross, Christians live in acceptance and trust in the suffering God who remains faithful in his love for the sinful human beings."[22] Since suffering is a pervasive narrative in people's lives and the Crucified or the Suffering One a pervasive icon, it is not surprising that Holy Week occupies a central place in the church's calendar. Perhaps more than Christmas Eve Mass, the Good Friday event draws a huge crowd—many of whom do not go to church on regular Sundays—on an extremely hot day to participate in an unusually long religious ceremony. This is generally true also of the Protestant churches.

Several Holy Week activities portray in vivid ways the suffering and agony that the Son of God endured. The *pasyon* (reenactment

**Fig. 1.3.** Religious procession, Samar Island: suffering with Jesus. Photo © Josephine A. Fernandez. Used by permission.

of life and death of Jesus through plays and readings) portrays the poor, lowly, and beaten Christ. This practice is more prevalent in certain parts of the Philippines, such as the Tagalog region, where the *sinakulo* (Passion play) and *pabasa* (readings) have had a long history. But the most vivid, if not gory, depiction of Jesus' suffering is the practice of self-flagellation during the Holy Week by those who have made *panata* (vow). The penitents (almost always male) walk barefoot in procession with their faces veiled and lash their backs with rope or bamboo sticks until they bleed. In some places, others are commissioned to do the lashing.

Why do they inflict pain on themselves? With theologies of atonement in mind, it is easy to arrive at the conclusion that the penitents do this as an act of penance for their own or others' sin. Penance may not be totally absent, but as Beltran's study suggests, the penitents do the self-flagellation primarily as a form of *damay*—sympathy with or participation in Jesus' suffering.[23] For them self-flagellation is an act of solidarity with the suffering Jesus.

## PEOPLE'S THEOLOGY

Popular religiosity is the day-to-day religiosity that informs and shapes the lives of people. If the Christian church neglects this reality, and if it is not integrated into the mainstream of the church's life, the people will continue to practice a split-level Christianity, one for the sake of official Christianity and another for their everyday living. Humility or knowing how to bow down to the religious intuitions of those who are not bred by the academy may be an expression of wisdom. As Cebuano-speaking farmers say, "*Ang humay nga may unod moduko; ang tahupon motuhoy*" (Like a stalk of rice, the more it bows down or bends the more substance it contains; when it goes straight up, it is actually empty [*tahupon*]). There is much that we can learn from the common people's religious intuitions that may contribute to our understanding of the Christian notion of Christ's salvific incarnation.

If we venture into the world of the common people, we may encounter a revelation—a widening of our own world. This reminds me of a mundane revelatory encounter that happened in one of the immersion trips to the Philippines I have led for students from the United States. In the house of one of the fisherfolks, I noticed an aquarium with very small fish, the size of a toothpick. I asked our hosts what kind of fish they were. The fisherfolks of Laguna de Bay (Philippines) told our group that the fish in the wider lake (the siblings of the fish in the aquarium) already weighed about two pounds. There was a big difference in size between the fish in the aquarium and those that were out in the lake. Then I turned to my students and explained the parable: just like the fish, if we stay within our aquariums we will not grow; our world will remain small and narrow. But if we take the risk and venture into the wider world, we open ourselves to the possibility of making our hearts as large as the world.[24]

A story attributed to Juan Flavier, who used to work as a rural physician, offers some insights.[25] In a conversation with a farmer in one of the rural communities he served, Flavier quizzed the man about his ability to tell time. Flavier told the farmer that he was ready to leave because it was already five in the afternoon. The farmer looked around and told Flavier that it was not five in the afternoon because the flower of the *patola* (gourd) did not fold yet. Wanting to test further

> **The Importance of the Mass**
>
> The rituals in folk Catholicism often function to validate and legitimate the existing cultural worldview and values. The Mass, for example, is commonly understood as a means to get indulgences or favors for a dead relative or friend. The person who requests a Mass would often tell the priest that the deceased came to her or him in a dream. It does not matter if the one requesting Mass for a dead relative or friend is present during the celebration. What is important is that the Mass be done for the benefit of the deceased person.
>
> —Benigno Beltran,
> *The Christology of the Inarticulate:*
> *An Inquiry into the Filipino*
> *Understanding of Jesus the Christ*
> (Manila, Philippines:
> Divine Word, 1987), 137.

the farmer's ability to tell time, the next day Flavier subjected the farmer to the same question. But before he did it, he cut the flowers of the *patola*. The farmer looked around in the direction of the *patola*, but there were no more flowers to tell the time. Flavier thought that he would outsmart the farmer this time, but then the farmer looked up at a big acacia tree and told him that it was not yet five in the afternoon because its leaves did not fold yet.

This story, I believe, gives us a glimpse of the hermeneutic attunement of the common people to the world they inhabit. With new eyes to see and ears to hear, we can discern that the people's religious intuition is very much attuned to their world and that the people's theological breathing and sensing are still one with the womb that has given birth to them. Moreover, this story tells us how we must think theologically with the people: we must be attuned to the world around us, to its rhythm and its pulse, its folding and unfolding.

## INTEGRAL SPIRITUALITY

As popular Christianity breaks the wall separating the sacred and the secular, it also points to a way of seeing that the world of nature is not outside of the purview of God but an embodiment of God or of the spirits. The colonizers brought with them a foreign religion that drove the spirits from nature, but another spirit came with them that is more rapacious in character than the indigenous ones. As a child living in a rural area in Hinunangan, Southern Leyte, I was afraid of the spirits that dwelt in the land, so I welcomed the new spirit that drove them away. But eventually I realized that the new spirit that came to our shores was more destructive; it was a spirit of destruction masquerading as development. By contrast, in making all space the realm of the spirit, popular religious intuition is pointing in the direction of ecological sensibility.

Along with an understanding of the natural world as God's embodiment calling for ecological sensibility, popular spirituality calls for a spiritual practice that is not isolated in certain places and moments considered sacred. With no financial means to buy a spirituality that requires performance at a serene and comfortable meditation center, the ordinary people practice spirituality in the most banal of places and times. They practice spirituality in the streets and agricultural fields, in the mountains and on the ocean—wherever they spend most of their time. Acutely aware that the forces of nature are beyond their control, rural farmers consider their small field to be symbolic of their faith. As Cebuano-speaking farmers say it, "*Diha sa daruhan giladlad namo ang among pagtuo*" (In the vulnerable field we lay bare our faith in God).[26] They match this faith with the sweat of their labor, leaving the final outcome to God (*bahala na ang Dios*—What will be will be as God wishes). The final outcome belongs to God, but hard work is not absent. "*Ang pinakamahusay na pataba ay yapak ng magsasaka sa lupa*," says a Tagalog proverb (The best fertilizer is the footprints of the farmer in the field). With the grain of rice or corn fertilized by the sweat of the small farmers, it is not a surprise that a popular wisdom saying has evolved: in Tagalog, "*Ang bawat butil ng palay ay pawis ng magsasaka*" (Every grain of rice is the sweat of the farmers). Hence, each grain of rice must be truly valued.

In a similar manner, the small-time fisherfolks have developed a spirituality that is consistent with their experience of life. Acutely aware, like the farmers, that they do not have full control of the forces of nature, they have learned to navigate life in the spirit of openness, harmony, and a sense of right timing. If the field is symbolic of the farmers' faith, the ocean plays a similar role among the fisherfolks. For them, the ocean is life; it sustains life. On the other hand its fierce whimsy can be unforgiving. Its buoyant force makes one float; but can also drown. Many have lost their lives in a storm. In spite of the ocean's unpredictability, the fisherfolks have continued to picture God's mercy with the imagery of the ocean because it has sustained them: in Cebuano, "*Ang kalooy sa Ginoo sama ka lapad sa dagat*" (God's mercy is as wide as the ocean). When God's ocean of mercy blesses them with a safe return and a catch, they are usually met by people on the shore—family members, friends, neighbors, as well as buyers.

Whatever blessings the people receive become an occasion of religious depth. An abundant harvest or catch leads to a fiesta celebration, but even an ordinary meal is a sacrament. When there is little harvest or catch, they still make it enough for the family. In a Filipino idiom

---

**The Role of Food**

*Kumain ka na ba?* (Have you eaten already?). This is one of the very first questions that a person gets to hear when visiting a friend in the Philippines. This tells us of the centrality of food and intestines in Filipino religious and social discourse. Close relationships among Filipinos are often described in terms of intestinal connections. The words *kapatid* (Tagalog), *igsoon* (Cebuano), and *bagis* (Ilokano), which mean sister or brother, have their roots in the word intestine *bituka* (Tagalog), *tinai* (Cebuano), and *bagis* (Ilocano). This relational notion of intestinal connection is often applied in larger settings that are way beyond immediate kinship.

—Melanio Aoanan, "Toward the Making of Filipino Intestinal Theology," in *Anumang Hiram Kung Hindi Masikip Ay Maluwang: Iba't-Ibang Anyo ng Teolohiyang Pumipiglas*. Dasmariñas, Cavite, Philippines: Union Theological Seminary, 2006.

---

in Tagalog, "*Kung maiksi ang kumot, matutong mamaluktot*" (literal translation: If the blanket is short, one must know how to curl up). A fisherfolk may prepare *kinilaw* (a raw seafood usually mixed with spices, vinegar, and/or coconut milk) and invite friends in the neighborhood. Poor families make sure that every member is present during meal time and that everyone has an equal share. Maybe because they barely have enough to get by, necessity has taught them that eating, more than filling one's stomach, is a communal event. One does not eat alone. Eating is an occasion for sharing not just food but life. Eating is a mark of relationship, of connection. In fact, deep connections among Filipinos are expressed through the language of food and internal organs. The word *kapatid* (brother or sister), suggests Melanio Aoanan, is a contraction of "*patid ng bituka*" (connected by a single intestine). Other Filipino languages, such as Cebuano (*sumpay sa tinai*) and Ilocano (*kapugsat iti bagis*), speak of this intestinal connection. Filipino theology, continues Aoanan, is truly an incarnational and, more specifically, intestinal theology—a *bituka* (intestine) and *pagkain* (food) theology.[27] Without romanticizing poverty, I say that it is ironic that those who have more material goods in life eat alone more often than those who have less. They may be eating more nutritious food, but not necessarily a communally and spiritually nourishing meal.

## WHO IS JESUS?

The Jesus who suffers occupies a central place among the marginalized Filipinos because they see in Jesus' plight their very own plight. Again, penance for sins is not the main focus of popular Christology, but rather *pakikiramay*, or identification with the suffering of Jesus, who in the first place embodied this quality. And closely associated with *pakikiramay* (sympathy or maybe empathy) is *malasakit* (suffering with). Following Beltran's point: "To make the truth of Jesus one's own is to have *damay* and *malasakit* with him, to be his disciple and share his destiny."[28]

*Pakikiramay* and *malasakit* with Jesus, I believe, are fitting responses of common Filipinos to Jesus because he embodied these qualities in his very own life. They belong to the attributes of Jesus that can be observed in his life, ministry, and death. Indeed, for the suffering and struggling common people, Jesus was a person for others, a person who came of age. Even with all the risks involved, he pursued God's cause of bringing about the reign of God in the midst of human destruction. Because Jesus' love for the world was expressed through his *pakikiramay* and *malasakit* with the disenfranchised, like many Filipinos who have raised their prophetic voices, he raised the ire of the power wielders and suffered a violent death. While *bahala na* (What will be will be) seems to be associated with *kapalaran*, the *bahala na* that is intertwined with the *malasakit* of Jesus forms into a *bahala na-malasakit*, that is, taking the risks involved in struggling with the disenfranchised of society.[29]

True, the image of the suffering and crucified Christ is prevalent and is often interpreted through the lens of passive acceptance and endurance of suffering, but a tradition of suffering as *bahala na-malasakit* is equally present in Filipino popular Christianity. Moreover, as embodied in the life of Jesus and in the tradition of the little ones, there is not only a *bahala na-malasakit* but also a *bahala na-su pakikibaka* (taking risk for the people's struggle). The Revolution of 1896 against the Spanish conquistadors and the People's Power Revolution of 1986 that toppled the Marcos dictatorship ninety years later both point to the tradition in which the love of the disenfranchised for the crucified Christ is a liberating force.[30] Reynaldo Ileto's *Pasyon and Revolution* points to the "Little Tradition" of the common people, in contrast to the "Great Tradition" (nourished by the *ilustrados* [literally, "enlightened ones"]—the elites during the Spanish colonial period), as an animating force in the past and in the most recent struggles of the Filipino people.[31] No one could miss the pervasive symbol of

---

### Mary, Mother of Jesus

Devotion to Mary—the Immaculate Mother, occupies a central place in the lives of common Filipinos. This was visibly true in the days of the famous People's Power Revolution (February 22–25, 1986). The Immaculate Mother was a central figure in this so-called miraculous event. As the people prayed with their rosaries and faced the loyalist troops and tanks, the image of the Blessed Virgin was with them. The triumph of the people's revolution was, for the common people, a victory or triumph of Mary.

—Teodoro Bacani, *Mary and the Filipino* (Makati, Philippines: St. Paul, 1985), 67–69.

---

the crucified Christ in the past and most current expressions of People's Power. Likewise, not to be missed is the image of the Virgin Mary—the mother of Jesus, who was *matimbang* (one who really matters) for the common people.[32]

While the resurrection tradition is not totally absent in popular religious expressions, it is weak compared to the crucifixion tradition. We can cite some reasons: People are already exhausted from the Good Friday event, and the weather itself (hot summer) does not suggest the emergence of a new life from winter to spring, as in temperate countries. Nevertheless, if the Holy Week celebration has the *pasyon*, the resurrection celebration has the *salubong*. *Salubong* is the reenactment of the dawn meeting of Jesus and his mother, in which the statues of the Risen Christ and the Sorrowful Mother are unveiled by a girl in the attire of an angel, singing the *Regina Coeli*. Then the removal of the veil during the meeting is accompanied by the release of doves and *bati*, a dance of joyful celebration.[33] Where the forces of death continue to reign, the *salubong* celebration is a source of inspiration, vision, and hope. It is founded on the belief that, like Jesus, the Filipino people will someday have their own resurrection. The *salubong* points to the dawn that ushers in the new day for the suffering people. Or in the idiom of the people, in Tagalog, "*Ang araw bago sumikat nakikita muna'y banaag*" (Early dawn precedes the sunrise).

## HOPE FOR THE FUTURE

The resurrection tradition is a living tradition of the common Filipino people. The common people's desperate situation and the Christian tradition have given birth to the *salubong*. Any faithful interpretation of the common people's resurrection tradition must be rooted in the people's desperate situation. It is out of the banality of crucifixions that the common people speak of resurrection. The notion of a grand

---

### Filipino Folk Sayings

*Ganyan talaga yan.* It is really like that, or That is what reality is.

*Bahala na.* What will be, will be.

*Wala itugot sa kahitas-an.* The all-powerful God did not grant it.

*Dili pa iyang panahon.* Its time has not yet come.

*Na sa Dios ang awa, na sa tao ang gawa.* Mercy comes from God, but labor belongs to humans.

*Bahala na ang Dios.* What will be will be as God wishes.

*Ubos-ubos biyaya, pagkatapos nakatunganga.* Spend lavishly, and you end up with nothing. Or, more literally, Spend all your blessings, and you end up not only with nothing but not knowing what to do.

*Madaling maging tao, ngunit marihap magpakatao.* It is easy to be a man/woman, but difficult to make oneself human.

*Ang humay nga may unod moduko; ang tahupon motuhoy.* A stalk of rice with substance bows down; an empty one goes straight up. Or, Like a stalk of rice, the more it bows down or bends the more substance it contains; when it goes straight up, it is actually empty.

*Ang pinakamahusay na pataba ay yapak ng magsasaka sa lupa.* The best fertilizer is the footprints of the farmer in the field.

*Ang bawat butil ng palay ay pawis ng magsasaka.* Every grain of rice is the sweat of the farmers.

*An kalooy sa Ginoo sama ka lapad sa dagat.* God's mercy is as wide as the ocean.

*Kung maiksi ang kumot, matutong mamaluktot.* If the blanket is short, one must know how to curl up.

*Ang araw bago sumikat nakikita muna'y hanaag.* Early dawn precedes the sunrise.

*Palay na, pinapatay pa!* Already dead, but killed again!

*Ang hindi marunong lumingon sa pinanggalingan ay hindi makararating sa paruruonan.* One who does not know how to look back to one's past will not reach one's destination.

*Daghan pa ang mangingisda kay sa isda.* There are more fisherfolks than fish.

*Kung walang tiyaga, walang nilaga.* If you do not persevere, you cannot expect something.

---

resurrection somewhere and someday may not be totally absent in the people's common discourse, understood either as hope or as escape, but this grand resurrection makes sense only when we reinterpret resurrection as what happens to people on the other side of the various kinds of deaths in the here and now.

Wherever we turn, the crucifixion and death of the common Filipinos is happening all the time and in all places. Theirs is a history of dreams betrayed and hopes dashed. While they continue to suffer from natural calamities, death caused by storm is infrequent among fisherfolks, death from shark attacks is also rare. The sharks that are killing more fisherfolks do not live in the sea but on land—the "loan sharks." Likewise, in the day-to-day Filipino discourse the killer crocodiles or alligators (*buayas*) do not live in the rivers but in public places. They devour the government coffers, and some varieties of these *buayas* collect money, or what is popularly called *tong*, from the meager income of the *jeepney* drivers. As if this situation is not already a death sentence, there are cases when even the dead are killed twice. Some seek donations for a dead person and then run away with the money afterward. As they say, "*Patay na, pinapatay pa!*" (Already dead, but killed again!).

Resurrection in the midst of the various kinds of deaths may be hard to find in the lives of the people and those who are dying before their time, but they are not totally absent. They are present in the midst of death—present even in the cemetery. This is true in the life of Aling Panchang. She has lived in

**Fig. 1.4.** Smokey Mountain 2, Manila. Photo © Eleazar S. Fernandez. Used by permission.

Manila's North Cemetery since 1955. Some time in 1960 she moved in with her son, who had acquired a small piece of land and a house at a relocation site. But the situation in the relocation site was so desperate that, in the words of Aling Panchang, "I couldn't stand it anymore. You know squatter areas are terrible! So much noise and so crowded. I came back to the cemetery after a month—and have not left since. I think I might stay here—forever."[34] Living in the cemetery where there was peace was, for Aling Panchang, a resurrection experience.

Indeed, it is hard to find grand moments of resurrection. For those who are barely making it in life, like Aling Panchang, survival is already a foretaste of resurrection. It is from this most banal experience of resurrection that the common people are making connections with the resurrection of Jesus. With Jesus' resurrection embodying their very own resurrection, the common people have started to read their history with new eyes, seeing it as a history of survival, struggle, and not giving up whatever little ray of hope is present. With this lens of reading history, the struggling common people have liberated the past from being a prison house. They engage in the retrieval of the past because they know that it is necessary for the journey toward a new and better tomorrow. Or as a Filipino saying puts it (in Tagalog), "*Ang hindi marunong lumingon sa pinanggalingan ay hindi makararating sa paruruonan*" (One who does not know how to look back to one's past will not reach one's destination). Looking back to one's past is a way of forging a new tomorrow through dedication to the present in acts of transformation. Here *kasaysayan* (history) is not only an *alaala* (memory) but also a *pangako* (promise).[35]

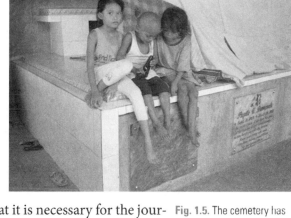

Fig. 1.5. The cemetery has been a home to many urban poor Filipinos. Photo © Josephine A. Fernandez. Used by permission.

What is this *pangako*? For the fisherfolks, it is not about the apocalyptic vision of sea or ocean disappearing (Rev. 21:1). That would not be a *pangako*, but a *bangungot* (nightmare) for those whose daily life depends on the ocean. An encounter with fisherfolks in Laguna de Bay points to this nightmarish possibility already slowly becoming a reality. One evening, in the hut where our immersion group rested for the night, one of the fisherfolks shared his fears tearfully as he thought about the death of the lake, a source of his livelihood and the future of his children, as a result of pollution coming from nearby factories. With a deep sigh he asked: "How will I support my children, and what will happen to them?"

The plight of the fisherfolks in Laguna de Bay is shared by fisherfolks in the Visayas and Mindanao. The destruction of coral reefs by illegal fishing and the death of mangroves have adversely affected the ocean's ability to support the lives of the small fisherfolks and their families. One has to go far to the open sea to get more catch. As fisherfolks in the Visayas and Mindanao say, "*Daghan pa ang mangingisda kay sa isda*" (There are more fisherfolks than fish). In Pasil (Cebu City), for example, a different form of *mananagat* (literally, one whose livelihood is associated with the ocean) has evolved. When I heard the word *mananagat*, I immediately associated it with fishing, as people commonly do. So my question to the wife of a *mananagat* was, "What kind of fish does your husband usually get?" Her answer surprised me: "My husband fishes or dives for scraps of iron or steel that fall into the ocean floor somewhere near the pier. Whatever catch he gets, he sells them by the kilo to the buyers." What a frightening image of the future: the ocean is not breeding fish but iron refuse as a result of the market's relentless pursuit of profits.

A more appropriate image of *pangako* for the lowly ones is that of a banquet—a popular image of Jesus' eschatological vision. For those who have barely enough to survive, like those who depend on *galong-gong* (round scad—a kind of fish more affordable to the common people), *daing* (dried fish), and *bagoong* (salted fish) for food, what could be the best expression of the *pangako* if not a banquet—a fiesta? The fiesta is characterized by an abundance of food—*lechon* (whole roasted pig), *embotido, hamonado, relyenong bangus, pancit, calderita,* and various kinds of desserts—and by joy, friendship, and sharing. In God's eschatological fiesta everyone has access to that which sustains life; it is an egalitarian meal.

Birthing the *pangako* is surely not an easy venture. The common Filipinos know that it requires a transformation of *loob* (core or center), a very important concept among Filipinos. They recognize that hardness of heart (*katigasan ng loob*), more than dullness of thought, is the greatest obstacle to transformation, which requires *pagba-balik loob* (repentance). For the lowly ones with diminished agency, transformation means the empowerment of *loob* so that they may develop *lakas ng loob* (courage). The development of *lakas ng loob* can, however, come only through a long gradual work of empowerment. While human effort is crucial, the common Filipinos believe that the transformation of *loob* is a *kaloob ng Dios* (gift of God) who has the attribute of *kagandahang loob* (compassion, willing the well-being of the people), says Beltran.[36]

Birthing the *pangako* (promise) requires patience, perseverance, and staying awake, qualities that are abundant in supply among those who have been seasoned by suffering and struggle. In the words of the common people: (in Tagalog) "*Kung walang tiyaga, walang nilaga*" (If you do not persevere, you cannot expect something). Small farmers know what patience and staying awake mean when they have to stay awake all night long to irrigate their rice field during hot summer months or when there is drought. *Jeepney* drivers know what patience and staying awake mean as they wait and find openings through the heavy traffic of urban centers in order to get to their destination. And fisherfolks know how to wait for the *habagat* (southwest wind) or the *amihan* (northeast wind) to subside or stop before proceeding to the ocean. They know that when *timog* comes (south wind), it is a sign that the typhoon is on its way out. The typhoon has been blowing for a long time, blowing away the people's dreams. The people are actively waiting for the opportune moment when they can synchronize their efforts with the power of *timog*, which can be interpreted as Spirit (good wind).

Moreover, birthing the *pangako*—a new and better tomorrow—requires faithful companions along the way. As the root of the word "companion" (Latin: *cum panis*) suggests, it means sharing the life nourishing *tinapay* (bread) or *baon* (meal prepared for the journey). The common people are aware that their dreamed-for new tomorrow can only come through the help of companions. They know the essence of communal endeavor through the *bayanihan* spirit (spirit of helping one another). Though this spirit is under assault, it is still alive in many areas, particularly in rural communities.

When we open ourselves to the lives of the common people, a revelation may happen. And there is no revelation without transformation. When we allow ourselves to be guests of the disenfranchised—taking popular religious history seriously—we open ourselves to the possibility of being transformed by the insights of those whose wisdom this world often despises.

## FOR FURTHER READING

Alejo, Albert. *Tao Po! Tuloy! Isang Landas ng Pag-unawa sa Loob ng Tao.* Quezon City, Philippines: Ateneo de Manila University, 1991.

Andres, Tomas, and Pilar Ilada-Andres, *Understanding the Filipino.* Quezon City, Philippines: New Day, 1987.

Bacani, Teodoro. *Mary and the Filipino.* Makati, Philippines: St. Paul, 1985.

Beltran, Benigno. *The Christology of the Inarticulate: An Inquiry into the Filipino Understanding of Jesus the Christ.* Manila, Philippines: Divine Word, 1987.

De Mesa, Jose. *In Solidarity with the Culture: Studies in Theological Re-rooting.* Maryhill Studies 4. Quezon City, Philippines: Maryhill School of Theology, 1987.

Fernandez, Eleazar S. *Toward a Theology of Struggle.* Maryknoll, N.Y.: Orbis Books, 1994.

Ileto, Reynaldo. *Pasyon and Revolution: Popular Movements in the Philippines, 1840–1910.* Quezon City, Philippines: Ateneo de Manila University, 1979.

Jocano, Landa F. *Folk Christianity: A Preliminary Study of Conversion and Patterning of Christian Experience in the Philippines,* Monograph Series No. 1. Quezon City, Philippines: Trinity Research Institute, 1981.

Mercado, Leonardo. *Inculturation in Filipino Theology.* Manila, Philippines: Divine Word, 1992.

Velunta, Revelation, ed. *Anumang Hiram Kung Hindi Masikip Ay Maluwang: Iba't-Ibang Anyo ng Teolohiyang Pumipiglas.* Dasmariñas, Cavite, Philippines: Union Theological Seminary, 2006.

# RURAL SOUTHERN BLACK WOMEN IN THE UNITED STATES

## ROSETTA E. ROSS

Recalling her youth as a tenant on a South Carolina farm, Victoria Way DeLee (b. 1925) once said, "Well, really, back then, we were treated like slaves. 'Cause when the white people said you had to go to work, you had to, whether you wanted to or not."[1] Though DeLee's experience was not indicative of that of all early twentieth-century southern rural African Americans, it was symbolic of a large number, especially those whose lives were marked by sharecropping and tenancy. Fannie Lou Townsend Hamer's (1917–1977) early experience of sharecropping was similar to DeLee's. So were her recollections about race: "I really didn't know what everything was about but I couldn't understand why Black people worked so hard and never had nothing. I just couldn't understand why the white people that weren't working were always riding in nice cars, two or three cars and a truck. I just couldn't understand why they had everything, and it seemed that we worked all the time and didn't have nothing."[2]

Although agribusiness predominates in the early twenty-first century, during the first half of the twentieth century many people in the United States lived in rural areas and interacted with family farms. DeLee's and Hamer's comments reflect the situation of many African Americans in relation to those farms. In the southern United States, most family farms were vestiges of nineteenth-century southern plantations. Eighteenth- and nineteenth-century southern colonial economies thrived off profits derived chiefly from enslaved agricultural labor. During the heyday of the colonial era, plantation profits made the South one of the wealthiest regions of the United States. By the time DeLee and Hamer were born, the elite splendor of the southern colonial economy was gone. Nevertheless, large family farms of the early through mid-twentieth century maintained relatively unbroken economic, social, and political connections to the plantation system of the colonial period. Civil rights activism by people like DeLee and Hamer challenged and helped interrupt twentieth-century continuity of colonial views and practices in the South. Cheap African American labor was the main engine driving the southern farm economy in the early twentieth century.

Two mechanisms of control preserved the status of early twentieth-century black labor: white supremacist cultural practices and the Jim Crow political codes they were coupled with. Violence and humiliation were interrelated cultural practices that aimed to maintain the colonial subordination and cheap labor costs instituted during the antebellum era. The combination of violence and humiliation—evident, for example, in verbal mockery during lynching and rape—emerged after Emancipation to mitigate potential gains of African Americans during the brief Reconstruction period. Implying that black persons did not deserve better treatment or fair compensation, racial humiliation sought to undermine the evolving identity of formerly enslaved persons as subjects and citizens. Racial violence combined with humiliation as a physical means of subduing self-conscious black agency.

When Reconstruction ended, subjugating cultural practices became more intense and were formally supplemented by Jim Crow legal codes that subordinated black persons politically. Born in the first three decades of the twentieth century, persons like DeLee and Hamer spent their childhood and early adult lives enduring these practices and negotiating the shared evangelical Christian reli-

**Fig. 2.1.** Victoria Way DeLee, c. 1971. Photo is courtesy *The State* newspaper of Columbia, South Carolina. Used by permission.

gious culture that both supported and opposed racial subordination. Once they engaged the civil rights movement, DeLee and Hamer, like other civil rights advocates, took on an interpretation of Christianity that challenged racism and made way for their development as important civil rights leaders and organizers. This chapter examines how DeLee's and Hamer's experiences in the Jim Crow South reflected the movement of rural black southern women from peonage to citizen leaders. Racial humiliation, violence, and restrictive political codes colored DeLee's and Hamer's experiences as low-wage farm laborers. As children, both engaged the southern evangelical Christian culture. As the civil rights movement entered their local areas, DeLee and Hamer combined tenacity, indigenous moral analysis, southern evangelical religious views, and liberal constructions of Christianity they encountered in civil rights activism. The combination helped DeLee, Hamer, and thousands of their contemporaries participate in bringing forth a new era of U.S. history.

**Fig. 2.2.** Fannie Lou Hamer at the Democratic National Convention, Atlantic City, New Jersey, August 1964. Photo by Warren K. Leffler, courtesy of the Library of Congress.

## AGRICULTURAL ECONOMY IN THE SOUTH

One of the most striking signs of the connection between nineteenth- and twentieth-century southern economies was the situation of African Americans and their labor in relation to the agricultural economy. During the early twentieth century an overwhelming majority of rural southern African Americans were part of the farm industry. African Americans interacted with the southern agricultural economy in three primary ways: as owners of small to moderate-size family farms, as sharecroppers, and as tenant-laborers (with the latter category including both field workers and household service workers). The majority were sharecroppers and tenants,[3] living the difficult, exploitative relationship that traded work for shares of crops, lodging, and, sometimes, meager wages.

> **Injustice and Self-Reliance**
>
> Black people who were living in the South were constantly living with violence. Part of the job was to help them to understand what that violence was and how they in an organized fashion could help to stem it. The major job was getting people to understand that they had something within their power that they could use, and it could only be used if they understood what was happening and how group action could counter violence even when it was perpetuated by the police or, in some instances, the state. My basic sense of it has always been to get people to understand that in the long run they themselves are the only protection they have against violence or injustice.... People have to be made to understand that they cannot look for salvation anywhere but to themselves.
>
> —Ella Josephine Baker, from Gerda Lerner, ed., *Black Women in White America: A Documentary History* (New York: Vintage, 1972), 347.

Based in economic practices that sought to keep labor costs as close as possible to enslaved free labor, sharecropping and tenancy systems were difficult for African Americans because the exchange of shoddy residences, paltry supplies, and meager income prevented most persons from realizing profitable benefits of their labor. Well-known southern farm economy activities reduced labor costs by extending sharecroppers' credit for seed, fertilizer, and other supplies (generally at an exorbitant markup) at the farm's supply store. Other means of reducing labor costs were cheating workers by using loaded counterweights to determine payment for picking cotton, paying tenant workers through (sometimes used) goods or with vouchers for merchandise, and extending credit for everyday goods. Young Victoria Way lamented low wages and payment through used goods, and as an adult Victoria DeLee recalled wondering why her grandmother had to "work for 25 cents a day. Why we had to go out there and bring a bag of those white people old clothes and stuff home and things like that."[4] Hamer—whose position as plantation timekeeper gave her some measure of authority—reported her resistance to defrauding practices by using her own counterweight whenever possible.[5]

At the end of the farming season, sharecroppers and tenants were often more heavily indebted to farm stores than their crop earnings or wages could cover. For many persons, this debt was perpetual. The ordinary resolution of this obligation was through the promise of labor to the farm for the following season. In what have become known as "Deep South" states, such as Mississippi and South Carolina, these labor practices were rampant. Some families were able to turn a profit and managed to escape the grip of the system. Others' hopes were dashed through cruelty such as destroying crops or killing farm animals. Hamer recalled, for example, the one year her father planned "to rent some land, because it was always better if you rent the land." That season Mr. Townsend "did get enough money to buy . . . mules, wag-

**Fig. 2.3.** Ella Baker speaking at the Democratic Convention, Atlantic City, New Jersey, August 10, 1964. Photo © 1976 George Ballis / Take Stock.

ons, cultivators and some farming equipment," but someone "killed the mules and our cows. That knocked us right back down."[6]

## LIVING WITH VIOLENCE AND HUMILIATION

In the early twentieth century many African Americans had no viable alternative to staying within the southern agricultural economy. Less than two generations past enslavement, the majority were descended from persons who had no resources to bequeath as generational assets. Moreover, social, cultural, and political structures compelled African Americans' conformity and helped secure their status as cheap labor for the southern farm economy. In addition to economic structures that kept African Americans tied to southern farms, violence and humiliation were para-economic mechanisms of subjugation and control.

Both DeLee and Hamer were familiar with indignities and violence that accompanied and supported southern agriculture. Brutal treatment of black women's bodies in the South and across the United States is well documented from the era of enslavement forward.[7] Presumptuous familiarity, especially in regard to touching and the manner of addressing black women, and the physical brutality of rape, often accompanied by coarse patriarchal verbal abuse, were forms of violence and humiliation aimed directly at black women. Disregard for African American parental authority and various forms of deprivation also may have taken on particularly gendered dimensions. Victoria DeLee described the personal experience of being struck in the head while her grandmother stood by because she disputed a white farmer's assessment of the way she picked cotton. The humiliating violence of being physically assaulted by the white landowner in her grandmother's presence was compounded by Victoria's being beaten by her grandmother, who, DeLee said, "just had to just beat me, 'cause she know if not he could, would have killed me."[8]

In addition to forms of violence and indignity targeting women, there also was, of course, the practice of lynching. Documented statistics on the number of African Americans killed through mob violence in the early twentieth century suggest that "on the average, a black man, woman, or child was murdered nearly once a week, every week, between 1882 and 1930 by a hate-driven white mob."[9] As a social and cultural instrument that supplemented political and economic practices to keep sharecropping and tenancy in place, lynching served not merely as "punishment." Booming in the early twentieth century (after Reconstruction and federal protections for African Americans were withdrawn from the South) lynching was a mechanism of terror used primarily to supplement other means of coercing African American subjugation. As they were inducted into the farm labor system, male and female children were introduced to the threat of mob violence and lynching.

DeLee's and Hamer's early knowledge of lynch mobs is evident through the vivid specificity with which they related lynching stories from their communities. Hamer recalled the report of Joe Pulliam, a black sharecropper who objected to, Hamer said, being "robbed . . . of what he earned." Initially wounded by gunfire for his objection, Pulliam lost his life when he defended himself. Hamer related details of Joe Pulliam being dragged by his heels on the back of a car through town and the severing of Pulliam's ears for display as a warning to others who might object.[10]

DeLee recounted particulars of a Mr. Fogle being castrated, having his organs stuffed in his mouth, then being hung and shot to death "piece by piece."[11] DeLee's account included both learning of the violence and experiencing humiliation and intimidation when Bub Cummings, the white farmer who reported the story, recounted details of the incident to intimidate her grandmother. Lucretia Way's being addressed with the familiar "Mom Cretia," use of the racial slur "niggers," and the threat that failure to comply could result in similar treatment all accompanied Cummings's story, which DeLee overheard. Furthermore, DeLee identified Cummings as intentionally including her as a child in the intimidation: "Here this man being killed, and I overheard. He didn't care. He talked right in front of us."[12] Practices of sociocultural racial violence persisted well into the civil rights era. Murders of student workers Michael Schwerner, Andrew Goodman, and James Chaney, NAACP leaders like Medgar Evers, volunteers such as Viola Luizzo, as well as beatings and mob attacks on protesters are a few examples of the violent intimidation aimed at curtailing civil rights activism.

> **The Bodies**
>
> During the time they were looking for the bodies of Chaney, Schwerner, and Goodman, they found other bodies throughout the state. They found torsos in the Mississippi River, they found people who were buried, they even found a few bodies of people on the side of roads.
>
> —David Dennis, quoted in *Our Enemies in Blue: Police and Power in America*, Kristian Williams (Brooklyn, N.Y.: Soft Skull, 2004), 110.

Childhood familiarity with sociocultural racial violence and participation in sharecropper and tenant indebtedness did not mean this situation was acceptable. Both DeLee and Hamer assert that as children they analyzed and protested injustice of African Americans' situation. DeLee's analysis yielded significant theological, social, and moral indignation. She protested her lack of control of her labor by compromising the quality of her work or by disobeying instructions. In response to being disciplined for her actions, DeLee verbally communicated disagreement with the morality of her grandmother's punishing her for such actions.[13] As a girl Hamer said she questioned the justice and value of hard work. "'Sometimes I be working in the fields and I get so tired I'd say to the people picking cotton with me, hard as we have to work for nothing, there must be some way we can change this.'"[14] The transgenerational nature of their experience as women particularly affected DeLee and Hamer. Both expressed anger, pain, and regret at their grandmother and mother, respectively, having such hard lives. As a child DeLee asked why "[God] let the people do what they was doing to her [grandmother]? Why she had to work so hard? . . . I was sayin', 'Don't you worry, I'll fix it for my grandmomma.'"[15] Similarly Hamer wondered, "why did it have to be so hard for [my mother]. . . . I vowed that when I got bigger, I'd do better by her. . . . If I lived to get grown and had a chance, I was going to try to get something for my mother and I was going

**Fig. 2.4.** Fannie Lou Hamer marching at a voter registration demonstration, Hattiesburg, Mississippi, January 22, 1964. Photo © 1976 Matt Herron/Take Stock.

to do something for the Black man of the south if it would cost my life; I was determined to see that things were changed."[16] As girls, neither had means nor access to effect change; however, both DeLee and Hamer resolved that things should change and, reflecting a normal familial sentiment, both wanted the changes for their parents. Both women carried this resolve into their adult lives.

In addition to their familiarity with racial violence as children, both DeLee and Hamer experienced violent practices of the civil rights era. During portions of their most active periods, repressive and retaliatory violence was common. DeLee once described a wall of her home as "like a polka dot dress where the bullet holes from where they would shoot in the house." During the same period her home was destroyed by arson.[17] DeLee and her husband, S. B., rotated sleeping at night to watch for terrorists who attacked civil rights workers' homes after dark. In one instance during school desegregation battles, a mob attacked DeLee and other African Americans who attended a high school basketball game. Harassed and beaten because of her activism, Hamer also experienced having shots fired into her home. This occurred shortly after her first voter registration attempt when she moved in with a friend. As her activism continued, Hamer said that the repeated violence "made us look like criminals. We would have to have our lights out before dark."[18] In one now infamous encounter, Hamer was brutally beaten while being held in a jail cell following her arrest with others in Winona, Mississippi. Returning from a civil rights training meeting, the group was arrested because they entered the "whites only" waiting room.[19] The severity of that beating has been said to have hastened Hamer's death.

## POLITICAL SUPPORTS FOR WHITE SUPREMACY

Limiting public education and denying civil enfranchisement were formal political mechanisms used to help subjugate black persons during the early twentieth century. Most rural black family life was shaped by the farm economy. American colonial perspectives about African Americans included narrow views about black children as well as adults. The colonial idea that African American children and youth were only potential field hands and servants remained in the imagination of many southern whites well into the twentieth century. In regard to education, formal political support of the lingering southern agricultural economy meant seasons for planting and harvesting determined African American school terms. Because planting began in early spring and harvesting continued through late fall, the school year for black children was only four months (generally November through February). While the shortened school period meant older children, youth, and adults spent planting and harvesting seasons in fields, infants and very young children who could not work spent days near the fields. Very young children generally were cared for by a slightly older child who was too young to work or whose work assignment was caring for the younger children.

Accompanying the shortened school term in limiting possibilities for rural black youth was the early age at which some children entered the labor market. Like their male counterparts, southern rural African American girls usually entered the farm economy as field laborers (and a smaller number as house servants). Fannie Lou Hamer recalled first taking on tenant indebtedness at the age children ordinarily entered school. "I started working when I was 6 years old," Hamer said. Distracted from play one day by the owner of the plantation where her family resided, Hamer agreed that she would pick thirty pounds of cotton when the farmer "called off the different kinds of things like Crackerjack and cake he would give me" if she were able to do so. The treats were things, Hamer said, "I'd never had . . . in my life." She immediately took on responsibility for the work she would engage in for the next three and a half decades, as her parents clarified their own impoverished situation that could not afford such treats: "They told me that I would have to pick that 30 lbs. of cotton myself, they wouldn't give it to me," Hamer remembered. While her parents

### On Registering to Vote

I applied for voter registration six times before I was able to be accepted. I was only able to be accepted after we had taken our registrar to court. In fact, all of my applications were used by the Justice Department in trying to have the registrar establish why I had not been registered in the beginning.

—Victoria Gray, from Henry Hampton and Steven Fayer, eds., *Voices of Freedom: An Oral History of the Civil Rights Movement from the 1950s through the 1980s* (New York: Bantam, 1991), 180.

were likely quite aware that their daughter would be indebted, the six-year-old girl was not. As Hamer found out, she became trapped in debt to the farmer, and, she later recalled, "I *never* did get out of his debt again."[20]

Civil disenfranchisement was another political mechanism for controlling African American labor. Although the thirteenth and fifteenth U.S. constitutional amendments abolished enslavement (1865) and granted black men the right to vote (1870), these constitutional changes were not secure. Postwar efforts to "reconstruct" social and political space for African Americans almost always were piecemeal and depended largely on the presence of federal troops for enforcement. The Tilden-Hayes compromise settling the 1876 election initiated withdrawal of federal troops from southern states.[21] Once the troops left, Jim Crow regression emerged. Alongside violence, southern state legislatures enacted a series of barriers to black male enfranchisement. The 1890 South Carolina state legislature, for example, abolished election of local government officials in favor of appointments, and required a poll tax, a literacy test, and property ownership for voting. In addition, the state legislature sought to strip African American men of the franchise labeling "offenses . . . blacks were thought especially prone to commit" as "disenfranchising offenses."[22] Southern black women fared no better after passage of the Nineteenth amendment (1920) enfranchising women.

## COMING OF AGE

One of the most dramatic changes brought by the civil rights movement was its disruption of social and economic connections of black labor to the southern farm economy. The resolve of rural blacks played no small role in causing this change. Women like DeLee of South Carolina and Hamer of Mississippi lived the southern legacy of the colonial era and ushered the civil rights movement into the rural South. Their civil rights activities helped sever the yoke linking the majority of southern African American labor to the southern agricultural economy. The civil rights movement altered what it meant for persons like DeLee and Hamer to fully come of age: it created a whole new meaning of entering adulthood for generations of black women.

During the early twentieth century coming of age for African American young women in the rural South included pragmatically enduring realities of continued poverty and farm work as part and parcel of considerations like marriage and family. Hamer's description of her early adult life reflects this: "My life has been almost like my mother's was, because I married a man who sharecropped." Fannie Lou Townsend met Perry Hamer in the cotton fields of Sunflower County, Mississippi. After they developed a friendship, when Fannie Lou Townsend was about twenty-four, the two married. Perry Hamer, a tractor driver for the W. D. Marlowe plantation, took his new wife to live with him; in addition to serving as a fieldhand, Mrs. Hamer was plantation timekeeper and performed housework (as did her mother) to supplement her family's income.[23] They did not have their own biological children, but the couple, while in poverty, adopted two children within the community whose families were unable to provide for them.

DeLee, who was seven years younger than Hamer, did not spend as much of her early adult life as a tenant. But she was as practical as Hamer and others of their generation in regard to the possibilities for her future. Frustrated by the way white supremacy circumscribed her life and wanting to overcome limits imposed by her stern, protective grandmother, DeLee decided getting married would give her freedom to "get what I wanted done." At age fifteen Victoria Way eloped with her suitor, S. B. DeLee, whom she met at church.[24] The DeLees had six children of their own and adopted two others. S. B. DeLee's employment with a federal agency outside his county of residence prevented the necessity of Victoria DeLee's continuing work as a tenant and provided economic security that insulated the family from financial repercussions of her civil rights activism. Still, DeLee had ongoing experience of sharecropping and tenancy, since her grandmother, mother, and siblings remained in the system.

## EVANGELICALS, JIM CROW, AND CIVIL RIGHTS

Practice of evangelical Christianity existed alongside and sometimes in support of the southern farm economy. Protestant evangelicalism was the religious tradition adhered to by most black and white southerners. Peter Paris and Latta Thomas[25] have noted that in most points of theology and doctrine African American Christian denominations acceded to the perspectives of the traditions from which they emerged. Scholars of U.S. religious history generally argue that black persons in North America took up Christianity as a consequence of at least three things: the disruption of enslaved Africans' sociocultural world, the plantation practice of imposing Christianity to indoctrinate docility, and the prohibition on practicing African traditional religions in the South.

Although they shared the same religious tradition, in general black and white southerners drew vastly different moral conclusions about the meaning of that religion for social and political life. On the one hand, many white laypeople and clergy argued that Christianity supported racial segregation and racial hierarchy. Riggins Earl and Eugene Genovese note that some clergy developed complex treatises arguing for this.[26] Moreover, as Charles Marsh points out, during the civil rights era Ku Klux Klan leaders used Christianity to substantiate their opposition to the movement.[27] On the other hand, African Americans connected their opposition to segregation and subordination with their understanding of Christianity. Although African Americans began to practice Christianity during the period of their enslavement and often encountered interpretations of Christianity that encouraged their compliance, as the religion developed among them, it was distinct from the prevailing southern white interpretations in at least one feature: African Americans held the widespread view that racial subordination and white supremacy were incompatible with Christianity.

It cannot be argued that to a person every African American arrived at the same moral conclusion about the social and political meaning of Christianity. Some did not disagree with their enslavement, and some blacks were themselves enslavers. Nor can it be ignored that some southern white Christians opposed enslavement and segregation. Nevertheless, the reigning tendency among the two groups in regard to the meaning of being Christian rests on this disparity about practical moral implications of the religion. The discrepancy proved to be the basis of what Vincent Harding has called "the river" of black resistance to bondage as well as the source of black and white abolitionist sentiments. It also was the origin of the civil rights movement activities in which Hamer and DeLee became involved.

Opponents of enslavement and racial subordination depended on shared aspects of the evangelical Christian religious culture to support their efforts for change. Although moral conclusions drawn by black and white southerners generally differed in regard to religion's implications for sociopolitical life, it was at least in part moral suasion based on religious ideas that accompanied the rhetoric of abolitionists and civil rights advocates as they aimed their arguments at white Christians. The location of South Carolina and Mississippi in the country's Bible belt meant evangelical Christianity held strong cultural significance in the rearing and identities of DeLee and Hamer. Like the majority of people across the South, from childhood on, both engaged Christianity as part of the ascribed cultural belief system.

DeLee and Hamer recall early religious inculcation that included prayers by women in their family. DeLee also remembered her questions about the utility of theological faith and prayer. She said her grandmother Lucretia Way believed in and prayed for divine intervention to change her circumstances, to "fix it." But young Victoria wondered, "What kind of God [would] let people do what they was doing to her [grandmother]?" At that point, DeLee said, she doubted the existence of any divinity.[28] DeLee's disbelief as a child broached the issue of theodicy. Taken up among some black theologians shaped by the civil rights era, theodicy emerges from the reality of centuries of black suffering in North America and remains an issue among theistic believers in the African diaspora. As a child DeLee challenged and debated her grandmother's God, ultimately declaring to that divinity, "Don't you worry, I'll fix it for my grandmomma. I'm gon' fix it."[29] DeLee's questions about divine care and intervention and her childhood determination that change depended on her own efforts resonate with views expressed by William Jones and Anthony Pinn in their treatises about African Americans' understandings of the relationship between God and suffering.[30]

Hamer's early recollections of religious instruction include her mother's praying for her children. In contrast to DeLee, Hamer describes her own childhood perspective as theistically affirmative. She anticipated divine assistance to support her desire to make changes. "I began to make promises to myself," Hamer recalled, "'cause I didn't really know who to make promises to, and . . . I really just asked God because I believe in God; I asked God to give me a chance to just let me do something about what was going on in Mississippi."[31] Although Hamer's "prayer" involved seeking divine help, she resolved to "do something" through her own efforts. In spite of Hamer's early theism, by questioning the value of hard work done by African Americans—"I just couldn't understand why Black people worked so hard and never had nothing"—she implied an interrogation of the Protestant work ethic that accompanied southern evangelical Christianity. Alongside its role as the source of wealth accumulation among some individuals, the Protestant work ethic became intrinsic to the dominant cultural perspective that poor and working-class manual labor warranted less financial reward. In this regard, as Hamer's observation implied, poor people's hard work served only to keep the poor *and* the privileged in "their places."

Having been inducted into the religiosity of southern and African American culture as children, both Hamer and DeLee integrated Christianity into their family lives. As an adult Hamer was a regular member at Williams Chapel Baptist Church in Ruleville, Mississippi. The DeLee family was active at St. John Baptist Church and then helped found the House of God Pentecostal congregation, both in Ridgeville, South Carolina. Notwithstanding their induction into the South's and African Americans' religious culture, both Hamer and DeLee demonstrated independent critical views in regard to the meaning and practice of religion for their lives. Hamer, for example,

---

### On Freedom Summer

For black people in Mississippi, Freedom Summer was the beginning of a whole new era. People began to feel that they wasn't just helpless anymore, that they had come together. Black and white had come from the North and from the West and even from some cities in the South. Students came and we wasn't a closed society anymore. They came to talk about that we had a right to register to vote, we had a right to stand up for our rights. That's a whole new era for us. I mean hadn't anybody said that to us, in that open way, like what happened in 1964.

—Unita Blackwell, from Henry Hampton and Steven Fayer, eds., *Voices of Freedom: An Oral History of the Civil Rights Movement from the 1950s through the 1980s* (New York: Bantam, 1991), 193.

articulated the complex perspective that both affirmed how Christian practices supported African Americans and criticized some black churches and black church leaders for "selling out" or failing to sufficiently use the church's moral and physical resources on behalf of the poor.[32] DeLee expressed critical disagreement with Pentecostals who disparaged social and political engagement as "worldly" and in conflict with the "holiness" emphasis of those traditions.[33]

## CIVIL RIGHTS ACTIVISM AS RELIGIOUS PRACTICE

The dawning of the civil rights movement and its progression into rural areas of the South dramatically changed the ordinary lives of people like Victoria Way DeLee and Fannie Lou Townsend Hamer. Conversely, individuals like DeLee and Hamer considerably affected the movement's momentum as they helped shift the meaning of becoming a black woman in the rural South. In addition to bringing legal expertise that challenged labor and other economic practices, the civil rights movement brought resources and activism that increased the number of independent black farmers and provided employment options for black workers. Moreover, the movement contributed to the enfranchisement of millions of African Americans whose participation in electoral processes changed the status of black persons from peons to citizens, thus altering southern politics. For some, the civil rights movement provided the option (and sometimes as a result of personal activism the requirement) to change jobs. In southern rural areas, for the more creative and assertive who saw opportunities to become full U.S. citizens and change the status of black persons, the movement meant they realized potentialities and opportunities that otherwise would have been swallowed up in poverty, indignity, and peonage.

Fig. 2.5. A student worker (Heather Tobis Booth) talks with a woman in a cotton field in Mississippi.

The shifts that occurred in DeLee's and Hamer's lives were quite dramatic, since both lived in close relationship to sharecropping and tenancy well into adulthood. This was especially true for Hamer, who, still living as a farm tenant, was forty-four years old when she first engaged civil rights practices in 1962. Because of their initiative and determination, by the time of the movement's waning both women had developed careers as community activists and public figures and had contributed significantly to setting in motion practices and ideas for a "New South." Christianity played no small role in changes that occurred in these women's lives.

Like many other black southerners who initially encountered the civil rights movement through their churches, Victoria DeLee first learned of civil rights practices from her Baptist pastor, Reverend R. B. Adams. As early as the 1940s Adams motivated congregants to attempt voter registration. Already predisposed to help change the South, DeLee responded to the potential she heard in Adams's recommendations. DeLee's successful registration and her pastor and congregation's celebration of that success perhaps sealed for DeLee—at that time still a young adult—her understanding of civil rights activism as religious practice.[34]

With the support of her pastor, congregation, and community, DeLee engaged the civil rights movement tenaciously. After formally securing her own enfranchisement, DeLee encouraged other African Americans to follow. Staying in the context of her initiation into the movement, DeLee began her civil rights activism by visiting and speaking to members at local churches. In addition to voter registration work, DeLee agitated for African American exercise of their franchise. In 1964, DeLee filed civil actions on behalf of her children, challenging Dorchester County's school segregation practices. Along with her husband, S. B., DeLee contested the racial and gender bias of Dorchester County's jury pool. DeLee's ongoing participation in a range of civil rights activities included leading boycotts and pickets to open employment opportunities for African Americans, organizing and encouraging African American participation in Democratic Party precinct activities, and cofounding a third party, the United Citizens' Party (UCP), in South Carolina. As the UCP's first vice president, DeLee was also the party's first statewide candidate. In 1971 she ran for Congress in the state's first congressional district but was unsuccessful in her bid.

In keeping with the then-predominant religiosity of the South and her identity as a Pentecostal laywoman, throughout her activism DeLee's self-representation was first and foremost as a religious person. She says she and her husband left behind Baptist traditions because they identified with the emphasis on "holy living" in the House of God denomination. In a 1971 interview DeLee cited her practice of "holiness" as a signature of her character and as defense against charges that she was physically and verbally abusive toward a police officer. The contrast of DeLee's "holiness" defense with the police report's depiction of her ("resisting arrest, striking a police officer, and cursing and abusing a police officer")[35] is a provocative example of the extent to which the colonial image of African American women justified white supremacy, violent retaliation for civil rights activism, and brutal treatment of black women. In addition to this self-conscious "religious" self-representation, during a 1992 interview DeLee expressed emphatic satisfaction that her moral reputation remained unblemished, especially in view of her interaction with men throughout her activism: "I've never been accused of nobody's husband, man or nothing," she said. Well aware of the pragmatic utility of her moral practice, DeLee observed that black women supported her because of this.[36]

The moral practice of "holiness" did not, however, become the whole meaning of DeLee's religiosity. Departing from the predominant emphasis in early twentieth-century black Pentecostalism and from an important concern of evangelical black Christianity, DeLee saw personal moral piety as the beginning and not the end of living a religious life. In the late nineteenth and early twentieth centuries, both whites who blamed black immorality and indolence for the plight of African Americans and black elites who advocated racial uplift understood moral piety as a combination of moral uprightness and industriousness. Moreover, in view of the postbellum and post–Reconstruction social status of black Americans, moral piety became the dominant mode of being an African American Christian. DeLee's departure from equating the whole of evangelical black Christianity with moral piety is important. By rejecting this viewpoint, DeLee, like many other black Christian civil rights activists, overcame the pious apologetic perspective that had long shackled the social power of African American

Protestantism. Furthermore, as one of a few women among mostly men in the movement, DeLee modeled in mid-twentieth-century Dorchester County a different way of being a woman. Although she was a wife and mother, owing to her primary participation in civil rights activism she was also a public figure. In taking up this role, DeLee broke with reigning conventions that prohibited all women's public participation and that particularly repressed black women.

As was true for DeLee, Hamer first engaged civil rights activism in a church. Hamer volunteered to attempt to register to vote after hearing of the possibility at a church meeting. Hamer's encounter with movement ideas and practices came not through her own pastor but through student ministers organizing for the Student Non-violent Coordinating Committee (SNCC) and the Southern Christian Leadership Conference (SCLC) in Mississippi. SNCC and SCLC student workers (including recent college graduates as well as active students who took short- and long-term leave from study) left northern and southern cities to support civil rights practices across the rural South. Student workers noted Hamer's leadership during her first registration attempt: she led gospel songs that calmed her peers when police began to harass the potential registrants. Students also encouraged Hamer by providing employment as an SNCC field secretary, which paid a regular, though meager, salary. In taking up full-time work for SNCC, Hamer shifted her sociocultural identity from sharecropper-tenant to community activist. While this altered identity proved beneficial, especially for future generations of rural black women, trauma prompted it for Hamer. Immediately after that first registration attempt, Hamer lost her job and home of eighteen years and began to experience repeated retaliatory violence. The significance of the SNCC salary for the Hamer family cannot be overestimated: the loss of her job and home with the advent of her civil rights career in August—during harvesting and preserving season—meant Hamer did not have time to prepare her family's ordinary winter food supplements. "That was a rough winter," she recalled.[37]

In many ways Fannie Lou Hamer is a paradigm of what the civil rights movement meant for southern rural African American women. Hamer's fame as an activist made her a searing example of the extent to which racial segregation and racial subordination divested people of opportunities and deprived society of their gifts. Once she began SNCC work, Hamer quickly moved from local to statewide to national prominence. In SNCC Hamer solicited others for voter registration, led citizenship training sessions to prepare potential voters for literacy tests that obstructed their enfranchisement, and organized relief for persons suffering retaliation for their activism. Hamer's natural intelligence combined with civil rights practices to make her an important leader of the Mississippi movement. Eventually she became a national civil rights speaker, traveling across the country to secure funds and other support for the movement.

After massive voter registration efforts across the state during 1963 and 1964, Mississippi organizers strategized to replace the exclusive and segregated state Democratic Party with the more inclusive, diverse, and newly formed Mississippi Freedom Democratic Party (MFDP). Because the MFDP held open precinct and county caucuses, its members argued their legitimacy over the "regular" Mississippi Democrats at the 1964 National Democratic Convention (DNC). As MFDP vice chairperson, Hamer riveted the national television audience with testimony before the DNC credentials committee. Unfortunately, power politics trumped moral justice, and the Freedom Democrats lost their bid to be seated at the convention. As a result of the MFDP challenge, Hamer joined other MFDP members as delegates at the 1968 DNC. After 1968 Hamer's civil rights activism took on a decidedly local, economic focus through organizing for affordable housing and cooperative farm programs.

Perhaps because she became so prominent and experienced many speaking and training

## The New Kingdom in Mississippi

To me, the 1964 Summer Project was the beginning of a New Kingdom right here on earth. The kinds of people who came down from the North—from all over—who didn't know about us—were like the Good Samaritan. In that Bible story, the people had passed the wounded man—like the church has passed the Negroes in Mississippi—and never taken time to see what was going on. But these people who came to Mississippi that summer—although they were strangers—walked up to our door. They started something that no one could ever stop. These people were willing to move in a nonviolent way to bring change in the South. Although they were strangers, they were the best friends we ever met. This was the beginning of the New Kingdom in Mississippi. To me, if I had to choose today between the church and these young people—and I was brought up in the church and I'm not against the church—I'd choose these young people. They did something in Mississippi that gave us the hope that we had prayed for so many years. We had wondered if there was anybody human enough to see us as human beings instead of animals.

—Fannie Lou Hamer, from the foreword to Tracy Sugarman's *Stranger at the Gates: A Summer in Mississippi* (New York: Hill and Wang, 1967), viii.

opportunities, Hamer developed sophisticated rhetorical constructions of her religious understanding of civil rights practices. She clearly articulated her belief that the nature of Christianity is "being concerned about your fellow man, not building a million-dollar church while people are starving right around the corner." In her foreword to Tracy Sugarman's *Stranger at the Gates*, Hamer distinguished the practice of Christianity from the church and church attendance. Saying she would choose the community of civil rights activists over the church, Hamer pointed to active compassion as a sign of Christianity: "They did something in Mississippi that gave us the hope we had prayed for so many years. We had wondered if there was anybody human enough to see us as human beings instead of as animals."[38]

## THE SIGNIFICANCE OF CLASS

Neither DeLee nor Hamer ever fully escaped poverty. Limited education coupled with their initial socioeconomic circumstances were so substantial that these social markers prevented them from ever completely realizing the benefits of their activism. A major focus of civil rights activism included the morally compelling argument that all persons should be treated equally; however, circumstances such as those at the 1964 Democratic National Convention revealed the trenchant difficulty of overcoming U.S. social class barriers. Hubert Humphrey's spontaneous expression of the ultimate reason for objecting to Fannie Lou Hamer's being seated during the 1964 convention ("The President will not allow that illiterate woman to speak on the floor of the convention"[39]) reflected his interpretation of President Johnson's perspective about the place of impoverished, poorly educated former tenants and sharecroppers in American society. Humphrey also articulated the reality that physically and verbally apparent social class markers could easily limit political opportunities and advancement.

In an important sociological text provocatively entitled *The Declining Significance of Race*, William Julius Wilson cogently observed what Humphrey's statement reflected: "the problems of subordination for certain segments of the black population and the experiences of social advancement for others are more directly associated with economic class in the modern industrial period."[40] Wilson also points out that the primary African American beneficiaries of civil rights advances were persons with formal education, which positioned them to take advantage of professional opportunities that unfolded as a result of the combined efforts of civil rights activists across the country.

DeLee's and Hamer's experiences of poverty and oppression presented striking evidence of problems lingering from the antebellum racial divide in the United States. Their willingness to become activists brought these problems to national attention. In this regard, rural southern African American civil rights participants like DeLee and Hamer helped change the meaning of becoming adults for rural southern black women (and men). They also opened doors for many other African Americans, doors that ultimately remained closed to DeLee and Hamer themselves. The challenge of providing opportunities denied to DeLee and Hamer remains. Rural and urban poverty persist as major impediments to meaningful social participation and advancement in the United States and around the globe. Collaborative relationships across social class (and other) dividing lines—frequently realized during the civil rights movement—are necessary to overcoming these barriers. Are there sufficient moral resources to help inspire this in any contemporary forms of Christianity?

## FOR FURTHER READING

Collier-Thomas, Bettye , ed. *Sisters in the Struggle: African American Women in the Civil Rights–Black Power Movement.* New York: New York University Press, 2001.

Crawford ,Vicki L., Jacqueline Anne Rouse, Barbara Woods, eds. *Women in the Civil Rights Movement· Trailblazers and Torchbearers, 1941–1965.* Bloomington: Indiana University Press, 1993.

Dittmer, John. *Local People: The Struggle for Civil Rights in Mississippi.* Chicago: University of Illinois Press, 1995.

Hampton, Henry, and Steve Fayer, eds. *Voices of Freedom: An Oral History of the Civil Rights Movement from the 1950s through the 1980s.* New York: Bantam, 1991.

Hine, Darlene Clark, and Kathleen Thompson. *A Shining Thread of Hope.* New York: Broadway, 1999.

Lerner, Gerda, ed. *Black Women in White America: A Documentary History.* 1972. Reprint, New York: Vintage, 1993.

Olson, Lynne. *Freedom's Daughters: The Unsung Heroines of the Civil Rights Movement from 1830 to 1970.* New York: Touchstone, 2002.

Payne, Charles M. *I've Got the Light of Freedom: The Organizing Tradition and the Mississippi Freedom Struggle*. 1995. Reprint, Berkeley: University of California Press, 2007.

Ransby, Barbara. *Ella Baker and the Black Freedom Movement: A Radical Democratic Vision*. Chapel Hill: University of North Carolina Press, 2005.

Ross, Rosetta E. *Witnessing and Testifying: Black Women, Religion and Civil Rights*. Minneapolis: Fortress Press, 2003.

# AFRICAN WOMEN THEOLOGIANS

## MERCY AMBA ODUYOYE

## CHAPTER THREE

I will make sure that someday
Things will be different
As different as a woman
Protecting a man.
—Jeremiah 21:22

The Circle of Concerned African Women theologians (the Circle) claims this promise that God made to ancient Israel and so seeks to achieve this vision of a different world. An Akan[1] symbol of hope is an open seed that means "There is something in the heavens; God let it reach us." This affirmation of hope for something beyond our present experience stimulates our work.

We date ourselves from 1989, but we stand on our holy scriptures, cultural texts, and all that is women-friendly in our African cultures and in our faith communities. The Muslims among us would say that a woman protected the Prophet (peace be upon him). Historians among us revive the memories of African women of note, and the Christians would cite a Mary or two. If we cite only our words and works in this account, it is because we found that our existence as women and as women theologians has not been recognized by others in African culture or in the church. Many have spoken and continue to speak their words not simply about us but often purportedly for us and on our behalf.

In October 1989 something happened at Trinity Theological Seminary (then College) in Legon, Ghana. African women in theological fields gathered at a conference organized around the theme "Daughters of Africa Arise." The convocation was planned as an inspirational event to motivate the participants to reflect on their lives as women of faith with a specific vocation to do theology. Bible studies were central, and cultural events featured storytelling and dramatics. At the deliberative sessions during the nine days of encounters, the study institute decided to inaugurate itself as a Circle of Concerned African Women Theologians.

This "outdooring" of African women theologians coincided with the Africa regional meeting of the World Council of Churches Ecumenical Decade of Churches in Solidarity with Women. This was organized by Omega Bula of All Africa Conference of Churches at Lome, Togo. Bula was also at the conference at Trinity. In Nairobi, the Pan African Christian Women's Association (PACWA) held its first conference, "Our Time Has Come." Founded in 1987, the PACWA is the women's forum of the Evangelical Association of Africa and Madagascar. The year 1989, then, was when African women rallied around the call to stand up.

What is new in the Circle's efforts and in the history of African women is that we tell our stories ourselves. The case is often made that traditional African religions and cultures make room for requisite and adequate participation for women. This ignores the fact of women's common experience in Africa that "by the time a woman has spent her energies struggling to be heard, she barely has the energy left to say what she wanted to say."[2] A people's history expands and changes when half the people whose voices previously have not been heard, whose experiences have not been recorded, begin to speak.

The historical, cultural, and religious contexts for the beginnings of the Circle can be found particularly in the last half of the twentieth century in Africa. During the first half of the century, the continent had endured the suffering of two "world" wars emanating from Europe. The afflictions experienced were far more traumatic than those caused by the previous colonial pillage. The growing awareness of the extent of these afflictions and the reasons for them resulted in an increase in global recognition of many different historical realities and the unmasking of the fact that historical writings had recorded only the stories of the powerful. "There began to emerge from the kitchen the stories of people who cooked in other people's kitchens so that the hostess might be complimented while the men who worked tirelessly for other men dropped their tools, saying they were not women."[3] Poles of opposition began to solidify: black and white, rich and poor, North and South. And there emerged as well the gender question, experienced by most cultures as one of the oldest struggles of humanity.

This question of the "natures" of women and men—What is woman? What is man?—and the relationships between them in African culture was sparked in new ways in 1985, four years before the founding of the Circle, when the world's women met in Nairobi on the continent where men at that time prided themselves on having women who had no need to seek liberation. While the Nairobi meeting was in session, African men were still snickering. But something new had touched the women of Africa, and they began to voice their presence. Women were standing up, abandoning the crouched position from which their breaths stimulated the wood fires burning under the earthen pots of vegetables they had grown and harvested. The pots, too, were their handiwork. Standing up

straight, women of Africa stretched their hands to the global sisterhood of life-loving women. In no uncertain terms women announced their position in the liberation struggle and their solidarity with other women.

Fig. 3.1. Logo of the Circle of Concerned African Women Theologians.

Before Nairobi there had been signs of solidarity, but it had been crouching under North-South economic, racist, and militaristic struggles for power. In Africa the move by women to seek more humane conditions for themselves was simply denied. When the women's efforts were detected, they were assigned to the cracked pot of Western decadence, unbecoming to Young Africa. Over time, African women had learned to know their oppressors but had held their peace: "When your hand is in someone's mouth, you do not hit that person on the head." But Nairobi stirred something new among the women of Africa, a desire to make themselves heard and their influence felt in the culture and in the church. The Circle is part of this history. It is also part of the history of the search by Africa's peoples for something new: not the changelessness of African tradition and not Christianity in its Western forms, but nonetheless a Christianity that is at the same time authentically African and authentically Christian.

In 1989, out of our cultural, social, religious, colonial, and missionary histories, the Circle stated its goals as follows:

- to create a forum of women whose interests are in the area of how religion and culture function in the lives of women;
- to publish documents for the academic study of religion and culture;
- to contribute to research that leads to policies affecting African women's development and their participation in religion and society;
- to work toward the inclusion of women's studies in religion and culture in the research carried out by institutes of African studies at African universities and other tertiary institutions;
- to enable African women in religious and cultural studies to contribute to cross-cultural studies of contemporary women's issues;
- to establish a network of women to monitor women's interest in this area and to serve as advocates for the inclusion of women in all deliberations in the field of religion and culture;
- to promote the inclusion of specifically women's concerns in the theory and practice of evangelism.[4]

If at first reading these goals sound more academic and abstract than "of the people," they resonate very deeply with the daily lives of most African women: women of different classes, non-Christian and Christian, urban and rural, rich and poor, educated and uneducated. They speak to the experiences of women all over Africa whose family, communal, and social lives are shaped by multiple forces, and "despite their differences," says Isabel Apawo Phiri, "they share a common experience of oppression from patriarchal practices in the African church and in society at large."[5] At the cultural-religious level folktales of African cultures admonish all women to be silent and sacrificing and always to put the corporate needs of family, clan, or nation ahead of the personhood and gifts of the individual woman. Numerous proverbs that are couched in formalized language function as potent, authoritative statements that in many different forms convey the sentiment "Fear women" or suggest that women are quarrelsome or demanding.

Equally powerful in their deleterious effects on African women are the drastic changes in their economic lives that have led to the association of women, and particularly mothers, with poverty. For example, in the mother-centered Asante culture, it is said that the child belongs to the mother. Mothers-to-be are safeguarded by taboos that insure their health and a safe delivery. After the child is born, her or his welfare becomes the responsibility of the community. These protections, born of ancient wisdom, have not been transported into the realities of contemporary economic and social life. Thus, the woman's capacity valued above almost all others in African culture— to bring new life into the world—is bringing with it "the penalty of motherhood," that is, to be poor. There are also the horrors of widespread AIDS and the issues of sexual trafficking.

Fig. 3.2. *Mother and Child* by Gerard Sekoto (South Africa, 1959). Courtesy National Archives (Contemporary African Art Select List collection #214).

And then there is the church, which still asks questions like "and women— where do they come in?" as if women were creatures apart from the rest of humankind and not partners in the theological enterprise. In response, the Circle asks, "Are women 'church' or not? Are women an integral part of the human race or not?"

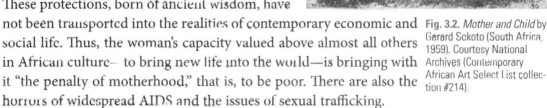

## STORIES OF ORIGIN

Over the years of its existence the Circle has become a phenomenon that intrigues people not only in Africa but abroad. Even while we were in the planning stages, we were already being stalked and

## Women's Leadership in African Churches

With only a few exceptions, African churches have resisted including women in leadership positions. The most common argument is no longer theological but cultural: African cultures do not allow women to lead men. African women theologians are saying that such an argument seems deliberately to ignore African cultures that allowed women to be leaders at shrines as priestesses and mediums, as well as those cultures that have female queens and chiefs. There is then a contradiction in the way that the church in Africa has preached about the equality of all humanity in Jesus Christ while in practice excluding women from the Eucharistic ministry. Women demand that the church return to a Christ-like understanding of authority and ministry—a demand for inclusiveness in ecclesial ministry and authority that is a quest for wholeness in the church of Christ.

—Isabel Apawo Phiri, "Doing Theology in Community: The Case of African Women Theologians in the 1990s," *Journal of Theology for Southern Africa* 99 (November 1997): 73–74.

evaluated. People wondered, "Who are these African women who call themselves theologians, and what are their concerns?" There are many perspectives from which to tell the story of the origins of the Circle. What one understands as the beginnings of the Circle depends on who is telling the story and for what purpose. Even as members of the Circle, we do not start from the same point.

Nyambura Njoroge begins with the World Council of Churches trajectory of women's participation in the church and specifically with the consultation of nine women theological students, including herself, held at Cartigny, Geneva.[6] Musimbi Kanyoro dates the beginnings to the initial group that met in Geneva to plan the 1989 meeting. Kanyoro notes specifically how the role of sexuality in African women's lives was introduced into the discussions, and out of this experience emerged her theological frame of "engendered cultural hermeneutics," that is, not taking cultural norms related to gender for granted but analyzing them in ways that will reveal what about them is life-affirming for women and what is destructive.[7] Bernadette Mbuy-Beya begins her Circle story with her shock and other responses to her discoveries in her work with women participating in transactional sex services and with children in her orphanage. At least one person—who cannot see how the African religious past, including its primal religious imagination and culture, can bequeath anything positive—has strained to locate the Circle in European Enlightenment and Christian missionary women's work in Africa and several other strands and roots outside Africa.

For some, the Circle's origins are more institutionally oriented than personal. The Brazilian theologian Virginia Fabella notes that many of the African women theologians who were members of the

Ecumenical Association of Third World Theologians (EATWOT), among them Daisy Obi, Isabel Johnston, and me, had leading roles in founding the Circle. From where Fabella stands, the Circle was designed on behalf of the African women of EATWOT, and, in effect, the Circle was in existence even before its formal founding. Indeed, the history of the Circle's origins is intertwined with EATWOT. The second EATWOT dialogue in Accra in 1977, twelve years before the official founding of the Circle, included African women who later became members of the Circle. In 1983 a commission on theology from a Third World women's perspective was formed in order to create awareness of the realities of women's subjugation, to challenge patriarchal elements in theology, and to make sure that theology works for liberation. There were efforts as well during these years to make sure that African women participated meaningfully in EATWOT as well as in the Ecumenical Association of African Theologians (EEAT). It was the 1981 EATWOT conference in New Delhi that made feminists of us. I was particularly struck by the use of misogynist folktales from Africa for entertainment at the conference.

Fig. 3.3. Musimbi Kanyoro, who is also former Secretary General of the World YWCA and currently director of the Population Program at the Packard Foundation. Photo courtesy of Musimbi Kanyoro and the World YWCA.

The politics of African women's representation in EATWOT also has a bearing on the prehistory of the Circle. As EATWOT grew, it became impractical to have all members present at every conference. A quota system was devised so that the three regions—Africa, Asia, and Latin America—would have equal representation and the "minorities," that is, North America and the Caribbean, would be present with a lesser quota. A quota system that gave Africa fifteen to twenty representatives naturally limited women's access. This became a strong motivation for us as African women in EATWOT to create our own platform from which we could launch the few who would be selected for these meetings. So we also worked on EATWOT themes while pursuing our chosen fields of religion and culture.

When women raised their voices in EATWOT, the numbers game shifted from continental representation to gender balance. EATWOT decided to try for one-third women delegates, though some men said there would not be enough women to fulfill the ratio.[8] Establishing the Circle revealed the lie to this assertion, often raised when women's participation is proposed anywhere, and the Circle has fostered a forum in which the many African women in theology could be connected with each other and have a voice.

All these different stories are well and good. After all, it is often said that "there is nothing new under the sun," and in Africa we say that if we stand tall to reach the heights we aspire to, it is because we stand on the shoulders of others. We made a conscious decision at the beginning to do our own thing until we knew who we were and what we were capable of. The aim of the Circle was stated as the quest "to end the isolation and marginalization of African women in the study of religion and culture." This was not to be study merely for its own sake but to begin the call for the integration of the study of religion and culture in deciding the direction of social change in Africa.

The postcolonial efforts to throw a fresh light on Africa using a torch held by Africans involved many aspects of life, but they were not gender-sensitive. The goal of the Circle has been to change this. We were so sure of our need to do this as African women that friends from Europe who wanted to come to our first meeting were asked to stay away. We needed space and could not tell what would happen if we were forced to play to the gallery. The Circle wanted to be an independent, multireligious association pursuing its own agenda and concerns. We did not want to involve others until we had shaped what we wanted to become. We made an exception for Africans in the diaspora and had three women from outside the continent: two, Jacquelyn Grant and Katie Cannon, from the United States and one, Verna Cassells, from Jamaica. We were able to hold to this policy until 1996, the year we had planned to evaluate our efforts and make new plans. In 1996, one British woman insisted on attending our meeting after being told specifically that it would be inappropriate for her to come. Later she interpreted this response as racism and neglected to acknowledge the presence of white South Africans at the meeting in Nairobi and in previous Circle publications.

With this in view, like the evangelist Luke, I say that many have told of these beginnings. To add to it all, I now tell my own experience of the history of the Circle. I see it as part of women's participation in shaping theology in Africa and therefore an attempt to touch the ethos of religion in Africa in general and Christianity in particular. For me, the Circle really began in 1976, when I felt the urge to find other African women in theology.[9] My friend and colleague Brigalia Bam of South Africa had tried in vain for three years, 1967–1970, to interest me in "women's affairs." We were both program staff working for the World Council of Churches and living in Geneva. It took marriage in a patrilineal world and interaction with other African cultures in Nigeria to motivate me. It was when I joined the Religious Studies Department at the University of Ibadan, Nigeria, that I became gender-sensitive. Women friends at the University of Ibadan who were also gender-sensitive helped me with the cross-cultural puzzles, but there were no other women in theology. I needed to find them.

## GENDER SENSITIVITY

In 1978, a conversation on women's liberation in the staff common room of the Faculty of Arts at the University of Ibadan led to a public lecture at the Institute of African Studies. I delivered a paper called "The Asante Woman: Socialization through Proverbs." I argued that African cultures have built-in beliefs, practices, and language that are oppressive to women.[10] The popular view, on the other hand, sparked off by the United Nations declaration of a year for women, was that the notion of women's liberation was foreign to Africa and that African women were not oppressed. The debate in the staff common room as to whether or not this was the case and the response to the public lecture convinced me that the time had come to seek out women who would study the phenomenon more closely.

The primary root of the Circle for me, then, is the search for community and solidarity with a focus on religion and culture. The Circle began its life as "an ever-expanding group of women, with or without formal education in theology, bound together in their common belief that religion and culture are key in the liberation of the humanity of religion."[11] I sought out women, but there were men who also shared this concern for women's liberation. Even at that time some men were willing to look positively upon the phenomenon of women's liberation beyond the sensationalism of popular opinion and mass media presentation of events. Soon thereafter, the theme of the annual religious studies conference at the university was "Women in Religion and Society." Although I was in charge of the conference at that time, the theme was not my idea. Walter Davis was the one who proposed it,[12] and the idea was debated by colleagues in the department—all men.

## FINDING ONE ANOTHER

The years from 1989 through 1996 were a period of finding one another through local and national workshops and doing so in the face of major obstacles. One of the major goals of the Circle was to challenge the physical isolation of African women theologians. How could women be brought together across the vast continent that is Africa? For many years we had no e-mail, and the postal service in Africa was more than precarious. We had to travel and meet in person; funding air travel was and remains a challenge. Related to distances, then, was the daunting task of financing all-Africa meetings. Another challenge was linguistic diversity: the multiplicity of languages indigenous to Africa as well as the European languages that are the heritage of colonialism. And then there was the matter of what models to use for our gatherings. First, there was the idea of institutes, for which the Oxford Institute of Wesleyan Studies was the model. The Institute was Euro-American but later became global in terms of the identity of its participants. A core group decides a theme in consultation with all interested parties, and a date is fixed to meet every four years or so, always at Oxford, to hear and discuss the results of individual research. This is an institute without its own physical structures, no academic board, no examinations, and no certificates, but it has shaped many lives and professions. The Circle was young, we were finding our feet, and we needed to meet more often, so the planners envisaged meeting every other year; hence the idea of biennial institutes.

The difficulties with financing an all-Africa meeting were met by the decision to make the biennial meetings zonal and to have three of them in six years. The zones took shape as follows:

- West Africa English-speaking: Sierra Leone, Ghana, Nigeria, and Cameroon (English). We were to make contacts in Gambia and Liberia.
- French-speaking: Senegal, Côte d'Ivoire, Togo, Benin, Cameroon (French), Zaire (Democratic Republic of Congo), Congo Brazzaville, Rwanda, Burundi, Madagascar, and Angola-Mozambique
- Eastern and Southern Africa English-speaking: Egypt, Ethiopia, Sudan, Uganda, Kenya, Tanzania, Malawi, Madagascar, Swaziland, Lesotho, South Africa, Angola, Mozambique, Botswana, Zimbabwe, Zambia, Lesotho.

In the seventh year we would evaluate and decide what to do next.

One of the major reasons for organizing around language zones was the cost of translating. We were trying to save that money for the pan-African meetings. Some countries had options, because individuals had facility with more than one language. We had also used Swahili at one of our planning sessions in Geneva. We still cherish the hope of communicating in African languages. So far this happens only on the local level and in small-group discussions in our own language areas. This enables the women with whom we dialogue to say their own words in their own idioms. This language issue is a challenge to all Africa, and we women who take most seriously women's experiences, words, and wisdom are caught up in it. The only theological work in an African language by an African woman we have thus far is *Jesus of the Deep Forest: The Prayers and Praise of Afua Kuma*. The author is a Ghanaian woman from an African independent church who was recorded and published in Ghana by two Roman Catholic priests. The Circle members have cited this book often to show that it is possible.

In the first seven-year period (1989–1996) the Circle had three biennial institutes, one in each of the three zones. Meeting in Nairobi in 1996, 124 conference participants affirmed the Circle but not the biennial institutes; the experiences of seven years had taught us other ways of organizing ourselves. That year we decided to stay together to do theology that responds to the challenges of life in Africa, especially those raised by women. Variety of history, perspective, and place continued to characterize our members. Many of the women remained in

## Grassroots African Theology

He is the one
Who cooks his food in huge palmoil
    pots.
Thousands of people have eaten,
Yet the remnants fill twelve baskets.
If we leave all this and go wandering
    off—
If we leave his great gift, where else
    shall we go?

Those words [translated from the original Twi] are those of Madam Afua Kuma in her *Jesus of the Deep Forest— Prayers and Praises of Afua Kuma* (English translation by Fr. Jon Kirby from the Twi original; see *Afua Kuma Ayeyi ne Mpaebo—Kwaebirentuw ase Yese*; Acrra: Asempa Publishers, 1981), 38. I have sought previously to show how the sort of "implicit" theology which is evident in her prayers and praises can become a liberating force for African Academic theology and for the academic theologian. Being an articulation of an apprehension of Jesus "where the faith has to live" at "the living roots of the church," this sort of grassroots or oral theology can deliver the academic theologian from the burden of imagining that it is his or her task "to construct an African theology" unaided.

—Kwame Bediako, *Christianity in Africa: The Renewal of a Non-Western Tradition* (Maryknoll, N.Y.: Orbis Books, 1995), 59–60.

EATWOT, while some never sought membership in that organization. We all carried on with other associations, theological and otherwise. As far as I know, we all remained committed to our faith communities. As political independence enabled erstwhile Christians, including politicians and academics, to come out as Muslims, so the boldness of finding our voices and learning more African primal spirituality and culture enabled some South African women, who had previously worn the label "Christian" to declare their allegiance to traditional religions. Many of us have become academics, and a few more have entered the ordained ministry of their churches. Many are serving in ecumenical positions as staff or resource persons. And at least one was listed for nomination to a bishopric. She lost the election, but I know she will offer herself again. When we said in Accra in 1989, "We are the church," we meant it.

The Circle's logo, the rising woman, was inspired by a popular tourist artifact in Ghana. We did our own interpretation: women are on their knees but with head and hands held high; they are confident that God will bring them to their feet. We related the logo to the *Talitha cumi* story in the Gospel of Mark, in which Jesus raises from the dead the daughter of Jairus: "Little girl, rise up," he said to her. The rising woman represents for us human potential and possibility to image the divine. The idea and the final form of the Circle's logo is the legacy of the late Reverend Sister Rosemary N. Edet of Nigeria.

In terms of its overall organization, the Circle imitates some of the features of EATWOT. We have no paid staff, and tasks are performed by volunteers. There is no permanent headquarters, and therefore the Circle "resides" where the coordinator lives. In fact, at the beginning the Circle did not have officers. There was just the initiator (me) and the team of people who organized the first convocation and were recognized as conveners. After the convocation, the members of the first institute went home from Accra and created whatever model was suitable to their context. The word "chapters" began to appear in Circle notes. Nigeria was the first to name itself a chapter, elect officers, and print letterhead. This was even before the Circle itself had created a logo. The form and designation of leadership have followed the changes in organizational models. The Circle remains flexible as it responds to the needs of its members, their faith communities, and the continent. To date a constitution is still in process.

## THEOLOGY AND SOCIETY

The connections that many Circle members brought with them from EATWOT meant that the Circle was to carry on the concern for the elimination of "life-denying forces in Church and Society, especially those rooted in ritual, racism, abject poverty and the neglect of the rural areas. We had on our hearts the need to work with all who seek to promote Christ's message in all its fullness."[13] Those of us who attended the 1980 Ibadan conference still nursed a vision of a two-winged (female and male) theology for Africa. We helped keep the Circle focused on women's full participation in ministry and a vision of the church as a community of women and men in the service of God's mission in Africa.

Theological themes such as Christology, ecclesiology, Mariology, pneumatology (the study of the Holy Spirit), and spirituality had come with us from EATWOT, but these traditional theological categories had taken on the specific questions of our contexts. Ecclesiology, or the doctrine of the church, has been a Circle issue that continues to challenge women's meaningful participation in their faith communities. The Bible and the interpretive strategies required to release its liberating message remain with us. The preparation women needed to enable women to be responsible participants in the church is a constant concern. We are learning to articulate faith reflections on

## African Women and Beads

Beadwork is an art form I associate with my paternal grandmother, Maame (Martha Aba Awotwiwa Yamoah). She participated in the fish trade in the Asamankese market and was happy nowhere else except in church. The market was her life and she clung to it until she could no longer see to get there. In the Methodist Church in Asamankese, she is remembered for her *Ebibindwom* (songs of Africa), the lyrics she wove together from Bible stories in church during sermons and sang at home while she made threaded beads. Beadwork and singing, that is how I remember her. She sorted beads out of an earthenware pot and threaded them for legs, waist, wrists and neck. Some of these beads were traditional hand-crafted ones whose names held world-views and philosophies of life—precious black *bota* beads fashioned from solid rock, mixed with mass-produced European glass trade beads made from sand.

As I look at the world of African women today and reflect on that life in these pages, I think of beadwork. When I look at the variety of beads, I think of the changing being of the African woman; my grandmother, my mother, my self, my nieces, and my grandniece: different beads from the same pot, different shapes, sizes, colours, uses, ever changing patterns strung on new strings. I hear the deliberate, gentle, instructing voices of the older women evoke the rhythm of *sam-sina*, the action of drawing a bead off the thread or pulling the thread through a bead. Women threading beads. I watch the different colours and I see a pattern emerge as they reject some beads and pick up others. Deliberate choices and delicate handling, for every bead is precious and none must be lost. Even those not needed at the moment will go back into the pot along with those we have not chosen. We appear only in beads of our choice, strung on strong strings in patterns of our creation.

—Mercy Amba Oduyoye, *Beads and Strands: Reflections of an African Woman on Christianity in Africa* (Maryknoll, N.Y.: Orbis Books, 2004), 102–3.

women's realities; we read the Bible in the context of African religion and culture and to discern what it tells women about who they are. We continue to search for what brings about full humanity for all, and we affirm that rituals and marital issues are subjects for theological reflection. As we seek life-renewing customs from African culture that we might retain as possible elements for transformation, we expose those that degrade women and provide stringent analysis of contemporary possibilities for undermining and eliminating them.[14]

Right from the start we chose an option stated by Musimbi Kanyoro "to dare speak and write about many subjects considered as taboo in African culture. The most courageous has been to talk openly about sexuality."[15] Kanyoro singles out sexuality "because it is the foundation for engendering cultural hermeneutics" that she has proposed and spearheaded. Sexuality, fertility, marriage, rites of passage, and several cultural practices such as polygamy that are harmful to women's well-being have been of deep concern to the women of the Circle. Sexuality is also critical because it involves issues of identity and relationships in one's community. It is also inextricably entangled with the AIDS crisis. In Africa, women's marginal participation in their faith communities and some Christian communities' resistance to the ordination of women have been traced to fear of women's sexuality,[16] and the cultural subordination of women has been used to exclude women from leadership in the church.

By the time we came together in Nairobi in 1996, after seven years of working in local, national, and zonal meetings, we found that membership had grown and also that members' interests had become more diversified. We therefore set up four study commissions to enable members to feel at home in their areas of interest. Each commission was coordinated by two women who had specializations in those fields. The four commissions created at Nairobi were the following: Ministerial Formation and Theological Education, Biblical and Cultural Hermeneutics, Women in Culture and Religion, and Women in History.

From the beginning, the Nigeria chapter described the Circle as "a human development project that will begin to provide a communication network among women in the Church and in academia and the rest of society who find religious and cultural issues crucial for the understanding of women's lives." The chapter's approach was interdisciplinary, using the model of traditional African women's solidarity groups. It was hoped that the Circle would become "a symbol of Africa's recognition of the necessity for a dialogical approach to religious and cultural plurality in Africa and their practical consequences for community harmony."[17]

The 1990 meeting held at the University of Calabar was intended to encourage participants to be univocal on issues that affect women, but it failed. The early euphoria of finding our voices and agreeing substantially on most human development issues seems to have resulted in unwarranted optimism. We know that we cannot sing in unison on all issues affecting African women, and we are, in fact, aware that this nondifferentiation of women dehumanizes us. In a 1979 lecture and later in a book, I disputed the Akan saying "*Mmaa nyinaa ye baako*" (All women are one).[18]

Today in the Circle we recognize and honor the diversity in the landscape. We still attract those who have our concerns. At the same time, we remain open to others, especially if they prove to be genuine dialogue partners. To date, however, no such formal dialogue has taken place. The tension of acknowledging global sisterhood and doing our own thing remains. As with the EATWOT Women's Commission, "while we create a new thing, and are anxious not to be classified as aping Western Women, we see the affinity, and the need to honor the work done in this [Western] context."[19] Wherever our work is, silence is no longer an option where women theologians are concerned. Even women's silence could not go unheard, because their lives spoke volumes. But now their voices are to be heard as well, and as Nyambura Njoroge says, these voices call churches to listen and to engage in conversation with Africa's women. Theology in Africa calls for acknowledging the role of gender in theology and for eliminating its debilitating effects so that the church might be true to its mission.

# SPIRITUALITY

The Circle promotes a spirituality of resistance and transformation. Total dependence on God makes us resilient. Anchoring our hope in God means that the future can be secure. We of the Circle have often been asked, "How do you cope, given all the many obstacles to the expressions of our humanity?" As African women theologians of Africa who form the Circle, we have decided to be open, to confront life realistically, to let go of the coping devices and the trickster life-styles that are often the strategies of the oppressed, and to intentionally face Africa's issues with the eyes of women fashioned out of its soil. We write from the perspective that the Bible is not the only text from God. Like Zechariah we open our mouths only to speak God's truth and to praise God. We use creation stories and myths of origins of our own lands. We read and listen to Islam and to Africa's primal religion.

We read the Bible cognizant not only of its patriarchal biases but also of its colonial and imperial stance. We look at mission history and ask, "Where are the Africans, what were their roles, and why?" We ask, "Where are the women, both traveling missionary and African?" In the midst of asking these questions, we hold on to the two Aramaic sayings from Jesus, *Talitha cumi* and *Eph'phatha,* from Jesus' admonition to the man who was deaf and mute to open our eyes, ears, and mouths. Claiming the power of the Spirit, we weave our own stories of healing and empowerment, confident that divine empowerment knows no gender boundaries (Joel 2).

The struggle is our life, and our freedom cannot be separated from that of our neighbor. We question all that has become accepted as normal, and we have out of the struggle created a Circle of women and a supporting group of men who believe in mutuality and empowerment for the sake of humanity and the environment. These are men who have been granted dreams of a new earth and a new heaven, men who like Jeremiah are willing to tell the world that God is doing a new thing in raising up women to speak up and to act out God's justice and compassion. They are men who like Joseph have been sent angels to open their minds to the liberating work God does through those willing to go counterculture when the particular cultural demand, provision, or norm stands in the way of the divine will for fullness of life. And wherever religion and culture affect human development, the Circle is sure to turn on the searchlight and call on others to face the issues involved.

Fig. 3.4. *Annunciation of the Angel to Mary* (carved wood panel) by Lamidi Fakeye (Nigeria). Courtesy National Archives (Contemporary African Art Select List collection, # 88).

## METHODOLOGY AND A "NEW THING"

We have been asked, "How do you work? What are your theological frameworks?" The Circle did not start its research with theses and theories. Circle women began with the realities of their African contexts, their own and other African women's experiences. We have sat with women where they are. We speak their languages and have had dialogue with them. Musimbi Kanyoro describes the Circle's method as that of storytelling—storytelling that leads to challenging cultural

associations based on fixed roles that are said to be divinely or culturally ordained for women and men. We have learned from their stories
and double-checked with others. Kanyoro has also acknowledged
that "telling these stories does not come easily," but oral transmission
of women's wisdom is an age-old method in Africa. Stories are the
basis of theology, and telling personal stories demands trust because
one is rendered vulnerable. Consequently, for the process to generate
not only theology but also healing, one has to create a safe environment. The individual's story becomes "our story," and from that we
proceed to do our communal theology. Ours is a circle of solidarity
and of mutual mentoring, so care, trust, and freedom are crucial to
our cohesion.

The cultural, religious, and economic realities behind the stories
have provided data on the women's lives. To understand and analyze
this data, we have resorted to the cultural and religious, especially
biblical, perspectives from which the women operate. We have listened to the stories, our own included, and tried to understand them.
We continue to do so. We did not begin by constructing conceptual
frameworks, whether of patriarchy or of hermeneutics. We were creating awareness of the existence of women's oppression. Theological
frameworks have come later.

The "new thing" that has been brought to theology mainly by
studies of women from Africa—a new aspect of feminist analysis that
deserves its rightful place among theological paradigms—we call cultural hermeneutics, in fact, gender-sensitive cultural hermeneutics. It
came originally from the work of Musimbi Kanyoro, and it addresses
African Traditional Religion (ATR), with attention to the gender
implications of shrouded cultural elements that male theologians took
for granted and did not question. The motivating question is whether
or not these cultural elements foster the full humanity of women or
whether they diminish them. For the Circle, the church and all other
religious institutions are part of this review. Its ways of proceeding
include the rereading of the Bible and doing communal theology. It
also requires the kind of storytelling that leads to challenging cultural socializations based on fixed roles—whether in ATR or in the
church—that are said to be divinely or culturally ordained for women
and men and therefore unchangeable. Denise Ackerman, another
Circle member, also calls attention to "lamentation" as another genre

that fits what Circle theology tries to do. This is a theology that challenges all to action for transformation, for "we cannot do liberation theology and locate it on non-liberating cultural practices."[20]

All of these give "African women our own voices and space . . . doing a theology inculturation for a gender and feminist perspective is a new thing."[21] Gender as a factor in postcolonial analysis has now been accorded its place in cultural analysis, and it gives African women a distinct voice. We did not want to be shaped by Euro-American feminism, as we felt it would undermine our credibility on the African continent and become the excuse for bashing us before we had been heard. We also did not see cultural analysis as playing a critical role in Western feminist analysis. We have had affinity with the womanist (African American) focus on class and the need to expose racism's strangleholds on all black people. But we were aware that our African religio-cultural issues that produce harmful traditional practices do not feature in womanism in the way we experience them. We therefore stayed on a neutral path by describing ourselves as African women theologians. This theology is communal but, as I have mentioned before, not univocal. We honor and learn from the differences among us as Africans as well as the differences between us and other women theologians. To communicate our findings, we have resorted not only to academic papers but also to liturgical, poetic, and story modes, depending on our audience and the occasion.

## MENTORING FOR WRITING

At the beginning, the focus on research, writing, and publishing presented the Circle to the outside as an elite group of women who were outside the rank and file of African women and whose research findings therefore were not worth publishing. That the content of the findings affects all African women, lettered and unlettered, rural and urban, salary earners and nonsalary earners, traders, farmers, and all other workers, young and old, was overlooked. We have persisted, because these findings are African realities that rule our lives as women in Africa irrespective of the diversity in social locations.

The convocation that created the Circle was a call for theological writings on the theme "Daughters of Africa Arise," anchored on the

*Talitha cumi* command of Jesus to the girl presumed dead (Mark 5:21-43). The planners wanted African women to write about themselves, their contexts, their faith, and their faith communities. They were motivated by the need to contribute to the theology being developed in Africa by Africans in such a way that it would indeed be a theology crafted by both women and men. At the convocation and subsequent meetings this need was repeatedly reiterated. The introduction to the nineteen papers of the 1990 Nigerian national conference stated that "the dearth of literature on women in Africa is an unacceptable reality. Not only is such literature unavailable in libraries in Africa, but also very little exists outside of Africa on what African women say about themselves. This is particularly true when it relates to religion."[22]

The Circle provides a safe space to create guidelines for research and writing, and the hesitation to put pen to paper has been overcome. We meet to discuss research papers and critique them to enable authors to finalize their thoughts. We search for publishing houses willing to give us space, and we very often work to raise funds to have our papers published. We are also trying to promote the Kenya Circle model of having Circle members contribute to the publication of their anthologies. We have had successes in the publication of Circle works by presses in the United States, Europe, and Africa. This mutual mentoring for writing and publishing has its roots in EATWOT, the liberation theology forum to which much of the core group of the founding members of the Circle belong. *With Passion and Compassion*, the outcome of a study by the EATWOT women's commission, was our first experience of this way of producing our own literature to share with the rest of the world. We have remained oral consultants to one another, reading each other's works and offering suggestions to enhance effective communication.

## AGENCY

One of the ten concerns of the Circle continues to be to insert gender-sensitivity into theological education. Up to the time of the creation of the Circle, there was no room for women's studies in religion, whether in the departments of religion of state universities or in church colleges and seminaries in Africa. Indeed, some church colleges and seminaries did not even entertain the notion of admitting women as students. At Trinity Theological Seminary, where the 1989 convocation took place, women were being admitted, but the college made no provision for their accommodation until women raised the issue. It is from this place that the Circle in Ghana is pioneering a continuing education program and center to work for gender sensitivity and gender justice in that institution as well as churches and other faith communities. Trinity's openness to this quest by women is demonstrated by the existence of the Institute of Women in Religion and Culture of the Seminary, the building of the Talitha Qumi Centre to house the institute and other society-related programs, and the beginnings of a master's program in women's theology.

The Circle's advocacy for women's concerns in the mainstream has had many practical results. The Kenya Circle is establishing a resource center at Limuru that began with a gift from Charlotte Graves Paton, which I received while participating in the Women and Religion program of Harvard Divinity School (1983–1984). With that money I purchased feminist books and lodged them in the Catholic Institute for West Africa, the Department of Religious Studies at the University of Ibadan, and the Department for the Study of Religion at Legon. The Institute at Trinity Seminary will also have a resource center. Indeed, it has already received many book donations and maintains bookshelves in the seminary's library. A Cameroonian project is on the drawing board to provide French-speaking women with a center. The Centres for Constructive Theology at the Universities of Durban-Westville and Pietermaritzburg have become places for excellence in women's studies in religion. The Department of Religious Studies at the University of Ghana and many others have begun women's and gender studies that focus on religion.

Not all the offspring are academic. The orphanage at Lubumbashi in the Democratic Republic of the Congo, founded by Marie Bernadette Mbuy-Beya, is an addition to her work with women sex workers. She is the same Circle member, a Catholic sister, who opened up the issue of sexuality for examination. She began by speaking with women in the profession and has remained an advocate and counselor ever since. The participation of the Lusophone (Portuguese-speaking) women is beginning another phase of Circle concerns. Women in Angola and Mozambique would love to research and write, but very few have the capacity or the means to do so. The Circle is developing a mentoring program in theological writing, but the project the Luso-phone women would like to take on is in the area of gainful participation in the economics of their countries; the Circle is seeking support and advice for this idea. To be relevant to our context is still our central motivating factor. However, research, writing, and publishing remain our raison d'être.

## THE CHALLENGES OF STAYING TOGETHER

The same challenges that made it difficult to find each other make it equally difficult to stay together. The Circle shares Africa's realities of vastness, linguistic diversity, and the lack of resources to cope with them. Poor communication and travel routes and cost can be a nightmare but are not insurmountable. In these days of e-mail, we tend to forget that when we began in 1980 and even in 1989, e-mail was not common. Africa's postal service was unreliable. With finances one can overcome the distances and even the language barriers at conferences. It is keeping in touch that is the real challenge. The linguistic groups came out of the need to save money when we really would have preferred to stay together. So we encourage those who can provide interpretation to offer their services.

Logistics have not been the only challenge. We have also had to address Africa's religious pluralism. The initiators of the Circle were Christian women, but those who were conscious that religion should be a major area of inquiry. They had Christian colleagues who had studied and were teaching Islam, but they were convinced that Muslim women in Africa have perspectives on feminism that the rest of the world needs to hear. It was not acceptable that we simply talk about them—Muslim women can speak for themselves. The colleague who made all this possible was Rabiatu Ammah of Ghana, who delivered a paper at the 1989 convocation and remains a Circle member. A few Muslim women from South Africa were to join later. There is not a critical mass of Muslim women who write, so the presence of many who have attended Circle events makes this an empowering aspect of our being together. Few members would say they are traditionalists, few are Jewish or Hindu, but all consciously operate with a multireligious understanding. Africa's triple religious heritage is honored in the Circle, but it is a real challenge to "strive for community within the context of difference."[23]

Plurality also takes many forms other than religious. It makes us accountable on so many levels. We are accountable to the nonwriting women whose wisdom we transmit in writing. We are accountable to the women's organizations whose praxis we participate in and upon which we attempt to reflect theologically. We are accountable to our faith communities whose best practices and teachings we adhere to but whose nonliberating stance we dare to critique. We are conscious that there is no such person as "the African woman," and yet we hold ourselves responsible for creating solidarity around our commonalities.

---

### May We Have Joy

May we have joy
As we learn to define ourselves.
Our world, our home, our journey.
May we do so telling our own stories and
Singing our own songs,
Enjoying them as they are or for what they
    may Become.
Weaving the new patterns we want to wear,
We continue to tell our tales of the genesis
    of our Participation.
We gather the whole household and begin a
    new tale.
*Nse se nse se o!*
*se se soa wo.*

— Mercy Amba Oduyoye, *Daughters of Anowa: African Women and Patriarchy* (Maryknoll, N.Y.: Orbis Books, 1995), 217.

---

## DIALOGUES AND ALLIANCES

In EATWOT, theological and cultural dialogue with others was always the last step. This makes sense to us. We need to stand firm as a group before leaping about. The women's commission of EATWOT followed this guideline. Eventually Circle members who are also members of EATWOT participated in a dialogue that included European and North American women, all meeting in Costa Rica. Dialogue happens whenever we are invited to talk about the Circle or contribute to theological debates. (To deepen our studies and widen our perspectives, we are now participating in an initiative on HIV and AIDS sponsored by Yale University.)

**Fig. 3.5.** Mercy Amba Oduyoye, the director of the Institute of African Women in Religion and Culture of Trinity Theological Seminary in Accra, Ghana, speaks to participants at the conference, "Access for All: Faith Communities Responding" in 2004. Photo: Paul Jeffrey/ Ecumenical Advocacy Alliance. Used by permission.

Slipping out of our own comfort zones to engage in religious dialogue with non-Christians is yet to happen. We are active participants in other theological forums in Africa that endlessly ask us to contribute and discuss our perspectives. The Circle hopes to expand and to interact with other circles, since the need to engage in dialogue and make alliances is basic to growth and creativity. We are people who take religion seriously and will work to make it a life-giving factor in human history. We are a circle, not a closed circuit.

So this is my story
A story rooted in an act of faith
A yearning for community
And the need to be in mission on God's side.

## FOR FURTHER READING

Dube, Musa W. *Post-Colonial Feminist Interpretations of the Bible*. St. Louis: Chalice, 2000.

Edet, Rosemary N., and Meg A. Umeagudosu. *Life, Women and Culture: Theological Reflections*. Proceedings of the National Conference of the Circle of Concerned African Women Theologians. Lagos, Nigeria: African Heritage Research and Publications, 1990.

Fabella, Virginia. *Beyond Bonding: A Third World Women's Theological Journey*. Manila: EATWOT and Institute of Women's Studies, 1993.

Kanyoro, Musimbi. *Introducing Feminist Cultural Hermeneutics: An African Perspective*. New York: Sheffield Academic, 2002.

———, and Nyambura Njoroge. *Groaning in Faith: African Women in the Household of God*. Nairobi, Kenya: Acton, 1996.

Oduyoye, Mercy Amba. *Beads and Strands: Reflections of an African Woman on Christianity in Africa*. Maryknoll, N.Y.: Orbis Books, 2004.

———. *Daughters of Anowa: African Women and Patriarchy*. Maryknoll, N.Y.: Orbis Books, 1995.

———, and Musimbi Kanyoro. *Talitha, Qumi!* Proceedings of the Convocation of African Women Theologians, Trinity College, Legon-Accra, September 24–October 2, 1989. Ibadan, Nigeria: Daystar, 1990.

Phiri, Isabel Apawo. "Doing Theology in Community: The Case of African Women Theologians in the 1990s." *Journal of Theology for Southern Africa* 99 (November 1997): 68–76.

# HISPANIC WOMEN:
# BEING CHURCH IN THE U.S.A.

## ADA MARÍA ISASI-DÍAZ

It was a cold Saturday afternoon in December. Gathered in the back of the unheated church were six women waiting patiently for the Advent retreat to begin. I arrived with Carmen, one of the parish leaders, who came loaded with a bag full of items to be used in the three-hour retreat. Both of us were there to facilitate the retreat. After the welcoming *abrazos* the group began to discuss where to meet. The parish priest had told us to use the parish center, but the women informed us there were no chairs. While Carmen went to the office to find out where we could hold the retreat, the conversation in the small group became a mixture of how busy the women were with Christmas preparations and how disappointed they felt that so few had shown up for the retreat. The women tried to encourage each other by remembering that Jesus had clearly assured his presence where two or three were gathered.

A few minutes after the announced beginning time for the retreat, the parish priest came in through a side door and, without greeting anyone, disappeared into the sacristy. Eventually Carmen returned with news that the group was to use a tiny room off the sacristy that serves as a cloakroom. When the priest came back into the church, Carmen went to talk to him, but he never greeted the other women or in any way acknowledged their presence.

By then a few more women had arrived. Slowly we all moved to the cloakroom and began to turn the space into a liturgical setting. Chairs were arranged around a table that was draped with a purple cloth Carmen had pulled from her bag. Three purple candles and a pink one, together with a small circle of plastic greens, became the

Advent wreath. A well-used Bible was placed on the table. Carmen set up a small tape player, and Christmas music filled the air. By the time the group was ready to start, half an hour late, sixteen women had gathered. Two more would arrive during the retreat. Including the facilitators, twenty women participated in the retreat.

Here they were, the pillars of this small church in El Barrio, the name for Spanish Harlem, one of the Hispanic neighborhoods in New York City. The Hispanic women's group of the parish, Las Madres Cristianas, had organized the retreat, as they have done for years in Advent and Lent.[1] They had to ask the priest for a place to gather, but they knew they themselves had to do all that was needed to make the event happen. They announced the retreat at Mass on Sunday and spread the word around in the neighborhood, and in the days immediately before the retreat they called their friends to remind them to come. The women had found facilitators, and they had bought with their own money two big bottles of soda, cookies, a cake, a loaf of bread, and cheese to make sandwiches for the *merienda* they always serve.

**Fig. 4.1.** Every Sunday, one by one, those gathered for the service on the sidewalk outside the closed door of the church come up to receive "spiritual communion"—an official Catholic tradition when consecrated hosts are not available— from the women who used to be Eucharistic Ministers at the closed parish. Photo © Ada María Isasi-Díaz. Used by permission.

Except for the sacraments, these women and a handful of men make everything happen in this church. On Tuesday evenings one of the women makes sure there is a small group in the church praying the Rosary. On Wednesday another one leads a group of those who have participated in the Life in the Spirit charismatic retreat. On Thursdays a third chairs the gathering of the Legion of Mary, whose members come together not only to pray but also visit the sick and others in need in the parish.

This particular year the Advent retreat was very important for the women. That they were gathering in this tiny cloakroom meant they had succeeded, for the time being at least, in keeping the church open. The archdiocese had announced nine months earlier that it was planning to close this parish along with several others. These women and some men in the parish had organized several protests. They demonstrated outside St. Patrick's Cathedral the day of the Mass of the Holy Chrism during Holy Week. They were able to attract the media, and when asked on camera why they had chosen such a solemn archdiocesan event to protest, they cleverly responded, "At the end of the Mass the Cardinal gives us the Holy Chrism to take back to our parish. If they close our church, where are we going to take the Holy Chrism?"

To protest the decision of the archdiocese they made posters to carry to the many meetings they organized. The posters read, "We are doing everything possible to keep our church open." They gathered to pray the Rosary on the steps of the church so the whole neighborhood would witness their struggle. They met with officials from the archdiocese and spoke powerful words about their community and the vital role their church plays in it.

> **On the Spirituality of Protest**
> Taking over our church so the cardinal of New York wouldn't close it and being arrested after staying for forty-eight hours—this is the most spiritual experience I have ever had.
> —Carmen Villegas in private conversation with author, February 2007.

## CONTEXT AND BACKGROUND

This small church has been a national parish since it was founded in the nineteenth century to serve the German community.[2] As waves of immigrants from different European countries swept north from the crowded Lower East Side of Manhattan, this church, a very simple building modeled after the Portiuncula (the tiny church St. Francis of Assisi used in the twelfth century as the motherhouse for his group), also served the Italian community that settled in this area after the Germans. By the 1930s, the neighborhood was crowded with stores, restaurants, and music shops reflecting a thriving Puerto Rican culture. By the 1940s, Spanish Harlem was a recognizable area of Manhattan. The church then began to serve the Puerto Rican community, celebrating Mass and other sacraments in Spanish. The Puerto Rican community, which is struggling to keep the church open, has been living in the area since the 1950s. The neighborhood is once again changing, and so are the parishioners. Surrounded by towering apartment buildings for low-income families, this church now also serves a growing Mexican community.

The present struggle to keep the church open is a new moment in the conflict that has existed all along between the Puerto Ricans and the institutional church in New York City. Puerto Ricans arrived in massive numbers in New York starting in the 1930s. This was a community with a deep religio-cultural Catholic foundation. However,

## The Church as Family

"Who is the mother of the Virgin Mary?" asked Margarita Barada, addressing the crowd getting ready to march to protest the closing of their church.

"St. Anne," shouted back the crowd.

"That's right; she is our grand-mother!" said Margarita. "And who is the mother of Jesus?" she continued.

"Mary," was the thunderous answer.

"Yes, Our Lady Queen of Angels is our mother!"

"And who is our savior?"

"Jesus"

"Yes, he is our brother."

"And this church is our home, and we will fight to keep it open," finished Margarita, as the crown broke into cheers.

—Reported by Carmen Villegas
to the author

unlike previous waves of immigrants, it did not bring its own native clergy. The priests assigned to ministry in El Barrio as well as the institutions of the archdiocese of New York have dealt with the Puerto Ricans using a so-called missionary mentality that does not value the faith of the people. The "very institutional Northern European Catholicism of the American Church" has clashed with Puerto Ricans' traditional ways of being Catholic.[3] Their Catholicism, celebrated and transmitted despite a historical shortage of priests, centers on rituals and traditions that have no need for an ordained minister. Celebrations in honor of saints, the Blessed Virgin Mary, and Jesus, among other religious practices inherited from the Spanish colonizers, are the way Puerto Ricans and other Hispanic people relate to the divine in their everyday lives without having to depend on the institutional hierarchy and a priest. These practices can be considered "an antidote to a highly clericalized religion that emphasized reception of the sacraments as the primary expression of faith."[4] It is also true that once Puerto Ricans found themselves in the U.S.A.[5] their traditional ways of being Catholic became a source of "identity and a way of connecting to their towns and the people back in their country of origin."[6]

The Catholic Puerto Rican ethos holds as extremely important being baptized, married, and buried "in the church," as the expression goes. However, other religious practices that are not official church sacraments do not need a priest but are led by the laity and are also of great significance for the whole community. They are important not only to those who go to church on a regular basis but also to those who do not assist at Mass with any regularity. For the latter, participation in these prayer services, such as novenas, processions, and Rosaries, is what allows them to consider themselves members of a Catholic community that upholds Catholic values—many of which are also considered cultural values. In fact, participation in popular religious celebrations is considered central to being a member of the community.[7]

Whereas the Catholic Church has served as an agent of "Americanization" for various immigrant groups, this has not happened with Hispanics. Catholic Hispanics continue to hold on to their Hispanic identity. There are geographic and historical reasons for this. Previous waves of immigrants, in the nineteenth and early twentieth centuries, came to the U.S.A. to settle and stay here, never

**Fig. 4.2.** Protesters gather outside a historic parish church in Spanish Harlem to protest its closing by the Archdiocese of New York. Photo © Ada María Isasi-Díaz. Used by permission.

going back to Ireland, Italy, Germany. Hispanics, however, relate to the U.S.A. differently. Some call themselves "Americans," but many think of themselves as Puerto Ricans living in the U.S.A., as Cubans living in the U.S.A., as Mexican-Americans—never just "Americans." For Hispanics what it means to be American is different from what it means to those of the dominant group. Hispanics are transnational people living and contributing politically, economically, socially to the U.S.A. but also relating to their countries of origin or those of their ancestors. A significant number of Hispanics travel back to visit family or the countries of their ancestry quite frequently. Another form of ongoing contact is the *remesas mensuales*—the monthly monetary contributions many send back to their families. The number of Hispanics sending *remesas mensuales* is so large that there are whole towns in various Latin American and Caribbean countries that have grown and developed economically thanks to the *remesas*. More than half a dozen countries list the *remesas* as either the main source or one of the main sources of national revenue. Politically, Hispanics from many different countries that live in the U.S.A. are allowed to vote in elections back in their country of origin, and they do vote.[8] A steady stream of people from Caribbean, Central American, and South American countries immigrating to the U.S.A. continuously revitalize Hispanic identity and culture in the U.S.A., which is why Hispanics do not "Americanize" the way other immigrant groups have done.

There are also historical reasons why Hispanics relate differently from other immigrant groups to the U.S.A. First of all, Hispanics settled in what is today the U.S.A. before the Mayflower pilgrims arrived, the event regarded as marking the beginning of this country.[9] Then there is the fact that large portions of what was México and all of Puerto Rico were "taken over" by the U.S.A. as the result of an expansionist mindset prevalent throughout the nineteenth century. All of these reasons give Hispanics a certain sense of entitlement about living in the U.S.A.

Other groups of Hispanics are here for political or economic reasons for which the U.S.A. bears significant responsibility. Though mentioned by only a few economists, today globalization involves not only the flow of capital but also the flow of laborers.[10] The ongoing political discussion about immigration, which flares repeatedly in the U.S.A., fails to acknowledge this flow of laborers as a worldwide phenomenon of globalization. It also adeptly ignores what can be confirmed by mere observation: were all those immigrants who are undocumented, the majority of them Hispanics, to be forced to leave the U.S.A., the service sector of the U.S.A economy would be severely hampered.

In New York City many of those cleaning Wall Street offices are Hispanics, as are the women who arrive on Fifth Avenue every morning to clean the homes of the wealthy. Many Hispanic men work on scaffolds in the heat of the summer and into the cold winter months repairing brick walls and roofs. They are the dishwashers in famous restaurants, they unload merchandise and restock shelves in grocery stores, and they bike frantically through New York City streets delivering take-out orders from restaurants. If Hispanic immigrants, particularly Mexican immigrants, were not able to come into in the U.S.A., the agricultural sector would be paralyzed, severely affecting the food production chain. For all of these historical, political, economic, and geographic reasons Hispanics relate to the U.S.A. differently from immigrants from other areas of the world. These are also the main reasons why Hispanics believe that they have a right to hold on to their identity instead of wanting or agreeing to being assimilated into the mainstream.

The fact that Hispanics have retained their identities has resulted in the Catholic Church becoming Hispanic.[11] Though the majority of U.S.A. bishops are not Hispanic, at the beginning of the twenty-first century 39 percent of U.S.A. Catholics are Hispanic, and it is projected that within the next two decades 50 percent will be Hispanics.[12] Contrary to what some may think, this does not mean a return to following without questioning what the *magisterium* (the official teaching office of the institutional church) teaches. Traditionally Hispanics have considered themselves Catholics *a mi manera* (in my own way). Orthodoxy, in the sense of following strictly official moral and theological teachings, is not any stronger among Hispanics than among Catholics from other ethnic backgrounds.[13] If it is true that Hispanics assist at Mass and other church services in greater number than other racial and ethnic groups do at present, this does not translate into strict observance of church commandments and rules. When one talks to Hispanic women, it is obvious that they follow their own interpretation of what the church teaches, accommodating it to their needs.

As a matter of fact, if there is one church teaching that Hispanic women seem to give priority to is that of "primacy of conscience." The primacy of conscience is a principle deeply entrenched in Catholic and Western moral tradition. According to this church teaching, though one is obliged to do everything possible to have a well-informed conscience, including knowing and paying attention to church teachings, one must ultimately follow the sure judgment of one's conscience even when, through no fault of one's own, it is mistaken. This teaching leaves room for Hispanic women to decide for themselves how they practice their Catholicism instead of unquestioningly following what the church tells them to do. Primacy of conscience is a church teaching that influences Hispanic women undoubtedly because of the influence Catholicism has on Hispanic culture. In Hispanic culture conscience is not something that comes into play only when considering matters of grave consequence or when making critical decisions. Conscience is invoked frequently but not lightly. *Mi conciencia me dice* (my conscience tells me) is a phrase often used by Hispanic women. It is not unusual for them to refer to conscience in regular conversations, in discussions, and even when arguing. You hear Hispanic women advising others to act according to their conscience, *haz lo que tu conciencia te indique* (do what your conscience tells you); shaming others for what they have done, *parece mentira que no te remuerda la conciencia* (it is a shame you have no remorse); and indicating disagreement with or condemnation of what another person has done, *la conciencia no le va a dejar tranquila* (your conscience is not going to let you have peace of mind). This use of "conscience" in common parlance is widespread.

To make it known that conscience plays a role in both minor and important decisions lets others know that one has considered the matter carefully and that one is invested in the situation. It is also a way of giving oneself importance, of making it known that one reflects seriously, has an opinion of one's own, and is able to decide for oneself.[14] Because conscience is their guide, Hispanic women follow church rules and teachings they agree with and ones that help them in their daily struggles. This is the "Hispanic way" of being Catholic, in contrast to the "U.S.A. way" of being Catholic, which Hispanic women see as more impersonal and much more institutionally oriented. The "Hispanic way" is personal, people-oriented, and community-centered.

## CHURCH AS FAMILY, CHURCH AS HOME

The idea that the church is the people of God, the community of believers, is primary among Hispanic Catholic communities. The institutional church should be at the service of the people of God. Though grassroots Hispanic women may not articulate it this way, if one pays close attention to what they say they need from the church and what they complain about, it is obvious that for them the church should be first and foremost a community and not an institution. There has always existed tension between Catholic Church as community and Catholic Church as institution, but that is not to say that we should settle for the latter. This is precisely what was happening that Saturday afternoon when the women gathered for the Advent retreat organized by Las Madres Cristianas. The women were not concerned with the lack of institutional support for the retreat, seen in the facts that the assigned place was not ready and the priest did not even greet them much less stop by to see how the retreat was progressing. The women were concerned with the lack of community participation, with how few had actually come to the retreat.

When Hispanic women are directly asked what they want from the church, their expectations are quite modest. For them, being Catholic has to do with their own relationship with God—a relationship fed by and expressed in their personal devotions, in the traditional ways in which the community relates to the divine. Their faith in God is unshaken, regardless of what those in charge of the institutional church do, no matter how the priests fail to minister to them and with them. Often when someone complains about priests, the women will simply say, "They are only human." It is moving to hear them excusing the priests. They overlook shortcomings, mistakes, and abuses because their religious understandings and practices do not hinge on priests and the institutional church.

Being Catholic for Hispanic women has to do with the religious practices they were taught at home when they were growing up. They have continued these practices throughout their lives, and they teach them to their children and grandchildren. The institutional church for them is important if it becomes a gathering point for them, if it helps the community with the many problems it faces, and if it appreciates their religious customs, participates in them, and helps to make them happen.

One of the leaders in this church of El Barrio puts it this way: "I am a little like my grandparents because they had a lot of faith. It was not a faith based on the church. . . . My grandparents did not go to Mass, and I go when I have to go, but if I am very tired or have something else to do, I do not go. The rules of the church did not matter much to them, and neither do they to me."[15] Rosa, another leader of this community, who died a few years ago, used to explain how the church as an organization provided a way of helping the community, an avenue for her to exercise her leadership.[16] There was little or no difference for her between the reason she became involved in politics and the reason she was involved in church groups. She explained how she took from the church what was life-giving for her. She did not depend on what the church says to know what was right for her to do in her own life.[17]

Margarita, also a member of this church, is involved in many of its groups and activities. In one of the meetings in which the community discussed ways to keep the church open, she was so exasperated with the priests that she stumped out, exclaiming that she was not going to put up any longer with all their stupid nonsense. This kind of open rebelliousness, however, is very infrequent. Women have survived so much that they are not fazed by anything that comes their way. They tend not to react forcefully, no matter how hurt they are. The fact that Margarita was so irate and walked out of the meeting indicates how hurt the community is by the possibility that the church might be closed. It is impossible for Hispanic women in this church and the community at large to comprehend that the archdiocese would even think of closing their church, much less without ever talking to the church members. The archdiocese's long study of shifts in Catholic population in New York meant absolutely nothing to Hispanic women, who do not think of the church as an institution but as home.

A few years ago Carmen, one of the leaders of the Advent retreat, was part of a small delegation from Las Hermanas, a national Catholic Hispanic women's organization, that met with a bishops' committee seeking input for a pastoral letter. Since the women believed that the church's ministry was sorely lacking, the presentation included a long list of grievances. One of the bishops asked the women why they did not leave the Church if they had so many complaints. Carmen was deeply insulted and hurt. Taking a deep breath, she blurted, "Leave the church? What do you mean leave the church? The church is our home. One does not leave one's home; one does not leave one's family!"[18]

This exchange is similar to what one hears time and again when people suggest that if Hispanic women wish to be ordained to a renewed priestly ministry, they need to join a Protestant denomination that ordains women. "I cannot leave my church. The church is my family. When you have disagreements in your family, you do not turn your back on the family. You do not stop being a Pérez, or a Rodríguez, or a Díaz. You work it out. Family is too precious to abandon over differences."

## BELIEFS, HABITS, AND PRACTICES

"The popular Catholicism I grew up with made no difference between life and religion. This was a time when we knew how to forgive and be forgiven embraced by the vulnerability of poverty that can indeed lead one to be self-centered. It was a time when we learned to depend on Divine Providence. Even for the rain, so essential for us, we depended on God, praying for it on Rogation Days. It was a time when we knew how to be part of the communion of saints by praying numberless rosaries for the souls of the dearly departed."[19] This way of believing and thinking is quite typical of many Hispanic women. Their religious beliefs are very personal, entrenched in *lo cotidiano*—the reality and struggles of everyday life—and always involving the community.

Who is God for Hispanic women? How do they relate to God? Here are, in their own words, some of the religious understandings of two Hispanic women from this parish in El Barrio.

> God for me is not a person. It is like a *sentimiento*—a deep feeling, a force that moves me, which pushes me in difficult moments. It is a force, something I cannot explain. But if they would ask me to draw God, I would draw my grandmother smiling because she is the only person that I believe has filled me so much that I can compare her to God. I would draw a picture of my grandmother with her hands open smiling, as if to say, "Come with me because I am waiting for you." God is strength for the *lucha*—the struggle—a strength that keeps you going ahead, that encourages. . . . For me it is always a force that moves me and even if everybody would say that I am bad, that I cannot do it, that force says that I can do it, that I am special, that I am capable of moving mountains. But it is something outside me that comes to me in the darkest moments.

> In difficult moments I pray to Jesus because I have him as my guide. But, though many times I do not dare to say this [publicly], I pray a lot to my grandmother. . . . [When my grandmother died] she never went away from me, she always stayed, and in difficult moments I pray to her. . . . Sometimes I feel that her strength [in me] is so strong that I can . . . [do] anything. . . . I never say this aloud, but she is my favorite saint. The other ones [saints] I respect but I never pray to them; only to her and to Jesus.[20]

As a child Rosa had been raised by her aunt, since the aunt did not have any children. She talked about God this way.

> I saw God as a compassionate being because in my childhood I suffered so much, I suffered so much. . . . After she [the aunt] took me in, she got pregnant and had a daughter. And, naturally, the world just flowered for her and she gave all her love to her daughter. She gave me all I needed materially, but that motherly love—no, I never knew it. God became that love of a mother and a father that I never had. . . . I see God as a brother, as a friend, as a father, as a mother, as a supernatural force. I am confident that God is with me always; the more down I feel, it is as if a supernatural force would lift me up; it gives me positive ideas on how to keep going; this force helps me to realize that I am not alone. No matter how alone I am, no matter how much it seems to me that the whole world is falling on me, and that maybe I have no means [of moving on], no doors to open, that all the doors are closed, I feel something that, at times I say, speaks to me. Especially when I am lonely, which is when one thinks about one's sufferings and problems the most, something places the thought in my mind that I can do it, that this is the road that I have to follow, or this is what I have to do in order to struggle with what is happening to me. . . . I see [God] as if thinking about so many problems which all of us throw on top of him . . . trying to find a solution to these problems. . . . I would definitely draw God as an extended hand, ready to lift up, to lift up whoever goes his way. . . . It is the hand that picks you up and gives you the strength to keep moving ahead.[21]

Grassroots Hispanic women have a sense of the divine that includes the Trinity as well as Mary the mother of Jesus, the saints, the faithful departed. They relate to all of them as friends and family. They talk to them in a casual way, and they strike deals with them as one does with friends and family. Though many might call the *promesas* Hispanic women make and keep superstitious, that is not so. Hispanic women are not ignorant or fearful of God. They do not trust in magic or chance or have a sense that they can cause God to act or not to act. Their *promesas*—lighting candles, saying prayers, dressing in the color of their favorite saint—are ways of relating to the divine. Just as one chats with family and friends, they chat with God and the saints in their prayers. When they share their troubles and heartaches with God, they are neither complaining nor expecting God to intervene in a supernatural way to fix what is wrong. They share with the divine for the same reason one does with other human beings: because they need support and encouragement.

An example of this is one of the favorite songs of Hispanic women to the Blessed Virgin Mary. In this parish it is sung during the service and procession of the Sorrowful Mother that takes place Good Friday evening when the women, and some men, come to accompany Mary, whose son, Jesus, has just died.

**Fig. 4.3.** The women of Spanish Harlem dress a large statue of Mary in a black velvet cape and put a white handkerchief in her hand. She is called La Dolorosa, "the Sorrowful One." When the women take her out in procession on Good Friday evening, they are accompanying the mother who has just lost her son. Photo © Ada María Isasi-Díaz. Used by permission.

| | |
|---|---|
| *Dolorosa, de pie junto a la cruz.* | Sorrowful One, standing by the cross. |
| *Tú conoces nuestras penas,* | You know our sorrows, |
| *Penas de un pueblo que sufre.* | Sorrows of a people who suffer.[22] |

In the song there is no petition for Mary to free one from suffering. The emphasis of the song is on empathy: the women empathize with the Sorrowful Mother, and they know that the Sorrowful Mother empathizes with them. They expect God, Mary, the saints, and the dearly departed to accompany them, to walk with them as they face the difficulties of *lo cotidiano*—everyday life.

Knowing that they are not alone, that they belong to a community that cares for them, is what gives them the strength to continue their daily struggles to survive, to provide for their children. Surviving as members of a minority group who are not given much importance by society or the church, Hispanic women hunger for God, Mary, and the saints to pay attention to them, to gaze upon them lovingly. This is the sense one gets when one sees Hispanic women kneeling before the statue of Mary: it is not so much a matter of their praying to Mary for what they need but of knowing that Mary is looking lovingly upon them.

Many Hispanic women now in their forties, fifties, and older were taught as children to fear God, to see God as judge and punisher. Yet they seem to have outgrown that negative understanding of God, and

**Fig. 4.4.** Women pray before a painting of Our Lady of Guadalupe on her feast day, December 12. Photo © Ada María Isasi-Díaz. Used by permission.

they relate to the divine in a very personal and positive way. Though they repeat all that the church teaches regarding salvation, they do not see themselves as horrible sinners. Their sense of salvation is not so much one of being redeemed from sin but one of participating in the divine.[23]

Gathered in the house of one of the parish leaders, a group of them talked about their relationship with God, about the meaning of their faith, of how they live their faith.

Two of the women were in their thirties, and the rest were in their fifties and older, the oldest was seventy-six. Most of them were from Puerto Rico; two were from Ecuador, two from the Dominican Republic. They all have lived in the U.S.A. for more than fifteen years; some of them arrived more than forty years ago. Two of them are single; the rest are married and have children and grandchildren. In the group there were several college graduates, while others' formal education was only at the grade-school level. All of them speak some English, but they continue to be most comfortable speaking in Spanish.

Most of these women had a very difficult time when they first arrived in the U.S.A. The oldest Puerto Rican present that afternoon captured all she had to go through at the beginning with a simple phrase: *y empezamos a luchar* ("and we began to struggle"). *Luchar*—to struggle—is the best way Hispanic women have of describing their daily lives. She continued, "Thirteen days after I arrived, a friend found me a job in a sewing factory." She married right away. She worked, had children, brought them up, and even went to school to learn enough to be able to help the children with their homework. "After the children came, I did not have much time to work with the church, but after they grew up, I went back to help. I went floor by floor in the buildings of the projects [housing subsidized by the government] with the nuns looking for people to baptize." Another of the participants emphasized how hard Hispanic women work by saying proudly, "They do say we are the labor force of New York City."

The ones who arrived in the 1950s worked in factories strewn all around Manhattan. They did not earn much, but those gathered believe that it was easier to survive at that time because five decades ago there were more entry-level jobs, and rent-controlled housing was available. The more recent arrivals, on the other hand, benefit from having an established community to receive them as well as government social services better geared to help them than they were decades ago. Some of the recent arrivals have received help from the church, mainly information about the different city services they can use and emergency help in the form of food and second-hand clothing.

One of the issues discussed by the group was God's role in suffering. Most of them think that God must have a reason for allowing suffering and that when they face obstacles they have to figure out "what is God trying to teach me" or they have to believe that "God must have other plans." One of the women spoke of how she rebelled against God when her father, to whom she was very close, died. "But now I have learned not to ask God why. Who am I to ask God to give me reasons for what happens?"

The oldest woman there was very clear that God does not want us to suffer. "We suffer but that does not mean God wants us to suffer. If we do not want anything bad to happen to our children, how much less is God, how is *Papa Dios* [Daddy God—a common way for adults to refer to God when talking to children and the regular way in which children address and refer to God] going to want us to suffer?" All of the women agreed that God does listen to their petitions, and they are convinced that when they do not receive what they ask for, it is because God knows it is not the best thing for them.

The group then discussed prayer. Only one of them reported using some formal prayers. But all of them understand prayer as speaking to God. The most senior member of the group spoke eloquently.

> From the window of my apartment I can see some trees— such beauty. And I am always there talking with God. Everyone who knows me looks up when they go by my apartment because they know they will find me at the window looking at the beautiful group of trees.
>
> In the morning I always say, the very first thing, "Good morning, Puerto Rico." Then I talk to God. I thank God for the miracle of life every morning. I thank God for my legs

with which I can walk, for my eyes, for having what I need to brew a cup of coffee. And at night I thank God for the spiritual and material food he has given me, and I ask God to give food to those who do not have any.

You know, people pray even when they do not have any food. I remember that when I was a little girl in Puerto Rico we lived better than we do now even if we were very poor. This was because the women prayed the Rosary. Everyday, shortly before noon a group of *viejitas* [an endearing term referring to elderly women] would come to my grandmother's house. They would sit on the wood we used for the kitchen stove and talk and talk until they heard the bell for the *Angelus* [traditional responsorial prayer to the Virgin Mary recited at noon and at six P.M.]. Then they would pray the *Angelus* followed by the Rosary. At the end they would have a little coffee and *serruchitos* [cornmeal mixed with water and a little sugar and fried].

Carmen, the parish leader who cofacilitated the Advent retreat, chirped in right away, saying, "I like to speak with God." She continued:

God understands me and is never going to be judgmental. I do not use formal prayers but lately, after I turned forty, I feel I need to reclaim what my grandmother taught me. I think it is a matter of vindicating all that one refused when young, which happened because we really did not understand. Now one wants to pick it up once again; now we are hungry for what we received when young.

Everything is a blessing from God. I have been given so many opportunities. What I have learned about community organizing and struggling for our rights I have learned from the church. The church has given me many opportunities, like inviting me to be a facilitator when John Paul II came to the Youth Congress here in the U.S.A.

I think, "If I do not defend the poor, who is going to do it?" And I get up, and I speak. And I feel very powerful. I remember that Scripture says that when we are the weakest, we are the strongest because Christ is in us. I believe that Christ calls me especially to struggle on behalf of the poor.

God is present in my life. Everything that comes from God is good. What is bad comes from me because I am human. People might say that it comes from the devil, but I think it comes from me, from my mistakes and weaknesses; from my selfishness.

The women gathered in that group believe that the majority of Hispanic people indeed have great intimacy with God. "Our culture continues to be a religious culture." One of them spoke about the procession of the Sorrowful Mother on Good Friday evening. "When we start, there are only a handful of us. But as we walk the streets around the church, more and more people join us, including teenagers, and by the time we return to the church, we have more than one hundred persons there to participate in the prayer service. If religion were not important to us, we would be the same or less by the time we return to the church."

The group then addressed the question, why do you think people ask you to pray for them? One woman said, "Well, they might think that God does not hear their prayers." However, the majority thought that it is a way for people to connect. "It is a way of making a human chain." One of them explained it as follows: "There are two reasons why people ask for prayers from others. When I would ask Angelita [elderly church leader who died the previous year] to pray for me when I was going to go to a conference, I asked her because I needed her support, because I needed to feel that she was in solidarity with me. Others ask for prayers because they feel so far from God and they believe you are closer to God."

Another theme the group addressed was what they think is most important in the Christian faith. One of the women immediately said, "To be authentic," by which she meant that one has to act according to what one believes. Another one talked about "fighting any kind of battle for Jesus."

> **On Suffering**
>
> We suffer but that does not mean God wants us to suffer. If we do not want anything bad to happen to our children, how much less is God, who is *Papa Dios* [Daddy God—a common way for adults to refer to God when talking to children and the regular way in which children address and refer to God], going to want us to suffer?
>
> —A seventy-six-year-old Hispanic woman

## Speaking to God

I like to speak with God. God understands me and is never going to be judgmental. I do not use formal prayers, but lately, after I turned forty, I feel I need to reclaim what my grandmother taught me. I think it is a matter of vindicating all that one refused when young, which happened because we really did not understand. Now one wants to pick it up once again; now we are hungry for what we received when young. Everything is a blessing from God.... I think, "If I do not defend the poor, who is going to do it?" And I get up, and I speak. And I feel very powerful. I remember that Scripture says that when we are the weakest, we are the strongest because Christ is in us. I believe that Christ calls me especially to struggle on behalf of the poor. God is present in my life. Everything that comes from God is good. What is bad comes from me because I am human. People might say that it comes from the devil, but I think it comes from me, from my mistakes and weaknesses; from my selfishness.

—Carmen Villegas

A third one spoke of carrying the Good News to the world. Four others talked about helping others. The first put it this way, "Jesus, being the son of God, came to serve. Why should we not do the same?" The next one referred to the fact that Jesus helped others and added, "I help anyone that I am able to help." Another one simply said what was central to the faith was to help others. The fourth one talked about reaching out for those who are in need. She added, "We are the arms of Jesus. He did much in a very short time, and I have to do the same."

One of the women indicated that the heart of the gospel message is, "Love one another." She went on to talk about each one having a special mission and about the need to ask Jesus to help us discover her mission. The others said that what they had identified as central to the faith is what they consider their mission. Only one of the women said she did not know what her mission was: "I know everyone has a mission, but I am still trying to find out what is mine. I am allowing God to guide me, to show me what is my mission."

## A DEPLORABLE AND SAD ENDING

Barely a month had gone by since I gathered with the women to reflect on our religious beliefs and practices as Hispanic women when the archdiocese communicated its intention to close the parish in a matter of weeks. The women immediately decided they were not going to accept the decision made by the officials of the archdiocese. They began to organize to take over the church until the archdiocese rescinded its decision. The closing Mass was to take place on the last Sunday of the month. But when church officials changed the locks of the building, the community decided it was time to move in.[24] A score of parishioners went to the regular Spanish Mass on Sunday and then simply stayed in the church. When after the last Mass in the evening the priest asked them when they were going to go home, they told him, "When the archdiocese changes its decision."

The community at large was very supportive, bringing food, blankets, and flashlights to the ones staying in the church. The second evening the archdiocese sent in security guards. The women had already informed the police of their intention to take over the church, so since the archdiocesan guard scared them, they called the police to protect them. The police remained in the church and were nothing but kind toward the protesters. But later that evening, when archdiocesan officials arrived and requested that they evacuate the church, the police informed the women that if they did not leave, they would be arrested. One of the police sorrowfully told the women he was heart-broken about what was happening to the church, where his mother had been a parishioner.

> ### Protecting What Is Important
>
> Margarita's daughter called me saying that they were taking the statues of the saints from the church and her mother had gone to stop them. I was very concerned for Margarita because she is into her seventies for sure. When I got there, she was confronting the men who had put big boxes in the truck. She kept telling them, "Open those boxes, you are not going to take our saints." All of a sudden she climbed into the truck and insisted that they take the boxes down. "You are not going to take our saints," she repeated time and again, thrashing around on top of the truck. I was worried she might have a heart attack. She is so strong, so strong. The men finally left without the boxes, even if they did not contain the saints.
> —Reported by Carmen Villegas to the author

The women who had taken over the church decided that the Mexicans in the group who were undocumented and could be imprisoned and expelled from the U.S.A. needed to leave right away. After praying together, some of the others also left. Six women who refused to leave were arrested and charged with trespassing on private property. Just before she was arrested, Carmen, my co-leader for the Advent retreat, said, "I can't believe I have to be afraid in my own church. I can't believe the church is not backing us up."[25]

Regardless of what they had endured, the community, led by the women, was not willing to give up. When Sunday came,

> about a hundred people gathered . . . on the slushy sidewalk in
> front of Our Lady Queen of Angels, a small Roman Catholic

church on East 113th Street that the Archdiocese of New York closed last week. The doors were locked, but parishioners and their supporters conducted an outdoor service, in Spanish and English, without a priest.

Nobody performed the sacraments, but the crowd sang hymns and recited the same readings heard yesterday in Catholic churches almost everywhere. . . .

"We are not going to move from here," said Carmen Villegas, a protest leader. "We don't care if there's snow, if there's rain." . . .

During the service yesterday, the parishioners, from infants to people in their 80s, were bundled in hats and scarves. A young man held aloft a wooden cross decorated with a painting of the Virgin Mary. Some of the elderly sat on folding chairs, and television news trucks were crammed into a cul-de-sac in front of the church. Among those who addressed the crowd was City Councilwoman Melissa Mark-Viverito. . . .

"What we are witnessing here today is not defiance," she said at the rally. "What we're witnessing is faith and love."[26]

Reflecting on what had happened the night they were arrested, the women were particularly hurt by the archdiocese sending private guards. "They have guards and we are armed with rosaries and Bibles," said one of the women arrested. "Really, what harm were we going to do?"[27] It was especially difficult for the women to experience the formality and coldness with which they were treated. "After the private guards arrived, a monsignor read a letter from the pulpit saying the church was closed. He didn't greet us or in any way show interest in us and why we were there," said Carmen Villegas. "He had a red book, opened it and said, 'The church is closed.' Then he began to tell us we could go to Mass at St. Ann's or St. Cecilia's. He told us we had to leave and that was that. As if this church were not our home, as if we had no rights in this family called the church."[28]

Hispanic women learned from the documents of Vatican II that the people of God are the church.[29] But the institutional church seems to ignore this teaching found repeatedly in the conciliar documents.

These Hispanic women see their resistance to the institutional church as faithfulness to what they were taught by the church. Their fight to keep their church open has to do with self-respect, with a deep belief that church authorities cannot close their church without consulting with them. They fight because they are afraid of what will happen to them as they lose the physical center of the community. They fight because this church is home for them; they cannot even begin to conceive that the archdiocese is doing away with their home.

What will happen to the church as it continues to alienate and mistreat those who have lived their Catholic faith without wavering? What will become of the institutional church as it continues to recentralize itself, taking back to Rome the decision-making power it had given to national bishops' conferences following Vatican II? What will happen to the institutional church as it continues to see itself as an end instead of seeing itself as being in the service of the community?

It is unimaginable that the cardinal of New York will rescind his decision, though the Hispanic women struggling to have Our Lady Queen of Angels reopen constantly remind themselves and everyone else that miracles are always possible. The hierarchy has never been willing to learn from those who do not bow to its authority. The male magisterium has never been willing to recognize the presence of the Holy Spirit in the community unless the community agrees with its authority. But as the elderly women always remind the community, "the cardinal and all the priests are only human. They might not want to know it, but we know God is with us—*Dios está con nosotros.*"

## FOR FURTHER READING

Badillo, David A. *Latinos and the New Immigrant Church.* Washington, D.C.: Johns Hopkins University Press, 2006.

Díaz Stevens, Ana María. *Oxcart Catholicism on Fifth Avenue: The Impact of the Puerto Rican Migration upon the Diocese of New York.* Notre Dame, Ind.: University of Notre Dame Press, 1993.

Gonzalez, Juan. *Harvest of Empire: A History of Latinos in America.* New York: Viking, 2000.

Isasi-Díaz, Ada María. *En La Lucha—In the Struggle: Elaborating a Mujerista Theology.* 2nd ed. Minneapolis: Fortress Press, 2004.

————, and Yolanda Tarango. *Hispanic Women: Prophetic Voice in the Church / Mujer hispana—voz profética en la iglesia*. San Francisco: Harper & Row, 1988. Reprint: Scranton, Pa.: University of Scranton Press, 2006.

————, Timoteo Matovina, and Nina Torres-Vidal. *Camino a Emaús—Compartiendo el ministerio de Jesús*. Minneapolis: Fortress Press, 2002.

Orsi, Robert. *The Madonna of 115th Street: Faith and Community in Italian Harlem*. 2nd ed. New Haven: Yale University Press, 2002.

Perez, Arturo, Consuelo Covarrubias, and Edward Foley, eds. *Así Es: Stories of Hispanic Spirituality*. Collegeville, Minn.: Liturgical, 1994.

Tweed, Thomas A. *Our Lady of the Exile: Diasporic Religion at a Cuban Catholic Shrine in Miami*. New York: Oxford University Press, 1997.

Vidal, Jaime R. "Citizens Yet Strangers: The Puerto Rican Experience." In Jay P. Dolan and Jaime R. Vidal, eds., *Puerto Rican and Cuban Catholics in the U.S., 1900–1965*, 11–143. Notre Dame History of Hispanic Catholics in the U.S., vol. 2. Notre Dame, Ind.: University of Notre Dame Press, 1994.

# TRADITIONS AND TRANSFORMATIONS

**Part 2**

# ORTHODOXY UNDER COMMUNISM

## PAUL MOJZES

CHAPTER FIVE

The Orthodox Church is profoundly hierarchical, with the lay-people at the bottom of the pyramid. Viewed theologically, the clergy are the sacred priesthood, while the *laos* (Greek for "people of God") are the royal priesthood of all members of the church of Christ. Indeed, the clergy cannot conduct formal divine worship without the presence of the laity, because in the eucharist the laypeople sacrifice concurrently with the consecrated priest, though they are decidedly not on the same level with the consecrated clergy in matters of governance and teaching the faith. Nor can there be a liturgy without the clergy. Viewed sociologically, in contrast, the hierarchical structure of the church is so firmly fixed that it appears as if the bishops and priests are the church, while the laity are merely passive spectators.

The Constantinian model of church-state relations created a situation in which the emperors, kings, patriarchs, bishops, priests, and monks were the only movers and shakers in the church. The people, or laity, were the consumers of religion who followed thoroughly traditional patterns of canonical regulations interlaced and often modified by ancient customs and folkways, sometimes intertwined with superstition and magical practices remaining from pre-Christian times. During the Byzantine period the concept of *symphonia* prevailed, under which the emperor was Christ's vicar on earth. His primary domain was the temporal affairs of God's people, while the patriarch governed the spiritual domain, ideally in perfect harmony with each other.

During years of Muslim overlordship, when the Christian emperor was replaced by the rule of the sultan, the *millet* system actually

> ### Christ's Church
>
> Members of the church of Christ are required to be all who have even once heard the preaching of the Gospel. Required are all because all are equally called by their nature in their religious association with God. . . . To Christ's church belong all who maintain Orthodox belief; not only the just but also the sinners.
>
> —Makarie, Metropolitan of Moscow, *Pravoslavno Dogmaticno Bogosloviye,* part 2 (Sremski Karlovci: Serbian Monastic Press, 1896), 166–67.

strengthened the role of the patriarch and the bishops (the hierarchy of the Orthodox Church) because the Islamic state dealt with people on the basis not of ethnicity but of religion. Therefore patriarchs and metropolitans were given not only religious supervision over their members but also judicial and administrative responsibilities. As a sign of their religious as well as secular prerogatives the Slavic Orthodox usually call their bishops *vladika* (ruler).

Orthodox churches, all of which consider themselves to be collectively the one, holy, apostolic, and universal church of Christ, are, unlike the Catholic Church (which makes an identical claim for itself), organized more or less along national lines. Usually the head of such a national church is a patriarch (or metropolitan bishop) who governs it along with the Holy Synod of bishops. Each autocephalous church is fully self-governing, and the patriarchs are equal, though the ecumenical patriarch of Constantinople is generally accorded the primacy of honor, while de facto the patriarch of Moscow has rivaled Constantinople, wielding occasionally more political clout among Orthodox nations.

Paradoxically, these hierarchical churches also practiced what the Russians call *sobornost*, a term not easily translated into English. One of its meanings is "conciliarity," with the additional connotation that matters of faith and practice become established only when the entire "gathered" (*sobranie* or *sobor*) church accepts them. All this changed after the Bolshevik Revolution and subsequent Communist takeover, first in Russia and other Soviet lands from 1917 to 1989 and then in other Eastern European Orthodox countries (except Greece and the Near East), from the latter half of the 1940s to 1989.

## THE *STARTSI* AND LAY THEOLOGIANS

Drawing an analogy from music, in which the virtuoso is distinguished from the orchestra, one may classify Orthodox laity into two or perhaps three groups. First there are the laypeople who by every measurement can be considered the Orthodox virtuosos: the *startsi*, the king or emperor with the nobility, and the lay theologians. Then there are the common or conventional believers who resemble the orchestra. And one may add that there is also the audience or the public—a large number of people who are passive recipients of the church's gifts but are mostly onlookers.

In Russian lands in particular one can find figures called *starets*, or "old man." It is a reference to men who practiced an intense spiritual and ascetic life, mostly living in forests or caves, dedicating themselves entirely to the Lord. Some may have been ordained, but most were not; they should be counted as laity because they played no role in clerical officialdom—they were not assigned any pastoral positions, did not come under jurisdiction of bishops or abbots, and conducted no official liturgies or mysteries, but led a life of prayer and fasting. Most had no theological or even basic education. They resembled the third- and fourth-century anchorite monks in Palestine, Egypt, and Asia Minor who left the cities to struggle against Satan on Satan's own turf, the desert. They sought no followers but somehow by word of mouth tended to gradually draw the attention of people near and then far, often against their own wishes. People were attracted by their simplicity and lack of pretension and fancy regalia. Sometimes people were simply drawn by the strange appearance of some of these desert figures, but often there were stories of miraculous healings. *Startsi* became confessors and counselors—wise men of God who could be trusted to provide unselfish and un-self-serving advice. Zosima from Fyodor Dostoyevsky's *Brothers Karamazov*, to whom the youngest brother, Alyosha, was so powerfully drawn, was the prototypical *starets*.

Unlike the Roman Catholic Church, in which until recently most theologians had been ordained clergy, the Orthodox Church produced trained lay theologians who equaled the ordained theologians

> ## The Possessors and the Non-Possessors
>
> At the end of the 15th and beginning of the 16th century in Russia there was a controversy between the "Non-Possessors" and the "Possessors." The Non-Possessors argued that the church should hold no lands, own no peasant serfs, and that the state should not intervene in religious matters as there must be no coercion in religion. The Possessors, who held opposite views, won.
>
> —Paul Mojzes, *Religious Liberty in Eastern Europe and the USSR: Before and After the Great Transformation* (Boulder: Eastern European Manuscripts, 1992), 51.

in erudition and profound theologizing. Among recent lay theologians are people such as Vladimir Soloviev, Nicholas Berdyaev, Sergei Bulgakov, Justin Popovic, and Nikos Nissiotis. These theologians, though not ordained, are part of the elite rather than the "people," and hence it will suffice merely to mention their important role.

Still another way for prominent laypeople, such as nobility and the wealthy, to promote the faith in pre-Communist Russia was to build chapels that were not part of the regular diocesan or parochial structure. The chapels were meant for the reading of the hours, a liturgical practice that did not require clergy. Some were roadside chapels, others

## Glossary

*Antimins*—a linen cloth in which the relics of a saint are wrapped.

*Antiphon*—a sung response, such as in liturgical chant.

*Autocephalous*—self-governing, independent Orthodox churches that maintain full ecclesiastical relationship with other Orthodox churches.

*Chistka*—Russian word for "purge." Usually referring to the elimination by imprisonment, concentration camps, and execution of Communists and non-Communists considered by Stalin to be enemies of the state. The Great Purge (*Velikaya Chistka*) took place between 1936 and 1939 and is considered the period of the greatest persecutions in the Soviet Union.

*Constantinian model*—the close relationship between church and state established during and after the reign of the Roman emperor Constantine the Great early in the fourth century.

*Dvatsatka*—Russian term for a group with a minimum of twenty people that was needed to apply for registration by the Communist authorities to permit the functioning of a church.

*Icons*—Stylized paintings considered windows to the eternal heavenly reality.

*Living Church/Renovationists*—a schism by a small section of the Russian Orthodox Church in the early 1920s with explicit Bolshevik sympathies and with some reformist ideas that the Bolsheviks used to subvert the patriarchal Russian Orthodox Church.

*Millet*—the organization of the Ottoman empire along religious lines, giving various Christians and Jews the right of limited self-government.

### Glossary (cont'd.)

*Old Believers*—a schism from the Russian Orthodox Church in the seventeenth century led by Archpriest Avvakum, who opposed the liturgical and other reforms instituted by Patriarch Nikon. The Old Believers later split into two groups, the *Popovtsy* (those retaining priests) and the *Bezpopovtsy* (those without priests).

*Parastos*—from Greek, "standing with." A memorial service when the family, friends, and other believers "stand with" the departed on the fortieth day after the death and a year after the death.

*Photian schism*—one of the earlier mutual anathemas between Pope John VII and Patriarch Photius of Contantinople in 863–867.

*Slava / krsna slava*—The family festival among Orthodox Serbs and Macedonians commemorating the saint's day when by tradition, centuries ago, the family was baptized, having converted from paganism to Christianity.

*Sobornost*—from the Russian *sobranie* or *sobor,* means "conciliarity," the gathered church. An Orthodox theological conviction that a doctrine is accepted only when the entire Orthodox church agrees with it.

*Starets/Startsi*—"old man/men." Saintly hermits who are adored by Orthodox laity and sought for miracles, counseling, and spiritual blessings.

*Symphonia*—the theoretically harmonious and equal relationship between the earthly and spiritual rulers of the Christian realm, such as the emperor and the patriarch. The Byzantine emperor was considered the vicar of Christ on earth and in practice tended to have more power than the patriarch.

*Tsar*—Slavic term for emperor, deriving from the word "Caesar."

*Uniate*—formerly Orthodox churches that had signed an act of union with the Roman Catholic Church, recognizing the supremacy of the papacy but retaining most other Orthodox characteristics. The Catholics call them Eastern Rite Catholics and look favorably upon them, whereas the Orthodox use it as a term of derision and regard them as apostates.

*Vladika*—Slavic term for bishops, meaning "rulers."

*Vrbica*—Slavic. An Orthodox holiday in the spring, named for young willow branches used in processions to the church, particularly popular with children.

were attached to an institution, and still others were part of a home or were free-standing structures, such as in the north of Russia, where there were fewer churches. Some in the last category became substitutes for churches. Technically this could not be the case because in order to celebrate a liturgy the church altar must have an *antimins,* a linen cloth in which the relics of a saint are wrapped, and these were generally lacking in chapels. No special liturgical blessing was needed for the chapels; they were dedicated the same way a home would be blessed. The chapel parishes were the smallest unit of Orthodox worship, but since they were independent and some had been associated with the Old Believers movement (see glossary, p. 131), the emperors and hierarchy succeeded in limiting the scope of the chapel movement.

## THE ORDINARY LAITY

*Ortho doxa* in Greek or *Pravoslavlje* in Slavic (right praise) is an appropriate name for this branch of Christianity: the central act of faith is the liturgy of divine worship. The act of worship is meant to temporarily lift the believer from the doldrums of daily life into a heavenly environment. All of one's senses are engaged. One's sight focuses on the walls and floors often covered with frescos or mosaics from bottom to top, icons, windows, splendid clergy vestments, candles burning. Sounds of the chanting by priests and deacons and the singing of one, two, or even three choirs singing responsively some of Christianity's most glorious music fill the sanctuary. The smell of incense is in the air. Worshipers taste the leavened bread that was baked by a lay family and the sweet red wine for the eucharist, which is mixed in a spoon and administered to people. (Those who do not partake of the communion are given pieces of the bread, so they are symbolically included in the church's fellowship.) Even skin is engaged in worship: those baptized are fully immersed three times in the water, and worshipers are sprinkled by holy water as part of the blessing by a priest. Lips touch the icons. Candles, mostly honoring the departed, are burning whenever there are worshipers in the church. Confession is whispered into the ear of a priest but in full view of other worshipers, who are queuing up to confess their sins and receive a pardon. Fasts are observed. On Good Friday at midnight boards are hammered to replicate the sound of Jesus being nailed to the cross. Orthodox ritual is dramatic, symbolic, vivid, sensory, and simultaneously affirming this life and focusing on eternity.

These acts cannot take place without a priest, yet Orthodox theology emphasizes that it is God's mysterious action rather than a priestly act that changes the common elements into avenues of grace, dispensed for the benefit of the gathered people of God. *Sobornost,* the Russian term for the gathered community of Orthodox Christians, is a powerful Orthodox theological concept: it maintains that a theological truth does not become a teaching of the church when it is promulgated by a patriarch, a synod of bishops, or a church council, but when it is received and accepted by the entire church. Thus, for instance, the signing of agreement for reunion by the Catholic and Orthodox bishops at the Council of Florence-Ferrara in 1438 1439 was never accepted by the Orthodox Church, despite the fact that only Bishop Mark of Ephesus refused to sign the document: the gathered church felt that it was not an authentic expression of the will of the entire Orthodox Church. The people were unwilling to accept the act of the hierarchy. The Feast Day of Mark of Ephesus is now celebrated as the Feast Day of Orthodoxy.

An important participation for the laity in liturgy was choral singing. Orthodox worship bans instrumental music—the entire liturgy consists of chants and choral music. While much of the chanting is by priests, as is choral music sometimes, in most churches there is but one priest, and therefore the choirs consist of laypeople. Sometimes there are as many as three choirs in a church, usually men's, women's, and one mixed, and they sing antiphonally, creating some of the most beautiful liturgical music ever performed. Certain songs are well-known by the congregation, which will join the choirs, making the task easier in the three-hour-long liturgy.

No church is as rich with ritual and ceremonies as the Orthodox. Typical Sunday liturgies last three full hours. Only a few of the most dedicated laypeople come for the entire liturgy. Most people arrive for the last hour, and even then there is a lot of milling around and going in and out—perhaps not surprisingly, since in most Orthodox Churches outside of North America there are no pews. Sometimes there are a few lean-on chairs along the side of the church wall for those who may be sick or invalid, but even that is not universal. Standing is the order of the day. Astonishingly, even in the midst of Soviet persecution of the churches, there were times when the churches were packed with elderly people—mostly *babushkas* (grandmotherly women), sometimes holding their grandchildren in arms, standing for hours devoutly transfigured by the holiness of the moment in contrast to the bleakness of their existence.

## COMMUNIST CONTROL

It is fair to say that the oppression and persecution of Christians was never so severe in the entirety of Christian history, even during the Roman Empire, as it was under Communism. And it is likewise a fair assessment that Communist control and persecution of religion was more severe for the Orthodox than for other religious communities and nowhere so thorough, cruel, and long-lasting as for the Russian Orthodox in the Soviet Union.

Lenin was convinced that the Orthodox Church was the main pillar of the tsarist system and that in order to demolish the Russian empire one had to crush the Orthodox Church. Hence the vast majority of the Orthodox churches in the Soviet Union were closed, destroyed, or converted to other purposes, sometimes as museums of atheism, thus perverting their very reason for having been built. Sacred objects, such as icons, chalices, vestments, and liturgical books, were confiscated from both church buildings and homes. At first these actions were justified by the argument that church gold and valuables were needed for the purchase of food during years of famine, but later the valuables were collected allegedly for storing and preservation in museums, to "protect" them from some imagined harm. In fact, the real purpose was to take them out of circulation in order to impoverish or prevent church worship and piety. Moreover, people were prohibited from attending churches if they were employed by the state (the state was the sole employer) and threatened with losing their jobs or being imprisoned. This law was especially rigorously applied to those who were employed in government and Communist Party bureaucracy and education. Those who desired to attend worship services despite the restrictions would usually do so in a distant place where they were not recognized. Children younger than sixteen were legally forbidden to have religious education or be taken to churches. Nevertheless, grandparents, particularly grandmothers, would take small children with them to worship. Under conditions of such repression the only thought was survival and the defense of valuable traditions, and therefore not much thought could be given to creative empowerment of laity. When some democratizing innovations were attempted by the schismatic Living, or Renovationist, Church, the Bolsheviks manipulated it to control the Orthodox Church, and before too long the main body of the church distanced itself from such experiments.

In other predominantly Orthodox countries (such as Bulgaria, Romania, and Yugoslavia) the Communist parties adopted this pattern from the Soviet Union, but it was less strictly implemented (except in Albania, where all religions had become constitutionally forbidden). The Orthodox churches were the most vulnerable to government pressures because they were too large to escape the notice of the government, as sometimes smaller Protestant churches could do. At the same time they were not as robust in opposition to the government as the Catholic Church, which was able to resist using the guise of papal primacy—namely that the head of the Catholic Church did not reside in a Communist land. The Orthodox hierarchies were directly pressured by the Communist government and sometimes caved in under duress. Their resistance was weakened by a long tradition of being submissive to temporal authorities, but also by the extraordinary cruelty by which they were persecuted.

The successful control, penetration, and muzzling of the official Orthodox Church leadership evoked disgust and condemnation by both laypeople and some hierarchs who were not under Communist control (for instance, immigrant communities in Western Europe, Americas, and Australia). This unfortunately led to inter-Orthodox antagonisms in which entirely new Orthodox denominations (such as the Russian Orthodox Church Outside of Russia) or schismatic eparchies were created with much political agitation. The schisms were political rather than theological, but they did have canonical consequences. Long legal battles as well as ugly physical confrontations

> **The Church and Nationalism**
>
> Ecclesiastical nationalism is often underpinned by a conviction that if the church is deeply rooted in the national ethos, then the national ethos, the national culture, cannot survive without the church.
>
> —Pedro Ramet, ed., *Eastern Christianity and Politics in the Twentieth Century* (Durham, N.C.: Duke University Press, 1988), 8.

resulted; these cast a shadow on the Orthodox reputation. After the collapse of Communism, when the extent of the cooperation of some of the church elite with the Communists became known, this also led to much recrimination and hostility within the churches. Gradually many of those schisms are being reconciled (such as the one between the Russian Orthodox Church Outside Russia with the Moscow Patriarchate), though new ones, again usually for nationalist reasons, are taking place (such as the Macedonian Orthodox Church breaking away from the Belgrade Patriarchate).

## TACTICS FOR SURVIVAL

The central Orthodox tactic for survival was a deep-seated belief among many clergy and laity that Christ's church had survived many empires and political and economic systems over the two millennia and that it would survive Communism as well. At times this did not seem convincing, as Communism claimed to be the wave of the future and its totalitarian approach appeared to swallow everything in sight. In retrospect, it was a trustworthy approach that helped the Orthodox and other Christians living under Communism endure even the harshest persecutions.

Orthodox experience under Communism varied from country to country, from extreme restrictions in Albania and the Soviet Union to greater permissiveness in Romania and Yugoslavia. In all cases the Communist Party exercised strict control and supervision over the activities of the churches. The persecution in the Soviet Union caused a sharp rift in the formerly Orthodox population. A segment of the population embraced a particularly intense, devout, mystical faith, including martyrdom, while a larger segment of the people rejected religion, becoming militant atheists. The majority retreated into a mode of passive survival, retaining vestiges of the ancient faith but manifesting little of it publicly. In the Balkans, except perhaps in

Romania and Greece, the laypeople followed outwardly Orthodox customs but tended not to be too engrossed in them. Atheists in those countries tended to be less militant.

During the darkest days of the Stalinist *chistka* (purges), the hierarchy of the Russian Orthodox Church was reduced to four bishops in the entire land. It is estimated that between 1917 and 1943 nearly three hundred bishops and forty-five thousand priests were martyred. No one knows the exact number of active laypeople tortured and executed, but their number was in the hundreds of thousands, if not millions. Having noticed the tendency for nominal believers to become ardent believers, Lenin feared fanaticizing believers and said "the harder you hit a nail the deeper you drive it in"; he ordered a temporary relaxation of the persecution. But when Stalin took control of the Bolshevik Party, the severest persecutions resumed, reaching their climax in the second half of the 1930s. It seemed that the Communists would succeed in eradicating religion.

In the Russian Federation of the Soviet Union many churches were sparsely visited, mostly by elderly women. Young people and working adults seemed entirely absent as a result of the great pressure exerted upon them—threats of losing good jobs or being denied entrance to the universities. Some of the worshipers, however, seemed to burn with zeal, showing occasional Western visitors icons with scenes of the apocalyptic final judgment—particularly the vivid depictions of the thousands heading for the burning fires of hell.

One of the tactics of survival was reliance on the utter devotion of elderly laywomen. Some of the few remaining "working" churches (the majority of the churches having been closed to all religious observances and consigned to other functions, such as museums, storage houses, concert halls, machine shops, bathhouses, youth clubs, stables, and so forth) were full during liturgies on holy days. When they came in from the freezing cold, worshipers—mostly older women

**Morality and the Orthodox Church**

[In Romania the Lord's Army] aimed to improve the morality of the Orthodox faithful. Alcoholism was a particular target. . . . [There was] the need for spiritual rebirth as an additional experience to participation in the sacraments of the church. Baptism needed to become a living experience for the adult believer, and personal devotion became a prime emphasis in his spiritual scheme of things.

—Alan Scarfe, "The Romanian Orthodox Church," in Pedro Ramet, ed., *Eastern Christianity and Politics in the Twentieth Century* (Durham, N.C.: Duke University Press, 1988), 217–18.

bundled up from head to toe—would warm up the sanctuary with their body heat. They stood in rapt attention, some for an hour, others for the entire three-hour liturgy. Many of the elderly women held grandchildren in their arms while they stood, and stood, and stood, displaying astonishing endurance and devotion. When foreigners would express concern to Orthodox clergy about church attendance consisting almost entirely of these elderly women, they usually replied knowingly, "there will always be elderly women." One might say with a fair degree of justification that it was the *babushkas* who kept the faith alive.

In the middle 1980s I attended a conference in Zagorsk, Russia at what has been renamed again as Saint Sergius Trinity Monastery, to which the Moscow Theological Academy had been moved during Soviet times. The monastery is actually a medieval fortification with many churches and other auxiliary buildings, including springs of holy water. It is a famous pilgrimage site. People came from great distances—literally thousands of miles and many days of travel—to attend the practically continuous liturgies, sometimes presided over by bishops and the patriarch. Most seemed poor and tired, some probably ill, but they stood in long lines filling bottles or containers with holy water, or sleeping under the open sky on one of the available benches, later to join the throng that pushed and shoved into the various sanctuaries, lighting candles, listening to the resonant priestly chants and the even more beautiful choral music so typical of Orthodox worship.[1] Frescoes and other types of paintings on church walls, floors, and ceilings instructed the often barely literate laity in biblical stories. Since the fall of

**Fig. 5.1.** Lay people on pilgrimage to St. Sergius, Holy Trinity Monastery, Zagorsk, Russia. Photo © Paul Mojzes. Used by permission.

Communism, what is new is the many souvenir stands outside the monastic walls, while among the pilgrims one can see soldiers and officers, schoolchildren with their teachers—namely, people of all ages instead of just the elderly women and an occasional old man.

Another tactic for survival was to emphasize the close connection of the Orthodox Church with the nation. For example, when Nazi Germany attacked the Soviet Union, it was the Orthodox clergy and laity urging the people to rally for the defense of the motherland that resonated more powerfully with the average Russian than the defense of the Communist system. Even during the repressive Brezhnev era one could observe some startling nationalist phenomena, such as the celebrations during a year in the 1980s in Tbilisi, the capital city of Georgia, when Orthodox Easter and the May 1 festival nearly coincided.

On Good Friday of that year I visited a large Orthodox church on the main avenue that had two levels. I went first to the lower level. The language of the liturgy was Slavonic, and a few older Russian-speaking women were in attendance. When I went to the upper level, I was in for a surprise. The church was overfilled with hundreds of mostly young males ages fifteen to thirty—the group that is hard to find in Christian churches anywhere. The language of the liturgy was Georgian. The youthful worshipers were in rapt attention but obviously unfamiliar with the flow of the liturgy. The explanation given was that "we are here to show that we are Georgians and do not want to be Russified and the Georgian Orthodox Church is one of the few public places where Georgian is spoken."

This provides an illustration of the important role that nationalism plays in Orthodox churches, particularly when this nationalism is suppressed, experiences crisis, or becomes incensed. When the nation is not threatened, there is less need for public identification with one's church, but if the nation feels threatened, laypeople head to the church. In Romania, for instance, even the Ceausescu regime encouraged church attendance in Romanian Orthodox Churches in order to offset the perceived rivalry with Hungarians and Germans of Transylvania. And, indeed, lay Orthodox Romanians frequented their churches in ways not seen in Bulgaria or Serbia, which are likewise Orthodox but did not feel as threatened in the 1980s.

Divine worship is not the sole locus of Orthodox faith and practice. Baptisms, weddings, burials, name days, feast days (such as the Serbian *slava*, or family saint's feast day), New Year, and others are also occasions to glorify God and create community. In Tbilisi after a church wedding, the guests met in the home of the Armenian groom. People were wall to wall; tables were covered with three layers of food and drinks. The groom's father delivered a flowery rhetorical toast as only people of the Caucasus seem to be able to deliver. He was careful to be politically sensitive, not knowing who might be among his guests. He toasted Brezhnev and the Communist Party; then with *much* greater passion and energy he pulled out the cross on a chain around his neck, spoke of Armenia's Christian roots and dedication to Christ, kissed the cross repeatedly, and did not fail to mention Armenian-American friendship for the benefit of American guests.[2] After this came the feasting, dancing, and merriment.

> ### A Handmaiden of the Government
> The Bulgarian Orthodox Church found itself in an asymmetrical relationship with the [Communist] government in which ... it became a close hand-maiden of the government in promoting patriotism yet was hard-pressed by the government's virulent atheist propaganda and control.
> —Paul Mojzes, *Religious Liberty in Eastern Europe and the USSR: Before and After the Great Transformation* (Boulder: Eastern European Manuscripts, 1992), 150.

Ironically the Bolshevik regime strengthened the role of laity in the Orthodox Church, though their aim was diabolic—to weaken or destroy the church by minimizing the role of the clergy. The 1929 Law on Religious Associations stipulated that a *dvatsatka*, namely a minimum of twenty adult members of a local church, may apply for registration (and could be denied without explanation). Church buildings were no longer owned by the church but by the state and might be leased to the registered applicants, but they had to be maintained as a personal responsibility of the applicants. The priest technically became an employee of the congregation and could be removed by the government at will.[3] The legislation about the *dvatsatka* could be and was abused by the authorities because the government frequently infiltrated the group that sought registration with its own spies, some of whom were atheists but were given the assignment to undermine the work of the church. Thus it was that some of the people of "the people's democracies" worked for the demise of the church while other people of God were heroic martyrs who sacrificed everything, including their lives, to preserve the church from extinction.

Other Communist governments, with the exception of Albania, did not pass such drastic legislation. In Albania all religion was prohibited in 1967, thereby making it the only country in the world that outlawed religious practice altogether in its Constitution of 1976.[4] Bulgaria sought to emulate the Soviet Union, and in that country the repression of religion was also very severe; in Yugoslavia repression eased after 1953, and church life, while not free, was not as severely curtailed. In Romania the Orthodox Church benefited most from the government's attempt to control its sizable Hungarian and German minority by privileging the Romanian Orthodox as a way of bolstering Romanian nationalism. Despite variations in repressive policies from country to country, from denomination to denomination, and from time period to time period it is an established historical fact that Communist authorities controlled, manipulated, restricted, and often brutally tortured and killed both common believers and church leadership throughout the region.

Another tactic of survival was abandoning the faith. One of the most common ways of dissuading people from participating in church activities such as worship was by threatening them with a loss of employment. This was particularly true of military officers, people who worked in government offices, and educators. Since the government was the sole employer, with the minor exception of certain trades, such as shoe repairmen or seamstresses, nearly the entire urban population was threatened with job loss; highly educated people were threatened with a transfer to menial labor (the deposed prime minister of Czechoslovakia, Alexander Dubček, became a streetcar conductor, some theologians were furnace stokers, and so on). Such threats were powerful restraints to participation in any public religious celebrations, driving religious sentiments into the private sphere—the family circle—or sending people to worship services in a city where they were not recognized. To prevent schoolchildren from participation in certain popular religious holidays, school administrations organized out-of-town field trips. This was particularly true at *Vrbica*, when children parade with weeping willow branches. Children's absence on Christmas Day, which was not a holiday, was particularly severely disciplined.

These and similar tactics caused very large segments of the Orthodox laity to distance themselves from the church and faith in

God. Atheization of many previously Orthodox societies tended to be greater than that of other religions under Communism. The retired people were the only segment of the urban population that to some degree overcame the fear of attending church services—hence the role of the *babushkas,* who somehow preserved the faith on behalf of the rest of society as if by proxy. Still, there were exceptions, such as the few courageous young men who participated in the annual custom of jumping into the cold or even frozen rivers to retrieve a cross chiseled out of ice—an ancient Orthodox custom.

Rural people had a different experience. In the Soviet Union public religious worship was almost entirely curtailed: church buildings were razed, and there were not enough priests to serve the villages (except the occasional exiled priests who were sent to a village in order to isolate their influence). Thus the only remnants of religion survived in the form of customs, private prayers, and hope for miraculous healings. The same can be said of Albania, both rural and urban. It was very different in Bulgaria, Romania, and Yugoslavia. There the government decided not to supervise as closely the religious peasant population. Most villages had churches and clergy. In fact, most priests came from village families; for them becoming a priest was a social advancement. Villagers tend to be much more traditional, because changes occurred more slowly and they were less susceptible to Communist propaganda, but they often obtained an inferior general education. It was the entire village *gestalt* that favored the retention of a much higher degree of religiosity in the villages. Villagers celebrated the various feast days that had been connected to the agricultural cycle (start plowing on a certain saint's day, apples are ready for picking for Saints Peter and Paul, harvest should be finished by another saint's day, and so forth).

One of the principal Marxist doctrines was that religion belongs in the private sphere, and the Communist governments attempted to impose it strictly. Having accepted this premise of privatization of religion, Orthodox laity succumbed to it as a tactic of survival and in order to become more successful. While many people discarded religion completely, others retreated into their homes. Many Orthodox homes retained an icon in the corner of a room with an oil lamp or candle burning at the base of the icon, and people prayed to God, the Mother of God, and their patron saint. When a child was born, often the mother alone or even the grandmother (sometimes surreptitiously) took the child for baptism.

People resorted to their Orthodox faith most tenaciously at occasions of death and dying. Sometimes even atheists asked for religious rites on their death beds, and their families gave them religious burials. There were, indeed, communist burials, but they were outnumbered by religious burials. The custom in most Eastern European countries is to have death notices posted in public places. From the death notice one could figure the broad religious affiliation of the deceased. A cross indicated a Christian (with different shapes for Orthodox and Catholic/Protestant), a crescent and star a Muslim, a star of David a Jew, and a five-pointed star a Communist. In multireligious cities people continued to be buried in their respective separate cemeteries. Rituals of death were probably the most successful way for the church to demonstrate its relevance to a religiously alienated population.

The Orthodox hierarchy emphasizes right belief and canonical procedure above all else, often sacrificing charitable work, and therefore laypeople generally have very little experience of it. Prior to the Communist takeover there had been Orthodox brotherhoods and sisterhoods charitable associations of Orthodox laymen and laywomen who promoted various charitable and cultural activities, such as hospital and prison visitations, choral or folklore societies, and literary circles. However, all these had been abolished by Communist legislation based on the premise that the state is to take care of all social and educational needs. In most parishes there was little or no community life. Church life was entirely restricted to worship. Only with the collapse of Communism did the government permit the reestablishment of some of these associations of Orthodox laypeople. Nowadays

Fig. 5.2. Russian Icon of Christ Pantocrator by Ivan Alexaev, c. 1900. Photo © Art Resource, N.Y. Used by permission.

they assist in hospitals, institutions for the mentally ill, prisons, shelters for the homeless, rehabilitation clinics, orphanages, and other social, cultural, and educational institutions.

Religious education was even more difficult. Catechism used to be taught in the pre-Communist period by priests in public and private schools. But Communists nationalized all schools. Religious education under Communism was often completely prohibited; when it was not, few Orthodox churches could provide such education in the parish. Schools were separated from churches, and priests had no access to schools. Thus, catechesis simply vanished. People learned, as in ancient times, from the many paintings and icons and from the sermons, though these were often poorly understood because they were typically delivered in an archaic form of the language (although Orthodox churches used the vernacular). Orthodox literature was practically nonexistent; only in Romania was there a number of theological journals and books, but these were usually intended for the elite rather than the laity.[5] The Bible was neither available nor read by the vast majority of the laity.

The Russian Orthodox and other Orthodox laypeople in the Soviet Union especially held strong apocalyptic notions, undoubtedly as a result of the severe persecutions by a government that many regarded as the Antichrist. Many had become quite fatalistic, not at all surprising given the powerlessness and even hopelessness of most of their situations. Their faith was expressed in mythological or miraculous terms that some scholars have called the first, or primitive, naïveté. In schools children were indoctrinated with rigid and dogmatic dialectical scientific materialism. Two dogmatisms collided in the minds of many people. Some ended up accepting Marxist dogmas, while others embraced insufficiently explained, presented, or understood Orthodox dogmas. Thus, many believed in a literal creationist story and did not accept the theory of evolution. Instead of using the widely available but often crudely delivered medical services, they would pray for miracles, travel long distances to search for a cure at pilgrimage places or to obtain bottles of holy water, or else resort to magical rites from dubious faith healers and fortune tellers. Fear of the devil and demons seemed for many nearly as powerful as trust in God, angels, the Mother of God, and the saints. Crossing oneself in the Orthodox manner (with three fingers and to the right and then left), burning candles for the departed, and celebrating *parastos* (forty days after death and then again a year later) were deeply ingrained folk observances. Their religious belief was by and large not only precritical but sometimes also an admixture of pre-Christian and literalist Christian.

Fig. 5.3. Receiving the Eucharist. Photo courtesy of Srdjan Srdic, www.mojkordun.com.

Relying on religious folk customs combined with ritual was another tactic of survival. For the typical Orthodox layperson religion is not primarily a matter of knowing the doctrines but of following rituals and customs. The liturgical year is replete with holy days, major and minor. For the major celebrations—Easter, Pentecost, Vrbica, All Saints, the Assumption of the Virgin Mary, Mother of God, and Christmas—there are colorful customs at home and in the church. For Easter parishioners bring bread, colored eggs, and other food to the church to be blessed—some eaten in the church, some taken home. At other times priests go to the homes to bless a newly built house, a family festival or celebration, a wedding, a funeral, or an anointment of the sick. Among the Serbs and Macedonians there is a unique holy day called *krsna slava* or simply *slava* (the same word for "glory" and "feast") that celebrates each family's tradition of its conversion from paganism to Christianity and baptism on a saint's day perhaps a thousand years ago. This becomes an occasion of a priestly visit and cutting of a special bread with

Fig. 5.4. Food brought the the church for blessing. Photo courtesy of Srdjan Srdic, www.mojkordun.com.

a coin hidden in it. The gathered family and friends rotate the bread and kiss it while the priest chants a liturgy and subsequently cuts or breaks the bread ceremonially. Each person gets to break off a piece of bread, and the one who finds the coin is regarded as being lucky in the coming year. This tradition was so deeply ingrained among the people

**Fig. 5.5.** Bring the yule log into the church. Photo courtesy of Srdjan Srdic, www.mojkordun.com.

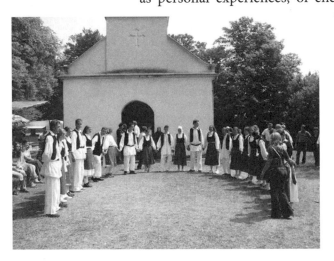

**Fig. 5.6.** Folk dancing outside the church. Photo courtesy of Srdjan Srdic, www.mojkordun.com.

that despite attempts at prohibition during the Communist period, even members of the Communist Party celebrated it, though stripping it of most of its religious components. For many laypeople the religious part seemed to take a secondary role to the celebration, which involved eating, drinking, live music, singing, and dancing folk dances; it lasted anywhere from one to three days.

An important role played by laypeople is *kum* and *kuma* (Serbian for "godfather" and "godmother," or at a wedding the best man and maid or matron of honor). This role, which no longer seems to have the same religious content as it did originally, is still of great social importance—sometimes equaling or even surpassing blood relationships.

One of the characteristics of people's Orthodoxy, which many would rather overlook, was the entanglement with superstition and magic. Particularly among the village folk and the less well educated there were countless stories, often claimed as personal experiences, of encounters with witches and warlocks, werewolves, demonic and benevolent spirits, haunted places, the evil eye, and all kinds of beliefs in good or evil fortune. Magical formulas were used during courting, weddings, births, illnesses and deaths. Even priests were involved in some rituals to drive out the devil, but usually such practices were more popular among the people. Particularly popular were the blessing of a new home as well as repeated blessings during various holy days, for which the presence of a priest was necessary. One might say that for many the more classical Orthodox religiosity was being replaced not with atheism but with superstition.

## OTHER CHURCHES AND RELIGIONS

The Orthodox Churches are firmly convinced that the Orthodox are the one, true, holy, universal, and apostolic church and that none of the non-Orthodox churches have the *pleroma*, or fullness of Christ's body, in them. This belief is consistently proclaimed by the bishops and the priests and fully embraced by the laity. Paradoxically the people's Orthodoxy may be a bit less antagonistic and simultaneously less dialogical toward the non-Orthodox. The lay Orthodox perceive themselves to be in the straight, uninterrupted line from Jesus Christ and his apostles—the only church that has preserved the fullness of the undivided apostolic church.

Roman Catholicism or "papism" (also called "the Latins" in the past) is regarded as the main threat against Orthodoxy—even greater than that of Islam—because the Catholic Church has asserted that it is the one, true, holy, universal, and apostolic church. Regarding the Orthodox as schismatics, the Catholic Church made numerous attempts prior to the Second Vatican Council to bring the Orthodox "back into the fold" and occasionally were successful in creating Uniate churches—that is, former Orthodox churches that had become Eastern Rite Catholic churches by accepting papal primacy. The word "Uniate" is a word of derision in Orthodoxy, and the Orthodox consider the Uniates to be a Trojan horse, often maintaining that no cooperation with the Catholics is possible until the Uniates are returned to the Orthodox fold, as they were after World War II in Ukraine and Romania. The experiences of the Photian schism, the Great Schism of 1054, the Fourth Crusade, the Council of Florence and Ferrara, the unions of Brest-Litovsk and Uzhgorod, and many others are vividly implanted in the minds of Orthodox. Even when both churches were persecuted under Communism, there was very little contact between them. Of course this did not necessarily mean that people in mixed neighborhoods did not get along during the calmer times, but it was always easy to embitter the believers, as happened in Ukraine, the former Yugoslavia, and Romania immediately upon the collapse of Communism, despite the ecumenical breakthroughs of Vatican II. In the 1990s, in the former Yugoslavia, the wars between Serbs and Croats were often perceived by the participants as wars of Orthodox against Catholics.

The Protestants are regarded as dangerous sectarians or even cult-ists. While the hierarchies of the Orthodox churches found ways to cooperate with some Protestant churches through the World Council of Churches, the Council of European Churches, or even on local ecumenical levels (for example, in Poland the Orthodox and Protes-tants had a joint theological school in Warsaw during the Communist period), people's Orthodoxy was not open to ecumenical cooperation and dialogue. Most Protestants, particularly the "free churches" (Bap-tists, Pentecostals, Methodists, Congregationalists), often targeted Orthodox believers for their evangelistic efforts since they usually considered an Orthodox layperson as not genuinely Christian ("born again") and therefore a fair target for conversion. Members of the Orthodox Church were frequently warned against associating with the "sectarians," and on the whole they heeded such warnings and were not tolerant toward the "heretics."

Islam was another monumental threat. All Orthodox countries had been at one time or another under the domination of Islam. The Russians were able to free themselves of the "Mongol Tartar yoke" that lasted from 1240 to 1480 and thereafter actually reverse the pattern by occupying many Muslim lands. But that was not the case in the Caucasus or the Balkans, where Arabic and later Turkish overlordship lasted into the nineteenth and twentieth centuries. The attitude toward Islam was one of bitterness and often hatred. Since collective con-sciousness still dominates people's psyches, many Orthodox felt that they ought to revenge themselves against not only the conquering for-eign Muslims but also Muslim converts in their midst, who were often considered traitors to their people and their faith. Even Communists whose heritage had been Orthodox sought ways of converting the Muslims back to the ethnoreligiosity of the mother group. Thus, the Bulgarian Communist government sought (usually unsuccessfully) to convert Pomaks (Muslims of Bulgarian ethnicity) and get them to change their names to Bulgarian/Christian and take other cultural steps to integrate themselves into the Orthodox milieu of Bulgaria.

The Orthodox Church's relationship with Judaism has not ben-efited from Jewish-Christian dialogue and post-Holocaust theology of the Catholic and Protestant churches. In Russia, Ukraine, Byelorussia, and Romania, anti-Semitism was pronounced among some hierarchs and the people. Among the Bulgarians, Macedonians, and Serbs, anti-

Semitism was not virulent, and the number of Jews living in those countries was small.

During the seventeenth century a serious schism split the Orthodox Church of Russia into the majority Russian Orthodox state church and the minority Old Believers. The Russian tsars and the official church mercilessly persecuted the Old Believers, who in turn split into two rival movements, *Popovtsy* and *Bezpopovtsy* (Priestly and Priestless). During the Soviet period the Old Believers were still subjected to persecutions—as were all the others—and many of these churches were left without formal clerical oversight, but they continued an often clandestine existence. Yet they are still not tolerated by the Orthodox.

Almost all Communist constitutions acknowledged the historical role of their respective Orthodoxies in the formation of national consciousness. It was this aspect of the Orthodox church-nation symbiosis that played an ambiguous or paradoxical role. To fully control the nation, the Communists felt that they needed to break the ethnoreligious symbiosis. But when they wanted to strengthen the role of their nation over that of other nationalisms, the Communists were eager to exploit the historic ties of the Orthodox Church to the nation and society and were willing, for instance, in Romania to give fairly free reign to the Romanian Orthodox Church in strengthening Romanian national consciousness. Toward the end of the Communist period (from about the 1980s onward) Serbian Communists sought to harness the influence of the Serbian Orthodox Church in their conflicts with Albanian, Boshniak, Croatian, and Macedonian nationalisms.

> ### The Church and Political Dissent
>
> Broadly speaking, the modern religious dissent movement [under Soviet Communism] was set off by the Khrushchev anti-religious campaign. Certain believers, both lay and clerical, began writing to the leaders of their churches, pleading with them to be bolder in standing up for the rights of the community in the face of intolerable state interference.
>
> —Philip Walters, "How Religious Bodies Respond to State Control," in Eugene B. Shirley Jr., and Michael Rowe, eds., *Candle in the Wind: Religion in the Soviet Union* (Washington, D.C.: Ethics and Public Policy Center, 1989), 125.

## RESURGENCE IN THE POST-COMMUNIST PERIOD

Since the collapse of Communism there has clearly been a return to explicit religiosity in Orthodox countries and an attempt to regain the privileged position of the Orthodox in their respective societies. Here are some anecdotal examples from my personal experience:

It is a workday in the middle of August 2006 around eleven A.M. at the Serbian Orthodox cathedral (*saborna crkva*; literally, council church) in Novi Sad, capital of the Vojvodina province of Serbia. No priests are at the church, but a small shop in the vestibule is open for the purchase of candles, church literature, and small icons. One by one, mostly younger and middle-aged women, some perhaps students, walk into the church, crossing themselves. Their dress is modern; some are in jeans. There is silence in the church. The women—and an occasional man—respectfully proceed to a platform on which lie diagonally two icons, one of Jesus Christ and the other of the patron saint. They bow and kiss the icon. One briefly kneels in prayer. A young woman prostrates herself full length on the floor. A few proceed to the iconostasis at the front of the church and briefly stop in front of some icons, occasionally crossing themselves. Just as quietly and without lingering, they leave the church. Some who had

**Fig. 5.7.** Church of Saint Sava in Belgrade. When it is finished, it will be the second largest Orthodox church in the world). Photo © Paul Mojzes. Used by permission.

purchased a few thin, yellow church candles go to the candle holder, where other candles are already burning, and ignite theirs on the flames, pausing a moment, perhaps uttering a prayer for a departed relative or friend or perhaps for someone sick, maybe praying for success on an exam. There is much veneration of the Mother of God, the Virgin Mary, who is venerated only slightly less than the Holy Trinity. During the Communist period in the same church there were distinctly fewer and usually much older women stopping for prayer, but essentially the same practice prevailed.

In 2003 I visited in Ekaterinburg (Sverdlovsk during the Soviet era) a very large, newly built church on the spot were the last tsar, Nicholas II, and his entire family were executed by the Bolsheviks. It is now well attended even at times when there is no holy liturgy. A few priests mill around but do not seem to engage the people, who are worshipfully moving around the cavernous sanctuary on two levels. Like in Novi Sad they pause to light candles, kiss the icons, and pray by bowing or occasionally kneeling or touching the floor with their foreheads. A large number of high school girls, curious and with a sense of awe, examine the interior, seemingly aware that in this location a historic tragedy has occurred, which is leading to the beatification of the tsar and his family.

A few years earlier, in an older church near the same location on a bitterly cold day (twenty degrees below zero), baptisms were held in the barely warm church. First, a baby was being totally immersed in the water by the priests three times; then an adult man also stepped into the large baptismal font—he was barefoot, and his arms and head were also wetted as he was being baptized, while his family and the curious crowded around the baptismal font.

People are no longer afraid of punishment, and many, but perhaps not the majority, are now declaring themselves as believers and are trying to catch up in being instructed in what it means to be Orthodox liturgically. A young woman in Skopje, Macedonia, heading into the cathedral states that she is doing it because she sees that young ethnic Albanians go to pray in the mosque and that perhaps Macedonians ought to show greater dedication to their church. A well-known Macedonian poet on the other hand emphatically told me that he is an atheist but is a Macedonian Orthodox. There are many like him throughout the Orthodox lands. During the Balkan wars of the 1990s many Serbs started to attend Orthodox churches, but it is not always clear whether this is a religious or a national affirmation. Perhaps it is both. Too little is yet being done to instruct them catechetically or theologically. Attendance at liturgies has gone up considerably, and more religious literature is being published. It will take time—twenty years at least, according to Bishop Irinej (Bulović) of Bachka—to raise a new generation of well-educated priests who will be able to help the people of God become mature, educated people of faith.

## FOR FURTHER READING

Bourdeaux, Michael. *Patriarch and Prophets: Persecution of the Russian Orthodox Church Today.* New York: Praeger, 1970.

Florovsky, Georges. *Ways of Russian Theology.* 2 vols. Belmont, Mass.: Nordland, 1972.

Lossky, Vladimir. *Orthodox Theology: An Introduction.* Crestwood, N.Y.: St. Vladimir's Seminary Press, 2001.

Meyendorff, John. *The Orthodox Church.* Crestwood, N.Y.: St. Vladimir's Seminary Press, 1981.

Mojzes, Paul. *Religious Liberty in Eastern Europe and the USSR: Before and After the Great Transformation.* Boulder, Colo.: Eastern European Manuscripts, 1992.

Pospielovsky, Dimitry. *The Russian Church under the Soviet Regime, 1917–1982.* 2 vols. Crestwood, N.Y.: St. Vladimir's Seminary Press, 1984.

Ramet, Pedro, ed. *Eastern Christianity and Politics in the Twentieth Century.* Durham, N.C.: Duke University Press, 1988.

Schmemann, Alexander. *The Historical Road of Eastern Orthodoxy.* Crestwood, N.Y.: St. Vladimir's Seminary Press, 1977.

Ware, Bishop Kallistos [Timothy]. *Orthodox Way.* Rev. ed. Crestwood, N.Y.: St. Vladimir's Seminary Press, 1995.

Zizioulas, John D. *Being as Communion: Studies in Personhood and the Church.* Crestwood, N.Y.: St. Vladimir's Seminary Press, 1985.

# EVANGELICALISM IN NORTH AMERICA

## MARK A. NOLL AND ETHAN R. SANDERS

CHAPTER SIX

In 1997 Zondervan, the evangelical imprint of HarperCollins, published *Sunday in America*, a book featuring about 150 photographs of American Christians at worship, at play, in the family circle, and in the world. For prose to intersperse among the photographs, Zondervan enlisted well-known personalities who could hardly be classified as ordinary Americans, including Senator Elizabeth Dole and former President Jimmy Carter. And the images, as inevitable for such projects, featured less the quotidian and more the distinctive, the poignant, the cute, the striking, the unusual, or the photogenic. Nevertheless, the book still provided an unusually illuminating glimpse into the religious lives of ordinary American believers, a great number of whom could be classified as evangelicals.

The book's approach was ecumenical, with much space devoted to Roman Catholics and mainline Protestants, and some to the Orthodox as well. Its many pictures of singing, preaching, baptism, family recreation, and deeds of mercy undertaken outside church walls were also generically Christian, or even simply generically human. But especially striking for those who could be identified as evangelicals were the images of people praying or attending to the scriptures.

Besides photos of Bibles held, addressed, or referenced by preachers, there were several scenes of Bible classes or Bibles being tenderly carried, including Baptist churches in Missouri and Mississippi, a United Church of Christ congregation in Bozeman, Montana, and the First Ukrainian Evangelical Baptist Church in Philadelphia. Bible readers or Bible carriers were also featured at a pre-game chapel service for minor league baseball players in North Carolina, a Salvation Army relief center for earthquake victims in California, and in a small family grouping (grandchild and grandparents) heading out the door to go to church. The images did not by themselves explain how the Bible was being used, but they did indicate its near omnipresence in the religious lives of those who were photographed.

Scenes of individuals at prayer—in evangelical postures or at evangelical churches—were even more common. In fact, it would take a pious Walt Whitman to do justice to the multiplicity of people at prayer as found in only this one volume:

> third-grade girls clutching Bibles newly presented at a Dallas Methodist church;
> a father and a son at a Promise Keepers rally in New Orleans;
> elderly black men at a Missionary Baptist church in rural Texas;
> leather-clad motorcyclists at a sunrise service in Denver;
> hundreds in New Mexico at a ranch retreat center sponsored by the Presbyterian Church (U.S.A.);
> a knot of teenagers at the National Youth Convention of the Church of the Nazarene;
> a family before Sunday dinner in Woodstock, Georgia;
> an elderly Mennonite pastor and his wife in Rowdy, Kentucky, before dinner;
> NASCAR drivers before a race at the Martinsville Speedway in Virginia;
> young people for a morning devotional at a North Texas Methodist youth camp;
> a crowd of the famous and not-so-famous pausing before work at a Habitat for Humanity site in Atlanta;
> a pastor kneeling with a couple "in crisis";
> a rodeo clown before entering the ring in Cody, Wyoming;
> Sunday School students at a Presbyterian church in Chattanooga;
> parishioners at Iglesia Resurrección y Vida Central in Grand Rapids, Michigan;
> black and white pro football players from both teams at the end of a game;

ex-gang members in Milwaukee; and
prisoners at a county jail in Fort Worth.

To the extent that such depictions were at all representative, there is a whole lot of praying goin' on.

What this one volume revealed about Sunday activities—and by extension, about religious lives during the days between Sundays— were the extraordinary variety, pervasiveness, and depth of religious practices engaged in regularly by white North American evangelicals.

For mostly historical reasons, the religious activities of African Americans differ considerably from those of their white counterparts, even though most black Protestants have always maintained convictions on doctrines and morals similar to the view of white evangelicals.

Yet when one turns from popular projects like *Sunday in America* in search of academic description or interpretation of

Fig. 6.1. This image from *Sunday In America* and others like it in the book show the centrality of prayer and the Bible in the life of evangelical Americans. From *Sunday in America* (Grand Rapids, Mich.: Zondervan, 1995), 13. Photo © Louis Deluca. Used by permission.

such practices, the scholarly cupboard—while not exactly bare—is hardly well stocked. As opposed to scholarly attention focused on evangelical media celebrities, evangelical cultural warfare, and evangelical participation in the bruising political partisanship of recent decades, serious inquiry into the specifically religious practices of North American evangelicals has been relatively rare.[1]

To be sure, a few well-researched case studies have illuminated the religious lives of evangelical or quasi-evangelical groups in specific localities.[2] And several sociologists have produced careful studies of specific dimensions of week-in, week-out religious life focused entirely or partially on evangelicals.[3] Social scientific polling has also made available an increasing quantity of relevant statistical material, though about such study it is important to keep in mind the sage words of Leigh Eric Schmidt: "Most of the things that count about Christianity cannot be counted, like the warmth or coolness of prayer,

**A Scholar's Interest in Evangelicalism**

I wanted to write a book about popular evangelicalism, to examine the ways evangelical theology and morality shaped individuals within the movement, how their participation in the evangelical subculture defined who they were and shaped the way they viewed the world. As a cultural historian, I was curious to see how evangelical theology functioned in various social contexts. Whatever contemporary evangelicalism has to commend it lies not in its media stars but in the sincerity and ingenuousness of the ordinary folk who consider themselves evangelicals.

—Randall Balmer, *Mine Eyes Have Seen the Glory: A Journey into the Evangelical Subculture in America,* 4th ed. (New York: Oxford University Press, 2006), 8.

the resonance or hollowness of scriptural words, the songs or silences of the saints in heaven, the presences or absences in the sacrament."[4] In other words, some help is at hand for examining the specific religious practices of evangelical groups. It remains nonetheless only a slight exaggeration to say that if formal academic studies were their only resource, contemporary observers would have better anthropological understanding of cock fighting in Bali than of the hundreds of thousands of baptisms each year in congregations of the Southern Baptist Convention; or closer attention to Roman Catholic street festivals among Italian immigrants in New York City than of scriptural study in the hundreds of thousands of small-group neighborhood Bible studies (usually organized by and for women) that take place weekly throughout North America.[5]

In light of the scholarly investigation that still needs to be done to document the ordinary religious lives of ordinary evangelicals, this chapter can be only a preliminary probe of a few aspects of a protean subject. Because of the numbers and social significance of evangelical communities, this subject is as critically important as it has been understudied. After taking up the always daunting challenge of defining and delimiting what is meant by "evangelical," brief reports follow on evangelicals at prayer, evangelical public worship, and evangelical material culture. The evidence for these subjects is spotty and conclusions only preliminary. Many critically important aspects of evangelical religious life—like the use of scripture, the growing turn to self-conscious "spirituality," and the calendrical rhythms that pervasively yet ironically mark the largely a-liturgical evangelical communities—are omitted. But what is treated may provide hints concerning both what does take place among evangelicals and what deserves more intensive further study.

For the purposes of the topics explored, the geography is intentionally North America, since several Canadian researchers have contributed unusual insights concerning the day-to-day unfolding of recent evangelical history.

## LOCATING EVANGELICALS

Given the increasingly slippery usage of the term, it is pertinent to note that "evangelical" has several legitimate senses, all related to the etymological meaning of "good news." For Christians of many types throughout history it has meant God's redemption of sinners by the work of Christ. In the Reformation the term became a rough synonym for "Protestant," which explains why several large denominations of European heritage like the Evangelical Lutheran Church in America use the term. Yet the most common usage today stems from renewal movements among British and American Protestants in the eighteenth century whose leaders —like the founders of Methodism, John and Charles Wesley, along with notable revivalists like George Whitefield—sought to renew "true religion" by stressing "gospel" or "evangelical" truths.

Evangelicals descended from these earlier movements have usually stressed the need for religious conversion ("the new birth"). They have held a high view of the Bible's authority. They have valued contemporary relevance over religious traditions. And they have emphasized in their formal teachings the person of Christ, especially his redeeming death on the cross.[6] Evangelical Protestants defined by these convictions made up the largest and most influential religious groups in the United States throughout the nineteenth century, and they were almost as strong in Canada. In both countries large numbers continue to the present. In keeping with the long evangelical tradition of independent or entrepreneurial action, the most visible evangelicals since the Second World War have been leaders of voluntary (or parachurch) agencies like the youth-oriented Campus Crusade for Christ or the relief agency World Vision, along with publishing companies like Christianity Today, Inc., radio-driven conglomerates like Focus on the Family, and educational institutions like Moody Bible Institute. Among the best known evangelical figures in recent decades have been the evangelist Billy Graham, the psychologist and broadcaster

James Dobson, the politician and broadcaster Pat Robertson, and Charles Colson, the one-time White House assistant to Richard Nixon who now heads a Christian ministry to prisons.

A major U.S. poll conducted in 1996 by the Angus Reid Group showed that adherents to Protestant denominations closely identified with traditional evangelical distinctives—like the Southern Baptist Convention, the Assemblies of God, the Church of the Nazarene, the Baptist Bible Fellowship International, the Churches of Christ, and many others—made up about 26 percent of the American population. These are the groups most likely to be called "evangelical," even though many in them do not use the term for themselves. Another 9 percent of the population were adherents of African American Protestant churches, where many religious beliefs and practices (but not political attitudes) are similar to those of white evangelicals. In addition, the same poll showed that significant numbers in other denominational families held to traditionally evangelical convictions concerning salvation in Christ, trust in the Bible, and the need to encourage non-Christians to become Christians—approximately half of the adherents of the older mainline Protestant churches (Presbyterians, Episcopalians, Lutherans, Methodists) and over a third of America's Roman Catholics. Whether defined by beliefs and practices or by identification with conservative Protestant denominations, evangelicals are strongest by far in the South, while weakest in New England and the far West.[7]

In recent decades, American evangelicals in conservative Protestant denominations have become closely associated with politically conservative movements. In other parts of the world and in earlier periods of North American history, evangelicals have been more generally nonpolitical and more widely spread across the political spectrum. A religious stream that in the United States includes Christian Reformed parishioners in Grand Rapids, Southern Baptists in Birmingham, and members of the Assemblies of God in Los Angeles (many Korean or Hispanic) cannot be summarized easily. But by heeding patterns of historical descent and intentional conviction, it is possible to bring at least nominal coherence to the broad and diverse evangelical stream.

## PRAYER

Prayer has always been central to evangelical experience, as to the experience of most adherents of all religions, but there has been little scholarly attention focused on the subject. Exceptions include a solid study by Richard Ostrander, who examined attempts by American Protestants early in the twentieth century to maintain religious traditions menaced by an increasingly scientific modern world, and an innovative report by George Rawlyk, who included consideration of prayer in extensive interviews of Canadian evangelicals that he supervised in the early 1990s.[8] They are the sources for most of what follows.

During the second half of the nineteenth century, a combination of the new higher criticism (which questioned older approaches to scripture) and the increasing prestige of natural science (which seemed to rule out the supernatural) took its toll on Protestant America's traditional notions about prayer. Most directly under attack was intercessory prayer, which Christians of all sorts had practiced through the centuries by petitioning God with requests that the petitioners felt could be answered with obvious results in their daily lives. This kind of prayer seemed especially suspect when judged by a scientific worldview in which it was assumed that God did not act visibly in the world. Such attitudes did not, however, level the walls of Protestant Christianity; among the holdouts remained many evangelicals who clung resolutely to one of the most personal and most prized aspects of their religion. Disputes about the

---

### The Importance of Prayer

The life of prayer in a world of science was indeed a difficult and important issue for turn-of-the-century Protestants. "Prove that prayer is of no avail," declared Charles Jefferson, "and you shatter the Christian religion." The Methodist writer E. S. Smith agreed with Jefferson: "At no point in the line of defense is the Christian faith more persistently assailed than at this; no doctrine is more vital to Christianity than that which this point covers." American Protestants of the early twentieth century may or may not have been interested in how many authors wrote Genesis, whether humans were descended from monkeys, or in the Social Gospel; but the serious Christian certainly prayed. This issue struck at the heart of the Protestant attempt to come to grips with modernity, not just among those in seminaries but among the rank and file as well. Yet while historians have devoted ample attention to the Protestant attempts to meet the intellectual challenges of biblical criticism and Darwinian evolution, not to mention the cultural challenges of a modern industrial society, the history of prayer in this era remains an untold story.

—Rick Ostrander, *The Life of Prayer in a World of Science: Protestants, Prayer, and American Culture, 1870–1930* (New York: Oxford University Press, 2000), 13.

Figs. 6.2–3. Hudson Taylor (top), founder of the China Inland Mission, and George Mueller (bottom) both published popular "answered prayer narratives" that served as an effective instrument to break down the barriers of religious skepticism and a powerful reassurance to believers in the goodness of God.

authorship of individual biblical books or adjustments in theological understanding were one thing, but for most evangelicals prayer was a lifeline to the divine that could not be ceded to the modernizing instincts of an increasingly rational world.

In the decades surrounding the turn of the century, evangelicals found a new devotional outlet to confirm their belief in the power of prayer. Narratives of answered prayer seemed proof positive against scientific suspicions. As speaking in tongues functioned for Pentecostals, so manifest answers to prayer functioned for a larger constituency to demonstrate the personal nearness of God. These narratives were also intended to demonstrate for doubters that there really was a God who truly answered prayer. They often appeared as full-length books, many from missionaries in foreign lands explaining how God had answered specific requests for material needs or specific petitions for converts in response to the preached message of Christian salvation. Two of the celebrity evangelicals figuring most prominently in these narratives were Hudson Taylor (1832–1905), founder of the China Inland Mission, and George Mueller (1805–1898), an expatriate German who had established a series of faith-based orphanages in England. Both published their own accounts of divine answer to prayer, and both became consistent material for others' commentary on prayer.

Naysayers, of course, abounded in response to the burgeoning evangelical literature on prayer. To the scientifically minded, recitals of answered prayer testified to simple coincidences, duplicity, or the triumph of hope over experience. In whatever event, direct causation could not be attributed to God, since none of the incidents could be repeated for a scientific test. The less empirically minded contended that, whatever the quantity of answered prayer, more petitions to God (for material needs, for health, for repaired personal relations, for peace in the world) went unfulfilled than were fulfilled. To the skeptics and even a few believers, the shooting of President William McKinley in 1901 offered a sobering lesson. As soon as the president was wounded by assassin Leon Czolgosz, and during the many days he lingered thereafter, churches and ad hoc groups gathered throughout the country to pray fervently for the recovery of McKinley, who himself had demonstrated a sincere personal piety. But, alas, the president did not recover.

Evangelical responses to skeptics tried to discriminate between the genuine and the fake. According to William Patton, author of *Prayer and Its Remarkable Answers* (first published in 1875, with ten reprintings soon thereafter), "multitudes 'say a prayer,' who yet do no praying. Many Christians and churches also pray so defectively . . . that they do not come within the scope of the Scriptural promises. What is their experience worth, then, in the matter before us? It should not be said that their prayers are not answered; but that they do not pray."[9]

During the Great War and directly after—a period marked by the fundamentalist-modernist controversy—many in the fundamentalist camp described the promotion of vibrant prayer as a more important activity than combat against the modernists. Reuben Torrey's *The Power of Prayer* (1924) and J. Oliver Buswell's *Problems in the Prayer Life* (1928) were two of the many books that urged believers to keep lists of prayer requests, which would help them realize when God answered specific prayers. The advice of Torrey, the popular evangelist and heir to D. L. Moody, and Buswell, the president of Wheaton College, spoke to a practice already well entrenched, and one that continues to this day in many evangelical circles.

Other evangelical leaders linked the practices of prayer more directly to the era's intra-Protestant struggles over doctrine and church practice. In 1924, James Gray, president of Moody Bible Institute, claimed that the fundamentalists' emphasis on prayer and their devotion to revival made them true successors of the seventeenth-century German pietists and eighteenth-century Methodists who had been God's instruments for revitalizing the dying orthodoxies of their day.

If frequently reprinted books can be any guide to what was happening in the homes of the book-buying public, the demonstrative appeal to prayer rode the back of intense interest. From the 1884 printing of D. L. Moody's *Prevailing Prayer: What Hinders It?* through the early 1900s, books on personal communication with God were well worn in the homes of conservative Protestants.

The centrality of prayer in evangelical life has continued to the present, where again popular literature provides an indication. Evangelicals make up the bulk of those who purchase such popular books as *Too Busy Not to Pray* (1988) by Bill Hybels, founding pastor of Willow Creek Community Church in Illinois, the prototypical late twentieth-century megachurch; *Prayer: Finding the Heart's True Home* (1992) by Richard J. Foster, a leading promoter of a more historical spirituality among evangelicals; *Prayer: My Soul's Adventure with God* (1995), an autobiography by Robert Schuller, who presided for many years over the Crystal Cathedral in California; *The Great House of God: A Home for Your Heart* (1997), a popular exposition of the Lord's Prayer by a widely read pastor from Texas, Max Lucado; and *Prayers from a Mother's Heart* (1999) by Ruth Bell Graham, wife of the famous evangelist.

The appearance in 2000 of Bruce Wilkinson's *The Prayer of Jabez: Breaking Through to the Blessed Life* soon became a sensation on the order of Hal Lindsey's *The Late Great Planet Earth*. Wilkinson, head of Walk Thru the Bible Ministries of Atlanta, Georgia, drew his inspiration from a little-noticed passage in 1 Chronicles 4:9-10 (quoted here, as in the book, from the New King James Version): "Now Jabez was more honorable than his brothers, and his mother called his name Jabez, saying, 'Because I bore him in pain.' And Jabez called on the God of Israel saying, 'Oh, that you would bless me indeed, and enlarge my territory, that Your hand would be with me, and that You would keep me from evil, that I may not cause pain!' So God granted him what he requested." To Wilkinson, Jabez set out a pattern that all later believers were intended to follow. Millions of readers from around the world agreed.

The specific teachings in these different books, as well as the various cautions, qualifications, and theologies found in them, differ considerably from each other. Yet as a group, their great popularity testifies to ongoing evangelical dedication to prayer as a foundation for life at home, at church, and in the world.

During the early 1990s, George Rawlyk of the Queen's University in Kingston, Ontario, sought to discover more precisely what prayer and other religious activities meant to Canadian evangelicals who were willing to speak about such matters with researchers from the Angus Reid Group. One of the most interesting results of the investigation that Rawlyk supervised was the discovery that these evangelicals reported a much more consistent practice of prayer than they did the reading of scripture. Where Canadians in general were more than three times as likely to pray daily as to read the Bible or other devotional material daily (29 percent to 8 percent), Canadian evangelicals, with much higher general levels of religious practice, were more than twice as likely to pray daily (87 percent to 42 percent). Of those who reported praying every day, about a fifth said they did so for at least an hour, another fifth twenty to fifty minutes, and the rest lesser amounts. The overwhelming majority of Canadian evangelicals reported that they directed their prayers to "God the Father" (90 percent). In a conviction closely related to prayer, 87 percent reported that they believed in divine healing, with half of that number reporting that they knew someone personally who had been healed as a result of prayer.[10]

While the numbers that Rawlyk discovered indicated the general importance of prayer to evangelicals, these numbers could not reveal the content, the intentions, or the meaning of the prayers. For that purpose Rawlyk looked to extended interviews, which followed up the polling. He found that men had greater difficulty articulating how and why they prayed, and what prayer meant, than did women. Men and women alike usually spoke of prayer as speaking informally with God. Some prayed in order to talk with God about what had happened during the day, while others stressed the peace of mind brought by the practice. One ordained minister said that he prayed to find the will of God, but also conceded that this search was often frustrating.

Most of the women interviewed spoke of prayer as simply talking to God, something they did informally and throughout the day. More

> ### Evangelical Canadians
> Over three times as many Canadians pray daily (29 per cent) as read their Bibles or other religious material daily (8 per cent). And one half of all Canadians (49 per cent) believe that "God always answers my prayers, even if the answer is no." . . . In fact, over twice as many evangelicals pray daily than those who read the Bible daily. As has been pointed out, 42 per cent of the evangelical sample read the Bible daily; 87 per cent, on the other hand, pray daily—78 per cent mainline Protestants, 87 per cent of the Roman Catholics, and 92 per cent of conservative Christians.
>
> —George A. Rawlyk, *Is Jesus Your Personal Saviour? In Search of Canadian Evangelicalism in the 1990s* (Montreal: McGill-Queen's University Press, 1996), 127.

specifically, several reported that prayer was like an ongoing dialogue with someone who was both understanding and caring toward them personally. The women also reported that prayer was a peaceful or relaxing activity that helped them to unwind or "get rid of the day's pressure." Many women stressed the need to pray throughout the day, being in constant communion with the Most High about the events of their daily lives, however trivial. Many of these same women also valued praying with others, which made them feel connected not only to God but to a broader church community as well.

Not surprisingly, for both men and women a significant factor in church adherence was the importance of corporate prayer. Rawlyk summarized that "feeling comfortable in a specific church seems to be more important than denominational loyalty," and also that the denominations that had successfully integrated small-group prayer into their church polity had been better able to retain their members.[11]

From the general study of Ostrander at the beginning of the twentieth century and the specific interviews of Rawlyk toward the end, it may be concluded that for evangelicals prayer remains one of the most personal aspects of Christian faith. Prayer connects believers to both God and the larger Christian community. It serves as protection for their beliefs and as an assurance of God's power in this world, but even more as a means of fostering identity and purpose. Although practices of prayer and the contents of prayer vary widely, and although there is no general evangelical consensus on what exactly occurs in prayer or on the best ways to pursue prayer, evangelicals devoutly believe that God hears prayers, that praying is essential to the Christian life, and that prayer has the ability to effect significant change in this world. In these conclusions evangelicals clearly resemble the adherents of other Christian traditions. If they are distinctive, it is probably in the informality, the individuality, and the demonstrative reassurances they find in prayer.

## PUBLIC PRAISE

If evangelical attitudes to prayer and their praying practices have remained relatively constant, it is different with evangelical public worship, where marked changes in recent decades have dramatically altered Sunday religious observance and particularly the sound of these services. Since the 1960s, evangelicals in North America, along with the Catholic Church and almost all mainline Protestant denominations, have witnessed significant movements of spiritual renewal that directly affect the shape of public worship. For many of the older denominations—as also for younger bodies, independent congregations, and the new megachurches—this development has led to fresh thought about the weekly worship service. The sermon, which remains a central feature of almost all Protestant worship, remains seriously understudied. Over the last fifty years sermons in general have probably become less formal in structure, less theological in content, more therapeutic in orientation, and more narrative in structure—though not necessarily shorter. The role of the Bible for sermons has doubtless changed, being used more for narrative and therapeutic purposes (but not being replaced by other authorities). Yet until further study of sermons is carried out, such conclusions must remain only tentative.[12]

By contrast, serious study, as well as great conflict, abounds concerning the great changes that have occurred in the musical life of congregations.[13] Most of the denominations issued new hymnbooks in the last thirty years, and there have been serious efforts at liturgical reform guided by more thorough study of the Christian past. Yet far and away the most dramatic changes in regular worship services have taken place in the evangelical churches in which—a major surprise when considering earlier antagonisms—styles of worship originating among Pentecostals and charismatics have become increasingly influential.

As described by Larry Eskridge of Wheaton College's Institute for the Study of American evangelicals, standard video footage of generic evangelical congregations, of megachurches, or of worship in the South and Sunbelt (which boast the greatest concentration of identifiable evangelicals) now regularly depicts about the same thing: "obligatory shots of middle-class worshipers, usually white, in corporate-looking auditoriums or sanctuaries, swaying to the electrified music of 'praise bands,' their eyes closed, their enraptured faces tilted heaven-ward, a hand (or hands) raised to the sky."[14] Behind such often-repeated images lies a lengthy evangelical tradition of populist worship innovation, but also a number of influential shifts since the Second World War.

The trajectory of evangelical worship habits has been determined by the populism of evangelical history. Evangelicals have always been about more than revivalism, but revival has nonetheless exerted a determining influence, especially as it points evangelicals toward emotional reassurance for those in the churches and effective appeal to those outside. For hymnody and the more general use of music, innovation aimed at capturing the attention of contemporary audiences has always been the key.[15]

This distinctly evangelical approach to public worship began in the early decades of the eighteenth century when the English Congregationalist hymn writer, Isaac Watts, took the daring step of producing hymns that went beyond the paraphrasing of psalms, which had long been the universal practice of English-speaking Protestant churches. Although Watts's hymns soon were transformed into classic exemplars themselves, they represented in their own day exciting and controversial new music, including popular examples like "Come, ye that love the Lord, / And let our joys be known"; "Jesus shall reign wher-e'er the sun / Does his successive journeys run"; and "Joy to the world! the Lord is come."

Hard on the heels of Watts, and as a driving engine of evangelical spiritual revival more generally, came the even more innovative hymns of Charles Wesley and a host of contemporaries who in the mid-eighteenth century self-consciously stressed the potential for personal engagement. So it was that Methodist adherents sang with fervor, hymns like Wesley's "Jesus, lover of my soul, / Let me to thy bosom fly"; "A charge to keep I have, / A God to glorify"; and "And can it be that I should gain / An interest in the Savior's blood?" To the audacity of writing hymns not taken directly from the scripture, Wesley and his hymn-writing peers added meters that deviated exuberantly from the common, long, and short that had monopolized almost all public singing in British churches. To their opponents, such hymns meant the sacrilegious breach of honored church traditions, but to the evangelicals they spoke of a revivified faith adapted to the interests of ordinary men and women.

Eager evangelical audiences took up the hymns of Watts, Wesley, and other eighteenth-century evangelical worthies like John Newton, William Cowper, Augustus Toplady, and William Williams so enthusiastically that this type of church music soon became canonical. The sustained popularity of the eighteenth-century hymns led to the ironic situation in which later generations of evangelical innovators had to overcome charges that *their* new works were a sacrilegious breach of honored church tradition.

But when innovators in the second half of the nineteenth century sought ways to reach out to urban dwellers who had left behind the small cities and rural regions where eighteenth-century evangelicalism had taken firmest root, they added a new kind of singing that once again featured the evangelical penchant for musical innovation. This time it was the gospel song—catchy, direct, sometimes sentimental, with lively choruses repeated after each verse—that once again brought the evangelical message of salvation into self-consciously contemporary churches for self-consciously deliberate purposes of outreach.[16]

Celebrity preachers with their equally celebrated song leaders, like the team of D. L. Moody and Ira Sankey in the United States and Britain, or Hugh Crossley and John Hunter in Canada, pushed past evangelical traditions in order to "rescue the perishing" or "throw out the lifeline," as the new songs put it. In Canada, the Methodist itinerants Crossley and Hunter developed the musical revival service into an immensely popular form of public entertainment as well as a greatly effective evangelistic tool. With their carefully planned multiweek services, the engaging monologues of Hunter, and the moving songs of Crossley (like "My Mother's Prayer" and "Papa, Come This Way"), this Canadian team became a mainstay of local spiritual renewal, but also a prod for reforming the regular worship service once they had left town.[17]

The same thing occurred wherever Moody and Sankey traveled or were publicized. Moody's down-home, lay-oriented preaching softened the gospel message and made it more appealing to the families and single individuals flooding into the hyper-busy cities of the industrial age. Sankey's *Gospel Hymns and Sacred Songs*, which appeared as a series beginning in 1875 and became very popular, retained some older standards (often abridged and with spruced up music) but also included a great number of new songs. Chief among the writers of these new pieces was the blind hymn writer Fanny Crosby. Her lyrics—like "Tell me the story of Jesus, / Write on my heart every word" and "To God be the glory, great things He hath done, / So loved He the world that He gave us His Son"—represented a simpler, more direct, and more easily remembered form of church music that came to define much of evangelicalism as surely as had the work of Watts and Wesley in the previous century.[18] Sankey's own work at the piano, and with other keyboard instruments, also struck out toward more expressive and singable music that came closer to the tunes of contemporary popular culture. (Neither then nor later did evangelicals ever become entirely comfortable with organs and organ music,

**Fig. 6.4.** Evangelical revival meetings of the late nineteenth and early twentieth centuries were marked by preacher / song-leader pairs. The best-known duo included the famed evangelist D. L. Moody (left) and the equally celebrated hymn writer and song-leader Ira Sankey (right). Image © Corbis. Used by permission.

for they were associated with high-church and formal church traditions that evangelicals associated with spiritual torpor.)

Outside the auditoriums where popular evangelists like Crossley-Hunter and Moody-Sankey did their work, yet another form of musical innovation was bursting onto the evangelical world. This contribution came from the Salvation Army, which after it "opened fire" in Canada and the United States in the early 1880s, was rapidly established as a mainstay of urban revivalism and urban social service.[19] From its earliest days under William Booth in what he called "darkest England," the public trademark of the Salvation Army had been the brass band on parade, in teeming public spaces, on stage for entertainment—in short, wherever it could be heard. The musical quality of Salvationist bands was often remarkably high, but they were at first regarded almost universally as a disruptive force. When, however, their music, and the well-rounded Christian action that accompanied it, began to draw crowds, change lives, and establish successful institutions, other evangelicals unbent enough to add some of the Army's musical verve to their own worship services.

At the start of the twentieth century, evangelical public praise represented a mixture of musical styles and preferences. Layers of Watts,

Wesley, Sankey, and the Salvation Army mingled in different proportions throughout North America. In the American South, these same tributaries were joined by regional influences, especially derived from shape-note singing, to create a distinctive worship sound. That sound was not well known outside of its region, but it would eventually contribute a great deal to the gospel music in white and black styles that became so popular in the last decades of the twentieth century.[20]

After World War II, musical stasis reigned in many evangelical churches, but it did not survive for long. At least four influences were critical in prompting change. The first, television, has not been systematically studied for its effects on week-to-week American religious life. Nonetheless, its presence by the late 1950s in most American homes, of whatever religion or none, meant that a powerful medium for shaping musical taste would work its influence in the churches as throughout all of the culture. For evangelical churches, television probably had much to do with rising expectations about professional musical quality, heightened self-consciousness in musicians' self-presentation, increasing tolerance for stronger rhythms, lowered levels of intellectual content, and intuitive assumptions about immediate singable appeal. Whatever the exact influence exerted by television, attendance by the 1990s at almost any evangelical church of any kind anywhere in North America would testify to the pervasive influence of this new medium.

Second, and better documented, are the explicit efforts by some leading evangelicals to attract younger people through music. Historian Thomas Bergler has shown, for example, how the Youth for Christ movement systematically and deliberately innovated in making its music as enticing as it could, yet without crossing the increasingly thin barrier between the pious and the worldly.[21] Youth for Christ, which began only in the last years of World War II, was active in thousands of localities by the early 1950s. Its main outreach was the Saturday night rally, in which lively music of all sorts—from near hip-hop to tuneful ballads to imitation Big Band—reached out, and with considerable effect, to members of the rising generation. Older evangelicals worried whether such innovation was appropriate, while few in the younger generation or those trying to appeal to them paid much attention.

A third factor in the renovation of contemporary evangelical music was the mainstreaming of Pentecostal influences. In the early decades of the twentieth century, when Pentecostal churches were multiplying rapidly, many evangelicals looked upon their special concentration on the work of the Holy Spirit as disturbing, fanatical, or worse. Over time, however, Pentecostal themes and Pentecostal personalities came closer and closer to the mainstream, with participation by leaders of the Assemblies of God at the formation of the National Association of Evangelicals in 1942 as a public mark of that process.

Pentecostal worship had always represented an analogue to the Pentecostal emphasis on healing and the gift of tongues, which is to say exuberant, spontaneous, and subjective. In addition, during the early decades of the movement a great quantity of new hymns appeared as expression of the heightened emotions resulting from direct contact with the Spirit. Pentecostal praise was marked by much more than just new words, however, for it also innovated ceaselessly with diverse musical expressions, including instrumentation from accordions, fiddles, banjos, and even (in a momentous development for evangelicalism) drums. Except for African American churches, rhythm in historical evangelicalism had always meant a down-beat on the first beat, never involved syncopation, and eschewed percussion as literally of the devil. But the Pentecostal movement was strongly marked by southern and African American origins; its lay leadership took orders from no highbrows; its great desire to palpably demonstrate the power of the gospel translated readily into musical styles that engaged body as well as mind, active emotion as well as passive sentiment. Although it took awhile for outside observers to notice the connections, the popularity of stars like Mahalia Jackson (with Southern Baptist and Sanctified Holiness roots) and Elvis Presley (raised in the Assemblies of God and a frequent attender at Sunday night gospel sings in Memphis) represented a forecast of more general musical trends in the evangelical churches as well as in American society as a whole.

Pentecostal patterns of worship and religious practice began to have a broader influence on the wider religious world when a pair of developments occurred after World War II. First was the rise in public meetings for healing. Evangelists William Branham (1909–1965) and Oral Roberts (b. 1918) were the figures best known in that "healing revival," but there were many others. These preachers, all from Pentecostal backgrounds, fanned out over especially the South, Southwest, and West to promote the healing of physical ills by a special work of the Holy Spirit.[22]

The second development, and the one that did the most to bridge the gap with evangelical congregations distant from Pentecostalism (or even hostile to it) was the charismatic movement that emerged in the late 1950s. This movement promoted some of the emphases of classical Pentecostalism but in typical American fashion: by presenting a kind of spiritual smorgasbord to sample as individuals chose. These emphases included a stress on personal conversion, physical healing, speaking in tongues, participation in small-group fellowships, and—above all—a profusion of freshly written, catchy, and very singable songs. Charismatic (in the sense of personal magnetism) leaders always played a major role in the charismatic movement. Some of those leaders, like Jack Hayford, minister of a Four Square Gospel Church in California, contributed significantly to the new music with songs like "Majesty" ("Majesty, worship His Majesty / Unto Jesus, be all glory, honor, and praise"). Charismatic renewal provided a bridge of common associations, songs, and attitudes between Pentecostals and non-Pentecostals. After the Second Vatican Council (1962–1965) it performed the same function in bridging the even broader historical divide between Catholics and Protestants.

The fourth important contributor to newer evangelical worship at the end of the twentieth century was the Jesus Movement, which took off in the mid-1960s and seemed to flame out after barely a decade. The Jesus Movement, strong at first on the West Coast but then broadening out to touch virtually all parts of the United States and many in Canada, represented old wine in new wineskins. Its youthful leaders stressed the need for a personal experience with Christ (the new birth), promoted disciplined study of scripture (but with little concern for what academics said about the Bible), stoutly resisted the loosening of morals (in some cases after personal experimentation), and displayed the single-minded zeal that marked leaders of earlier evangelical revivals. At the same time, the Jesus Movement did not lead to the traditional evangelical division between church and world. It was a movement that fully engaged popular culture, was fully a part of the postwar recognition of youth and young adulthood as independent stages of life, and simply took for granted Christian use of much in popular culture that earlier generations of evangelicals had disavowed.

Above all, the Jesus People embraced modern musical idioms—at first the gentler sides of folk and jazz, but then increasingly the louder and amplified rhythms of rock as well. Larry Eskridge has described the music that came out of the Jesus Movement to influence the broader subculture as "equal parts folk, pop and light rock—simple songs and choruses that, in the recollection of one early musician . . . , 'sang themselves.'"[23] Significantly, many of the new tunes were written in order to sing small portions of scripture, often from the King James Version.

For American evangelicals, the Jesus People were strategic brokers between age and youth, and also between churchly culture and American culture. Their ability to set strict standards in matters of doctrine and practice while opening themselves to postwar popular culture led the way for many others. The Jesus Movement was gone as a recognizable organism by the late 1970s, but the youth-oriented attitudes, the reliance on pop culture, and a well-stocked repertoire of new tunes remained.

Several important associations of churches drew directly on the emphases of the movement, including a network of Calvary Chapels under the leadership of Chuck Smith. In 1965, Smith became the minister of a small independent congregation in Costa Mesa, California, and immediately opened the church door to "hippies" and other countercultural folk. Through a mix of informality, soft rock music, biblical exposition, and the standard charismatic options, Calvary Chapel took off and within a generation had spawned a network of nearly a thousand other chapels around the world.

A similar story describes the Association of Vineyard Churches, which was connected to Smith's Calvary Chapel in its early days. Under the leadership of John Wimber, this California-based evangelical movement stressed divine healing and promoted nontraditional forms of worship. Its loose-leaf collections of new songs were used by many churches far beyond its own movement and served as inspiration for similar new ventures by even more. The Vineyard has grown to hundreds of congregations with hundreds of thousands of members and with congregations in many countries.[24]

The great changes in evangelical church music that have accelerated since the 1960s rested securely on long-standing traditions of popular innovation but were driven especially by television, evangelical willingness to embrace popular youth culture, the Pentecostal and charismatic movements, and the Jesus People. Under these influences church musicians by the 1980s were exploiting a full range of pop, folk, and even rock styles as settings for this new wave of song. Without knowing yet what will survive and what will simply fade from sight, the following are almost random example of such lyrics: "I love you, Lord / and I lift my voice / to worship You / o my soul, rejoice"; "Hosanna, Hosanna, Hosanna in the highest! Hosanna, Hosanna, Hosanna in the highest! Lord

## Music and the Jesus Movement

Given the centrality of music to the Jesus movement, its rise came at an opportune time in terms of the musical trajectory of American evangelicalism as more upbeat, youth-friendly musical forms began to make some inroads into the subculture during the '60s. However, it would be the Jesus People themselves who drew naturally upon the rock and folk-oriented musical forms of popular culture to create their own body of "Jesus Music" to enhance worship, to use as an evangelistic tool, and to serve as a form of sanctified musical entertainment. Overall, this sanctified version of rock music provided a common ground within the movement and a potential bridge between the Jesus People and their peers in "the world." As the movement grew across the country and found itself on a more solid footing, it promoted the growth of not only more musicians playing for a growing audience, but also an expanding infrastructure of local venues, home-grown promoters, and a rough-hewn recording and distribution "industry" that in its early days placed more emphasis on evangelism and discipleship than on marketing and sales.

Soon, however, the marketing potential of the new "Jesus Generation" began to swing the dynamics of the Jesus Music away from its informal, countercultural roots toward the trappings and business practices of the mainstream music and entertainment industries. While still but a shadow of big-time rock 'n' roll, by the mid-'70s recording contracts, improved production values, better distribution and packaging, large Jesus Music festivals, and a tiny—but increasing—amount of radio airplay all pointed to a growing professionalism and corporate control over what had once been a casual, homegrown element of "Jesus Freak" life. "Jesus Music" provided the foundations for a significant new musical presence within evangelicalism and the lynchpin for the emerging and future evangelical youth cultures: the "Contemporary Christian Music" industry.

—Larry Eskridge, "God's Forever Family:
The Jesus People Movement in America, 1966–1977"
(Ph.D. diss., Stirling University, Scotland, 2005), 254–55.

we lift up your name with hearts full of praise. Be exalted O Lord my God! Hosanna in the highest!"; "Holy fire, living flame are you. / Our desire is to honor you."

The increasingly standard practice of singing with a combo made up of guitar, drums, and synthesizer has made the organ an anachronistic relic in many Protestant and some Catholic churches. Songs projected onto a screen have replaced the hymnbook in many places. The same set of religious forces has provided the foundation for a multimillion dollar industry of contemporary Christian music that has made stars out of individuals like Amy Grant and groups like D. C. Talk, P.O.D., and Switchfoot.

The proliferation of megachurches since the 1980s is not unconnected to this chapter of musical history. These churches, defined by an ability to maintain a regular weekly attendance of two thousand or more, now exist in every state and province. Megachurches are spiritual shopping malls designed intentionally to provide religious resources for people caught in the tense circumstances of modern life. The model for such congregations is the Willow Creek Community Church in South Barrington, Illinois. It began in 1975 with services in a rented movie theater as an outreach for youth and their parents. The mission of its leaders, including founding pastor Bill Hybels, is explained on its webpage: "to build a church that would speak the language of our modern culture and encourage non-believers to investigate Christianity at their own pace, free from the traditional trappings of religion that tend to chase them away."[25] From the start Willow Creek avoided churchy language and sought professional standards. Also from the start, upbeat music, newly written songs, and professional-level musical talent were central in communicating its message. Within

**Fig. 6.5.** In many regards the Willow Creek Community Church of South Barrington, Illinois, is the prototypical model of the modern North American megachurch. These churches have contributed to popularizing the new modes of praise and worship music in North America during the last quarter of the twentieth century. Photo © John Gress / Reuters / Corbis. Used by permission.

a year weekly attendance was over a thousand, and by the mid-1990s as many as fifteen thousand were attending weekend services on its 127–acre campus in Chicago's northwest suburbs.[26] The sound that comes from such megachurches—usually meeting in multiple services on Saturday nights and Sunday mornings—is no longer Watts, Wesley, and Sankey set to eighteenth- and nineteenth-century tunes. It is rather music expressing nearly the full range of styles from contemporary popular American culture.

Critics of the charismatic movement, the megachurches, and other Protestant adaptations to modern sensibilities are not shy about expressing their disapproval of the new music.[27] They charge that charismatic worship focuses on the self and not on God. They see the megachurches as catering to the transitory felt-needs of a pleasure-driven population. They hold that the new songs obscure the realities of human sinfulness and the holiness of God, while pampering the fragile postmodern self, and so make it impossible to grasp the true character of divine grace.

Contemporary debates over modern innovations in evangelical song resemble earlier controversies between Methodists and the traditional churches of the eighteenth century, or Pentecostals and their critics early in the twentieth century. The debates are important because they address the twin, but sometimes competing, strengths of North American evangelical Christianity. These strengths are its connection to the historic Christian faith and its impulse to adjust the faith in order to gain a broad hearing among the populace at large.

The future of weekly worship certainly hinges on what happens in the volatile evangelical dance with American popular culture. It may also hinge even more on what happens in the rest of the world. The fastest growing segments of evangelical or evangelical-like Christianity are now found in sub-Saharan Africa, China, Korea, the Pacific Islands, and Latin America. Where once British and North American evangelicals dictated styles of worship to a missionary world, now majority-world evangelicals are nearly at a place to exert a countervailing influence on the former evangelical homelands. If that outcome actually occurs, it will doubtless affect the sound (and more) of North American worship.

## MATERIAL CULTURE

Whatever influence the majority world may come to exert, it is likely that the material culture of North American evangelicals, which has come to mirror the material values of the American host culture, will remain distinctive. Throughout the twentieth century, commercialization reached unprecedented heights in North America generally, while at the same time commercial promotion of religiously oriented products became commonplace in evangelical circles. This commercialization exploded during the last quarter of the century. By the late 1970s stores specializing in the sale of Christian merchandise were growing at nearly double the national retail average.[28] By the 1990s Christian retailing amounted to a $3 billion annual enterprise. As with other parts of the American economy, when sales reach such figures, it inevitably follows that the mom and pop stores would be squeezed out by national retail chains. This well-known American process has now witnessed the rise of the Christian megastore, with one chain boasting average retail space of thirty thousand square feet per outlet.[29] In fact, the market for Christian goods and objects has become so lucrative that many nonreligious retailers now routinely stock Christian-designated items in order to meet the demand.

Given traditional Protestant warnings about the dangers of trusting in money, the temptations of idolatry, and the allure of "the world," it may seem strange that American evangelicals have created such a booming industry at the start of the twenty-first century. Historically, evangelicals rained criticism on their Catholic contemporaries for what they perceived as Catholic susceptibility to material and idolatrous temptations. Yet now they themselves are taking part.

Persuasive explanations for this apparent anomaly have been provided in a wide-ranging book by historian Colleen McDannell. Its title, *Material Christianity*, points to her thesis that American Christian believers of all sorts have regularly expressed a desire to "see, hear and touch God"[30] by incorporating religious objects into their daily lives and the physical landscape of those lives. Her examination of what evangelicals have actually done, as well as what they have said, allows her to demonstrate that Protestant evangelicals have never been as successful at dividing the sacred from the profane as their speech might indicate. Instead, for many evangelicals the line between the two has always been blurry, and for some it has now passed away entirely. As suggested by McDannell's provocative book, full evangelical engagement in the manufacture, merchandising, and display of material objects can best be understood as a search for identity. By examining the terrain of what has become the burgeoning material culture of a burgeoning religious subculture, it is possible to see more clearly how evangelical religious life has come to interact with the national material culture.

Evangelicals have embraced a culture of religious objects primarily for self-identification and for demonstrating to others what the Christian faith means to them. These overarching purposes have been manifest in different ways. Its development is perhaps most obvious in the Jesus Movement, whose effects in shaping evangelical worship were matched by effects in influencing evangelical materiality. In striking measure, the Jesus People separated themselves from popular American life even as they embraced it fully. Jesus People wanted it known that they had found something more life-fulfilling than sex, drugs, and rock 'n' roll, but they used the paraphernalia that had arisen around sex, drugs, and rock 'n' roll to make that statement. Thus, emblazoned T-shirts, bumper stickers, and buttons with dayglow Christian symbols used the cultural trappings of the counterculture to show the counterculture a better way. Among the most popular icons were a hand pointing toward heaven accompanied with the words "one way" or "Jesus is the one way"; a smiley face with the slogan, "Smile. God loves you!"; and the sketch of a fish (in reprise of an ancient Christian symbol) with the name Jesus lettered on the inside.

During the 1980s and 1990s, organization replaced anarchy in the merchandising and display of Jesus objects. Huge retailing conferences like the annual convention of the Christian Booksellers Association

> **Religious Belief and the Concrete**
> American Christians . . . want to see, hear and touch God. It is not enough for Christians to go to church, lead a righteous life and hope for an eventual place in heaven. People build religion into the landscape, they make and buy pious images for their homes, and they wear special reminders of their faith next to their bodies. Religion is more than a type of knowledge learned through reading holy books and listening to holy men. . . . Throughout American history, Christians have explored the meaning of the divine, the nature of death, the power of healing, and the experience of the body by interacting with a created world of images and shapes.
> —Colleen McDannell, *Material Christianity: Religion and Popular Culture in America* (New Haven: Yale University Press, 1995), 1.

and, later, the International Christian Retail Show, allowed hundreds of vendors to exhibit their wares in spacious convention centers. In the competition that resulted, products became more elaborate, and more costly, and also turned from the slogans of the Jesus People to knockoffs of mainstream merchandising giants like Nike, Pepsi, Ford, and Reebok.

The growth of Christian retail in the 1990s produced a variety of predictable responses. When the cheap, brightly colored bumper stickers of the '70s gave way to more elaborate and professional products, one of the favorites of baby boomer evangelicals was the fish (or *ichthus*, after the symbol in the ancient Roman catacombs) with Jesus' name etched on the inside. This emblem became so widespread that other wily merchandisers provided their own parody—a footed fish with "Darwin" etched inside. Nothing daunted, Christian retailers responded with a new larger *ichthus* designated "Truth" that was shown swallowing the Darwin creature—and all for display on the back of a car, van, or truck.

An even more widely noticed evangelical icon in the 1990s was the WWJD (What Would Jesus Do?) bracelet. This phrase had been popularized originally in a novel from 1897, *In His Steps*, by a Social Gospel minister, Charles Sheldon. The book described the transformation of a city whose church people made WWJD their guide for daily life. A century later, bracelets with these letters were being sold in both Christian and secular outlets and were being worn by hundreds of thousands of evangelical young people and adults. Among the many parodies that inevitably followed, "We Want Jack Daniels" and "What Would Elvis Do?" were among the least vulgar. Parody grew serious when environmentalists, both religious and secular, asked "What Would Jesus Drive?" in an effort to raise consciousness about the responsible use of natural resources.

By the turn of the millennium, religious retailers were moving in many directions. Although Christian takeoffs of commercially popular products remained in vogue, increasing numbers of Christian-defined companies moved beyond sloganed T-shirts into the production of complete product lines. Thus, for evangelicals who choose this way of proclaim-

Fig. 6.6. The popular WWJD? (What Would Jesus Do?) bracelet. Photo © Scott Speakes/Corbis. Used by permission.

ing their identity, there now exist blazers, hoodies, skirts, pants, jackets, capris, beanies, wrist wear, socks, belts, belt buckles, hats, wallets, messenger bags, laptop cases, purses, necklaces, rings, earrings and toe rings—all from Christian retailers and bearing some form of Christian identifying symbol.

The growth of an evangelical fashion industry has been greatly stimulated by the internet. Hundreds of Christian retailers now push such products online, where enterprising shoppers can even create their own Christian gear. If accumulating the accoutrements of a distinctive lifestyle has become American big business in general, it is also increasingly common for younger evangelicals to do the same. Whether it is skateboarding or snowboarding, alternative rock or punk rock, merchandise is available that ostensibly allows evangelical consumers to be both in the world but not of it. Sales of such items are often keyed to Christian rock festivals, where Christian vendors sell Christian clothing, Christian music, Christian accessories, even Christian tattoos that let consumers impress a Christian identity on the personalities they are creating.

Christian biker clubs, primarily on the West Coast, carry the process of self-identification a step further. Members in dozens of such clubs display coordinated belt buckles, leather jackets, and vests with Christian messages. They ride together, organize prayer and study groups, and share the gospel at Sturgis. One Pentecostal-specific group is called the "Azusa Street Riders." Much more widespread are marketing efforts connected with the Fellowship of Christian Athletes, which promotes Christian-logoed water bottles, lacrosse helmets, golf balls, sports bags, and so forth.

As McDannell shows convincingly, the recent reach of evangelical merchandising into the marketplace represents not so much a new development as an expansion of material culture from private spheres to the public. Since the early to mid-nineteenth century, the desire to create a distinctly Christian home has prompted especially evangelical women to unusual efforts at decoration.[31] Needlework with Bible

**Fig. 6.7.** Christian retailers have moved beyond parody-logo T-shirts to creating their own fashion lines that are more in touch with modern trends. Companies such as C28 (one of whose hoodies is pictured here) have both major shopping mall and online retail outlets where they sell all sorts of Christian-themed gear such as wristbands and wristcuffs, sandals and sunglasses, and belt buckles and button-downs. Photo courtesy of C28.com.

**Fig. 6.8.** Christian rock festivals such as this one are hubs for evangelical material culture. Beyond the music, concert goers can browse dozens of vendors selling Christian apparel, snowboards, tattoos, and skateboards. Some ventures even have art galleries and poetry readings or other outlets for evangelical expressions of the arts. Photo: Scott Stahnke.

verses or Christian slogans began even earlier; in the first years of the twentieth century that particular practice was successfully promoted to a wide public by the Gospel Trumpet Company. The display of religious books, hymnals, and especially the family Bible is also a practice with roots deep in the nineteenth century.[32] More recent are religious figurines available from the Precious Moments collection.

In what looks like a sharp break from former anti-Catholic animus, evangelical homes by the second half of the twentieth century were also increasingly likely to display a decorative cross, particularly one affixed to the wall. Although these objects are available singly, or as individual receptacles for candles, others come in sets for clustering. The decorative cross has also sparked a collecting hobby, especially among travelers who return from trips with new examples for their collections. So popular has the business in decorative crosses become that they are now sold in major home retailers like Pier One Imports or Kirkland's as well as in stores specializing in Christian merchandise.

For evangelicals, like adherents of almost all other religions, physical objects also serve as agents of memory and memorial. Decorative crosses, for instance, are often just as much a way of remembering a significant journey to Mexico, Ireland, or Spain as they are of evoking a biblical image. (The fact that evangelical crosses are not crucifixes—they are invariably bare—helps explain their plastic associations.) Evangelicals, again in common with humanity in general, collect objects that remind them of faith and family. Although the family piano, or even family organ, is now less common in an age of individualized interior space than it was when families gathered in parlors or living rooms, clusters of photos, crosses, or hymnals on a piano have long served to connect present generations to those gone before. Similarly, popular pictures of Jesus, preeminently Warner Sallman's *Head of Christ* (see p. 7), function both as contemporary reassurance and links to a past when the portrait was also displayed.[33]

Religious objects associated with special events such as weddings, funerals, or the birth of children also abound in evangelical homes. These mementos not only occupy a special place in memory but also work to strengthen the Christian community. Gift-giving supports that community linkage, as it also stimulates merchandising, in the form of a religious journal for graduates, a devotional book for Christmas, a picture frame for baby showers, or a family Bible for weddings.

A special item that can be rescued from the realm of mere kitsch by following McDannell's approach is the refrigerator magnet. When these ubiquitous icons of contemporary American life display religious mottoes or inspirational messages, they reinforce at a persistent daily level both faith and community. Among evangelicals a distinctive kind of magnet is the prayer reminder for foreign missionaries. Such magnets may feature a portrait of the missionary family, the name of the country or region in which they are serving, and perhaps a biblical reference spelling out ideals of the mission. The act of displaying these humble mementos takes on significance when it stimulates prayer for the missionaries, increases solidarity with a local church where other members are doing the same thing, and perhaps even provides some sense of fellowship with far distant members of the worldwide Christian community. Such decorations also mark the household as a "Christian home" with distinctive Christian interests.

The community-building aspect of material culture is often overt among evangelicals. Community building through the display in the home of missionary or local church reminders is sometimes matched by self-conscious choice of retailers outside of the home. When evangelical mechanics or carpet cleaners put an *ichthus* on their business

Fig. 6.9. Decorative crosses adorn the walls of many evangelical homes. The crosses can be bought at most major home furnishing stores as well as local retail shops. They can serve strictly decorative purposes as collectibles or mementos from travel or as reminders of one's faith. Photo © Ethan R. Sanders. Used by permission.

cards, they are both making a statement about themselves and looking for business from fellow believers. Beginning in the 1970s and 1980s, evangelical organizations began publishing business guides (sometimes called "Christian Yellow Pages") in order to direct the Bible-believing populace to Bible-believing proprietors. Entire sectors, like the Christian cruise business, now exist to cater to the Christian market exclusively.

The construction of evangelical identity and community happens from an early age and is strongly influenced by material culture. Thus, most Christian retail stores offer a wide array of products for the very young, including objects for home or Sunday school instruction like play sets of Noah's Ark, nativity sets, puzzles, picture books, lesson plans, and flannel boards. For a subculture more at home with words and general images, the depiction of Jesus is a regular exception to the evangelical wariness of icons narrowly defined. Christian retailers have come to provide a parallel universe to American merchandising in general, with videos such as *Veggie Tales* or *Wemmick Stories*, Christian figurines like Bibleman or Davey and Goliath, Christian plush toys, Christian video games, Christian board games, and even Christian candy.

The roots of contemporary evangelical material culture extend back at least two centuries, as indicated by the wide range of goods offered for sale in the first generation of mass evangelical periodicals in the nineteenth century.[34] By the start of the twenty-first century, however, the fruits had grown in directions undreamt of in those earlier days. Especially from the 1960s the vehicles of evangelical merchandising and the vehicles of more general American merchandising have come very close together.

Critics of these developments fear that evangelical faith has been co-opted by mainstream commercialism, with the result that the sacred is trivialized beyond hope.[35] Yet as McDannell notes shrewdly, North American evangelicals have rarely displayed much interest in the kind of critical thinking that worries about such trivialization. Rather, the emphasis among evangelicals has always been on "*doing* religious activities and *identifying* oneself as Christian."[36] A surprising proportion of evangelical homes would have some familiarity with solid middlebrow authors like C. S. Lewis or John Stott, many more would be familiar with what populists like James Dobson, Chuck Colson, or Billy Graham are saying, but almost all would know what WWJD on a child's bracelet means and would be pleased to see such a bracelet worn. If children are more familiar with Bob the Tomato and other *Veggie Tales* characters than with the biblical figures they are meant to represent, the theology has definitely become materialized and commercialized, but it has not vanished altogether. In the increasing homogeneity of contemporary commercial society, self-identification by refrigerator magnet does not sound heroic, but it may still be effective. If evangelicals have acceded to an unprecedented commercialization of their lives, they have not given up the evangelical conviction (which drives the missionaries memorialized on so many magnets) that the Christian gospel can find a home in any culture, even a culture of unprecedented commercialization. As Colleen McDannell has noted perceptively, for a religion organized around the incarnation of God in human flesh, it is not in principle a false step to work at incarnating that religion in contemporary commercial culture. Questions of integrity, of quality, of priorities, or of self-criticism do, however, remain—not so much about whether this kind of evangelical material culture is acceptable in broadly evangelical terms, but how and why and to what end it is taking place.

## THE INFLUENCE OF EVANGELICALISM

Brief examination of prayer, public worship, and material culture is not enough to chart a full peoples' history of North American evangelical Christianity. The very diversity of the movement militates against that possibility, since every trend spotlighted as typical in the preceding pages is challenged by some recognizably evangelical voices. Moreover, these three aspects of ordinary religious life, though of great importance, by no means encompass the whole of evangelical lived religion.

What this chapter's analysis does suggest, however, is that evangelical engagement with broader North American culture continues along lines laid down in earlier generations. American and Canadian evangelicals were in the vanguard of creating their national civilizations, especially in the first two-thirds of the nineteenth century. Despite the push early in the twentieth century by some members of the fundamentalist movement to distance evangelical religion from the secular world, even fundamentalists maintained the traditional evangelical symbiosis with the host culture. Sometimes, by pioneering in the use of radio for mass communication or organizing locally without heeding guidelines from national denominations, for example, fundamentalists extended evangelical engagement with American material culture.[37]

That engagement has only expanded over the course of the last century, and with mixed results. Evangelicals, with Pentecostals and the Jesus People showing the way, have accomplished a significant baptism of popular music. In the process, theological depth has been sacrificed, but the compensation is broad access to a broad range of ordinary Americans with a gospel message that retains many features of the historical faith. In other venues, the exchange has been more one-sided. North American evangelicals once observed Sunday with nearly universal understanding about what it meant to honor the Lord's Day.[38] When the inner drive of evangelical religion motivated such observance, Sundays could be luminous. When evangelicals turned to public legislation to enforce Sunday observance, it looked like a sign of cultural strength but was probably the beginning of the end. After the Second World War, evangelical acceptance of standard American practices—television, commercialization, leisure, the shopping mall, and the other options fueled by unprecedented wealth—doomed the evangelical Sunday to near extinction.

It is an old question whether evangelical efforts at reaching the populace have done more to Christianize the society or socialize the Christians.[39] But whether for itinerant preachers in the eighteenth century, mass advertisers in evangelical magazines during the nineteenth century, fundamentalist radio preachers in the early decades of the twentieth century, or Christian merchandisers in the early twenty-first century, it remains a good question.

## FOR FURTHER READING

Ammerman, Nancy Tatom. *Pillars of Faith: American Congregations and Their Partners.* Berkeley: University of California Press, 2005.

Balmer, Randall. *Mine Eyes Have Seen the Glory: A Journey into the Evangelical Subculture in America*, 4th ed. New York: Oxford University Press, 2006.

Eskridge, Larry. "God's Forever Family: The Jesus People Movement in America, 1966–1977." Ph.D. diss., Stirling University, Scotland, 2005.

Hangen, Tona J. *Redeeming the Dial: Radio, Religion, and Popular Culture in America.* Chapel Hill: University of North Carolina Press, 2002.

McDannell, Colleen. *The Christian Home in Victorian America, 1840–1900.* Bloomington: Indiana University Press, 1986.

———. *Material Christianity: Religion and Popular Culture in America.* New Haven: Yale University Press, 1995.

Miller, Donald E. *Reinventing American Protestantism: Christianity in the New Millennium.* Berkeley: University of California Press, 1997.

Ostrander, Rick. *The Life of Prayer in a World of Science: Protestants, Prayer, and American Culture, 1870–1930.* New York: Oxford University Press, 2000.

Rawlyk, George A. *Is Jesus Your Personal Saviour? In Search of Canadian Evangelicalism in the 1990s.* Montreal: McGill-Queen's University Press, 1996.

Warner, R. Stephen. *New Wine in Old Wineskins: Evangelicals and Liberals in a Small-Town Church.* Berkeley: University of California Press, 1988.

# PENTECOSTAL TRANSFORMATION IN LATIN AMERICA

## LUIS N. RIVERA-PAGÁN

## CHAPTER SEVEN

## FATED TO POVERTY

Sidney W. Mintz's *Worker in the Cane: A Puerto Rican Life History*, published in 1960, is a classic text in anthropology. It follows the life and travails of Anastacio (Taso) Zayas Alvarado, a cane worker of poor origins and dismal prospects who from his childhood was destined for the crushing manual labor typical of Caribbean sugarcane plantations. This is, sadly, the story of many Latin Americans who struggle to overcome grievous poverty while striving to confer meaning to a human existence at the margins of any social hierarchy.

Most scholars who examine the text stress the futile efforts of Taso Zayas to forge a brighter economic future for his family. But they frequently have disregarded what truly astounded Mintz: Zayas's unexpected conversion to Pentecostalism. From that dramatic religious experience arose Zayas's profound conviction that, despite the severe social conditions of his life, his existence had now gained an eternal significance, and he had been blessed with heavenly salvation, had become a child of God and temple of the Holy Spirit.[1]

This story of extraordinary healing, both physical and spiritual, gives us a view into the sudden and dramatic irruption of Pentecostal Christianity in Latin America. This charismatic way of conceiving of and living the Christian faith has transgressed the boundaries of what for centuries had been the normative dogmatic and ecclesiastical expression of Christianity in the region. It has reconfigured the self-understanding, family life, and communal existence of millions of working-class men and women.[2] In short, it is a narrative of unexpected transformation that in its particularity becomes paradigmatic of a religious revolution for Latin American Christianity.

Mintz's initial interest in Taso Zayas's life had nothing to do with religiosity. Neither the scholar nor Zayas seemed to care much about sacred issues, matters of doctrine, liturgical rites, or theological creeds. Mintz's scholarly concern was typical of the mid-twentieth century, namely, how the process of modernization and industrialization affected and shaped the existence of rural workers. Taso was one of a multitude of men and women in Latin America who lacked schooling, land, and house, who from cradle to grave were in bondage to an accelerated capitalization of one product, geared toward export and controlled by foreign corporations. In the Caribbean during the first half of the twentieth century, that meant sugarcane. The region had become a huge plantation devoted to sweetening the consumption habits of metropolitan cities all over the world while embittering the lives of so many native workers, modern versions of the African slaves who used to sweat and die in the fields of the islands.[3]

Taso Zayas was nothing more than another worker at a sugarcane plantation, constantly striving and yet failing to make ends meet as he worked from sunrise to sunset to provide food and clothing for his common-law wife, Elizabeth, and his twelve children, of whom three died in their early childhood. Fatherless at the age of ten months (in 1908) and motherless when he was twelve (1920), he suffered from painful aches caused by the hard labor he had to perform daily. His domestic life was plagued by continual bickering with Elizabeth—not exactly an image of happiness and comfort of any kind.

Zayas was not a passive pawn in the winds of social destiny, for at times he was very active in Puerto Rico's general confederation of workers and in the reformist Popular Democratic Party. The 1940s were for him a decade of intensely felt social disillusionment, followed by bitter frustrations. Everything promised to change; everything remained the same. Zayas did not seem to fit well into the social patterns of power struggles. Labor union organizing and political activism resembled Sisyphus's curse.

## CONVERSION, SPIRITUAL BAPTISM, HEALING

Yet in 1950, as he was plagued by poverty, pain, and frustration, something astonishing happened in Zayas's life: a radical disruption of his previous self-understanding and existence. As was so frequent though paradoxical in Latin American patriarchal society, the women of the house took the first step. Elizabeth and their oldest daughter, Carmen Iris, went to a Pentecostal healing crusade. They came back with amazing stories of miraculous healings, charismatic happenings, and conversions. Extraordinary events seemed to be taking place, bringing joy where suffering prevailed and hope where despair ruled.

Elizabeth's life was haunted by the sinister memory of her father, who had drunk heavily and mistreated her mother, and by her constant fights with Taso, caused by her suspicions about his possible dalliances with other women. One night in the midst of a Pentecostal revivalist session, she felt herself possessed by a supernatural power that gave her the exceptional capability of speaking in tongues. The preacher's interpretation, to the joyful exclamations of the congregation, was that Elizabeth had been baptized by the Holy Spirit. She had been transformed into a new creature, her soul had been redeemed, and she was assured of eternal salvation.

Mintz was astute enough to perceive the significance of female priority in the religious conversion of this family. Indeed, as happens throughout Latin America, conversion to evangelical Protestantism or to Pentecostalism usually entails a sweeping reconfiguration of family life. It is probably too much to claim that it fundamentally alters the patriarchal hierarchy of authority, for the biblical literalism to which it is closely linked is suffused with notions of masculine primacy. But it frequently transforms the patterns of behavior of the husband/father, who adopts a sterner moral discipline and now abstains from investing money and energy in drinking, womanizing, and betting.[4] The patriarchal hierarchy might be left in place and even theologically reinforced by biblical allusions to female submission in the New Testament epistles (1 Cor. 14:34, Eph. 5:22, Col. 3:18, 1 Tim. 2:11-12, 1 Pet. 3:1), but the shape of masculine behavior is nonetheless substantially reconfigured. The patriarchal household code acquires a benevolent aspect.

Zayas had always considered himself Roman Catholic, but throughout his life he had regarded church activities as something alien to his daily labors, sorrows, and illusions. He heard with some reservations the strange stories narrated by his wife and daughter but decided to attend one of the evangelistic campaigns of a visiting North American preacher. As the evening progressed, Zayas experienced something strange and unexpected: "Brother Osborn[5] began to pray for the sick. . . . I felt something in my body, a thing—an extraordinary thing—while he was praying for the sick. And later, after he finished that prayer, I felt an ecstasy—something strange. . . . And afterward I did not feel that pain that I had been feeling. . . . And up to the present, thank God, I have never felt that pain again."[6]

Miraculous healing is nothing new in Latin American religious traditions. There are several sites considered sacred, where healing divine grace is implored and received. The most famous of all is the basilica of the Virgin of Guadalupe, in Mexico. The basilica brims with thousands of ex-votos of gratitude for the healing miracles performed by the Guadalupe.[7] Since her first alleged appearance to the indigenous man Juan Diego, in December 1531, countless acts of divine healing have been attributed to the Patroness of Mexico and Latin America. Though the Guadalupe has also fulfilled a meaningful role in the formation of the Mexican national identity,[8] it is probably true that common people throughout Mexico, Latin America, and the Hispanic diaspora in the United States look to the Virgin more as a maternal source of extraordinary favors in situations of grave distress than as a patriotic icon.

Fig 7.1. Healing of blind girl: Photo of Victory Christian Center, Crucade in the Dominican Republic, 2005. Photo © Victory Christian Center, Tusla, Okla.

Miraculous healings are usually attributed to a holy person, most of the time the Mother of Christ, and happen in a sacred place, in this case the Tepeyac. Both the holy person and the place are linked

**Fig. 7.2.** Blessed Virgin of Guadalupe mural, Mexico City. Photo © Rene Sheret/ Stone/Getty Images. Used by permission. Tradition says that the first apparition of the Virgin in Mexico dates from December 1531, when the Virgin appeared to Juan Diego and told him: *"You should know, son, that I am the Virgin Mary, Mother of the true God. I want a house and a chapel, a church to be built for me, in which to show myself a merciful Mother to you and yours, to those devoted to me and to those who seek me in their necessities."* Adapted by Luiz Nascimento from *Mexican Phoenix: Our Lady of Guadalupe: Image and Tradition across Five Centuries* by D. A. Brading (Cambridge: Cambridge University Press, 2002), 60.

to a sacred myth of origin that first circulated orally and then was recorded in writing. Zayas's healing, however, belongs to a different genre. Stories now abound in Latin America of healings that occur in many scattered places, with no sacred myths of origin, performed after the intercessory prayers of evangelists unrecognized by mainstream churches. Such healings take place under the aegis of churches and congregations of relatively new origins and picturesque names (such as Iglesia del Buen Pastor, Iglesia del Getsemaní, Fuente de Agua Viva, Roca de Salvación), many of them founded by self-appointed preachers. They might take place anywhere—a football stadium, a recently opened storefront church, the town square, places not usually considered sacred—and are performed by ministers not accredited by any theological academy or any of the traditional Christian confessions. One might speak of a radical democratization and popularization of divine healing.

The healings are usually perceived as extraordinary events. But as happens so frequently in the history of the Christian faith, this movement is also a process of the retrieval of a tradition not entirely erased from the memory of the believing community. After all, miraculous healings abound in the Gospels and the chronicles of the first apostles. "Signs and wonders" (John 4:48) were part and parcel of the early Jesus movement and were considered indications of a decisive irruption of divine power and mercy in human history. When John the Baptist had doubts about the identity of Jesus, he sent some of his disciples to question the Galilean. Jesus, true to form, replied indirectly by signaling his acts of healing: "Go and tell John what you hear and see: the blind receive their sight, the lame walk, the lepers are cleansed, the deaf hear, the dead are raised, and the poor have good news brought to them. And blessed is anyone who takes no offence at me" (Matt. 11:2-6). Jesus' first commission to his disciples, according to an early memoir, included the performance of similar "signs and wonders": "Cure the sick, raise the dead, cleanse the lepers, cast out demons" (Matt. 10:8).

The first controversial public act of the apostles Peter and John was to cure someone lame since birth (Acts 3:1-10). The religious authorities were strongly annoyed, not only because an act of divine grace had taken place outside the margins of the sacred place, in the portico of Jerusalem's temple, but also because the authors were "uneducated and ordinary men" (Acts 4:13) who lacked the social, academic, and ritual credentials traditionally required to mediate divine grace. The "wonders and signs" (Acts 2:43) of those "uneducated and ordinary men" were construed as a serious challenge to the authority of the priesthood and scribal experts.

The "signs and wonders" of Pentecostalism that bewilder so many of its observers are an expression of a characteristic common to most Christian reform movements—an attempt to recover lost dimensions of the early Christian apostolic community. In this case, those lost dimensions are physical healings, reception of the Holy Spirit, glossolalia, passionate devotion to the faith, and priority of the poor ("uneducated and ordinary") people in the worshiping community.

> **Healing**
>
> In the moment when Brother Osborn began to pray for the sick, my own case came immediately to my mind. When he began to pray, he spoke in this way: "All those who have sickness in any part—put your hands on the affected place, whoever has different illnesses." And I lifted my hand to the spot where I really felt pain. And while the brother prayed, I felt something in my body, a thing—an extraordinary thing—while he was praying for the sick. And later, after he finished that prayer, I felt an ecstasy—something strange—and then it went away.
>
> —Taso Zayas, quoted in Sidney W. Mintz, *Worker in the Cane: A Puerto Rican Life History* (New York: Norton, 1974 [1960]), 211.

Zayas's healing was neither unique nor peculiar. In twentieth-century Latin America healing divine grace seemed to abound, manifesting itself in multiple forms outside the boundaries of the established church. Acts of healing and exorcism occurred thanks to the intercession of evangelists whose ministry was ignored by most mainstream churches, and they benefited common people like Taso Zayas. Once again, as so many times before in history, divine grace seemed to surpass and overwhelm the hierarchical patrolling of ecclesiastical frontiers.

Despite the constant attribution to Latin American Pentecostalism of ethereal spiritualism and otherworldliness, researchers are astounded by the importance of corporeal healing for many charismatic Pentecostal churches. The body recovers the centrality that it enjoyed in the early Jesus movement. There are sensible reasons for this. These are

**Fig. 7.3.** Honduras Church Leaders Conference and Crusade with Rev. Dr. Jae-Rock Lee. Photo © Urim Book USA. Used by permission.

men and women whose physical and social survival is predicated upon their ability to perform hard manual labor and who therefore need to have strong and healthy bodies to provide for the well-being of their families. They are poor and do not have the financial resources to pay for expensive medical services. They are also denizens of nations lacking adequate social health institutions. Thus, a debilitating illness becomes a matter of life and death. In such a grave situation, sometimes the only hope of the powerless appears to be divine intervention. For countless rural and urban poor workers, serious sickness becomes the occasion to implore the Virgin or to attend a healing crusade with anxious hope in their hearts that they might become beneficiaries of merciful divine power.

In the twentieth century new and more accessible healing competitors to the Virgin suddenly began to spread across Latin America. Divine grace took a more popular and democratic shape. Dozens of uneducated and ordinary men and women became mediators of divine healing power.[9] This process simultaneously implied a critical downgrading of the Virgin Mary's role in creedal faith and religious rites, a dimension of the antagonism of Latin American evangelicals and Pentecostals toward Roman Catholicism.

Physical healing might have been the starting point, but conversion, as Zayas explained to Mintz, entailed other decisive dimensions. After attending the worship services of the Pentecostal chapel in his barrio for several weeks, Zayas experienced an extraordinary event usually known in that ecclesiastical tradition as baptism by the Holy Spirit. He was a man of few words, but his narration of the blessing of the Holy Spirit had subtle tinges of deep spiritual gratification: "And while one is praying one feels as if something comes and fills one. . . . I received a blessing . . . at the same time one receives the tongues. And when one is baptized with the Spirit . . . one feels most content. . . . When a person thus receives the blessing of the Holy Ghost, it is a great joy that a Christian feels. . . . One is exceedingly happy."[10] A man whose life had been extremely difficult—in continuous bondage to strenuous work and poverty, plagued by debilitating pain, in perennial marital stress, and with a history of disappointments in labor union and political affairs—suddenly felt joyful thanks to the divine blessing of baptism by the Holy Spirit. His taciturn and somewhat trite witness lacks eloquence but nonetheless expresses the radical newness of his self-understanding by stressing that he felt "full": "One receives the Spirit . . . that comes and fills one. . . . Yes something comes and fills one."[11] Plenitude has displaced hollowness at the core of his mind and heart.

The experience of an uneducated and ordinary person speaking in divine tongues under the blessing of the Holy Spirit is not only memorable; it also leads to a momentous reappraisal of his or her entire existence. The hearing of the gospel, preached in clear, simple words, awakened in Zayas a deep sense first of guilt and then of absolution. "In truth at times one feels, eh—guilty of many things. . . . All of those things must be changed."[12] Zayas was not one to belabor the things he used to do that he now considered sinful, and it would be unfair to attempt to fill in the blanks, but the idea is emblematic of many similar experiences: a rejection of a former lifestyle now perceived as violating God's will, the sense of having been forgiven, and the decision to lead a holier life. Sanctification is taken seriously as a necessary consequence of spiritual baptism.

In this narration, the emphasis is not upon the traditional baptism by water, but upon the spectacular event of the reception of the Holy Spirit. Elizabeth was more loquacious, more expressive with words, and her description of the baptism by the Spirit was more dramatic than Taso's. "There came this peculiar thing. It invaded my whole body. . . . I began to tremble. . . . My body was moving more . . . until at last something . . . compelled me to dance. . . . I could not control myself. . . . And then I spoke in other languages, like Hebrew or something like that. . . . Meanwhile . . . there were

> **Guilt and Absolution**
>
> Now, in that moment that I felt—eh—oh—guilty, it was because I used to do many things they prohibit. That is the guilty part of what I was feeling. Before, as I said, Elizabeth and I used to have our differences and we used to quarrel and such things. And when they explain these things, then one feels guilty. I felt guilty, and she [Elizabeth] must have too.
>
> —Sidney W. Mintz, *Worker in the Cane: A Puerto Rican Life History* (New York: Norton, 1974 [1960]), 217.

those strong movements in my body . . . and for the sheer pleasure of it, one goes speaking in tongues. . . . I felt as if my face were being lighted up by a flashlight. And I felt more alive than ever, and happier than ever."[13]

A poor woman—who had seen her mother mistreated by her drunkard father, felt disregarded by her husband, had suffered three of her children dying in their infancy, and was overworked in caring for her other children—suddenly felt "more alive than ever, and happier than ever" after being baptized by the Holy Spirit. She felt that divine power—"there is something powerful . . . beyond the firmament one sees"[14]—had entered into her and conferred on her amazing gifts.[15] Elizabeth and Taso describe their incorporation into a Pentecostal church, but curiously neither mentions the traditional sacrament of water baptism. It probably took place, but as a sacramental event it was overshadowed by the spiritual baptism. This constitutes an important, though usually overlooked, recasting of the theological understanding of baptism. Baptism by the Spirit, not by water, becomes the decisive transforming and empowering experience.

One important outcome of conversion and spiritual baptism is peace of mind. Joy and hope displace anger and frustration. It is first expressed in family life. The bitter fights between husband and wife disappear. "When you seek God," according to Taso, "then you are made a new creature and then you have peace in your home, then you have contentment."[16] But his wider communal context also changed. This is signaled mainly by his continual references to the members of his church as "brothers" and "sisters," an indication that Taso and Elizabeth are now members of a new

**Figs. 7.4 and 7.5** A large-scale Protestant religious ceremony at the Maracaña soccer stadium in Rio de Janeiro, Brazil, in the summer of 2004. Although this ceremony was open to all denominations, most Protestants in Rio de Janeiro are Pentecostals. Photos © Marshall Roderick.

type of family and that their church functions not only as a place for common worship but also as a network of vital support and solidarity. For Taso, the solutions once searched for in the labor union or in the political party are now to be found in the community of believers. Indeed, Pentecostal congregations in Latin America frequently perform useful services of solidarity in situations of social distress so common in the lives of their members.

## BECOMING PEOPLE OF THE BOOK?

Conversion did not drastically change the socioeconomic situation of Zayas and his family. They were poor before it and remained poor afterward. "His work takes him to the cane, along the railroad tracks and on the spurs, eight hours a day in the sun. . . . He and Elí and seven of their children live in their little house, eating their rice and beans and drinking black coffee, entertaining themselves with the Bible and the tambourine and the gossip of the barrio."[17] In fact, one might suspect that the midcentury decline of sugarcane production on the island and its replacement by small manufacturing plants requiring higher levels of technological skills possibly placed his family under even worse economic stress.

Despite the connections that some scholars predict, in a too-facile optimistic Weberian mood, between conversion to a morally stern religiosity and socioeconomic upward mobility, more frequently than not the poor remain poor. After all, modern economic globalization never truly intended the elimination of poverty. Its preferred biblical mantra is probably Matthew 25:29 ("for to all those who have, more will be given, and they will have in abundance.")

And indeed, the second half of the twentieth century was not generous to the Latin American poor. The glad tidings of socialist revolution, national security military juntas, liberation theology, and neoliberal globalization had all been proclaimed, leaving behind a trail of broken promises and frustrated hopes. However, millions of Latin Americans, in the midst of dreadful poverty and turbulent revolutions, still believed firmly that their lives had changed significantly. They held fast to the conviction that, thanks to the Holy Spirit, they possessed a new identity and were now "children of God," members of the community of saints, chosen for eternal salvation. They gathered assiduously in austere temples and chapels, built by their own hands and devoid of the grandeur of Roman Catholic sacred architecture, to praise God, study the Bible, perform acts of exorcism, heal the sick, and share in the tribulations and good news of their fellow brothers and sisters.

The story of Zayas and his wife is superbly narrated by Sidney Mintz, but the anthropologist could not hide his surprise at their conversion to the newly introduced Pentecostalism. Mintz was no apologist for the newcomer evangelists, and his last sentences poetically betray his secularist perspective. "Taso's story has no moral. . . . Or perhaps the reader will see the waste I think I see: the waste of a mind that stands above the others as the violet sprays of the *flor de caña* tower above the cane."[18] A wasted mind? Maybe from the perspective of an academician who values intellectual achievement, but that is not how Taso and Elizabeth perceived themselves. When asked, they emphasize the healing of their bodies and the salvation of their souls. They have been healed, have received the blessing of the Holy Spirit, and have the Bible, as the word of God, constantly within reach. They are now members of the community of believers and possess the assurance of eternal redemption. They have come to see themselves as privileged citizens of the kingdom of heaven. They even learned to play the tambourine.

At the core of all of these phenomena lay another crucial change in the minds of people like Taso and Elizabeth that seems to have escaped Mintz: They have become *readers*. In the more than two hundred pages of Mintz's study of Taso's life before his conversion, it is obvious that Taso did not care for books or any type of reading. He apparently was not analphabetic, but certainly illiterate. Totally absorbed in daily labors, he had neither time for nor interest in books or journals. After their conversion, he and his wife may still not be people of books, but they have certainly joined the company of the people of the Book. Now Taso and Elizabeth read the Bible constantly, in the congregation and in their house.

Conversion entails a novel source of certainty regarding the place of humanity in the divinely ordered cosmos. The Bible is now perceived as the word of God. In the middle of the twentieth century, evangelicals in Latin America could be distinctly recognized by a book they carried constantly and quoted ceaselessly, the Bible. It was always at the center of the congregation and in the living room of the house. It was seen as an infallible font of firm convictions and ideas. It functioned symbolically as a talisman, an apotropaic (intended to ward off evil) amulet, when risky activities were to be undertaken. Only after the reforms approved by Second Vatican Council, in the mid-1960s, would the Roman Catholic Church promote a similar mass publication of the Bible in easily accessible editions.

Zayas explains how in his church they gathered around the Bible and in a collegial way conversed about biblical doctrines. "Any other doubt I might have I resolved in the Scriptures," he affirms with confidence.[19] Notice the prominence of the "I" in this statement; it is not the case that the believers receive a body of doctrines from a hierarch equipped with credentials of ecclesiastical authority. What they now share is a sacred book to be read and interpreted by many uneducated and ordinary men and women—people like Zayas. They have become the people of the Bible, but the Bible has also become the book of the people.

Merely one book is indeed a rather limited intellectual horizon. Yet if someone, no matter his or her educational background, diligently reads the poetry of the Psalms, the biographical narrations of the Gospels, the irate apostrophes of the prophets, or the subtle theological deliberations of Paul, it is difficult not to surmise that such a practice would indeed expand their repertoire of words, images, and ideas. Taso and Elizabeth did not become biblical scholars by any means. Their textual interpretations might be naïve, but it is hard to imagine their not acquiring a wider stock of linguistic and intellectual skills simply by reading what is, after all, not an undemanding text. Their reading of the Word increases their repertoire of words and, what for them might be even more decisive, simultaneously transforms drastically their understanding of the world.

## THE KINGDOM OF GOD AND THE KINGDOM OF THIS WORLD

Several scholars currently take a critical view of Christian Lalive d'Epinay's thesis about the otherworldliness and lack of political awareness of the Pentecostal churches in Latin America. This rethinking takes place in the wake of the emergence of Neo-Pentecostal megachurches and evangelical political parties all over Latin America. Demographic growth has increased their political power and influence. Numbers do make a difference when votes are counted.[20] The time has come when many Pentecostal churches take more interest in the kingdom of this world and in earthly citizenship, and the debate is now shifting its focus to the shape of their social engagement (including the intriguing question about the possible emergence of a Pentecostal theology of liberation).

The political awareness and activism of the Pentecostal churches in Latin America, however, is a rather new process that has mainly taken place since about 1990. In the mid-twentieth century the community of the saints stressed separation and distinction from the world, functioning as a refuge from its sorrows and temptations. When prompted and challenged to confront controversial political and social matters, most evangelical and Pentecostal churches would quote Jesus' words to Pilate as the legitimizing text for their political abstention: "My kingdom is not of this world" (John 18:36). The severe Johannine strictures against the "world" were some of their favorite biblical leitmotifs. The "world" was conceived as ruled by demonic powers, under the tyranny of Satan. The most that could be asked of the state was its protection of the right of the new churches to preach and expand. Religious freedom might indeed have important consequences for the democratization of any society, and mainstream Protestant churches were usually aware of the link. Yet the concern of most midcentury Pentecostal congregations was their right to proclaim their charismatic version of the gospel free from restrictions by the state or any legally established church.

For their part, Taso and Elizabeth seemed undisturbed by the midcentury political and social turbulences taking place in Puerto Rico, including the formation of a strong independence party, a nationalist insurrection, the industrialization of the island, and the establishment of the Commonwealth of Puerto Rico, an ambiguous juridical relationship with the United States.[21] In the midst of poverty and sociopolitical transformations, Taso and Elizabeth were relatively serene, for their minds and hearts revolved around the community of saints, the joy of the Spirit, and the promise of eternal salvation. In political issues, they tended toward quietism rather than activism.

Taso did not continue his work in union-related and political matters. He sees those activities as part of his former self, from which he has been freed. The church now became the center of his aspirations and exertions. We cannot tell from Mintz's account whether at a later date Taso became disenchanted with the church as well, but it can be ascertained that some years after his unexpected and dramatic conversion, he still felt at home immersed in church activities. "He seems serene" is Mintz's terse description.[22]

## TRANSFIGURING LATIN AMERICAN CHRISTENDOM

The spread of evangelical charismatic Christianity across Latin America has not left the social situation intact. The growth of these congregations has indeed changed the continental public landscape considerably.

Since their colonial inception, Latin American nations were characterized by an official linkage between the state and the Roman Catholic Church. The royal patronage exercised by the Iberian crowns entailed the acknowledgment by the church of the sovereignty and authority of the metropolitan state, but also the state's recognition of the Roman Catholic Church's exclusivity in religious affairs.[23] It was sometimes the source of acute conflicts, whenever the ethical conscience of priests, missionaries, and theologians clashed with the severe exploitation of the native communities.[24] Yet it was a convenient arrangement for both partners, for it conferred a sacred aura to the metropolitan sovereignty and conversely provided the church with state protection.

The governments of the new states, which emerged after the nineteenth-century wars of independence, promptly recognized the advantages of royal patronage and tried to preserve it. This heritage forged a particular brand of Christendom closely linking the state and the Roman Catholic Church in Latin American countries, a condition juridically inscribed in many national constitutions and Vatican concordats.[25]

This official connection between church and state was venerable but also vulnerable. It became embroiled in countless disputes of jurisdiction that sometimes resembled the renowned dispute between Henry II and Becket, though most of these never produced martyrs deserving similar fame or memory. Sometimes archbishops and bishops became decisive protagonists in the national drama, diminishing the powers of the state and restricting the possibilities of religious competition; at other times, the sword of the state curtailed severely the rights and powers of the church. In a critical phase of the Mexican Revolution, the church lost legal recognition, its property was nationalized, and religious houses were closed. During the Colombian civil war, on the other hand, Catholics massacred members of the evangelical minority under the excuse that the Protestants usually aligned themselves with the Liberal faction. In general, only the Roman Catholic Church had the legal and political credentials to influence national destinies.

Conversion experiences like those of Taso and Elizabeth have substantially changed and dramatically complicated the religious landscape of Latin America. Titles like that of David Stoll's book—*Is Latin America Turning Protestant?*[26]—might be hyperbolic and misleading, but it is indeed true that evangelical and Pentecostal churches of all kinds and varieties are sprouting up all over Central America. In Guatemala, Nicaragua, Costa Rica, Brazil, and Puerto Rico, on any given Sunday morning possibly more hymns are sung, sermons are preached, exorcisms are performed, and prayers are offered to God in Protestant churches than in Catholic ones. The exceptional growth of the variegated Pentecostal expressions of the Christian faith has indeed reshaped the religious configuration of the entire region.[27]

In changing the religious landscape, widening the horizons of religious liberty, and forging a ferocious competition for the souls and hearts of believers, these charismatic congregations have fragmented the traditional Latin American model of Christendom. Their presence and activities constitute one of the most important transformations of the Latin American human landscape of the past century. No history of twentieth-century Latin

**Fig. 7.6.** Mother Church of the Christian Congregation in Brazil, located in the Italian Braz District, in Sao Paulo, Brazil. The Christian Congregation in Brazil is also called Congregação Cristã no Brasil.

**Plate A.** *Christ in the Manger* by Francis Musango (Uganda). The African setting of *Christ in the Manger* evokes the ongoing creation of a Christianity on that vast continent that is authentically African in its theological, liturgical, and cultural interpretations. Courtesy National Archives (Contemporary African Art Select List collection, #137).

**Plate B.** *Peace Be Still*, He Qi (China). The painter He Qi places himself in a fifth generation of Chinese Christian artists, a lineage that began with seventh-century Nestorian Christians of the Tang Dynasty. Well known in both East and West, he uses bright colors, modern art styles, and folk art in his non-Western depiction of Bible scenes and stories. Used by permission. For more information and art by He Qi, please visit www.heqigallery.com.

**Plate C.** *"Mary . . . Rabboni" . . . John 20:16* (batik, 1999) by Hanna-Cheriyan Varghese (Malaysia). Malaysian Christian artist Varghese sets Jesus' and Mary Magdalen's Easter morning encounter in a brightly colored eastern garden: "Jesus said, 'Do not cling to me, for I have not yet ascended to the Father. . . . Mary of Magdala went to the disciples with her news: 'I have seen the Lord.'" © Hanna-Cheriyan Varghese. Used by permission.

**Plate D.** Their arms stretched to the sky, delegates from the ecclesial base communities of Liberation Theology come together for their sixth meeting, generating fervor and fresh initiative for the implementation of social reform at the grassroots level, Trinidad, Brazil, July 1986. © Bernard Bisson/Sygma/Corbis.

**Plate E.** *Feeding of the 5,000* (1999) by Laura James. Ethiopian Christian iconography is a major inspiration in the art of Laura James, a self-taught American artist of Antiguan heritage, who was commissioned in 2001 to create thirty-five images for a new, multicultural reading of the Book of the Gospels by Liturgy Training Publications. © Laura James. Used by permission.

**Plate F.** *Black Madonna II (Classic)*, April 1998, by Elizabeth Barakah Hodges. Tradition and innovation come together in this late twentieth-century icon-like Black Madonna, which is a work in mixed media. Iris Rose Hart Collection, © Elizabeth Barakah Hodges / SuperStock. Used by permission.

**Plate G.** *The Rapture* by Charles Anderson. The Conservative Christian belief in the Rapture is complicated by several different biblical, theological, and historical plot-lines. At its most basic it posits an unexpected moment in the future when Jesus returns and true Christians disappear from the earth in the midst of their everyday activities. Image courtesy of Bible Believers' Evangelistic Association (www.bbea.org).

**Plate H.** *The Creche* (ca. 1929–1933) by Joseph Stella (1879–1946). The intriguing work by Italian-born American Modernist/Futurist painter Joseph Stella offers a vision of people from all over the world and all walks of life gathered in community around the manger scene. Photo © The Newark Museum / Art Resource, N.Y. Used by permission.

America is complete if it leaves outside its margins the evangelical and Pentecostal reshaping of the continental religious configuration. It has become a meaningful part of the story of many men and women who, in very severe socioeconomic straits, strive simultaneously to create an earthly home for their bodies and to affirm their belonging to a heavenly home.

Some scholars have made the case that despite their initial isolation from the public and political arenas and their tendency toward a conservative stance regarding ethical issues, the evangelical and Pentecostal churches widen the democratic character of Latin American societies. They point out, first, that to become a member of any of these congregations, which lack the aura of traditional social legitimation, requires a free and conscious decision—a crucial building block of any democracy. Second, these churches' tend to be more participatory and less restricted by a professional clergy, thus inspiring a less passive attitude on important community issues.[28]

It is probably safer to say that the jury is still out regarding the political consequences of the increase in the diversity of evangelical and Pentecostal expressions of Christianity in Latin America. Some of these new churches tend to be very congregational and participatory; others, however, are under the iron-fisted control of their founders and self-designated apostles and tend to mirror the autocratic character of traditional haciendas and plantations. Some might question traditional norms of social conduct; others, on the contrary, espouse very conservative social and sexual ethics. What is undeniable is that traditional monopolistic Christendom, as known for centuries in Latin America, has been superseded by a bewildering variety of forms of living and thinking the Christian faith. The actions of the Holy Spirit, contrary to Augustine's restriction of the Spirit within the confines of the Catholic Church, seem to promote diversity, division, and, from time to time, even bitter competition for the hearts and souls of the

> **Speaking in Tongues**
>
> And while I was glorifying, I know that at one point I wanted to say, "Glory to God, Hallelujah," and I could not. I swallowed my tongue, and then I spoke in other languages, like Hebrew or something like that. The pastor said I was going to something in tongues; and then I heard Brother Juan say, "She has received it! She has spoken in tongues, in spiritual tongues." And meanwhile, while I was in that state, there were those strong movements in my body. Something comes—comes to where one is, and for the sheer pleasure of it, one goes on speaking in tongues. One does not know what one is saying, and one is left speaking that way without knowing how.
>
> —Sidney W. Mintz, *Worker in the Cane: A Puerto Rican Life History* (New York: Norton, 1974 [1960]), 242.

people. Under the proclaimed aegis of the Spirit, Latin American Christendom is indeed undergoing a dramatic and profound religious transfiguration.

## PROVISIONAL PREDICTIONS

It is too early to predict with a high degree of confidence the long-range consequences of the impressive growth of Pentecostal Christianity in Latin America, but some provisional suspicions can be suggested.

There has been a dramatic battle for the spirit of the poor between the Pentecostal churches, with their pneumatological emphasis, and the Catholic ecclesial base communities inspired by liberation theology. Liberation theology made the preferential option for the poor a cardinal theological and ecclesiastical principle. It also foregrounded the primacy of the hermeneutical perspective of the poor. Ernesto Cardenal's famous *The Gospel in Solentiname* (first published in 1978) became its poetical hermeneutical paradigm. Many poor, however, have opted for the religiosity of the Spirit rather than for a theology of political and social resistance. This tendency does not necessarily lead us to the dirge of liberation theology prematurely sung by some conservative critics. But it certainly complicates the image of the historical protagonism of the poor, in the midst of continuing poverty and the new waves of enthusiasm for drastic social transformation shaking Latin America during the first decade of the twenty-first century. Intriguingly enough, since the 1990s there have been increasing signs of an emerging Pentecostal Latin American theological production.[29] The script of Latin American liberation theology might yet be redrafted, this time with surprising charismatic contours.

If we speak of the Latin American poor, then their racial and ethnic identities must also be taken into account. Many of them are indigenous (most prominently in Guatemala, Bolivia, Peru, Ecuador, and Mexico), African Americans (in Haiti, Brazil, Dominican Republic, Cuba, and Puerto Rico), or mestizos, generated by the multiple forms of miscegenation that have taken place during the past five hundred years. These ethnic and racial communities have suffered social discrimination and degradation, and many are now attracted to the promise of spiritual dignity conveyed by the religions of the Spirit.

"Syncretism" has always been a risky and potentially misleading term in religious matters, but it is difficult to avoid the impression of certain intimate interactions, in several autochthonous (indigenous) communities, between the spirits of the ancestors and the Spirit of the new Pentecost thriving all over Latin America. The boundaries between the Christian Spirit and the spirits of indigenous and African religiosities are frequently porous and symbiotic. It is not necessarily a conscious synthesis, but the primacy of orality in their liturgy, the narrative style of their homilies, and their flexibility in integrating popular rhythms and melodies into their worship constitute points of contact of many Pentecostal churches with the spirituality enshrined in the aesthetic traditions of autochthonous peoples. This has led some scholars to perceive indigenous Pentecostalism in Latin America, the Caribbean, and Africa as part and parcel of a process of ethnic revitalization.[30]

Religion matters in Latin America. And it matters even more in its increasing and astounding variety. The traditional binary confrontation between the secular state and the Roman Catholic Church is now being displaced by an array of multiple relations among religiosities of assorted theological and ritual configurations. The proliferation of many of these congregations with their tendency to break off from each other suggests a complex and confusing Latin American religious map in the future. Such a spiritual configuration promises to become a bewildering and ever-winding maze analogous to the fantastic labyrinths found in some of Jorge Luis Borges's stories. Diversity and complexity seem to be decisive hermeneutical keys in the religion of the Spirit of this postmodern zeitgeist.

Scholars and missiologists have recently stressed a crucial change in the global demographics of Christianity.[31] While the proportion of Christians in the Western and Northern churches diminishes, the churches in the South are growing geometrically. Some even predict the emergence of a "next Christendom," dominated by the churches of Latin America, sub-Saharan Africa, and Southeast Asia. If that is a valid point, then much of the credit belongs to the explosion of indigenous Pentecostal churches throughout the Third World. Future historians might consider twentieth-century Pentecostalism as the most significant global religious upheaval since the birth of Islam and the Protestant Reformation.

What this might entail for the political and social conflict engendered by neoliberal globalization is hard to envisage. The leadership of many of these churches is frequently authoritarian, conservative, isolationist, and fundamentalist. As has been shrewdly observed, the hierarchies of some Pentecostal churches, influenced by the North American "theology of prosperity," seem more interested in apostolic success than in apostolic succession. Nevertheless, a growing body of critical Pentecostal literature, open to political radicalism, challenges the prevailing socioeconomic powers and is ready to engage in ecumenical dialogue with other Christian partners. The future might be less bleak than the one foreseen by many contemporary Cassandras.

Indeed, the vigorous spread of Pentecostal churches and movements in the twentieth century has complicated enormously another of the main dimensions of that century of Christianity—the ecumenical movement. Ecumenical dialogue has taken place mainly among mainline Protestant churches, Roman Catholicism, and Eastern and Oriental Orthodox churches. With few exceptions, the Pentecostal movement, the fastest growing sector of Christianity during the past hundred years, has kept its distance from the ecumenical dialogue and has frequently viewed it with some degree of distrust. The Pentecostal churches are very young and still rather anxious to forge a clear sense of their own identity. They have emerged and developed in a social and ecclesiastical environment of contempt and disdain, engendering their tendency toward isolation and clear boundaries of separation.

The time may come when many of them will look more positively toward dialogue and ecumenical collaboration with other Christian churches. The success of Pentecostalism has promoted a mimetic reaction in other branches of Christianity, as attested by the increasing popularity of the charismatic renewal movement in many Roman Catholic Latin American dioceses. The enthusiastic Pentecostal style of worship is also strongly influencing mainstream Protestant congregations. This has led some scholars to perceive, in analogy to Paul Tillich's "Protestant principle," a Pentecostal principle, a tendency toward "pentecostality" that is not restricted to Pentecostal denominations but is shaping the liturgical practices of many other Christian churches.[32] This liturgical convergence might constitute a bridge of ecumenical dialogue and rapprochement between churches that usually have stressed their doctrinal and theological differences.

Several times in the history of Christianity, an age of the Spirit has been foreseen, predicted, and desired. The hierarchical church, with its emphasis on orthodox doctrine, traditional liturgy, and accredited priesthood, has frequently looked with distrust at these enthusiastic aspirations, for it well knows how difficult it is to control and restrain their possible consequences. The Spirit tends to overwhelm and transgress the boundaries so carefully drawn by ecclesiastical hierarchies. "For the *pneuma* [spirit/wind] blows where it chooses . . . but you do not know where it comes from or where it goes" (John 3:8).

This chapter began with Sidney Mintz's engaging story of the astounding conversion to charismatic and Pentecostal Christianity of Taso Zayas and his wife, Elizabeth, two "uneducated and ordinary people" from the Latin American Caribbean. Some skeptical minds might recall John Locke's ironic observation regarding this type of charismatic enthusiasm: "I ask how shall any one distinguish between the delusions of Satan, and the inspirations of the Holy Ghost?"[33] Still, for many other trustful believers, their story of healing, spiritual baptism, and conversion was one of many similar signs that the age of the Spirit had finally arrived. Like the wind from the Caribbean Sea, whose storms bring disarray and redesign so many constructions in the sands of human affairs, the new Pentecost of the Spirit seems to be reconfiguring in unexpected ways the contours of the people's history of Christianity.[34]

## FOR FURTHER READING

Anderson, Allan H., and Walter Hollenweger, eds. *Pentecostals after a Century: Global Perspectives on a Movement in Transition.* Sheffield: Sheffield Academic, 1999.

Chesnut, R. Andrew. *Competitive Spirits: Latin America's New Religious Economy.* Oxford: Oxford University Press, 2003.

Cleary, Edward L., and Hannah W. Stewart-Gambino, eds. *Power, Politics, and Pentecostals in Latin America.* Boulder: Westview, 1997.

Escobar, Samuel. *Changing Tides: Latin America and World Mission Today.* Maryknoll, N.Y.: Orbis Books, 2002.

Gutiérrez, Benjamin, and Dennis Smith, eds. *In the Power of the Spirit: The Pentecostal Challenge to Historic Churches in Latin America*. Arkansas City: Asociación de Iglesias Presbiterianas y Reformadas en América Latina; Centro Evangélico Latinoamericano de Estudios Pastorales; Presbyterian Church (U.S.A.), Worldwide Ministries Division, 1996.

Míguez Bonino, José. *Faces of Latin American Protestantism*. Grand Rapids: Eerdmans, 1997.

Shaull, Richard, and Waldo Cesar. *Pentecostalism and the Future of the Christian Churches: Promises, Limitations, Challenges*. Grand Rapids: Eerdmans, 2000.

Sigmund, Paul E., ed. *Religious Freedom and Evangelization in Latin America: The Challenge of Religious Pluralism*. Maryknoll, N.Y.: Orbis Books, 1999.

Silveira Campos, Leonildo. *Teatro, templo e mercado: Organização e marketing de um empreendimento neopentecostal*. Petrópolis, Brazil: Editora Vozes, 1997.

Stoll, David. *Is Latin America Turning Protestant? The Politics of Evangelical Growth*. Berkeley: University of California Press, 1990.

# APOCALYPTICISM IN THE UNITED STATES

## BRUCE DAVID FORBES

At the very end of the twentieth century in the United States, an explicitly Christian series of novels about the end-times, Left Behind, sat atop most major best-seller lists. These lists did not chart sales at conservative Christian bookstores; they indicated purchases by the general public at stores like Borders, Barnes & Noble, Target, and Wal-Mart. When journalists and mainline religious leaders eventually became aware of the Left Behind publishing phenomenon, most ensuing discussions centered on disagreements among Christians about whether they shared the theology, biblical interpretation, and social and political perspectives espoused by the books. Yet few commentators noticed that the Left Behind series represented more than just an example of controversy within formal Christian theology. The books also represented the culmination of an unofficial, informal theology expressed in American popular culture throughout much of the twentieth century about cosmic battles between good and evil and about the elimination of evil through violence. The Left Behind books were accepted and thus popular because they resonated with well-established beliefs and assumptions long expressed in American popular culture, in examples such as the American western and comic book superheroes. Along with an interplay of influence between popular culture and organized religion, repeated motifs within popular culture also are revealing: in essence they hold up a mirror that reflects a network of basic beliefs embraced by many Americans, inside and outside Christian churches. What the general public *really* believes often finds expression more in the trends of popular culture than in the statements of elite, formal theologians.

## LEFT BEHIND BOOKS

In 1995 Tim LaHaye and Jerry B. Jenkins published the first volume of their series, titled *Left Behind: A Novel of the Earth's Last Days*. LaHaye was the best known of the two authors, prominent and often combative in decades of evangelical Christian efforts, serving on the board of the Moral Majority, advocating a literal reading of the Bible, and opposing what he saw as the dangers of secular humanism, including globalism, evolution, feminism, and homosexuality. One commentator claimed that LaHaye was the most influential American evangelical of the last quarter of the twentieth century.[1] Left Behind book covers identify LaHaye as the person who "conceived" the series, but the actual writer was Jenkins, who previously had published over one hundred less famous books of all kinds, especially for the Moody Bible Institute. Jenkins completed coauthoring Billy Graham's autobiography, *Just As I Am,* and then began work on the series that was to vault him into public attention he had not experienced before.[2]

The original intention was a short series of novels, but when sales exceeded expectations, the plan expanded to twelve volumes, with titles like *Tribulation Force: The Continuing Drama of Those Left Behind* (1996), *Nicolae: The Rise of the Antichrist* (1997), *Soul Harvest: The World Takes Sides* (1998), and so on. From initial print runs of 150,000 or 200,000 for the early books, later print runs started with two to three million each. *The Indwelling* (2000), the seventh volume, reached the number one position on four best-seller lists in fiction, in the *New York Times, Publishers Weekly,* the *Washington Post,* and *USA Today. Desecration* (2001), the ninth novel, was the best-selling fiction title in the United States in 2001, dethroning John Grisham, who had held that honor for several years. A widespread public mood of general speculation about the significance of the turn of the millennium in 2000 and 2001 probably helped sales, but the authors and their publisher, Tyndale House, were eager to continue their successful venture as long as possible. When the initial series of twelve books was completed in 2004, the authors and publisher decided to add a prequel, then expanded the prequel into a trilogy, plus one last sequel. By that time even the most avid fans seemed exhausted, sales sputtered, and critics suspected a greater interest in profits than prophets.

Yet at the height of the books' popularity, at the turn of the century, their exposure in the general population was extensive. The Barna Research Group conducted a study in May 2001 that provided some striking data. While the survey was commissioned by Tyndale, and the Barna group is known for its work in conservative Christian circles, Barna nevertheless is an independent firm that uses generally respected methodologies. The study found that 24 percent of American adults were aware of the Left Behind books, and 9 percent had read at least one of the volumes.[3] In other words, almost one-tenth of the adult population in the United States had read at least one of the Left Behind books. Public attention to the books continued to grow for at least a couple of years beyond the date of the study, so later results undoubtedly would have been even higher. The Harry Potter books admittedly have had much greater recognition and readership, but the Left Behind statistics would be the envy of almost any other author or publisher.

Barna's research also found, not surprisingly, that readers of the Left Behind books tended to be born-again Christians who attended nonmainline Protestant churches in the South and the West. Yet the study also revealed millions of readers who did not fit those categories, including Catholics, mainline Protestants, and adherents of other world religions or no religion at all. George Barna concluded that the series "reached a larger unduplicated audience of non-believers than most religious television and radio ministries draw through their programs."[4] The Left Behind books successfully crossed over from a predictable audience of conservative Christians to reach major portions of the general public in the United States.

Fig 8.1. *Left Behind* by Tim LaHaye and Jerry B. Jenkins. The readers of the Left Behind series include not only born-again Christians but also millions of Roman Catholics, mainline Protestants, members of other world religions, and those who claim no religious affiliation at all. Image used by permission of Tyndale House Publishers.

What was the story line of the books that interested so many people? It was based upon a particular view of the end-times that modern evangelicals call dispensational premillennialism, or simply dispensationalism (discussed further in the following section). Essentially, it consists of a complicated series of events beginning with a rapture, an unexpected moment when all true Christians instantly and mysteriously disappear from the face of the earth. Those who remain behind then experience a seven-year period of increasing difficulties, war, and chaos, a period called the tribulation, in which the Antichrist rises to prominence, is indwelt by Satan, and persecutes all who do not conform to his one-world government and religion. At the end of the seven years Jesus Christ then returns to earth in a glorious appearing to defeat Satan and to begin a thousand-year reign of peace and harmony on earth, the millennium.

LaHaye and Jenkins wanted to imagine what it would be like to live through all of these events, and they acknowledged that the story they created was fiction, with characters and specific incidents they invented, but both creators insisted that the basic outline of the story was consistent with biblical prophecy. Three major characters in the story were Rayford Steele, an airline pilot, Chloe Steele, Rayford's adult daughter who emerges into leadership, and Cameron "Buck" Williams, a journalist. Within the first twenty pages of the first book the rapture occurs. Several passengers instantly disappear from Steele's plane in midair, leaving clothing and even a hearing aid behind, and after some initial hysteria and confusion, many of the remaining people conclude that it was the rapture. The entire plot of the twelve books, then, becomes the story of those who were "left behind." Some persons, including the three mentioned above, take the rapture as a wake-up call, convert from nominal Christianity to a born-again acceptance of Christ, and form a Tribulation

Force to battle against evil. Nicolae Carpathia arises as the Antichrist, initially with a deceptively charming demeanor (looking very much like Robert Redford, the authors say), becoming secretary general of the United Nations, and eventually inflicting oppression, violence, and death upon the world. The novels are filled with dramatic struggles and outright battles between good and evil, and part of the suspense of the story is wondering which of the familiar cast of characters might die next. (Many do.) The first half of the twelfth volume, *Glorious Appearing*, is particularly filled with blood and gore as the climactic finale approaches. When Jesus appears, one motion of his hand causes an incredible chasm to open up, into which all unbelievers tumble to hell, "howling and screeching," and then the millennium begins. Fans of the books found it to be a satisfying conclusion, while critics objected to the image of Jesus as a warrior, and they also dissented from the authors' apparent certainty that all members of other world religions, and many mainline Christians without a born-again experience, will be consigned to hell.

## FORMAL THEOLOGY

When most theologians and religious studies scholars seek to place these novels into context, they usually discuss the history of doctrines about millennialism and apocalyptic thought, which certainly have a long tradition. In the words of historian Eugen Weber, "Apocalypse— the revelation or unveiling of the world's destiny and of mankind's— has fascinated Jews and their Christian offspring at least for the last 2200 years."[5]

"Apocalypse," from the Greek word *apokalypsis*, meaning "disclosure," "revelation," or "unveiling," refers to the revelation of divine mysteries, generally about how things will turn out in the future, often including punishment of one's enemies and rewards for those who were faithful. Historians note that apocalyptic thought tended to arise when Jews or Christians faced difficulties, because the apocalyptic visions promised that no matter how bleak things appeared to be, God offered hope in the future. Thus, the Book of Daniel in the Hebrew scriptures was written in a time of persecution, when traditional

**Definitions of "Apocalyptic Literature," "Apocalypticism"**

Certain portions of the Bible (including Daniel 7–12 and the book of Revelation) are often categorized as apocalyptic literature, a genre or type of Jewish literature that became popular during the intertestamental period and extended into the [New Testament] era (c. 400 B.C. to A.D. 100). The writers of apocalyptic literature sought to disclose "heavenly secrets" concerning how the world would end and how the kingdom of God would suddenly appear to destroy the kingdom of evil. Apocalyptic writers made extensive use of visions, dreams, and symbols as instruments of revealing what was hidden. Apocalypticism has been variously defined as a social movement or ideology arising out of an oppressed subgroup in a society, whether ancient or modern, which in defining its identity seeks release from oppression by seeing a future reality as more important than the present state of affairs.

—Stanley J. Grenz, David Guretzki, and Cherith Fee Nordling. *Pocket Dictionary of Theological Terms* (Downers Grove, Ill.: InterVarsity, 1999), 12–13.

Jewish culture seemed threatened by the imposition of Hellenistic values and customs, and the Revelation to John in the Christian New Testament was written in a context of Roman persecution of early Christians. The following generalization is of course oversimplified, but throughout the history of Christianity apocalyptic literature tended to arise in eras when Christianity endured threats or turmoil, and among smaller, marginalized Christian groups. When Christians enjoyed status or power, they were likely to deemphasize apocalyptic theology or treat it allegorically.

The term "millennialism" arises from some references in Revelation 20:2-7 in which John saw a vision of an angel who bound and threw the Devil or Satan into a pit for a thousand years (a millennium), a period during which Christ and Christian martyrs reigned over the earth. Millennialism is the strain of thought that looks forward to an ideal time in the future when problems are resolved and life is perfect, under the reign of Christ. Some Christians expect such a thousand-year period to occur literally upon the earth, within human history, while others see it more as symbolic language expressing hope about the future. Sociologists have generalized the term "millennialism" to refer to religious movements even beyond Christianity, when any culture holds religious beliefs about some kind of future deliverance to a better life, even if it does not involve a thousand-year period. In that wider meaning, the Ghost Dance among nineteenth-century Native Americans might be called a millennial movement. Among all the variations, the consistent motif is hope in the future.

There was an ebb and flow of millennial, apocalyptic thought throughout the history of Christianity, but one period when it played a major role was in the founding of European colonies in the New

World and in the development of the United States into a nation with a sense of religious calling. Christopher Columbus himself wrote, "God made me the messenger of the new heaven and the new earth of which he spoke in the Apocalypse of St. John . . . and he showed me where to find it."[6] New England Puritan beliefs that their colonial experiment was part of God's plan, American convictions that their young nation was a New Israel, and later expressions of manifest destiny all were conveyed repeatedly in millennial language.

In the American context, it is helpful to distinguish between "premillennialism," "postmillennialism," and "amillennialism," because they played contrasting roles in American history. The first two terms refer to differing beliefs about whether Christ's second coming would occur before or after the millennium. Postmillennialism posits that Christ's return will come after the millennium, that it will be "postmillennial." In this view, positive developments on earth, including conversions to Christianity and improvements in society, can help prepare the way for Christ's second coming. This perspective tends to be optimistic about what can be accomplished on earth, motivating Christians to spread the gospel and also to work for reform of economic, social, political, and cultural aspects of life, believing that a regeneration of human beings by the Holy Spirit can lead to a gradual coming of God's kingdom on earth, which would then be followed by Christ's second coming. This was the most common perspective in much American Protestantism from colonial beginnings into the twentieth century. An essay in the *American Theological Review* in 1859 referred to postmillennialism as the "commonly received doctrine" among American Protestants.[7]

Premillennialism reverses the order, arguing that Christ's second coming will be "premillennial," with Christ's intervention causing the sudden beginning of the millennium in dramatic fashion. This perspective tends to be more pessimistic about what human beings can accomplish, expecting life on earth to deteriorate into warfare, immorality, and godlessness until Christ returns to set things right. Historian Jeanne Halgren Kilde summarized premillennial beliefs in this way: "No perfecting activities or good works could improve the world or usher in the millennium. Individuals, replete with sin, had only one hope of avoiding damnation: to convert to Christianity as quickly as possible, before Christ's imminent return. Thus, while post-millennialists saw divine history as a process of improvement, these premillennialists . . . saw history as a struggle between good and evil in which human society was inherently corrupt and which only Christ could resolve."[8]

Premillennialism emerged in the nineteenth and twentieth centuries to become the predominant perspective among American fundamentalist and evangelical Christians, but not among mainline Protestants and Catholics. The viewpoint of the latter groups often is labeled "amillennialism," which interprets the millennium symbolically instead of as a literal thousand-year period to be expected at the end of human history. Theologian Stanley Grenz notes that "from the fourth century to the present, amillennialism in some form or another has reigned as the quasi-official teaching of most mainline Christian traditions, whether Orthodox, Roman Catholic, or Protestant."[9]

Clearly the Left Behind books represent the premillennial perspective. Within the premillennial camp there are many disagreements about the precise details of how the end-times will unfold, but the theological view named earlier, dispensational premillennialism, or simply dispensationalism, was the particular form of premillennialism that became dominant among American fundamentalists and evangelicals in the late nineteenth century and throughout the twentieth century. Historians generally regard it as a fairly recent view in the history of Christianity, arising especially through the teachings

Fig. 8.2. Portrait of John Nelson Darby. Image courtesy of the National Portrait Gallery, London.

of John Nelson Darby (1800–1882). Darby, a former Church of Ireland priest who was one of the founders of the Plymouth Brethren, predicted a "secret rapture." Although earlier Christians may have had ideas about Christians being lifted up into the air at a time of judgment (based especially upon 1 Thess. 4:16-17), Darby helped give it a name not found in the Bible, a "rapture," and he separated the rapture from the final judgment day as two distinct events. The entire dispensational package of details combined together, including a rapture, a seven-year tribulation, the glorious appearing, and then the millennium, had not appeared in Christian theology prior to the nineteenth century, although its advocates argue strongly that it is the proper understanding of biblical prophecy. In the United States these dispensational views became part of a "Princeton theology" that advocated biblical inerrancy and literal reading of the Bible, were expressed during the Niagara Bible Conferences, and influenced the notes of the *Scofield Reference Bible,* all of which were important in the emergence of American fundamentalism. In the 1970s, the dispensational view spread further through the popularity of Hal Lindsey's *The Late Great Planet Earth* and through an extensively viewed, low-budget Christian film, *A Thief in the Night.*[10] The Left Behind books built upon the influence of these predecessors, extending dispensational views beyond conservative Christians even further into the general public.

As the Left Behind series grew in popularity at the end of the twentieth century, mainline Christians who held alternate views were either unaware of the books or uninterested in responding, which left a vacuum for LaHaye and Jenkins to fill. Mainline Christian leaders belatedly realized that many members of their churches, Catholic and Protestant, assumed that all Christians believed in a rapture and that all Christians interpreted the Book of Revelation as a coded prediction of literal future events. Only after the turn of the century did critiques begin to appear, from Catholics Carl Olson (*Will Catholics Be Left Behind? A Critique of the Rapture and Today's Prophecy Preachers*) and Paul Thigpen (*The Rapture Trap: A Catholic Response to "End Times" Fever*), Lutheran Barbara Rossing (*The Rapture Exposed: The Message of Hope in the Book of Revelation*), and Protestant evangelical Gary DeMar (*End Times Fiction: A Biblical Consideration of the Left Behind Theology*).[11] The formal theological debate was joined in books written for general audiences and in radio, television, and church discussions. Supporters of the Left Behind books were pleased to advance their perspectives, and critics argued for alternate biblical interpretations and theological beliefs. The discussions also spilled into social and political issues, because critics charged that the books were linked with a George W. Bush foreign policy that was suspicious of global cooperation and dismissive of the United Nations and that saw most choices as black and white. In addition, critics asked, if one holds a belief that only Christ's return can change the inevitable deterioration of the world, why would anyone work to alleviate poverty or protect the environment? Historian Paul Boyer, whose book about prophecy belief in modern America was published in the early 1990s, wrote in a later article that "all of us would do well to pay attention to the beliefs of the vast company of Americans who read the headlines and watch the news through a filter of prophetic belief."[12]

## POPULAR THEOLOGY

The foregoing discussion is a summary of some of the terminology and perspectives that historians and formal theologians would bring to an analysis of the Left Behind books. They tend to focus on the influence of the books: supporters of the Left Behind series were excited about the possibilities for evangelization and conversion to what they saw as proper belief that arose from the popularity of the novels, and critics worried that the books were theologically misleading and socially and politically dangerous. Yet a discussion of the influence of the books, good or bad, does not address a further question. *Why* were the books popular? Why did so many people in the general public respond to them?

This is more than a question of idle curiosity, because the answer may help us glimpse some aspects of the beliefs of "average" Americans. When analyzing popular culture, one of the most basic axioms is that popular culture both influences us and reflects us. Assessments of popular culture seem to focus most often upon how it shapes or influences individuals and society. For example, does violence in the mass media help create a violent society? If women are portrayed consistently as victims or helpless bystanders in movies and television programs, does this repeated pattern influence the way young women envision themselves? Does television news coverage of events around the world contribute to a heightened global awareness? Such questions focus upon the influences of popular culture, whether evaluated positively or negatively.

But examining what is popular has potential to tell us about society in another way. Popular culture also reflects us. Examining what is popular is like holding up a mirror to see ourselves. The public decides what movies, television shows, music, and clothing styles become popular, sometimes surprising the pundits. The largest advertising budget does not necessarily bring the best results, indicating that the general public makes choices and cannot be seen as mere pawns of the creators or producers. Why does the public make the choices it does? In part, what we choose must resonate in some way, thus revealing our fears, hopes, yearnings, or assumptions. Admittedly, it is a speculative task to figure out what those are, but widespread patterns in popular culture can at least provide clues.

Two classic and frequently neglected books provide a theoretical framework for recognizing an unofficial belief system within the expressions of popular culture. The first is *Your God Is Alive and Well and Appearing in Popular Culture*, published in 1976 by John Wiley Nelson, a theology professor at Pittsburgh Theological Seminary. He claimed that there exists, alongside the traditional religions that many people acknowledge, an "American cultural religion." "Functioning societies in their most stable periods of self-understanding and expression," he wrote, "produce a single dominant set of values which unifies all the shared individual or small-group beliefs into one characteristic belief system." That dominant set of values is the basis of an American cultural religion. This sounds a bit like the thesis of Robert Bellah's famous essay "Civil Religion in America," written nine years earlier. But while Bellah focused mostly on the nation's symbols and leaders, Nelson examined examples of culture such as television, films, music, and popular literature as the expression and reaffirmation of the American cultural belief system.[13] Traditional religious institutions are explicit in stating what they believe and "in scheduling the ritual dramas

**American Politics and Apocalypticism**

Academics do need to pay more attention to the role of religious belief in American public life, not only in the past, but also today. Without close attention to the prophetic scenario embraced by millions of American citizens, the current political climate in the United States cannot be fully understood.

Leaders have always invoked God's blessing on their wars, and, in this respect, the Bush administration is simply carrying on a familiar tradition. But when our born-again president describes the nation's foreign-policy objective in theological terms as a global struggle against "evildoers," and when, in his recent State of the Union address, he casts Saddam Hussein as a demonic, quasi-supernatural figure who could unleash "a day of horror like none we have ever known," he is not only playing upon our still-raw memories of 9/11. He is also invoking a powerful and ancient apocalyptic vocabulary that for millions of prophecy believers conveys a specific and thrilling message of an approaching end—not just of Saddam, but of human history as we know it.

—Paul S. Boyer, "John Darby Meets Saddam Hussein: Foreign Policy and Bible Prophecy," *Chronicle of Higher Education* 49, no. 23 (February 14, 2003): B12.

of reaffirmation, that is, the worship services. American cultural religion is much less recognizably explicit, but no less powerfully pervasive in our lives." For Nelson, popular culture, such as watching television in the family room of a suburban home, is the worship experience for the American cultural religion.[14]

When Nelson attempted to discern a creed of basic beliefs in the American cultural religion, he used a template of questions that obviously arose from his own background in Christian theology. In each example of popular culture, he asked:

- What was unsatisfactory about the present situation?
- What was its source (the nature and the source of evil)?
- What was the delivering force that defeated the evil?
- What would a resolved situation look like?
- What is "the way," the path to follow in the interim?

The common answers to these questions, found in broad patterns of popular culture, would reveal the beliefs of the American cultural religion. Interestingly enough, while Nelson considered many examples of American popular culture in the twentieth century, he gave special emphasis to the western. He called the American western movie the "high mass" of the American cultural religion, because it communicated society's dominant belief system so effectively.

The second classic book, *The American Monomyth*, appeared only a year after Nelson's. More recently, authors Robert Jewett and John Shelton Lawrence published a substantially revised edition of the work under a new title, *The Myth of the American Superhero*. Many elements of their thesis were compatible with Nelson's views, but their initial volume was essentially completed before the appearance of Nelson's book, and they made no reference to his work. They discussed a similar dominant pattern in popular culture but extended it beyond the western.

Jewett and Lawrence were aware of Joseph Campbell's studies of myths, in which he found a single recurrent pattern in traditional mythological story lines. In *The Hero with a Thousand Faces*, Campbell summarized the plot of the *classical monomyth* as follows: "A hero ventures forth from the world of common day into a region of super-

natural wonder: fabulous forces are there encountered, and a decisive victory is won: the hero
comes back from this mysterious adventure with
the power to bestow boons on his fellow man."[15]
When Jewett and Lawrence surveyed American
popular culture they became convinced that this
plot did not describe most of what they saw. They
could detect a common plot or story line, but it
was different from the classical one. They argued
that a distinctively American monomyth had
emerged, and they summarized it in this way: "A
community in a harmonious paradise is threatened by evil: normal institutions fail to contend
with this threat: a selfless superhero emerges to
renounce temptations and carry out the redemptive task: aided by fate, his decisive victory restores
the community to its paradisal condition: the
superhero then recedes into obscurity."[16] This
outline of the dominant plot in American popular
culture sounds very much like a western, and it is
no surprise for Jewett and Lawrence, who traced
the American monomyth's development through
Indian captivity narratives, pulp fiction, westerns,
and comic book superheroes.

> ### American Cultural Religion
> All religions offer a system of beliefs
> and values, but so does American
> society. And the set of beliefs and
> values offered by American culture
> are not beliefs and values to which we
> are converted. We grow up believing
> that they are true. That's part of what it
> means to be an American. In fact, we
> learn them so well that most of the time
> we are not even fully conscious that
> we believe them. Every time we watch
> TV, read popular magazines or detec-
> tive fiction, listen to country music, go
> to the movies or professional sports
> events, we are having these American
> cultural beliefs and values reaffirmed.
> We are in fact attending worship ser-
> vices of the American cultural religion
> fifteen to twenty hours a week.
> —John Wiley Nelson, *Your God
> Is Alive and Well and Appearing
> in Popular Culture* (Philadelphia:
> Westminster, 1976), 16–17.

Jewett and Lawrence also noted the influ-
ence of religion upon these story lines. While the classical monomyth is essentially an initiation rite, the American monomyth is
a tale of redemption. The American monomyth "secularizes the
Judeo-Christian redemption dramas that have arisen on American
soil, combining elements from the selfless servant who impassively
gives his life for others and the zealous crusader who destroys evil.
The supersaviors in pop culture function as replacements for the
Christ figure, whose credibility was eroded by scientific rationalism.
But their superhuman abilities reflect a hope of divine, redemptive
powers that science has never eradicated from the popular mind."[17]
Thus, in the back-and-forth interplay between popular culture and
organized religion (especially Christianity as the majority religion

> **The Western as American Myth**
> The dominant belief system in American life has found a normative ritual form of expression in "the Western." In no other type of mythological drama is this dominant American salvation myth more comprehensively fixed.
> —John Wiley Nelson, *Your God Is Alive and Well and Appearing in Popular Culture* (Philadelphia: Westminster, 1976), 16–17.

in the United States), formal institutionalized religion has helped shape the basic form of the popular culture narrative, while popular culture in turn reaffirms, replaces, and revises aspects of the religious assumptions.

While Nelson, Jewett, and Lawrence all emphasize a singular dominant pattern in American popular culture, they also recognize that what is popular varies from subgroup to subgroup (arising from gender, race, ethnicity, social class, region, and more). In addition, various examples of popular culture intentionally spoof or seriously critique the dominant patterns, attempting to establish their own counterdominant traditions. However, even such variety highlights the presence of an overarching common pattern of pervasive beliefs and tendencies, as the alternative perspectives push against it.

## WESTERNS AND COMIC BOOKS

Throughout the twentieth century two patterns in American popular culture have been especially prominent: the western and the comic book superhero. Both have been pervasive and influential in the shape of American popular culture. Both are redemption dramas. Both express assumptions about the conflict between good and evil. Both resolve the conflicts through violence. A brief discussion of these two traditions should help demonstrate that the Left Behind books stand as much within the context of these patterns of popular culture as within a context of formal theology. Part of the reason that the general public could embrace the Left Behind series is the books' reaffirmation of messages long preached by American popular culture.

The western as a genre represents a long tradition in American popular culture, from Indian captivity narratives to dime novels to Buffalo Bill's Wild West Show; in fiction ranging from James Fenimore Cooper to Louis L'Amour; in countless radio dramas, movies, and television shows; even in the presidential styles of Teddy Roosevelt and Ronald Reagan and the "New Frontier" of John F. Kennedy. In 1902 what might be considered the prototypical example of western fiction was published: Owen Wister's *The Virginian*, which sold more than two million copies. By the middle of the century westerns literally flooded movie theatres and television screens. *The Virginian* became a Gary Cooper movie in 1929, and *Shane*, starring Alan Ladd and Jack Palance, appeared in 1953. Both films are considered classics of the western formula, representing innumerable movies that appeared in theaters from the 1930s through the 1970s. On television, westerns were important from the beginning of the medium in the 1940s and 1950s, reaching their peak in 1959, when twenty-six westerns aired in prime time. Many series from that time and thereafter are legendary: *Gunsmoke; The Lone Ranger; The Rifleman; Wanted Dead or Alive; Have Gun, Will Travel; Rawhide; Bonanza; The Big Valley; Maverick;* and more.

Fig. 8.3. The immensely popular 1953 movie *Shane* (with Alan Ladd and Brandon DeWilde, above) is a prototypical example of the Western with its dramatic and often simplistic depiction of the battle between good and evil. Photo © Underwood & Underwood/Corbis. Used by permission.

When looking for ways that popular culture either influences or reflects society, the strategy is to examine common patterns rather than exceptional unique examples. Thus, it is helpful to analyze the formula of the genre. In the case of the western, first of all the setting is the frontier, "the meeting point between savagery and civilization." In the words of John Wiley Nelson, "here the untamed, often savage wilderness makes its stand against the forces of law and order, who fight for the farmer, the schoolmarm, and the future of us all."[18] And the result is not in doubt, because everyone knows that the civilizing forces will win. The western is a ritual drama that repeats over and over that the mature, responsible, law-abiding forces will prevail. It is in a sense an eschatological setting, at the border between good and evil, with the result of the conflict already a foregone conclusion.

> ### The Popularity of Superheroes
>
> The characters [comic book superheroes like Superman and Batman] are popular not only because they embody childhood dreams, but because they provide us a way of fulfilling fundamental human yearnings that we carry with us no matter what our age.
>
> —Jenette Kahn, Introduction to Les Daniels, *DC Comics: Sixty Years of the World's Favorite Comic Book Heroes* (New York: Little, Brown, 1995), 12.

Regarding the characters in the drama, "the adversaries in the Western form are simplistically good and evil foes."[19] In the classic western, heroes and villains wore white hats and black hats. The villain was such a chilling personification of evil, expressing sadistic cruelty with a contemptuous sneer, that no force of kindness would ever be able to transform him. The evil villains came from the outside, such as the outlaw gang that rode into town or the scheming banker who represented corrupt politicians or heartless absentee bosses. The threatened townspeople were basically innocent but helpless. The only hope for deliverance came from the morally pure, respectful, self-sacrificing hero who appeared from elsewhere, destroyed the villains, reluctantly through violence, and then usually departed.

Most people assume that a western necessarily takes place in the American West of the 1800s. However, if the formula briefly outlined here provides the basic criteria for a western, it might be possible to claim that other stories beyond the American west are "westerns" too. Thus, several commentators have called *Star Wars* a space western, and John Wiley Nelson argued that the movie *Casablanca* was just as much a western as *Shane*. In this view, James Bond movies and numerous action adventure stories represent a continuation of the western genre in settings beyond the American West.

The rise of westerns in American popular culture was followed by comic books and their spandex superheroes, and their formula was remarkably similar to the western. Superman was the breakthrough character, created by Jerry Siegel and Joe Shuster, appearing for the first time in the June 1938 issue of *Action Comics*. Superman provided the model for most superheroes who followed, having amazing super powers, a secret identity, and a dramatic costume with capes and flourishes. Comic historian Les Daniels wrote of Superman that he was "an instant triumph, a concept so intense and so instantly identifiable that he became perhaps the most widely known figure ever created in American fiction."[20] Batman followed in 1939, along with Sandman,

Hawkman, and The Spirit. Flash, Green Lantern, The Shield, Captain Marvel, and White Streak appeared in 1940, and Wonder Woman, Captain America, Plastic Man, and Sub-Mariner came in 1941. It was a flood of characters, or, as comic book fans call it, the Golden Age of comics. Other "ages" followed, when Marvel Comics and Stan Lee introduced superheroes like Spiderman and the Fantastic Four with more personal struggles and foibles, and when some comic books moved beyond the superhero genre. Yet the superhero comic books retain a prominent role in American popular culture. Many who have never touched a comic book have seen television shows or movies based upon the genre.

In a comparison of superhero stories with the western formula, the setting is still the frontier between good and evil, but when supervillains as well as superheroes serve as the antagonists, the battleground is more cosmic. In the superhero stories frequently the nation, the world, or the entire universe is threatened by evil, not merely a town. Other characteristics are also present: the community is helpless in the face of danger or evil and needs help from outside, the superhero intervenes as a savior or deliverer, the characters tend to be simplistically good and evil, and in the end evil forces seldom are transformed. Resolution comes instead through the destruction of evil characters, or, when they are needed for sequels or continuing story lines, they are at least vanquished temporarily. (One reason Jewett and Lawrence personally are critical of this dominant narrative is that they believe it undercuts democracy. If the townspeople always need an outside deliverer, then they never take responsibility themselves, and after the superhero defeats evil and leaves, the community is no better prepared for the next threat than it was before.)

Over the years, comic book stories increasingly have used explicitly mythological language and visual symbols, consciously recognizing their religious connections. Perhaps the most dramatic example came from Jack Kirby, who worked for decades with both DC and Marvel comics, creating legendary characters and superhero teams. In the 1970s, he invented an entire mythological universe eventually dubbed the Fourth World, with comic book series titled "The New Gods," "The Forever People," and "Mister Miracle." The stories arose from a planet blown in half, creating two new conflicting worlds: New

Genesis, led by the benevolent Highfather, and Apokolips, led by the villain Darkseid. Beyond Kirby's creations, other comic book series carried titles like "Millennium" and "Zero Hour: Crisis in Time," and superheroes appeared in thinly disguised crucifixion poses on comic book covers.[21]

Westerns and comic book stories also were decidedly male-dominated, both in the demographics of their audiences and in the gender of the heroes, consistent with the patriarchal character of society and churches throughout much of the twentieth century. Yet just as gender emerged as an issue in society, it arose among comic book creators as well. The classic example comes from psychologist William Moulton Marston, best known for inventing the lie detector, who also published an article critical of comic books. Among other complaints he wrote, "It seemed to me, from a psychological angle, that the comics' worst offense was their blood-curdling masculinity."[22] An editor invited Marston to write a comic book of his own, and Wonder Woman was the very successful result, appearing in 1941–1942. While Marston wanted to provide a role model for girls, others complained about undertones of submission to men and even visual portrayals of bondage. At a minimum, Wonder Woman at least helped bring discussion of gender issues into the comic book world.

What religious messages or beliefs have the traditions of westerns and comic books repeatedly affirmed? A compelling case can be made for the presence of the following:

1. *Evil comes from the outside.* An external source of evil, such as an outlaw gang or aliens from another planet, is psychologically comforting for the public to accept, because it assures that "we" are not the problem.

2. *An outside redeemer brings deliverance.* When the threat to individuals or the community seems too overwhelming, the prospect of a Clint Eastwood or a Superman brings hope where none seemed otherwise possible. It also suggests that the community is incapable of solving the problem.

3. *People are good or evil, not both.* The villains in a *Lone Ranger* television show, a Batman comic book, or a James Bond movie are not the kind of people one could expect to change their ways as the result

of a heart-to-heart conversation. Terrorist villains in more recent action-adventure stories are also beyond redemption. People on both sides may have foibles or deceptive charm, but at heart they are either good or bad.

4. *The solution is the destruction of evildoers.* When the distinction between good and bad people is clear-cut, and when bad people cannot be changed, there is only one way to eliminate evil: kill the evildoers. In how many action-adventure movies are the villains transformed to a new way of living. (Very few.) How often do they die? (Most of the time.) Situations are resolved through "redemptive violence."[23]

Such assumptions or beliefs are at least a portion of the creed of what John Wiley Nelson called the "American cultural religion." The apocalyptic fiction of LaHaye and Jenkins stands directly in the tradition of the American monomyth, the dominant story line represented by westerns, comic books, and more. The setting of the Left Behind books is literally eschatological, on the frontier of good and evil; the adversaries are simplistically good and evil foes; the evil comes from the outside (the Antichrist, indwelt by Satan); humans are incapable of resolving the situation; and deliverance must come from a savior (in this case, Christ himself) through the righteous destruction of evil and the evildoers. In addition, the Left Behind leaders are overwhelmingly male, although the roles of women are more complicated than one might expect.[24] The Left Behind books reaffirm every one of the four beliefs or assumptions numbered above. In a sense, the Left Behind books bring the discussion full circle, back to explicit religion, because Jewett and Lawrence contended that the American monomyth was basically a redemption drama rooted in Judeo-Christian traditions that had been secularized.

Thus, even though it is relevant to analyze the Left Behind books in light of formal Christian theology, such as the differences between various Christian understandings of millennialism, it is equally important to recognize that the books represent themes long repeated and reaffirmed in American popular culture, throughout the twentieth century. Seen in this context, the Left Behind books are yet another Arnold Schwarzenegger or Indiana Jones movie, with explicit religious imagery added. Because many of the Left Behind messages resonate so well with a pervasive unofficial, informal theology revealed in popular culture, they lead us to consider what many ordinary Americans believe, within the Christian church and beyond it.

Various Christian leaders may be disturbed by the four beliefs outlined above, wanting to argue instead that human beings are mixed, simultaneously saints and sinners, and that humans might be transformed, not just condemned and destroyed. Critics also may be dismayed by the advocacy of violence in the name of God. The point here is that the Left Behind books did not originate these debated themes, which are deeply embedded American assumptions and beliefs revealed and reaffirmed in long traditions of American popular culture.

## FOR FURTHER READING

Boyer, Paul. *When Time Shall Be No More: Prophecy Belief in Modern American Culture.* Cambridge: Harvard University Press, 1992.

Forbes, Bruce David, and Jeanne Halgren Kilde, eds. *Rapture, Revelation, and the End Times: Exploring the Left Behind Series.* New York: Palgrave Macmillan, 2004.

Frykholm, Amy Johnson. *Rapture Culture: Left Behind in Evangelical America.* New York: Oxford University Press, 2004.

Jewett, Robert, and John Shelton Lawrence. *Captain America and the Crusade against Evil: The Dilemma of Zealous Nationalism.* Grand Rapids: Eerdmans, 2003.

Lawrence, John Shelton, and Robert Jewett. *The Myth of the American Superhero.* Grand Rapids: Eerdmans, 2002.

Nelson, John Wiley. *Your God Is Alive and Well and Appearing in Popular Culture.* Philadelphia: Westminster, 1976.

Slotkin, Richard. *Gunfighter Nation: The Myth of the Frontier in Twentieth-Century America.* Norman: University of Oklahoma Press, 1998.

Weber, Eugen. *Apocalypses: Prophecies, Cults, and Millennial Beliefs through the Ages.* Cambridge: Harvard University Press, 1999.

# CATHOLICS
# IN CHINA

## JEAN-PAUL WIEST

CHAPTER NINE

The situation of the Catholic Church in China at the very end of the twentieth century was complex and constantly evolving.* The most common view of the church highlights two extremes: the church that is recognized by the government, and the underground church that is in hiding. In fact, increasing numbers of Catholic believers belong to a large gray area between these two. The government-recognized part of the Catholic Church functions openly in churches registered with the government and is linked to the *Zhongguo Tianzhujiao Aiguohui*, or Chinese Catholic Patriotic Association (CCPA). It is therefore often referred to as *guanfang* (or *gongkai*) *jiaohui*, the open church. The other extreme, often referred to as *dixia jiaohui*, the underground church, refuses any control by the CCPA and usually operates in private homes or buildings without seeking government approval.

There are no perfect terms to identify these two clearly distinct manifestations of the Catholic Church in China. I would recommend avoiding labels such as "patriotic church" to describe the government-recognized segment of the church because it implies either that all its members wholeheartedly support the CCPA or that the underground church is not patriotic minded, neither of which is true. Likewise, the names "suffering church" and "loyal church" to describe the underground segment of the church are wrong and divisive, as they falsely imply that the government-recognized church has not suffered or is not loyal to the pope.

Chinese Catholics all love their country. Their moral values and habits of hard work make them model citizens. In this sense they are

*This chapter was originally published as "Catholics in China: The Bumpy Road toward Reconciliation" by Jean-Paul Wiest. Reprinted from the *International Bulletin of Missionary Research*, January 2003, by permission of the Overseas Ministries Study Center, New Haven, Conn. For details, visit www.InternationalBulletin.org.

231

clearly patriotic. The vast majority worship openly or would like to, provided they would not be controlled by the CCPA. Many, even in the government-recognized churches, remain suspicious of the CCPA and would like to see it disappear.

In this chapter, then, I view the Catholic Church in China as one church, not as two (one faithful to Rome versus one that is not). It is certainly a wounded church, but the division did not lead to the formation of a schismatic church because the difference never amounted to a doctrinal deviation or a total breach of communion with the worldwide Roman Catholic Church. The Holy See has never issued a formal declaration of a Chinese schism, nor has it explicitly excommunicated any "patriotic" bishop.[1] In fact, there are increasingly hopeful signs that healing between the different groups is in the making, though the road toward reconciliation has recently included some unpleasant bumps.

## GOVERNMENT-RECOGNIZED SEGMENT

The roots of the division between the two parts of the Chinese Catholic Church can be traced to the emergence of the CCPA in 1957. Formed on the model of the *Sanzhi Aiguo Yundong,* or Three-Self Patriotic Movement—a Protestant group organized in 1954 under the control of the government to force the churches to break their economic and political ties with the West and become thoroughly self-governing, self-supporting, and self-propagating—the CCPA was to serve as a bridge between the church and the state.

By late 1957, because of the prior expulsion of foreign bishops and the subsequent imprisonment of Chinese prelates who opposed the regime or rejected the CCPA, 120 out of 145 dioceses and prefectures apostolic were without ordinaries. The clergy in several districts considered filling the vacancies a real apostolic need and, at the urging of their local CCPA branch, began the process of choosing a new bishop. After electing a candidate each, the Dioceses of Wuchang and the Wuhan in Hubei Province telegraphed the names to the Holy See for the pope's approval. The Congregation for the Propagation of the Faith turned down their requests, however, because it saw these selections of bishops by the Chinese as an attempt to put in place "patriotic" ordinaries who would simply carry out the Communist government policy.

There is no doubt that the Chinese government was, and still is, trying to exercise a large measure of control over the church. In all fairness, however, one must also acknowledge that the requests came from a Chinese clergy who, in the midst of intense pressures, still acknowledged the pope's privilege to appoint bishops. Only when their plea was rejected did they decide to proceed anyway, on the ground that the Holy See had failed to realize the difficulty of their situation. On April 13, 1958, "patriotic" bishop Li Daonan of the neighboring Diocese of Puqi performed the consecration of the two bishops in the Hankou cathedral. Thus began the ordinations of bishops sponsored by the CCPA but not recognized by the pope. In church parlance, such bishops are "illegitimate." In canonical terms, however, their consecration, although "illicit," remains perfectly valid.

Saddened by the news of the consecration of the two new bishops, Pope Pius XII issued the encyclical *Ad apostolorum principis*, in which he expressed his disapproval of the CCPA and reiterated that the authority for making episcopal appointments was his alone. Not unexpectedly, the Chinese government reacted by forbidding church authorities to have any further contact with the Vatican. A question was even inserted in the ritual of episcopal ordination that made new bishops-elect promise to "be detached from all control of the Roman Curia." The intention of the question, as explained by a "patriotic" bishop, was not to reject papal authority but to object to the Vatican's rejection of Chinese-elected episcopal candidates.[2] Bishops, priests, sisters, and laypeople who refused to go along with the government and the CCPA stance were sent to jail or labor camps. In 1958, prayer for the pope was removed from the public prayers of the church. By 1962, the number of "patriotic" bishops had reached forty-two, while those formerly appointed by Rome had fallen to about twenty.

The division between the two groups became fully apparent only after the end of the Cultural Revolution (1966–1976), during which all public religious activities ceased and all church properties were confiscated. By 1979, clergy were allowed to return to their dioceses. The new policy of the government allowed them to function in public, rather than in hiding, and many began doing so. With fewer than thirty bishops still alive, some prelates who had been imprisoned for their unswerving loyalty to the pope and had refused any relationship with the CCPA were now more willing to cooperate with the association for the future of the Catholic Church in China.

After 1981, the requirement to swear independence from Rome was dropped, which resulted in more priests willing to accept episcopal ordination. In addition, several of the "illicit" bishops have secretly obtained legitimization of their status from the pope. Some even actively sought higher positions within the CCPA in order to influence its decisions and curb its tendency toward unilateral control.

In late May 1980, more than two hundred delegates representing the government-registered Catholic Church gathered in Beijing to attend the Third National Convention of the CCPA and the National Catholic Representatives Assembly. These two meetings resulted in a major reorganization of structures within the open church with the creation of two additional national organizations: the Chinese Catholic Church Administrative Commission and the Chinese Catholic Bishops' Conference. From this point forward, the CCPA relinquished its role as overseer of all church concerns, relegating itself to external affairs and church-state relations. Responsibility for doctrinal and pastoral affairs was given over to the clergy and church leaders. In 1992, further reorganization placed the Bishops' Conference on an equal footing with the CCPA while reducing the Church Administrative Commission to a committee responsible for pastoral affairs under the control of the Bishops' Conference. Five additional committees were also set up to oversee seminary education, liturgy, theological study, finance development, and international relationships. Initiatives in the areas of pastoral work, training of clergy, and the social apostolate of the church indicate that the new structures have been effectively implemented.

With many ups and downs, the open church's attitude toward papal primacy has gradually improved. The prayer for the pope was reintroduced into the Collection of Important Prayers in 1982. In February 1989, the government allowed spiritual affiliation with the Holy See, and in April of the same year the new Bishops' Conference promptly acknowledged the pope as the spiritual leader of the Chinese church. By the end of the decade, most congregations had also restored the prayer for the pope during Mass.

## UNDERGROUND SEGMENT OF THE CATHOLIC CHURCH

Many clergy released at the end of the Cultural Revolution were still unwilling to join any Catholic organization registered with the government. They refused to live at a church with other priests who had married, betrayed others, or publicly denied the primacy of the pope. They therefore carried out religious activities in private and gradually attracted a great number of Catholics to join with them. Bishop Fan Xueyan of the Diocese of Baoding in Hebei Province was released in 1979 and acted as the leader of the underground church. Recognizing the urgent need for bishops in several dioceses, he ordained three bishops in 1981 without first securing approval from the government or the open church. When the pope learned of the circumstances that prompted such a procedure, he legitimized the new bishops and granted them and Bishop Fan special faculties to ordain successors as well as bishops for vacant seats of neighboring dioceses. By 1989, the underground church had more than fifty bishops, who in November of that year set up their own episcopal conference. Rome also gave underground bishops the authority to ordain priests without the required lengthy seminary training. This concession has accounted for the overall poor theological instruction of priests in the underground church. Moreover, signs of excess and lack of coordination have appeared, with some dioceses having as many as three bishops claiming to be the legitimate ordinary.

Fig. 9.1. Catholics in Shaanxi Province, 1999. Photo © Yang Yankang /Agence VU. Used by permission

Since 1989 the underground church has been the target of mounting pressure from the government. The same government document of February 1989 that recognized the

spiritual leadership of the pope also spelled out how to deal with the underground church. Communist cadres were asked to differentiate between underground forces that clung to their hostility and stirred up believers and those who did not join the open church because of their faith in the pope. The former, said the document, must be dealt with severely, while patience should be used with the others. Accordingly, the government regarded the setting up of an episcopal conference by the clandestine bishops as a provocation. This evaluation resulted in the arrest of several leaders, including Bishop Fan. At the local level the implementation of that policy has remained vague and vacillating, resulting in sporadic destruction of unregistered religious buildings, temporary detention, and the levy of heavy fines. Since the ban of the Falung Gong in July 1999, however, repressive measures against Catholic communities not officially registered have also greatly increased. Several priests and bishops remain in prison or have had their activities curtailed.

Many underground Catholics play a prophetic role by their refusal to participate in a government-sanctioned organization. They dare to challenge the government policy regarding human rights and freedom of religion from a Catholic standpoint.

## RECONCILIATION IN THE MAKING

The bitter division has pitted those who choose to worship under the supervision of the government against those who refuse to do so. During the past twenty years the two sides have gradually moved away from mistrust and bitter accusations to an attitude of understanding respect and to concrete acts of cooperation and genuine efforts at reconciliation. The dividing lines between the two are becoming increasingly blurred. Fidelity to the Holy See has become less of an issue, since the pope has legitimized most of the bishops in the open church, and a number of new ones are being ordained with his approval.

For an ever-growing number of clergy, sisters, and ordinary Christians, the division does not make much sense anymore. In a courageous and prophetic manner many act as bridges between the two sides of the church, and the late Pope John Paul II made repeated pleas to the Catholics of China to display toward one another "a love which consists of understanding, respect, forbearance, forgiveness and reconciliation."[3]

The more serious reconciliation issue involves the still-unresolved tensions between the People's Republic of China and the Vatican. Informal talks between the two sides about the normalization of diplomatic relations have taken place intermittently since the late 1980s. Beijing realizes that it has much to gain from restoring such ties but insists on two main points: Rome must first sever its relations with Taiwan, and it must not interfere with the election of Chinese bishops. The Vatican sees diplomatic normalization as leading to greater freedom for the church and to possibilities for a solid implantation.

Church officials have indicated that they are ready to establish relations with Beijing, but first an agreement must be reached over the Holy See's relationship with Chinese Catholics. In late 1999, the news spread that both sides had made substantial progress toward bridging the gap between Beijing's demand for a total and complete independence of the Chinese church and Rome's insistence on an autonomous Chinese church in communion with the pope and the universal church. But during the course of the year 2000, two events—the ordinations of bishops without papal mandate on January 6 and Rome's October 1 canonization of 120 martyrs who died in China—seriously undermined the process. These misunderstandings point to the distance that still separates the Holy See and the Chinese government.

## AN OFFENSE TO ROME: NONAPPROVED ORDINATIONS

The ordination on January 6, 2000, of five bishops approved by the CCPA but not approved previously by Rome represents a major source of contention between China and the Holy See. Canon Law 377 states clearly that "the Supreme Pontiff freely appoints Bishops or confirms those lawfully elected." The Vatican thus refuses to sanction any bishop named independently by Chinese or any other civil authority, while Beijing, in defiance of church law, claims the right (since 1958) to appoint bishops.

**Fig. 9.2.** Catholic ceremony in Shaanxi Province, 1994. Photo © Yang Yankang / Agence VU. Used by permission

Circumstances surrounding this ordination, however, point clearly to a rift within the open church. We know now that original plans called for an even larger ordination ceremony, but several open church bishops disapproved and refused to attend the ceremony, as did the teachers and seminarians of the national seminary in Beijing. Accordingly, all but five ordinands bowed out of the ceremony. These five, however, felt the pressure of the government and the national CCPA to be ordained without seeking prior papal approval. This incident shows clearly that the prevailing mood within the open church inclines toward full support of existing church laws. Repressive measures from the government have been unable to reverse the trend.

How the Vatican chooses bishops in China remains a problem, but not an insoluble one. A likely compromise is for the Vatican to choose bishops in consultation with the Chinese government. No agreement can be reached, however, until the two sides resume dialogue.

## AN OFFENSE TO BEIJING: CANONIZATION OF MARTYRS

On October 1, 2000, as a proud China celebrated the fifty-first anniversary of its founding as a republic, the worldwide Roman Catholic Church proclaimed as saints 120 Catholics who died on Chinese soil, 86 of them during the Boxer Uprising in 1900. The timing of this canonization resulted in a bitter exchange of words between the two parties that once again derailed precarious efforts toward reestablishing diplomatic relations.

The history of turbulent relations between China and the Roman Catholic Church is littered with elements of cultural disparity; in this instance the problem centers on the meaning attached to dates. For Chinese people, October has a special meaning. On October 18, 1860, British and French troops burned down the magnificent summer palace resort known as the Yuanming Yuan. Forty years later, precisely during this same month of October, another rampaging foreign force was in the midst of pillaging the capital. By contrast, October 10, 1911 (the Wuchang Uprising against the Qing Dynasty, the beginning of the overthrow of the imperial regime), and October 1, 1949 (the birth of the republic), stand as symbols of the indomitable spirit of the Chinese people and their resolve to forge their own destiny.

October is likewise a unique month for Roman Catholic devotion. First, it is the month of Our Lady of the Rosary, a designation based on a key naval battle at Lepanto, Greece, on October 7, 1571, when Christian forces defeated Ottoman Muslims. Western missionaries brought to China the cult of Mary and the recitation of the Rosary, so much so that in some parts of Hebei, Catholics are known as Old Rosary Sayers. Today, the two most common pictures found in Catholic churches and homes are still those of the Sacred Heart of Jesus and the Virgin Mary, and the most popular form of devotion remains the prayers of the Rosary. October is also referred to as Mission Month because special emphasis is put on reminding Catholic faithful of their responsibility to ensure that Christian belief is spread to the entire world. The month opens with the feast of St. Theresa of the Holy Child, patron saint of missions, who spent her life praying for the conversion of non-Christians. Chinese Catholics have a great devotion to St. Theresa, with whom they readily identify because, not being allowed to preach the gospel openly, they too rely on the power of prayer.

Each October, the third or fourth Sunday is set aside as Mission Sunday to promote mission awareness among the faithful and to secure funding for the missionary enterprise. Since it was established in 1926, Mission Sunday has been closely related to China because it was on October 28, 1926, that the first six Chinese bishops of modern times were ordained by Pope Pius XI. Mission Sunday is emphasized by a papal message that always pays special tribute to those who died a violent death because of their faith. In 2000, John Paul II opened Mission Month with the canonization of 120 martyrs who died in China. What prompted the decision was the fact that close to three-fourths of the people added to the list of saints were killed by the Boxers exactly a hundred years earlier. Rome acknowledged that the canonization had been postponed several times in the past because it was a "highly sensitive question." Yet it went ahead in 2000, insisting that the decision was "a purely religious matter" with no political overtone. It simply "rendered justice to the historical reality" of 30,000 innocent people killed by "Boxer rebels."

Pointing to another historical reality, Beijing, for its part, denounced the event as a painful reminder of how, until recently, missionaries and Chinese converts had been agents and lackeys of colonialist and imperialist nations. It called the canonization ceremony of October 1 an "open insult" to the Chinese people, who on that same day celebrated the fifty-first anniversary of their throwing off foreign control and aggression. In stark contrast to this response, when a few months earlier the Russian Orthodox Church canonized 222 Chinese Orthodox martyrs, the Chinese government did not raise any criticism. Many of these Christians were killed during the nights of June 11 and 24, 1900, during the same Boxer Uprising.

On October 24, 2001, a year after the canonization dispute, the pope acknowledged that historically members of the church had had to work within the context of "complex historical events and conflicting political interests," and that their work "was not always without errors." These errors, the pope said, "may have given the impression of a lack of esteem for the Chinese people on the part of the Catholic Church, making them feel that the church was motivated by feelings of hostility towards China. For all this I ask forgiveness and understanding of those who may have felt hurt in some way by such actions on the part of Christians." But this response was not enough for China. On October 30 a Chinese spokesperson, although viewing the apology as "a positive move," said that the pope had "not made a clear-cut apology for the canonization incident, which seriously hurt the feelings of the Chinese people."[4]

## LOOKING FORWARD TO THE TWENTY-FIRST CENTURY

In 1950, China had a Catholic population of about three million, with 1,900 Chinese priests and 3,700 Chinese sisters. In 1980, it was estimated that fewer than 1,300 elderly Chinese priests were actively engaged in ministry. The situation of Chinese sisters was even more discouraging: by 1980 just over 1,000 remained. Obviously the training of new church leaders and the reopening of seminaries and novitiates were most urgent priorities. Sheshan Regional Seminary near Shanghai was the first Catholic house of formation to reopen in 1982.

At the turn of the twenty-first century, twenty-four major seminaries were allowed to operate with government permission, and another ten existed in the underground church. Altogether they prepared 1,700 seminarians. Sisters in formation totaled 2,500, spread over forty novitiates in the open church and twenty in the underground. With a total of 2,200 priests and 3,600 sisters, the number of religious workers seemed to be on the rebound. Churches and chapels reopened for public worship with government approval had multiplied and stood at 5,500. The Catholic Church population was estimated at more than twelve million, a rate of growth that had only kept up with the population growth since 1949. By comparison, Chinese Protestants displayed much more vitality by growing from less than three million to at least twenty-five million members, or twice the population growth. Factors behind the relatively slow growth of the Catholic Church are many and complex, and certainly include the bitter inner dispute that has been so divisive.

Fig. 9.2. Catholic woman in Shaanxi Province, 1998. Photo © Yang Yankang / Agence VU. Used by permission

The Catholic Church's educational activities came to an abrupt end in the 1950s. Private schools reemerged in the early 1980s under the impetus of Deng Xiaoping, but the government has made a clear distinction between private schools as houses of religious formation and training and private schools as alternative options within the public education system. While the five recognized religions (Taoism, Buddhism, Islam, Protestantism, and Catholicism) are permitted to open the former under certain conditions, they are barred from any involvement in public education.

Yet in a country where church educational activities remain drastically curtailed, Catholic publishing houses such as Sapientia Press in Beijing, Guangqi Press in Shanghai, and Hebei Faith Press in Shijiazhuang, together with the Protestant Amity Press in Nanjing, are important means for reaching and educating a great number of Christian and non-Christian Chinese. They publish Bibles, Christian literature, and journals and have also reprinted in simplified characters many of the Chinese translations arriving in recent years from Taiwan and Hong Kong, such as the documents of Vatican II, the liturgy of the Mass, the new code of canon law, and the new universal catechism. Unfortunately, except for *Zhongguo Tianzhujiao* (The Catholic Church in China), the official journal of the CCPA, church publications remain subject to the government censor and may legally be sold only on church premises or through mail order.

The Hebei Faith Press also publishes a biweekly newspaper called *Xinde* (Faith). In spite of the restriction just mentioned, it has a distribution of forty-five thousand copies throughout most of the provinces of China, which amounts to a readership of over half a million people in the underground and the open Catholic Church, as well as among non-Christians. Besides relaying news of the church within and outside China, the newspaper also encourages readers to act responsively by sending funds for various charitable causes and major catastrophes. Responses have been so enthusiastic that they have led to the establishment of *Beifang Jinde* (Progress), a Catholic social service center formed to handle donations for charity work in society.

Some outside organizations foster a confrontational and adversarial position on the situation of the Chinese church. Such groups, however, are in direct defiance of the pope's pleas for understanding, forgiveness, reconciliation, and unity among Chinese Catholics. The Chinese Catholic Church today is quite different even from what it was in the 1980s, when it emerged from long years of repression. It is growing in numbers, enjoying relative freedom of worship, and experiencing a renewal of vocations to the priesthood and religious life. At the same time, Chinese society is undergoing profound social and economic changes. This transformation is confronting the church with new issues and challenges as it begins to shed its ghetto mentality and to fulfill a more meaningful role for various segments of the society.

Pope Benedict XVI sent a letter to Chinese Catholics on Pentecost Sunday 2007.[5] It may signal a point of no return at several levels: first within the Chinese Catholic Church itself; second, in the dialogue between the Chinese government and the Vatican; and third, in relations between the government and the Chinese Catholic Church.

Concerned above all with the unity of the Roman Catholic Church, Benedict XVI speaks not of the "official church" and the "underground church" but only of the "Church which is in China." He offers all Chinese Catholics an invitation to pardon and reconciliation: "the purification of memory, the pardoning of wrong-doers, the forgetting of injustices suffered and the loving restoration of serenity require moving beyond personal positions or viewpoints. These are urgent steps that must be taken to signify authentic bonds of communion with the local Church and with the universal Church." The pope also gives a clear answer to burning questions that have divided the Chinese Church internally for twenty years. For instance, the Eucharist celebrated by priests and bishops who are both in communion with the pope and recognized by the civil authorities is valid, and so are also all the other sacraments they administer.

In his letter the pope addresses not only Chinese Catholics but also government authorities. He invites them to dialogue that would transcend misunderstanding and incomprehension and make way for new forms of communication and collaboration for the good of the Chinese people and for peace in the world. He assures them that he is not a political authority and that the mission of the Church in China is to proclaim Christ, not to change the internal structure of the state. The Church invites Catholics, he assures civil authorities, to be good citizens who contribute respectfully and actively to the common good. Likewise the Church expects the state to guarantee Catholic citizens the full exercise of their faith and not to interfere in matters of faith and discipline.

While offering an olive branch of peace, the pope also states clearly where no compromise is possible. Without naming it specifically, the pope denounces the Patriotic Association's claim to place its members above the bishops and to guide the church community, particularly condemning its declared purpose to foster independence and autonomy, self-management, and democratic administration of the Church.

To the Chinese Church the letter gives the pastoral directives it greatly needs to overcome its division and achieve reconciliation To the civil authorities, it brings a new offer of dialogue based on mutual respect and deeper understanding. On December 18, 2007, during a study session of the entire Polit Bureau on religion, China's president Hu Jintao spoke of religion's role in the construction of a harmonious society and of the necessity for the communist party to take that into account. Time will tell of the full impact of the pope's letter, particularly on the ordinary Catholics of China, but its historical significance seems already certain.

## FOR FURTHER READING

Chan, Kim-Kwong. *Towards a Contextual Ecclesiology: The Catholic Church in the People's Republic of China (1979–1983), Its Life and Theological Implications.* Hong Kong: Chinese Church Research Center, 1987.

Kindopp, Jason, and Carol Lee Hamrin. *God and Caesar in China: Policy Implications of Church-State Tensions.* Washington, D.C.: Brookings, 2004.

Lam, Anthony S.K. The Catholic Church in Present-Day China: Through Darkness and Light. Hong Kong: The Holy Spirit Centre, 1997.

Lambert, Tony. *China's Christian Millions: The Costly Revival.* Grand Rapids: Kregel, 2000.

Lee, Joseph Tse-Hei. "Christianity in Contemporary China: An Update". Journal of State and Church 49, no. 2 (Spring 2007): 277–304.

Leung, Beatrice, and William R. Liu. *The Chinese Church in Conflict: 1949–2001.* Boca Raton, Fl.: Universal, 2004.

Lozada, Eriberto P., Jr., *God Aboveground: Catholic Church, Postsocialist State, and Transnational Processes in a Chinese Village.* Stanford: Stanford University Press, 2001.

Madsen, Richard. *China's Catholics: Tragedy and Hope in an Emerging Civil Society.* Comparative Studies in Religion and Society 12. Berkeley: University of California Press, 1998.

Minter, Adam. "Keeping Faith". *The Atlantic,* July/August 2007. See website, http://www.theatlantic.com/doc/200707/chinese-bishop.

Mooney, Paul. "Faith in the Countryside: Catholics in China." *National Catholic Reporter* 42, no. 10 (January 6, 2006): 12–13.

Tang, Edmond, and Jean-Paul Wiest. *The Catholic Church in Modern China: Perspectives.* Maryknoll, N.Y.: Orbis Books, 1993.

# EXISTENTIAL RITUALIZING IN POSTMODERN SWEDEN

## VALERIE DEMARINIS

Living in and being myself a product of the country that is considered the most secularized in the world, does not mean that spiritual questions or questions about existence are not important. In fact, they may be even more so here because everything is so private around this topic. . . . However, what we really need in Sweden are safe places where people can go and maybe new kinds of groups they can join so that they can feel they belong somewhere and get renewed. This in my opinion is the function of a "sacred place" today. In my medical office I can provide support, information, treatment, and medication, but I cannot and should not try to provide a community of comfort and caring. That is outside my responsibility and competency. How to build such safe and sacred places is another question. I only know the need for such is very great.

—A consulting psychiatrist in urban Sweden[1]

The primary religious response to secularism in postmodern Sweden is what I call "existential ritualizing." My approach to the subject matter here is shaped by my research in the psychology of religion as informed by cultural and health psychology. The central focus in this approach is trying to grasp how people are creating existential meaning in their lives, where in this process difficulties are occurring, and how the problems are addressed. The term "existential" is used here as an umbrella term for the different expressions of meaning-making that may include or exclude a specific transcendent aspect, or may combine elements of different belief traditions. It is a functional orientation using a wide filter, with the intention of catching the many-faceted dimensions of how people are struggling to make existential meaning in this cultural context. The term implies what an individual or group considers to be of ultimate concern, what would commonly be included under the term "spiritual" in English-speaking countries as interpreted with a wide lens. The term "ritualizing" is used here to mean special actions that have a symbolic value for the person involved. When combined with the adjective "existential," ritualizing refers to meaning-making actions that help the person or group feel connected to the source of life, however that is imaged. The term "postmodern" describes the perspective on the nature of things and how they are to be approached. This vantage point is one of choice, which stands for critical questioning, innovation, confrontation of absolutes, and the necessity of raising  suspicions. In reality, however, this situation of choice in the extreme can become a burden leading to an inability to find existential meaning and identity.[2]

## SWEDISH VALUES

Data from the World Values Surveys and the European Values Surveys, measuring the beliefs and values of most of the world's peoples, have been collected at intervals after the initial study in 1981. Factor analysis of national-level data from the forty-three societies included in the 1990 World Values Survey and supported by the 1995 and 2000 waves, from eighty societies, identified two main dimensions that account for more than half of the cross-national variance in more than a score of variables that tap into basic values across a wide range of domains, including politics, economic life, sexual behavior, and religion. The first is the Traditional/Secular-Rational dimension, which reflects the contrast between the relatively religious and traditional values that most often prevail in agrarian societies and the relatively secular, bureaucratic, and rational values that most often prevail in urban, industrialized societies. "Traditional societies emphasize the importance of religion, deference to authority, parent-child ties and two-parent traditional families, and absolute moral standards; they reject divorce, abortion, euthanasia, and suicide, and tend to be patriotic and nationalistic. In contrast, societies with secular-rational values display the opposite preferences on all of these topics."[3] Thus Sweden, scoring high on the Secular-Rational dimension, places less importance on organized religion, has a large percent of the population living together though not married, respects the rights of children, and permits both divorce and abortion. Euthanasia and suicide are not permitted, though the rate of suicide is high. Though proud of being Swedish, ethnic Swedes generally are not nationalistic.

The second dimension is that of Survival/Self-Expression. Societies ranking high on Survival values tend to emphasize "materialistic orientations and traditional gender roles; they are relatively intolerant of foreigners, gays and lesbians and other out-groups, show relatively low levels of subjective well-being, rank relatively low on interpersonal trust, and emphasize hard work, rather than imagination or tolerance, as important things to teach a child. Societies that emphasize Self-Expression values display the opposite preferences on all of these topics."[4] Ranking high on the Self-Expression dimension, Sweden is well-known for its generous immigration policy, equality for men and women, a strong welfare state, and high subjective well-being, high degree of interpersonal trust, and the encouragement of a well-balanced life in which work is balanced by interests and familial as well as social activities. Sweden is the society that represents the extreme of the Secular-Rational and Self-Expression dimensions. Sweden also is the country that has consistently had the lowest scores for church-oriented religion in these surveys.[5]

In this country with a population of just over nine million people, the welfare state model remains one of the most advanced in Europe. This means that the taxation system is high, as are the educational, social and health care benefits. Sweden is the only one of the Scandinavian countries that has, in modern history, never been occupied or directly involved in a major war. It has a high standard of living, and the encompassing dimension of the welfare state has included a model of care from the cradle to the grave.

## THE CHURCH OF SWEDEN

In this welfare model, up to the year 2000, Sweden had a state church: the Church of Sweden, based on the Protestant evangelical Lutheran tradition. To glimpse the importance of this transition at the turn of the current century, a very brief historical overview is required.

From the twelfth century all Swedish kings were Christian, and Christianity was the official religion. Sweden was a province of the Roman Catholic Church. A large number of churches were built throughout the country. The national format with locally organized church districts became the social governmental format that still exists today. During this period the cloister system developed that played a significant role in providing social welfare, education, and dissemination of knowledge and cultural information from other parts of the world.

> ### The Church of Sweden and Meaning-Making
>
> The Church of Sweden until the year 2000 was the state Church of Sweden and thus has had—and still upholds—a national meaning-making function which cannot be compared with any other of the meaning-making institutions in Sweden. Since, in other words, the Church of Sweden maintains a vicarious meaning-making function; I believe it is accurate to see this church as the meaning-making background against which the institutionally un-affiliated make their individual choices.
>
> —Maria Liljas, *Ritual Invention: A Play Perspective on Existential Ritual and Mental Health in Late Modern Sweden* (Uppsala: Uppsala University Press, 2005), 120.

In the sixteenth century the Protestant Reformation brought an official transition from the Roman Catholic to the evangelical Lutheran orientation. Swedish became the language used in church services, and the Bible was translated into Swedish. The church and state were joined in the seventeenth century, and the Evangelical Lutheran Church became the official and the only permitted religion. During the eighteenth century both internal and external opposition to the religious monopoly of the Church of Sweden arose and led in the nineteenth century to the creation of splinter groups within and outside the official church. The Swedish Baptist, Methodist, Mission, and Salvation Army movements became separate worshiping communities. In 1860, it became possible to leave the state church in order to worship in another evangelical organization. In 1862, the church and state districts became separate organizations, resulting in the state assuming responsibility for education and social welfare. In accordance with the freedom of religion law in 1951, it became possible to leave the state church without joining another religious organization.

In 1991, the national tax office assumed responsibility for all national and local registers. From 1996, baptism became the requirement for state church membership, previously an automatic affiliation from birth. In 2000 the Church of Sweden transitioned from the official state church to an independent religious organization, yet with powerful ties to the state.[6] The Church of Sweden remains, for the majority of ethnic Swedes, a living part of their cultural if not always active religious heritage.

But long before this official change, church attendance began to decline, with currently only about 5 percent of the population attending Sunday worship services regularly. The Church of Sweden, even after the official split from its state function, remains in a privileged position socially, and its rituals of baptism, marriage, and burial remain in wide use. In addition to traditional church services, which are poorly attended, especially in large urban areas, church buildings are widely used for musical and other cultural events and remain open to all those interested in finding a quiet place for contemplation. On occasion, the buildings are also used for combination events such as expressive dance and meditative exercises that include a brief worship service.

Fig. 10.1. Twelfth century church in Gotland, Sweden, one of more than ninety on the small island and part of the Christian cultural heritage of Sweden. Photo courtesy of Harry Benjamin.

The lack of church attendance and the label of secularization, however, especially when viewed from a more functional perspective, do not mean that existential ritualization is extinct. In fact, in Sweden, as in many other countries where traditional religious expressions are decreasing, there is evidence, from the same World Values Survey research presented earlier, of a rise in broader spiritual concerns. "The need for meaning becomes more salient at high levels of existential [here meaning economic] security so that, even in rich countries, although church attendance is declining, spiritual concerns are not disappearing."[7]

The above profile of the Swedish population is linked to those who are ethnic Swedes. To this image needs to be added the diverse immigrant population, which includes those with ethnic roots in Africa, the Middle East, South America, North America, and other parts of Europe as well as Scandinavia. These individuals and groups reflect various types of meaning-making systems, with different means for expressing existential ritualization. At points, the very open, secular, and tolerant Swedish society, with its policy of religious freedom, comes into conflict with ethnic groups whose religious expressions are apprehended as being too different or too extreme. In the most recent debates since the beginning of this new century and against the background of global events, ethnic groups with a religious and/or cultural base in Islam are among those refugee groups often having a challenging time making Sweden a new homeland. This is certainly not a situation unique to Sweden. Nevertheless, the way in which religious myths and misunderstandings are fueled by media and popular culture in this very secularized and still dominantly monocultural society are tangible. Other ethnic minority groups in Sweden, especially those with a Christian heritage such as the Suroyo (see case 3 presented in the next section), have experienced a more tacit acceptance in Sweden as a result of their Christian background and a different cultural climate concerning refugees when they first arrived in Sweden.[8]

Globalization and cultural diversity in cultural contexts such as Sweden are contributing to the emergence of new questions relating to existential meaning and its ritualized expression. To some degree traditional religious institutions are identifying these questions and trying to make decisions about future directions of service. To a great degree, individuals and groups of the dominant ethnic Swedish and other ethnic backgrounds are consciously living the challenge to find pathways to new or renewed expressions of existential ritualization.

## EXISTENTIAL RITUAL EXPRESSION

The need for existential ritual expression is not in any way a new phenomenon. From a developmental psychological perspective, this need is basic to human survival, to the formation of personal and social identity, and to the socio-cultural signals and codes that define group membership. This type of ritual expression, encompassing cultural rites of passage, seasonal celebrations, and community worship, has been more or less automatic to persons born and raised within a particular group cultural context. To be a part of the group or community has meant to be a part of its existential ritual expression. The given worldview—the lens by which reality is viewed and ordered—surrounding a given system of ritual expression has been most often inherited and not consciously chosen. This worldview affects all aspects of how life is lived and also perceptions of physical, psychological, and spiritual health and illness.[9]

Fig. 10.2. This newer commercial building in Stockholm appears to reach higher into the heavens than the church spires behind it, a visual evocation of changing dynamics between religion and secular culture. Photo © Peder Bjorkegren/Etsa/Corbis. Used by permission.

One of the critical differences in the existential ritual process happening now in Sweden, but also in many other cultural contexts as well, is that the element of choice is being introduced. It is this aspect of postmodernism that is creating the biggest challenge. For many, the postmodern period presents new opportunities and new means for existential exploration. For others, it presents a time of lostness, when there is an almost desperate searching for an existential home, a sense of belonging. Often times the search leads to actions and efforts of belonging that have detrimental consequences for psychological and existential health and development. A young ethnic Swedish man expressed his feelings about his existential search in this way:

Growing up my parents didn't have any belief structure or special activities. I tried to invent my own as a child, but you can't do this in isolation. Later I got into different things with alcohol and smoking, but it didn't feel like anything to build on. And then I went through a real period of depression, partly because of being abandoned by my father but also because I didn't have any way to make meaning and still don't. I feel this huge emptiness just drifting without a base. I can't decide things, and I feel very alone. The medicine I sometimes take does not give me an answer to meaning only a temporary escape.[10]

This example is not an isolated one. Growing numbers of persons in this postmodern context are struggling and searching to find ways of making meaning that reflect a worldview and existential ritual expression that provide a sense of well-being and life-affirming identity. It is not uncommon for these existential struggles and searches to lead to the need for psychiatric intervention.

A natural question the reader may be asking at this point is: "Where is there existential hope and direction in this postmodern context?" The following section discusses three examples of hope and direction that are not exhaustive of the different types of existential ritual experimentation, but are representative.

## THREE EXAMPLES

All these examples are kinds of ritual experimentation. This designation is meant to signify the searching nature of those involved in the struggle to express their existential beliefs in significant actions, and to strengthen their beliefs through these actions. Each case reflects, in a unique way, the kind of identity issues, struggles, and ways of coming to terms with existential ritualizing in the postmodern Swedish cultural context. The cases reflect the lives of ordinary people struggling to find ways of expressing and living their faith in a somewhat extraordinary situation. The cases all draw from a Christian heritage, using common Christian symbols and stories, yet each necessitates a new translation of these symbols and stories in order for them to function as living expressions of faith. In each example, those involved are struggling to find and/or create new stories in order to stop, at least for brief periods of time, patterns of what can be experienced as relentless questioning. They are also trying to find a sense of community together, a means for meaningful renewal and existential nurture.

### The Sann Människa Network

The term *sann människa*, which directly translates from the Swedish as "true human," alludes to a phrase in the Nicene creed: "True God, true man."[11] The organization Sann Människa began in 1992 as a joint effort of Petter Wingeren, a priest of the Church of Sweden, and Ulf Ståhlhandske, a teacher at Sigtuna, a local community college. The project from its inception was focused on understanding how to be truly human in church: how to make use of bodily, creative, relational, and sexual energies of being human in a more fundamental way in church life and in its liturgy. Nature and the natural environment were also very important. Over time the original idea of the project changed. It began as the core of a movement within the Church of Sweden to liberate the body in faith, life, and practice, with a primary focus on church services and rituals, and shifted to a more participant-centered core, less a church movement and more a network to meet the ritual needs of the participants. Though links remained to the church, the more the project evolved, the less the organized church was interested—apart from individual church members, both clergy and laity, who were a part of the network.

The Sann Människa network organized twelve ritual workshops between 1992 and 1997. The network consisted of just over a hundred people, and about seventy to eighty attended one or another of the Sann Människa meetings. At each of the individual meetings between eleven and twenty-five people participated. There was a core group of ten persons. The age range in the network and core group ranged from twenty to fifty. The core group and network were dominated by women, a not uncommon phenomenon. People from all over Sweden were involved, but the majority came from the regions around Stockholm and Uppsala (the capital and the central university city on Sweden's east coast). The majority of participants were ethnic Swedes. Many of the younger participants were university students, and most of the older had a university degree.

The participants' relationships to the Church of Sweden varied. Most had at least some cultural or religious connection, having gone through the church's rituals of baptism and confirmation. The spectrum ranged from active engagement to absolute disengagement. During the time of participation, the Sann Människa ritual experience became for some a complement to the church, or a substitute for church rituals as they moved away from the church, and for others a new search for ritual fulfillment as they had not ever been active in church rituals.

Sann Människa's rituals were all based on improvisation in some way, and over time guidelines, or rules, for the rituals were developed. The ritual rules concerned instructions for forming the ritual room, ritual time, entrance and exit practices, silence, a special talk-space, a rest-space, and leaving and stopping procedures. Four types of ritual forms were used by the group:

- rituals planned with a specific theme (certain of the communion rituals, for example);
- rituals planned without a theme, where form but not content was decided beforehand;
- unplanned with a theme, such as rituals around "masculinity-femininity"; and
- unplanned without a theme (most of the ritual events).

The ritual planning process was leaderless, and all members had a voice in the process. True to Swedish form, many of the rituals were held outdoors in beautiful natural settings often near a large lake, or combined both inside and outside sequences.

### Feminist Liturgies[12]

The feminist liturgical movement in Sweden represents a type of religious revival more than one of secularization. During the twentieth century a sacramental renewal and liturgical revival was associated with both the high church movement in the Church of Sweden and with the ecumenical movement. This resulted in a much higher frequency of Eucharistic celebration, especially in contrast to the beginning of the 1900s, when this liturgical function had almost disappeared from weekly services. Along with this renewal came a sacramental change in the interpretation of the liturgy, influencing both the Church of Sweden and the Free Churches (Protestant denominations, such as the Swedish Baptist, Methodist, and Mission Churches, with prominent spiritual-evangelical expressions of belonging and worship).

Feminist liturgies are both dependent upon and a reaction against the verbalist tendency, the tendency to devalue the role of the congregation, and the tendency to focus on sin and forgiveness. An interesting paradox is that the liturgical renewal, to which the feminist liturgical movement is indebted, was closely related to resistance to the ordination of women. Ironically, important and empowering liturgical advances were accompanied by the negation of gender equality with respect to women's ordination. This needs to be understood against the background of Sweden as one of the most advanced countries in terms of gender equality, women's rights, and women's representation in the power-making structures of all societal institutions.

Feminist liturgies in Sweden have not developed as the result of an organized movement, although steps in this direction have been taken in recent years through the organization of national conferences on feminist liturgy. The liturgies have instead developed as spontaneous expressions, emerging out of

> **Women in the Church of Sweden**
> Women priests, upholding tradition in the same way as men, is one side of the present reality in the Church of Sweden. There is, however, also another current, more in line with cultural or radical feminism, where the stress lies on valuing the specific gifts and experiences of women.
> —Ninna Edgardh Beckman, "The relevance of gender in rites of ordination," in Hans Raun Iversen, ed., *Rites of Ordination and Commitment in the Churches of the Nordic Countries: Theology and Rerminology* (Copenhagen: University of Copenhagen, Museum Tusculanum Press, 2006), 545.

Fig. 10.3. Sophia Mass in Sweden. Photo © Jim Elfström. Used by permission.

**Fig. 10.4.** Sophia Mass in Sweden. Photo © Jim Elfström. Used by permission.

women's gatherings from the 1970s onwards.

The *Sofia-mässa* (Sofia Mass) is named for Lady Wisdom, Sofia, in the Jewish and Christian tradition, and represents a form of liturgy introduced by women as an alternative to the traditional and androcentrically labeled forms of worship. These masses are inclusive of both women and men. The first of these masses, celebrated on December 4, 1994, in Stockholm, was attended by 250 people and received much attention in the Swedish media. These masses are held two to four times a year in Stockholm, and have spread to other parts of the country. The Sofia Mass includes most components of a traditional high Mass, but with a new understanding of God and humanity, of gender relations, and of the Bible. Words, gestures, and dance are used to embody these understandings.

### Third-Generation Suroyo Acculturation

This example is of a generation of children, now young adults, of religious refugees to Sweden who are struggling to negotiate the postmodern landscape in a largely secularized cultural context. The term "Suroyo" (including those identifying themselves as Arameans, Assyrians, Chaldeans, and Syrianer) refers to those sharing the Syriac Orthodox Christian tradition.[13]

During the twentieth century a Suroyo migration took place within Middle Eastern countries such as Turkey, Syria, Lebanon, Iraq, and Iran, and also to developed countries internationally. The migration from each country varied in its characteristics, but there are common patterns related to economic, religious, political, labor, and social factors. Increased violence toward and discrimination against the Suroyo in the Middle East are shared factors common for the group.[14] In the 1970s, a large wave of Syriac Orthodox Christian religious and political refugees from Turkey and other countries of the Middle East came to Sweden. In comparison to other ethnic groups, the Suroyo as a group has a strong resolve to remain in Sweden. This is in no small part due to the reality that they have no country to which they can return.[15]

As psychologist of religion Önver Cetrez notes, the Suroyo migration to Sweden took place in several phases. The first phase began in 1967, with Suroyo coming to Sweden from different Middle East countries as quota refugees, defined as those who prior to arrival have been granted residence permits within the refugee quota framework executed through the Swedish Migration Board. A second phase took place in the first half of the 1970s, with residence granted for political and humanitarian reasons. Phase three was in the late 1970s, with special emphasis on Suroyo from Turkey and with a quota system for reuniting families. Political turmoil and war brought Suroyo in the 1980s from Syria and Lebanon and in the 1990s from Iraq.

It is difficult to find satisfactory demographics on the total population of Suroyo in Sweden; there are complications because of the immigrants' different countries of origin, and Sweden's national statistics do not classify by ethnicity or religion. The ethnic group itself gives a figure of seventy thousand to eighty thousand for the total population in Sweden (when using a broad approach to the different minority groups that are included in this labeling of Suroyo).[16]

While the Suroyo in their countries of origin were an internal minority characterized by religious difference, being a Christian minority among Muslims, in Sweden the Suroyo have become an immigrant group among others, being differentiated more in ethnic than in religious terms. Despite this change of minority positions, "the ethnic relations in Sweden are far more

> ### Suroyo Youth in the Churches
>
> The ethnic church or associations are for the youth, in comparison to their parents and grandparents, not necessarily the only providers of care, information, social meeting points, and rites of passage. Institutions in mainstream society and new technologies also meet some of these needs. Quality places for the youth may still be found in church buildings, but also in centers of recreation, in sports arenas, and in traveling to countries of origin. Religion and kinship for the 3rd generation Suroyo youth are better approached as personal and cultural resources and practices of differentiation for meaning-making, among other resources and practices, than as all-encompassing spheres of meaning.
>
> —Önver Cetrez, *Meaning-Making Variations in Acculturation and Ritualization: A Multi-Generational Study of Suroyo Migrants in Sweden* (Uppsala: Uppsala University Press, 2005), 312.

just in juridical terms than they were in the countries of origin."[17] Nevertheless, this minority group, as others, has been negatively portrayed. Debates about immigrants often include topics such as "gang rape, honor killings, forced child marriages and female genital mutilation."[18]

For the majority of members of the third generation (and even of the second generation to some degree) of Suroyo in Sweden, negotiation of cultures, worldviews, and existential ritualized activity is not optional. These negotiations, an everyday occurrence, for members of this minority cultural group are energy-draining, ongoing, and with no certain outcome. They need to be understood against the power structure of a dominant as distinct from a minority culture.

The third generation, born and raised in Sweden, have Suroyo religious and kinship culture at home. It is important to note that, in terms of the categories of the World Value Surveys, this cultural group represents a near-opposite orientation to traditional values and self-expression than that found in mainstream Swedish culture. In the classic Suroyo culture, traditional family and religious patterns are valued. A collective in contrast to an individual focus is the norm. During childhood, for the third-generation Suroyo, traditional cultural forces, including the Syriac Orthodox Church, are the primary shapers of how worldviews are formed and how existential ritualizing is practiced. Especially for those families living in close-knit Suroyo communities in the suburbs of large cities in Sweden, these influences continue to shape and guide values, behaviors, and existential ritualizing into adolescence and beyond. But as this generation is educated in Swedish schools and becomes accustomed to the dominant Swedish culture's meaning-making strategies, its members will have to make certain choices. As Cetrez has written:

> They [members of the third generation] have to choose elements from or ways of interacting with each specific cultural system they encounter: the agricultural of their grandparents, the modern or industrial of their parents, and the postmodern society in the mainstream Swedish context. Acculturation for the 3rd generation becomes much more complicated, consisting of different or sometimes even contradictory worldviews, as well as worldviews

having different validity. At the same time as collective safety, economical welfare, and social safety are important, the 3rd generation being children of Swedish society also value life quality or life-meaning as do the mainstream youth of their age.[19]

The words of one young woman on her worldview negotiation and existential ritualized activity provide a glimpse of the kind of challenge cultural negotiation at this level entails.

My worldview is not just from one way of thinking, but several. Somewhere in the background I am Christian from an Orthodox Catholic church in my country of birth. But after coming to Sweden I rebelled against the church. I tried the Lutheran church but it wasn't much better. For me the church and God are not the same. I tried to find a home for my questions and doubts but I felt as an outsider. I find strength from a feminist group which I have been involved in for three years. We have our own symbols and small rituals of meaning and belonging. I've given up trying to decide WHICH is the one I want. I now just accept that I belong to both but in my own way. I don't feel this is wrong. It works for me and keeps me from going crazy with all the uncertainty in the world around me.[20]

## AN AGENDA FOR THE TWENTY-FIRST CENTURY

These three examples illustrate the need and desire for a type of onto logical security in an age and context that do not, and in reality cannot, readily provide such. Psychological and existential needs and desires are what these groups have in common. However, the particular solutions and types of ontological security will vary in ritualized forms and faith expressions. In this kind of postmodern cultural context, the individual and group need to re-create the stories and symbols that will provide such security. In addition, stories and symbols need to come alive in sacred and safe spaces for individual and communal expression.

Critically important questions concerning existential health and existential dysfunction in this Swedish welfare state were raised at

> ## Cross-Cultural Experience and Meaning-Making
>
> The homogenous model of culture is but one dimension of cultural reality today. . . . Cross-cultural reality exists for immigrants and refugees living in those places [the new homeland]. For such persons developmental-preventive concerns involve both the unconscious and conscious activities of negotiation and balance between the different cultural worldviews and meaning-making frameworks.
>
> —Valerie DeMarinis, "Psychological Function and Consequences of Religious Ritual Experience". In *Rit, symbol och verklighet: Sex studier om ritens function,* ed. Owe Wikström (Uppsala: Tro och Tanke: Svenska kyrkans forskningsråd), 16.

the close of the twentieth century. Since Sweden is one of the remaining and relatively well-functioning welfare states, a public health agenda in response to these questions would seem in order, especially considering the mental health consequences of existential dysfunction. This type of development would certainly seem like a logical development of the World Health Organization's understanding of the current (also referred to as third) public health revolution: "The third public health revolution recognizes health as a key dimension of quality of life. Health policies in the 21st century will need to be constructed from the key questions posed by both the health promotion and population health movements. 'What makes people healthy?' Health policies will need to address both the collective lifestyles of modern societies and the social environments of modern life as they affect the health and quality of life of populations."[21] What I am proposing is an existential preventative public mental health agenda. Such an agenda will require the participation and coordination of many public and private actors, including primary and secondary schools, religious and worldview institutions (such as humanists), and university systems.

In many ways, attention to existential need can be incorporated into the public school setting. As world religion and world affairs are already a part of the school curriculum, these classes can be expanded to include more intentional work on students' own expressions of ontological security, existential ritualization, and worldview construction.

Religious and worldview institutions can provide, in addition to organized worship and gatherings for members, safe spaces for those who do not belong to an organized group, where one is able to ritualize and create or re-create stories of meaning that will help to provide a base of ontological security. These institutions, such as the Church of Sweden, can also provide existential caring, since their leaders are trained to hear the existential needs expressed in the stories of doubt, sadness, and ontological longing of persons struggling in this post-modern context.

This kind of existential caring requires the type of education and training best suited to a university context. Specially designed training and continuing education courses can thereby be constructed to meet this need for professionals like priests, pastors, deacons, and hospital chaplains, directed toward a needs-based approach. A preventive approach to existential development in cultural context can become a part of the training process for elementary and high school teachers, where applied learning modules could be included in required courses related to religious and worldview perspectives. Mental health professionals also need training in order to recognize the dimension of existential need based on ontological insecurity as distinguishable from other dimensions of, for example, depressive symptoms. Such courses are being developed in psychology of religion at Uppsala University.

## FOR FURTHER READING

Cetrez, Önver. *Meaning-Making Variations in Acculturation and Ritualization. A Multi Generational Study of Suroyo Migrants in Sweden.* Uppsala: Uppsala University Press, 2005.

DeMarinis, Valerie. "Existential Dysfunction as a Public Mental Health Issue for Post-Modern Sweden: A Cultural Challenge and a Challenge to Culture." In *Tro på teatret: Essays om religion og teater,* edited by Bent Holm, 229–43. Copenhagen: Copenhagen University, 2006.

———. *Pastoral Care, Existential Health and Existential Epidemiology: A Swedish Postmodern Case Study.* Stockholm: Verbum, 2003.

Edgardh Beckman, Ninna. "Lady Wisdom as Hostess for the Lord's Supper: Sofia-Mässor in Stockholm, Sweden." In *Dissident Daughters: Feminist Liturgies in Global Context,* edited by Teresa Berger, 159–74. Louisville, Ky.: Westminster John Knox, 2001.

Liljas, Maria. *Ritual Invention: A Play Perspective on Existential Ritual and Mental Health in Late Modern Sweden.* Uppsala: Uppsala University Press, 2005.

Pettersson, Thorleif. "Religion in Contemporary Society: Eroded by Human Well-being, Supported by Cultural Diversity." In *Measuring and Mapping Cultures: 25 Years of Comparative Value Surveys,* edited by Yilmaz Esmer and Thorleif Pettersson, 127–54. Leiden: Brill, 2007.

# INNOVATION
# AND AUTHENTICITY

# Part 3

# ORDINARY CHRISTIANS AND THE HOLOCAUST

## VICTORIA J. BARNETT

God simply made me an outsider.

> —Gertrud Staewen, a Protestant member
> of a Berlin resistance group helping Jews[1]

In order to lead the National Socialist German struggle against world Jewry, the quick and thorough implementation of the dejudaization of the Christian church is of high and essential significance. Only when the dejudaization of the Christian church is completed can the German people join in carrying out the fight of the *Führer* . . . and can the divine commission of the German *Volk* assist in its fulfillment

> —Hugo Pich, Thuringian church superintendent[2]

Our church, which has been fighting in these years only for its self-preservation, as though that were an end in itself, is incapable of taking the word of reconciliation and redemption to humankind and the world. Our earlier words are therefore bound to lose their force and cease, and our being Christians today will be limited to two things: prayer and the doing of justice.

> —Dietrich Bonhoeffer, May 1944[3]

A growing body of scholarship on the behavior of ordinary people during the Nazi years of terror between 1933 and 1945 has focused primarily on German citizens and, after 1939, the populations of Nazi-occupied countries. The range of behavior was wide, including that of bystanders and perpetrators, and was shaped by each country's history, culture, and particular experience of war and occupation. Although few of these studies focus extensively on the religious underpinnings of people's reactions to Nazism, any study of the behavior of ordinary people during this era is in fact also a study of ordinary Christians. Throughout Europe as well as in the United States, over 95 percent of the population was Christian.

The most instructive case study—and the one in which the record of both the church leadership and lay members has been documented most extensively—is that of Nazi Germany itself. This chapter will focus primarily on the reaction of ordinary Christians in Nazi Germany, then offer a brief overview of some of the responses of Christians outside Nazi Germany, and conclude with observations of what motivated Christians who responded to the persecution and genocide of the European Jews.

## NAZI GERMANY

The picture of ordinary people that has emerged from the study of Nazi Germany is one of widespread complicity, ranging from passive acquiescence to active involvement. The instances of resistance against Nazism and rescue of its victims were the actions of a small minority. Even more troubling, most research reveals that the cooperation of the majority was not coerced but voluntary, reflecting an active affirmation of at least some aspects of Nazi ideology and the values it expounded.[4] As historian Peter Fritsche writes, "It should be stated clearly that Germans became Nazis because they wanted to become Nazis and because the Nazis spoke so well to their interests and inclinations."[5] After January 30, 1933, the rapid conformity of ordinary Germans to Nazi regulation of daily life, including the new measures that targeted and isolated their Jewish neighbors, is striking and well documented.[6]

Over 98 percent of the German population in 1933 was Christian. Over 95 percent belonged either to the Roman Catholic Church or to the German Evangelical Church (the Protestant church of Germany, which included churches from the Lutheran, Reformed, and United traditions). The so-called free churches (Mennonites, Methodists, Baptists, and other denominations) were quite small, as were religious groups considered to be sects, such as the Jehovah's Witnesses and Christian Scientists. The Jewish minority was less than 1 percent.

In the early postwar years in Germany, the Christian churches often portrayed themselves as having heroically opposed Nazism. When church leaders did acknowledge their failure, they portrayed it as a failure to live up to their Christian principles, accusing themselves, in the words of the Protestant church's 1945 Stuttgart Declaration of Guilt, "for not witnessing

Fig. 11.1. Thousands attend a convention of the German Christian movement at the Berlin Sportpalast. The banner that hangs from the balcony says, "The German Christian Reads 'The Gospel in the Third Reich.'" November 13, 1933, Berlin. Photo © ullstein bild / The Granger Collection, New York .

more courageously, for not praying more faithfully, for not believing more joyously, and for not loving more ardently."[7] Yet just as there is now more research on the behavior of ordinary people, there is also a solid body of research that refutes this early hagiography and documents the pervasive complicity of the Christian churches with Nazism. Far from having opposed Nazism from the beginning, most church leaders either actively welcomed the new regime or quickly made their peace with it. Many of them publicly condoned the measures against Jews, citing Christian teachings.[8]

## THE INSTITUTIONAL CHURCH AND ITS LEADERS

To understand the behavior of ordinary Christians under National Socialism, we must understand the institutional context in which this occurred, particularly the so-called church struggle (*Kirchenkampf*) within German Protestantism. We must also understand the larger ideological dynamics of the time, particularly the way in which the widespread popular affirmation of a German *Volksgemeinschaft* (community of the German people) shaped Christian behavior. *Volksgemeinschaft* was the ideological cornerstone of Nazi society and its understanding of the role of citizens, fostering the emergence of what historian Claudia Koonz has called "an ethnic conscience" that was based upon a "communitarian morality."[9]

The religious implications of this communitarian morality were articulated in paragraph number 24 of the 1920 Nazi party platform, which espoused the party's commitment to what it called "positive Christianity":

> We demand the freedom of all religious confessions in the state, insofar as they do not jeopardize its existence or conflict with the manners and moral sentiments of the Germanic race. The party as such upholds the point of view of a positive Christianity without tying itself confessionally to any one confession. It combats the Jewish-materialistic spirit at home and abroad and is convinced that a permanent recovery of our people can only be achieved from within on the basis of common good before individual good.[10]

Paragraph 24 made most ordinary Christians and their clergy feel that there was a place for them within the Nazi party and, after 1933, within the Third Reich. "Positive Christianity" seemed an affirmation of the central role that Christian belief could play in the new *Volksgemeinschaft*, and the importance of the "common good" seemed to emphasize a positive new communitarian principle. Few Christians at the time were troubled or offended by the paragraph's anti-Semitism.

The main problem that would emerge for the churches was expressed in the first sentence of the statement, with its affirmation of the kind of religious belief that would not conflict with the "manners and moral sentiments of the Germanic race." In fact, Paragraph 24, although it was only one section in a larger document that laid out the Nazi agenda, revealed how the party viewed the link between religious sensibility and racist ideology. The foundation of National Socialism was its ideology of racial superiority and its various policies, including the genocide of the Jews, which were designed to create a pure "Aryan" race that would dominate Europe. Christians were thus challenged by the regime to reconcile their religious beliefs with the Nazi agenda. A fierce struggle within the German Protestant church soon broke out between those who embraced racial ideology and sought a nazified,

Aryan church and those who viewed this as an ideological corruption of Christian values and belief.

While the primary source of tension between the Nazi regime and the two major churches was the conflict between Nazi ideology and Christian belief, others factors contributed to the division. Church leaders were distressed by the more extreme Nazi ideological purists, who viewed religion as an outmoded superstition that would be superseded by National Socialism. In particular, the writings of party propagandist Alfred Rosenberg alarmed church leaders. Rosenberg's *The Myth of the Twentieth Century* attacked both Jews and Christians for undermining German values and the *Volksgemeinschaft*, and his book was censured by the Vatican. Rosenberg's outspoken anti-Christianity was a minority opinion within the party, however, so many church leaders dismissed it as not being symptomatic of party attitudes.

They were far more alarmed by the Nazi policy of *Gleichschaltung*—the synchronization (essentially the nazification) of all sectors of society under the authority of the party; this threatened church institutional independence. For the churches, *Gleichschaltung* was epitomized by the move to create a unified Reich Church that would ultimately incorporate both the Catholic and the Protestant churches and propagate the nonconfessional Christianity described in the party platform. The attempt at a Reich Church soon foundered because of the strong opposition of church leaders. They were not nearly as outspoken, however, in their direct dealings with the Nazi state. Here the response of both Catholic and Protestant leaders was to work out compromises with the Nazi state as they attempted to retain their independence. The most prominent example was the 1933 Concordat signed by Catholic leaders and Nazi state officials. The Catholic Church viewed this as a state guarantee that the church would retain sovereignty over religious institutions, including schools. Yet such agreements—as well as the corresponding photographs of church leaders alongside Nazi officials—gave the regime an added legitimacy. Throughout the Nazi era, moreover, the churches' strategy of cautious compromise with the state would mean a consistent and deliberate avoidance of any direct criticism of the government, particularly on political matters.

The Protestant situation was far more complex than the Catholic one, given the lack of a centralized leadership that could make agreements with the state and the significant diversity in the leadership and membership of the twenty-seven Protestant regional churches. The greatest challenge in the Protestant church, even before 1933, was the division among different theological and ideological factions. After 1933, this division led to the German church struggle, or *Kirchenkampf*. The *Kirchenkampf* was very much a grassroots phenomenon and actually had its beginnings in the 1920s, when several revivalist movements throughout Germany sought to reinvigorate German Protestantism during an era of great social and political change and instability. During the Nazi era these different movements took Protestants in opposing directions. The pro-Nazi German Christians (*Deutsche Christen*) embraced the nationalist and ethnically defined understanding of Christianity that had been articulated in Paragraph 24. The opposing group became known as the Confessing Church (*Bekennende Kirche*), which opposed the ideologically defined religion of the German Christians and called for a church based solely upon the confessions and the scriptures.

The *Kirchenkampf* ignited over the attempt to create a Reich Church and most particularly over the status of baptized "non-Aryans"—people of Jewish descent whose families had at some point converted to Christianity. Germany had one of the most highly assimilated Jewish populations in Europe, and there were actually almost three times as many non-Aryan Christians as there were secular or observant Jews. Almost 90 percent of them were Protestant.[11] With the Nazi ascent to power, these people were now subject to Nazi racial laws, and the German Christians immediately supported the establishment of a Reich Church that would not only bar non-Aryans from the

**Fig. 11.2.** Ludwig Mueller, standing on a podium on the steps of the Berlin cathedral, addresses a group of German women in traditional dress during his formal installation as Reich Bishop, September 23, 1934, Berlin. Photo © Süddeutsche Zeitung Photo. Used by permission.

ministry and other church positions, but also create a church (and Christianity) more reflective of Nazi values.

The German Christians defined themselves as a populist movement dedicated to aligning German Protestantism with "Germanic" values and culture. They created new liturgies and hymns as well as an insignia that superimposed the swastika over the cross. They incorporated the highly gendered rhetoric found in Nazi propaganda about the role of women and the necessity for a strong "manly" and militaristic Christianity that could stand up to the rest of Europe.[12]

The aspect that was most controversial was their attempt to "aryanize" Christian doctrine and scripture, even eradicating the Hebrew scriptures and all references to Jesus' Jewishness. This met with strong opposition from most Protestant leaders and theologians. (The setting of ethnic criteria for church membership and baptism antagonized Catholic leaders as well.) Although they agreed with nationalism, support for the new state, and much of the cultural rhetoric, traditional Protestant bishops could not tolerate theological heresy. Nonetheless, they hoped to retain the German Christians in the Protestant fold. At the height of the movement in late 1933, the German Christians comprised about one third of the Protestant pastorate, and their popular following was strongest in the regions where the Nazi party had the most support. While these numbers would subsequently drop, the German Christians retained control of several regional churches, prominent seminaries, and theological faculties, and they continued to be influential throughout the Third Reich.

The Confessing Church was initially founded as the Pastors' Emergency League to help non-Aryan church employees who were in danger of losing their jobs. As the radicality of the German Christian worldview became clearer, a number of theologians and church leaders joined forces to compose a theological and ecclesiological response to what they viewed as the ideologization of Christianity. In May 1934, representatives of all the regional Protestant churches met in the town of Barmen and unanimously approved the Barmen Declaration of Faith, a six-point document written by the Reformed theologian Karl Barth. The declaration decried the ideological Christianity of the German Christians and laid the foundation for potential opposition to the state, claiming that a true church could only follow one Lord, not a worldly Führer.[13] The Barmen Declaration was the founding document of the Confessing Church.

While those who met at Barmen included Lutheran bishops and the heads of United and Reformed churches, the meeting actually led to much broader changes in the Protestant church, driven largely by lay members and the emerging generation of theological students, which included the first generation of women permitted to attain theological degrees. Within months, the more outspoken members of the Confessing Church were being harassed by German Christians and coming into conflict with state authorities. This sector of the Confessing Church argued that it represented the true church and that the mainstream leadership, by compromising with both the state and the German Christians, had ceased to have any integrity. As the radicalization of this sector of the Confessing Church intensified, the leaders who had met at Barmen retreated to more neutral ground. By 1935, mainstream Protestant leaders viewed the German Christians and the Confessing Church as equally problematic extremes that threatened to bring about a church schism and, in the case of the Confessing Church, risked antagonizing Nazi state authorities.

Both the German Christians and Confessing Church were popular movements that energized hundreds of thousands of Christians. In a church that had traditionally been strongly hierarchical, the outspoken and ongoing struggle between them raised theological and political issues that permanently altered the nature of German Protestantism, particularly in the Confessing Church's challenges to the traditional alliance of church and state authority.

Thus the behavior of Protestant leaders paralleled that of their Catholic counterparts—a cautious accommodation to the Nazi state. Criticism of the state, usually confined strictly to church-related matters, was coupled with expressions of support for National Socialism. All too often these statements of support explicitly agreed with the anti-Jewish measures. When Bishop Wurm of Württemberg, in a letter to a state official, privately protested the violent pogroms of November 1938 (also known as Kristallnacht), he added, "I contest with no word the right of the State to fight Judaism as a dangerous element."[14] In particular, the churches—even the Confessing Church—avoided any kind of solidarity with persecuted Jews. The church protests on behalf of non-Aryan Christians deliberately avoided addressing the plight of observant or secularized Jews; throughout the Third Reich, the concern even of the Confessing Church would be restricted to members of the Christian church. In September 1935, a small group of Christians submitted a memorandum to a Confessing synod meeting in Berlin. The memorandum documented the persecution of Jews in Berlin and called upon the Confessing Church to protest; the synod leaders refused to even include it on the official agenda.[15]

Catholic and Protestant church leaders' caution toward Nazi authorities meant that the opposition to the state that did emerge among Christians—including acts of rescue and resistance on behalf of persecuted Jews—was generally carried out by ordinary people, often in opposition to the church leadership and certainly without their support.[16]

## ORDINARY PEOPLE AND RESCUERS

Of those who helped persecuted Jews, many were women working in the helping professions as social workers, deaconesses, and educators. This is particularly evident in the little we know about the isolated cases in which Jews, Catholics, and Protestants worked together to help those victimized by the Nazi regime.[17] Most of these people seem to have been involved in social ministry—working with the poor, in soup kitchens, in hospitals and institutions. These kinds of charities traditionally see the most interreligious cooperation and also mark the intersection of religious and social movements.

In 1911, Friedrich Siegmund-Schultze, a Protestant pastor and social worker, had established an organization in the slums of east Berlin that by the 1920s had developed into a group of welfare centers, drawing volunteers from the ranks of pacifists, political leftists, Quakers, Catholics, and Protestants. Many of these volunteers eventually found their way into circles that helped Jews, including the Protestant Grüber office in the late 1930s, which helped Jews emigrate as long as that was possible. In July 1933, Siegmund-Schultze himself was deported for his efforts on behalf of Jews.[18] From exile in Switzerland he began to help refugees and became part of a loose network of

### Memo to the Confessing Church

*The following is an excerpt from a memo submitted by Protestant church social worker Elisabeth Schmitz to the 1935 Steglitz Synod of the Confessing Church. The bishops at that synod refused to include the memo on the official agenda.*

What should we answer to the question, "Where is your brother Abel?" We in the Confessing Church have no better answer than Cain's. . . . Why must we continually hear from the ranks of the non-Christians that they feel the Church has abandoned them? . . . Why doesn't the Church pray for those suffering guiltlessly, those under persecution? Why aren't there prayer meetings for the Jews, like there were prayer meetings when the pastors were arrested? The Church makes it bitterly difficult for us to defend her. Since when was it anything other than blasphemy to contend that it is the will of God for us to promote injustice? Let us take care that we do not enthrone the evil of our sins in the Temple of the Will of God.

—Theodore Thomas, *Women against Hitler* (Westport, Conn.: Praeger, 1995), 39–40.

Christian and political groups throughout Europe that in the following years would become important in both rescue and resistance activities in Germany, France, Switzerland, Holland, and the Scandinavian countries.[19]

This network of rescue and resistance ultimately involved a number of efforts usually thought to represent individual and isolated cases. One was the White Rose student group in Munich, which included Hans and Sophie Scholl, a brother and sister who distributed anti-Nazi leaflets and who were executed in 1943. Another was the village of Le Chambon in France, a village of French Huguenots that rescued thousands of Jewish children. During the war the French Protestant Cimade group worked to help thousands of Jews imprisoned in concentration camps in occupied France. The link between each of these cases was a group of key but little-known Christians with connections throughout Europe, each of whom within his or her own circle was carrying information and trying to promote the activities of localized resistance groups. Tracy Strong, the American general secretary of the YMCA, traveled throughout Europe carrying messages between different groups and trying in particular to help the work of the Quakers in France. Laura Livingstone was a British Quaker who worked with Jews in Berlin and then headed refugee efforts in Britain once the war began. Adolf Freudenberg was an exile from Nazi Germany who headed the ecumenical refugee offices in Geneva. Gertrud Staewen, the self-described outsider cited in the epigraph on p. 265, was a Christian socialist who worked with a small resistance group in Berlin that helped several Jews escape Nazi Germany. Gertrud Luckner, a Catholic and a trained economist and social activist, was incarcerated in the Ravensbruck concentration camp until the end of the war as a result of her efforts to rescue Jews.

**Fig. 11.3.** Group portrait of Jewish and non-Jewish refugee children sheltered in various public and private homes in Le Chambon-sur-Lignon during World War II with some of the French men and women who cared for them, 1943. Photo © United States Holocaust Museum, courtesy of Peter Feigl.

This network was one level of the activism of ordinary Christians. The more common phenomenon throughout Europe was rescue by individuals: decent people who decided, often at great risk, to hide Jews or help them escape. Certainly not all of those who rescued did so on the basis of Christian conviction in fact, the research on rescue during the Holocaust shows that religion was not a significant factor in shaping the motivations of the rescuers. In the seminal study of rescuers conducted by Samuel and Pearl Oliner, only 15 percent cited religion as a motivating factor.[20] While the research on rescue doesn't yield any single predicting factor, the Oliners came up with a personality profile that seemed to fit rescuers; its dominant characteristic was a pronounced "sense of attachment to others and their feeling of responsibility for the welfare of others, including those outside their immediate familiar or communal circles."[21] In the occupied countries (the Oliners primarily studied rescuers from Poland) many rescuers had some personal connection with the person they rescued. Others, particularly in France and Scandinavia, viewed rescue as a

### A Petition of Protest

*The following is an excerpt from a 1943 petition protesting the deportation of German Jews that was sent by a Bavarian group, the "Lempp Circle," to Bavarian Bishop Hans Meiser, who refused to sign it.*

As Christians, we can no longer bear that the church in Germany remains silent about the persecution of the Jews. . . . Every "non-Aryan," whether Jew or Christian, has "fallen among murderers" today in Germany, and we are asked whether we meet him like the priests and Levites or like the good Samaritan.

—Victoria Barnett, *For the Soul of the People* (New York: Oxford University Press, 1992), 199.

Fig. 11.4. A priest and several nuns pose with a group of children at a Franciscan convent school in Lomna, Poland where Jewish children were hidden during the German occupation, April 24, 1946. Photo © United States Holocaust Museum, courtesy of Lidia Kleinman Siciarz.

patriotic form of resistance against German occupation.

Another striking pattern among rescuers that emerges was the marginality of many of those who found their way into rescue or resistance. Many were women. They were laypeople, not church leaders. They were often found in groups that had been politically marginalized and targeted by the Nazis: leftists, homosexuals, pacifists. Among religious groups, the ones with the greatest record of opposition to National Socialism and activism on behalf of its victims are the ones with a history of religiously grounded opposition to authority, such as the Quakers.

It is important to remember that those involved in rescue and resistance activities were in the minority. The vast majority of Catholic and Protestant citizens in Nazi Germany conformed to the regime and supported its rules. The work of historian Robert Gellately documents the degree to which the Nazi police state apparatus, including informants who turned in Jewish neighbors, was based upon the extensive and voluntary cooperation of private citizens. With the onset of the war in 1939 and the German invasion of Eastern Europe, Jews in those countries suffered horrific violence, not only at the hands of invading German soldiers but all too often from their neighbors, who witnessed and sometimes joined in the violence. This violence sometimes carried the explicit sanction of Christian church leaders in those regions. In Slovakia, President Jozef Tiso, an ordained priest, defended the deportations of over fifty thousand Jews, sparing only those who had converted to Christianity.[22] Archbishop Karol Kmetko of Slovakia refused the pleas of a local rabbi to protest the deportations of Jews, saying that the only way the Jews could save themselves was to convert to Christianity. Bishop Brizgys, head of the Lithuanian church, told his clergy not to help Jews who asked for help.[23] In Poland, some Christians continued to base their anti-Semitism on Christian teachings, even after the Holocaust ended.[24]

## CONCLUSION

What do the reactions of ordinary Christians during the Holocaust tell us about the intersection of religious belief, prejudice, and behavior? Studies of the Holocaust often focus on Christian theology, particularly Christian teachings about Judaism, to explain the poor record of Christianity under National Socialism. Church historians tend to emphasize the institutional and ideological dynamics of that complicity, especially in terms of church and state relations. Both of these perspectives are valid and give insight into the complex dynamics of complicity. Anti-Semitism was pervasive in that era and was certainly part of the mentality of many Christians throughout Europe. In Nazi Germany it was augmented by patriotism and nationalism, especially among Protestants.

Thus, the reaction of Christians to the Holocaust is an instructive case study in the intersection of ideology and religion, belief and behavior, and above all in the conformation of Christian theological and ecclesiological understandings in alignment with state power. Examining the behavior of ordinary Christians brings these larger dynamics into a different light by altering our perception of the role of belief and even theology, for we see how easily theological and doctrinal precepts became fluid and were adapted to the larger political movements of their time. Even leading theologians revised their theologies to conform to the new Nazi spirit and the political priorities of the *Volksgemeinschaft*.[25] The endorsement of a racist and genocidal ideology by prominent figures, as well as by church leaders, had a profound effect on ordinary Christians, for it legitimated the actions of the Nazi state and made it much harder for individuals to stand up on behalf of victims. The history of Christian behavior under Nazism is in many ways a cautionary tale about the seductive power of a popular religiosity, and it illustrates how pliable religious belief really is and how easy it is for people to use religion to reify their prejudices and nationalism. This was why the theologian Dietrich Bonhoeffer, writing from prison in 1944, concluded that Christianity, particularly its institutions, had been profoundly tainted, and that all that remained for ordinary Christians was "prayer and the doing of justice."

### The Seelisberg Address to the Churches, 1947

We have recently witnessed an outburst of antisemitism which has led to the persecution and extermination of millions of Jews. In spite of the catastrophe which has overtaken both the persecuted and the persecutors, and which has revealed the extent of the Jewish problem in all its alarming gravity and urgency, antisemitism has lost none of its force, but threatens to extend to other regions, to poison the minds of Christians and to involve humanity more and more in a grave guilt with disastrous consequences.

The Christian Churches have indeed always affirmed the un-Christian character of antisemitism, as of all forms of racial hatred, but this has not sufficed to prevent the manifestation among Christians, in various forms, of an undiscriminating racial hatred of the Jews as a people.

This would have been impossible if all Christians had been true to the teaching of Jesus Christ on the mercy of God and love of one's neighbour. But this faithfulness should also involve clear-sighted willingness to avoid any presentation and conception of the Christian message which would support antisemitism under whatever form. We must recognise, unfortunately, that this vigilant willingness has often been lacking.

We therefore address ourselves to the Churches to draw their attention to this alarming situation. We have the firm hope that they will be concerned to show their members how to prevent any animosity towards the Jews which might arise from false, inadequate or mistaken presentations or conceptions of the teaching and preaching of the Christian doctrine, and how on the other hand to promote brotherly love towards the sorely-tried people of the old covenant.

—From the Address to the Churches, Seelisberg, Switzerland, published by the International Council of Christians and Jews, http://www.jcrelations.net/en/?item=983.

Most of those who withstood the lure of this revised theology were in some way outsiders and thus better able to hear and respond to the needs of the Jewish victims of Nazism. The cases in which we find Jews and Christians actually working together in resistance and rescue are so rare throughout the historical literature that they fairly jump off the page. Yet in the wake of the Holocaust these were the very individuals who opened up a new era of Christian-Jewish conversation, a crucial but immensely difficult relationship in the wake of the genocide of the European Jews. In 1947, a group of sixty-three Jews and Christians met in the Swiss village of Seelisberg and, on the basis of a study paper by the French Jewish historian Jules Isaac, issued the Seelisberg Address to the Churches, which outlined ten points for Christians to affirm in the wake of the Holocaust.[26] The background of most of its signers is little known, but what is striking about many of them is that they had firsthand experience of the Holocaust—and the failure of the churches. Isaac and most of the Jews who attended had lost family members. Many of the Christians in attendance had attempted to help Jews. These ordinary people issued an early document that established the foundation of post-Holocaust theology as we know it.[27] Their experience and wisdom, as well as their courage in confronting the Holocaust's immediate challenges to Christianity, stand in stark contrast to the complicity of many Christians during the Nazi era. Nevertheless, the Seelisberg meeting, like the engagement of those Christians who resisted Nazism and attempted to rescue its victims, is a reminder of the power of ordinary people.

## FOR FURTHER READING

Barnett, Victoria. *For the Soul of the People: Protestant Protest against Hitler.* New York: Oxford University Press, 1992.

———. *Bystanders: Conscience and Complicity during the Holocaust.* Westport, Conn.: Greenwood, 1999.

Bergen, Doris. *Twisted Cross: The German Christian Movement in the Third Reich.* Chapel Hill: University of North Carolina Press, 1996.

Ericksen, Robert R., and Susannah Heschel, eds. *Betrayal: German Churches and the Holocaust.* Minneapolis: Fortress Press, 1999.

Fritsche, Peter. *Germans into Nazis.* Cambridge: Harvard University Press, 1998.

Gellately, Robert. *The Gestapo and German Society: Enforcing Racial Policy, 1933–1945.* New York: Oxford University Press, 1990.

Gushee, David. *Righteous Gentiles of the Holocaust: Genocide and Moral Obligation.* St. Paul: Paragon House, 2003.

Haas, Peter. *Morality after Auschwitz: The Radical Challenge of the Nazi Ethic.* Philadelphia: Fortress Press, 1988.

Hockenos, Matthew D. *A Church Divided: German Protestants Confront the Nazi Past.* Bloomington: Indiana University Press, 2004.

*Journal of Contemporary History* 42, no. 1 (2007), special issue on Christianity in Nazi Germany.

Phayer, Michael. *The Catholic Church and the Holocaust: 1930–1965.* Bloomington: Indiana University Press, 2000.

# ECUMENISM OF THE PEOPLE

## PATRICK HENRY

CHAPTER TWELVE

Ecumenism, said Archbishop of Canterbury William Temple in 1942, is "the great new fact of our era."[1] The registering of that fact in histories, news stories, and encyclopedias gives the impression that ecumenism is a matter of organizations and large gatherings, of scholars meeting for years to find points of convergence, of agreed communiqués, and church unions. That story is grand, it is momentous, and it is not the whole story.

Many people are part of "the great new fact of our era" without knowing it, because the term "ecumenism" is over the horizon of common vocabulary. Indeed, one of the greatest ecumenists, Father Thomas Stransky, CSP, when asked, "What is ecumenism?" replied, "Ecumenism is something which, if we had a better name for, we would have more of." Father Stransky is himself a wizard at helping people realize they are ecumenists even if they don't know the word.

"Ecumenism" is linguistically noble and colossal—it comes from Greek and means "the whole inhabited world." In a Christian framework, ecumenism resonates with "God so loved *the world*" and Christ's prayer that *all* his followers be *one*, and it names the effort by members of specific denominations to overcome the splintering of the church of Jesus Christ by acknowledging and claiming the gift of unity. While the theological motive for ecumenism is the unity Christ prayed for, much of the energy of popular ecumenism comes from experience with neighbors, friends, family. Faithful Christians today say, think, feel, and believe positive things about other Christians that their ancestors a century earlier would have recoiled from. And almost universally these faithful Christians, whether they call themselves ecumenists or not, report that the more they appreciate the faithfulness of others, the more they grasp the faithfulness of their own traditions. Unity does not require uniformity; indeed, it is allergic to it.

## THE "CANNOT"

Benedictine Sister Joan Chittister, who has published thirty books, was set on an ecumenical course when she was in second grade. Her mother was Catholic, her stepfather Presbyterian. Joan rushed home from school one day. "What did you learn in school today that has you so wound up?" her mother asked. "Sister said that only Catholics go to heaven." "Oh, really? And what do you think about that, Joan?" "I think Sister's wrong." "And why do you think Sister would say a thing that's wrong?" "Because Sister doesn't know Daddy." "Sister," says Sister Joan recalling this moment, "was missing some of the evidence."[2]

The people's history of ecumenism is many things, but at root it is the story of countless experiences like Joan's, a conviction that what was taught was wrong, based on someone's "missing some of the evidence," and that one could not in fact believe it. To condense the experience into a single word, we can say that the people's history of ecumenism is grounded in a "cannot"—not "I will not believe" or "I choose not to believe," but "I cannot believe." And the ripple effect of that "cannot" has extended far. Today it would be difficult to find a Catholic nun who thinks the gate of heaven barred against Presbyterians (or even Buddhists, for that matter). To round out the irony, I know a Presbyterian nun.

When Herbert Chilstrom was a boy growing up Lutheran in Litchfield, Minnesota, about the time Archbishop Temple was declaring ecumenism the new fact of our era, he would quickly move to the other side of the street if he saw a Catholic priest or nun walking toward him. When, toward the end of the twentieth century, Chilstrom retired as the first bishop of the newly united Evangelical Lutheran Church in America, Archbishop John Roach of the Archdiocese of Saint Paul and Minneapolis was an honored guest at the retirement party.[3] What happened in the intervening half century

> **An Approach to Ecumenism**
> Organize as if there is no prayer; pray as if there is no organization.
> —John R. Mott (1865–1955), a founder of the World Council of Churches, winner of the Nobel Peace Prize in 1946.

was a seismic shift in Christian identity, and it is a measure of the power of the "cannot" that most Christians would find it as unthinkable today that Archbishop Roach would not be at that party as they would have understood in an earlier era why Catholics and Protestants didn't want to encounter one another on the sidewalk. The people's history of ecumenism is an account of how something that many would not have dreamed of—except in their nightmares—has come to seem the most natural thing in the world.

# BACKGROUND

The ecumenical movement is generally portrayed as a twentieth-century phenomenon, though there were periodic (and mostly episodic) efforts at Christian reconciliation in earlier times. The seedbed was in the missionary movement. In Africa and Asia, when Christian missionaries of various denominations attempted to perpetuate the distinctions and antagonisms of their churches back home in Europe and North America, potential converts were both mystified and scandalized. The missionaries came to realize that in their new context, so like that of the earliest Christians in the Roman Empire, the differences paled, and they were forced by their circumstances to recognize each other as sisters and brothers in the faith—*the faith*, deeper than any of their particular expressions of it. Ecumenism was born in the missions, not in libraries and seminar rooms; it began when people who were preaching the gospel grasped that they could no longer talk about other people who were preaching the gospel the way they had been taught to talk about them.

While the mission field was the arena in which doctrinal differences began to move to the periphery of concern, the traditional center of Christendom, the North Atlantic, saw a burgeoning of common social effort by Christians, initially in the devastation following World War I, and then in the vaster catastrophe of World War II. To the issues labeled "Faith and Order" were added those called "Life and Work."

These latter, in so many ways expressions of the mandate from Jesus in Matthew 25 to feed the hungry, give drink to the thirsty, welcome the stranger, clothe the naked, care for the sick, and visit the imprisoned, have been and remain a particular focus of popular ecumenism. That Christians would not work together (and also with persons of other religious traditions or none) in soup kitchens, AIDS shelters, and the like is today as unthinkable as Lutherans and Catholics avoiding each other on the street.

The movements of Faith and Order and Life and Work developed independently in the first decades of the twentieth century; they came together in 1948 at the founding of the World Council of Churches. The World Council is the centerpiece of ecumenical history, joined in the 1960s by the revolutionary Second Vatican Council of the Roman Catholic Church, and this story has been told often and well.[4] While it has many of the marks of institutional history, the story also intersects time and again with popular history, because what the World Council and the Second Vatican Council stand for, promote, and nurture resonates with the wide and deep effects of the ecumenical "cannot." The most intense moment of intersection came in 1982, with the publication of a document, *Baptism, Eucharist, and Ministry*, that was the fruit of fifty years of erudite theological work by eminent scholars—and the book became a runaway best seller and was the focus of thousands of small-group discussions around the world. This document is discussed in more detail below; it is mentioned now to signal that there is no clear line of demarcation between history as we are used to it and people's history. It is a matter of focus and emphasis.

The strands leading up to 1948 are many. An important one was highlighted by Robert S. Bilheimer in *Breakthrough: The Emergence of the Ecumenical Tradition*: that much of the leadership of the movements that coalesced in the World Council of Churches was provided by

> **The World Council of Churches**
>
> The World Council of Churches is a fellowship of churches which confess the Lord Jesus Christ as God and Savior according to the scriptures, and therefore seek to fulfill together their common calling to the glory of the one God, Father, Son and Holy Spirit.
>
> It is a community of churches on the way to visible unity in one faith and one eucharistic fellowship, expressed in worship and in common life in Christ. It seeks to advance towards this unity, as Jesus prayed for his followers, "so that the world may believe" (John 17:21).
>
> —From "Basis of the World Council of Churches," see www.oikoumene .org/en/who-are-we.html.

Fig. 12.1. The logo of the World Council of Churches. Courtesy of the World Council of Churches, Geneva, Switzerland.

laypersons and by young people. The Student Christian Movement, the Worldwide YMCA, and the Interseminary Movement galvanized energies and shaped careers. John R. Mott, credited by many as the chief architect of the World Council, was a Methodist layperson, and formulated what most practical-minded ordinary Christians would immediately recognize as an appropriate plan of action, free of theological gobbledygook and pious posturing: "Organize as if there is no prayer; pray as if there is no organization."[5]

It is hardly surprising that a movement that began among laypersons was soon being managed by clerics and denominational officials. Ordinary Christians could be heard complaining about bureaucracy, about out-of-touch professionals, and either about too much concern with theological quibbles in the face of the world's crying need or about excessive social action without attention to theological fundamentals. Ecumenism, like so many vital human motivations and actions, came to seem like something "they" do: this meant that it could be left to "them," and/or "they" could be blamed for whatever you did not like. At the height of the Cold War, the World Council of Churches was subjected to a blistering attack in *Reader's Digest*, a powerful reflector and shaper of popular attitudes not only in the United States but also around the world.[6]

## WAKING UP

Positive popular engagement with ecumenism, like so much else in a people's history, is hard to document. People were doing ecumenism without writing a lot about it, and those who wrote were often angry about something. It was my privilege over a period of thirty years (twenty as its executive director) to be closely involved with the Collegeville Institute for Ecumenical and Cultural Research, which is committed to discerning and nurturing popular ecumenism, and much of this chapter will draw on my experience. A people's history of ecumenism is necessarily impressionistic and idiosyncratic.

My predecessor as executive director, Bob Bilheimer, often said that the job of the ecumenical movement in general, and of the Institute in particular, is to help people who are already ecumenical but don't know it recognize their true identity—in short, to wake them up. These are people who have more in common with their counterparts in other denominations than with many in their own traditions. In some instances, ecumenical identity is a recovery of something they knew as children, as Sister Joan did, but may have forgotten as they grew older. In others, it is a confirmation of what has come clear only with mature experience, as in Herb Chilstrom's case. In Bob Bilheimer's own story, it was a paradigm shift in thinking that confirmed something he "knew" but didn't know he knew.

> One day, while I was an undergraduate, I was walking across campus with a remarkable man, the secretary of the Student Christian Association. We were talking about the church, and I said I had no use for it. In reply to his question, "Why not?" I spoke of my church back home to which I had had to go and which had meant very little, and of what seemed to me the general insignificance of churches. "But that is not what I mean by 'church,'" he said. "What do you mean?" "The church," he said, "is the Body of Christ, and you are a member of it." I stood still and looked at him; we walked on. I had never thought about that before.[7]

Before long Bilheimer understood, as Chittister and Chilstrom did, that one's church is too small—that there is more than one family room in God's house, and that each family room, if not sealed off from the others, is a good place to be.

Richard Mouw, president of Fuller Theological Seminary and a major voice in evangelical

---

**Pope John Paul II on Ecumenism**

The commitment to ecumenism must be based upon the conversion of hearts and upon prayer, which will also lead to the necessary purification of past memories. With the grace of the Holy Spirit, the Lord's disciples, inspired by love, by the power of the truth and by a sincere desire for mutual forgiveness and reconciliation, are called to re-examine together their painful past and the hurt which that past regrettably continues to provoke even today. All together, they are invited by the ever fresh power of the Gospel to acknowledge with sincere and total objectivity the mistakes made and the contingent factors at work at the origins of their deplorable divisions. What is needed is a calm, clear-sighted and truthful vision of things, a vision enlivened by divine mercy and capable of freeing people's minds and of inspiring in everyone a renewed willingness, precisely with a view to proclaiming the Gospel to the men and women of every people and nation.

—Pope John Paul II, introduction to the encyclical *Ut Unum Sint* (1995), 2–3.

Christianity, learned through sustained contact and conversation that people in other rooms are not as scary as he once thought. "Now when I speak about other groups of Christians, I remember that I have friends in those groups." Indeed, "there are also times, now, when I take part in groups with members of my own denomination and wish my Orthodox and Roman Catholic friends were there, because they would understand what I was saying. I have built up new loyalties to Christians from those other traditions. I have very much needed them to help me explain who I am as a Christian."[8] Mouw has discovered spiritual kinfolk among those he used to think of as aliens and has learned one of the fundamental ecumenical truths—that people can use very different language to mean much the same thing, and the same language to mean something very different.

Chittister's, Chilstrom's, Bilheimer's, and Mouw's are twentieth-century ecumenical stories. There are also tales that reach back directly into earlier eras. Margaret O'Gara, a leading Roman Catholic ecumenist, coined a phrase that captures the surprise of popular ecumenism: "the ecumenical gift exchange." To illustrate it, she recounts a moment in a class she was teaching in the 1990s. The final day's discussion turned to personal reminiscences. A woman mentioned the name of her great-grandmother. A man said his great-grandmother had the same name. A rapid genealogical excavation unearthed the connection.

Two sisters had grown up in an Anglican family in Nova Scotia. One had become Catholic and married a Catholic. Her Anglican family cut off all contact with her. The two sisters never saw each other again; all the knowledge their descendants retained was that a branch of the family was missing. Those two sisters were the grandmothers of the two students who were seeking priesthood, he as a Catholic, she as an Anglican. That summer there were two ordinations, and both families attended each. The ceremonies included a prayer that their ministries would be an instrument for the reconciliation, not only of their families, but also for their whole church families, so that they could live again as sister churches.[9]

Popular ecumenism, then, has many chronologies and choreographies. It can trace its roots to childhood, adolescence, young adulthood, middle age—or all the way back through several generations. And while the stories recounted here are experiences of highly articulate and theologically trained individuals, the experiences they recount resonate with countless narratives I have heard from people who have no bibliography and hold no position in a hierarchy. Popular ecumenism is accessible to all sorts of elites. "Ecumenism is not something that is done to the people of God. It is something we do together."[10]

## ECUMENISM AMONG US

In Collegeville, Minnesota, in the summer of 1994, the powerful reality of popular ecumenism became especially vivid. In our planning for a large conference sponsored by the Institute, we thought first of calling it "Transmitting the Ecumenical Tradition." As the program committee talked, the center of gravity shifted. We realized that the proposed title embodied an assumption needing to be challenged, namely that there is something called *the ecumenical* tradition that can be transmitted, with the clear implication that it is the norm against which anything else that might claim to be ecumenical would be measured and judged.

In earlier years we had already done boundary crossing, involving in our discussions members of churches that were not part of the "official" ecumenical movement (indeed, some from churches that were highly, even caustically, suspicious of the World Council of Churches), so we knew people who were genuinely ecumenical whose story was not part of what would be generally understood as "the ecumenical tradition." At the conclusion of the committee's meeting we realized that our conference would be "Ecumenism Among Us"—no one's story would be privileged, and something would be discovered, not transmitted. The conference would not presuppose that we or anyone knew for sure what ecumenism is; we would discern it together. The conference was attended by 208 people, ranging in age from seventeen to eighty-seven and shaped by more than forty Christian traditions.

The report of the conference mirrors our intention. It is not by any stretch of definition an agreed communiqué. I was especially eager to avoid such a formal result because of an experience nearly a decade earlier, where popular ecumenism ran headlong into official ecumenism. I was one of twenty-six participants from thirteen countries in a World Council of Churches consultation in Singapore on the relation between the church's unity and its commitment to justice (it often happens that competing understandings of what is just and unjust divide churches from one another, and even within themselves—Life and Work can be just as contentious as Faith and Order). We were not "ordinary" Christians in a people's history sense—our professional and ecclesiastical positions and our academic pedigrees would set us apart in mixed company—but we were acutely aware of the particularities of our individual experiences, and our conversations were spirited, provocative, and inconclusive. As we approached the final day, those in charge of the meeting proposed that we issue an agreed communiqué, and they presented a draft. The members of the consultation immediately mounted a stiff resistance, insisting that we would not put our names to something so clearly manufactured. The consultation members prevailed, but only after presenting an opposition that was unfamiliar to ecumenical officials who were accustomed to being deferred to as the "experts."[11] Our effective "popular" resistance anticipated something an Ecumenism Among Us conference participant said eight years later: "I believe the pressure from daily experiences will be the only effective force in catalyzing denominational change."[12]

Among the seismic changes in church life in the twentieth century that were registered at "Ecumenism Among Us" is the shift from denominational divisions to ideological divisions within denominations as the place where most Christians experience disunity. "We seem to be splintering within as we seek to heal without. The best way for healing with other communions is to learn to live with pluralism within. Reconciliation and grace are virtually impossible to communicate when the institution of the church is so visibly broken."[13] Herbert Chilstrom, who as a boy crossed the street when he saw a Catholic coming, was later, as a bishop, denounced by fellow Lutherans who believe that ordaining gays and lesbians destroys the church. It is not so much that the old ways are entirely out of date, but they are only one part of a complicated, ever-shifting scene.

> I see no one united ecumenical movement, but several streams diverging farther from one another: interfaith dialogue and work; institutional church union work; Christian unity prayer and practice in the lives of individuals, families, and congregations; the continuing reformation of denominations; churches working together to feed the hungry and heal the sick; multidenominational rural parishes; marriages that succeed across denominational lines; multidenominational teaching faculties of seminaries. In this process there is an opportunity to let go of older formulations of the ecumenical movement.[14]

In some ways, indifference is a greater threat than division itself to popular ecumenism. "Most Christians worship comfortably and in good conscience in their own setting without being pained by the state of church division."[15] It is unfortunately true that "ecumenical activity" is often the first line item in a church's budget to get cut when times are tight, but the pain of church division is inescapable every time a marriage crosses denominational lines. Couples in such situations know that ecumenical discussion needs to shift from how the traditions can help them to how they, on the basis of their experience, can help the traditions find creative, even revolutionary ways beyond the historical impasses.

At "Ecumenism Among Us" many additional features of popular ecumenism surfaced.

- Members of Orthodox churches expressed unease with the individualism of Protestants, and even of Catholics: "The coming together of the church must be the reconciliation of traditions, not individuals. I desire unity as much as anybody, but I cannot move on my own."[16] For the Orthodox, "We believe" is identity, not simply grammar.

- The deeply ecumenical nature of twelve-step programs, especially Alcoholics Anonymous, was offered as a model of repentance, reconciliation, and renewal.

- Choirs sing together even if they can't comfortably pray together. Music is an ecumenical bridge.

- Multiculturalism was highlighted as experience, not simply sociological observation: "It's peculiar to me to hear about multiculturalism as a *change*; as an African American, I've grown up in a multicultural situation, in which I've had to know more about you than you about me."[17]

- The center of gravity shifts from generation to generation: "The middle-aged and older tended to choose the session, 'When does dissent in the church become unfaithfulness?,' the younger, 'How can the ecumenical situation abroad help us in North America get perspective on our own?' Is this because young people have experienced more religious pluralism than many older persons and therefore this is more of an issue for them because they are less familiar with significant doctrinal divisions, or, because they have grown up in an era of dissent, they view dissent as usual and expected?"[18]

- Boundary crossing is not so much a challenge to be faced as a given to be acknowledged: "Is there room in the ecumenical movement for people who live on the boundaries of several traditions?" "People tend to agree or disagree without any reference to the church to which they nominally belong."[19] I recall a gathering of forty Sunday school teachers in a Presbyterian church at which the pastor asked, "How many of you are 'cradle' Presbyterians?" Three hands went up.

- Hurt and healing deserve as much attention as disagreement and truth: "We need to tread gently upon one another's 'holy ground.'"[20]

- We must repeatedly go back to the beginning: "Regardless how many times I have had an ecumenical conversation, or how many times I have considered these questions, each time I have it with someone new, I have it for the first time. For me, intentional willingness to go again and again into dialogue is a first, next, and last step. Conversation doesn't happen just to move on to a next point."[21]

- "Being the church and fighting injustice are inseparable." "It strikes me as ironic that concerns for economic, racial, social liberation, fundamental to the lives of millions of Christians (and non-Christians), many (if not most) of whom are people of color, can be labeled 'issues,' regarded as separate from the gospel, or treated as if auxiliary to the Christian faith. Yes, I make space in my own life for contemplation, study, silence, etc., but I also come from an African people who do not/did not dichotomize the world into secular/sacred, public/private, and I also am in the heritage of Black American Christians who heard God through the word call them into action, on their own behalf and in behalf of God's world. In faithfulness to those heritages and all that God has enabled me to know, experience, and become, the integrity of my Christian faith is caught up with my faithfulness to serving the downtrodden and freeing the captives (not just in a spiritualized sense)."[22]

- Arrogance undermines ecumenism. "Any kind of prophetic protest needs to be spoken with the recognition that we can be wrong. The longer I was in a stance of defending myself, the more I was becoming the mirror image of the people who were attacking me. You have to avoid becoming what you hate." "When I feel irritation, fear, or hostility as my response to another, I can ask those emotions to be my teachers, to show me what part of my spirit is frightened, in pain, and feels the need for security and protection, to ask what steps will open me to healing, to be more fully re-membered with Christ's body."[23]

## BAPTISM, EUCHARIST, AND MINISTRY

The year 1982 stands out in the popular history of ecumenism because the "official" ecumenical movement and the disparate but powerful expressions of the ecumenical "cannot" came together in an

### Statement from an Orthodox Commission

*Members of the Joint Commission of the Eastern Orthodox Churches and Oriental Orthodox Churches included official representatives of the Coptic Orthodox Church, the Syrian Orthodox Patriarchate of Antioch and All the East, the Supreme Catholicosate of All Armenians at Etchmiadzin, the Armenian Catholicosate of Cilicia, the Malankara Orthodox Syrian Church of the East, and the Ethiopian Orthodox Church from the Oriental Orthodox family; the Ecumenical Patriarchate, the Greek Orthodox Patriarchate of Alexandria, the Greek Orthodox Patriarchate of Antioch, the Russian Patriarchate, the Romanian Patriarchate, the Serbian Patriarchate, the Bulgarian Patriarchate, the Georgian Patriarchate, the Church of Cyprus, the Church of Greece, the Church of Albania, the Czechoslovakian Orthodox Church, the Polish Orthodox Church, and the Finnish Orthodox Church from the Byzantine Orthodox family.*

We have now clearly understood that both families have always loyally maintained the same authentic Orthodox Christological faith, and the unbroken continuity of the apostolic tradition, though they have used Christological terms in different ways. It is this common faith and continuous loyalty to the Apostolic Tradition that should be the basis for our unity and communion.

—"Second Agreed Statement" (1990) from the Joint Commission of the Eastern Orthodox Churches and Oriental Orthodox Churches.

unprecedented way that surprised nearly everyone. The World Council of Churches published a booklet with the rather dry title of *Baptism, Eucharist, and Ministry*—and it became almost instantaneously a bestseller, with over 450,000 copies in print in dozens of languages.[24]

The fundamental reason for this breakthrough of official ecumenism into popular conversation was a decision taken in 1964 to shift the focus of official ecumenical attention. "Instead of taking general themes and trying to deduce from them elements that would point the way for a new practice in the churches, . . . the churches' practice was to be the focus of joint theological reflection." And it was the Roman Catholic Church that showed the way, "for the proceedings [of the Second Vatican Council] had begun not with a general debate about the nature of the church but with the question of the renewal of the liturgy. Why not also apply this approach to the ecumenical movement?"[25]

The worshiping life of the church—that is, the church where people experience it, what people actually do, not an "understanding" of what they do—was to take precedence over theory. As a participant in "Ecumenism Among Us" put it, "There is something cleansing about worshiping the Lord together. Something miraculous happens when I bow my head in prayer or raise my voice in song together with a person I've been arguing with or about whom I've been having ungenerous thoughts. Worshiping with that person does more for the state of my heart towards him or her than any amount of wonderful dialogue."[26] As worshiping together across denominational lines—the sheer fact of praying with others was a crossing of traditional boundaries in many cases—became more common, especially after Vatican II, people started asking whether this new fellowship could be expressed in the eucharist.

In the 1960s and 1970s, many high-level meetings were devoted to the refinement of texts on baptism, eucharist, and ministry, texts whose origins in some instances could be traced back for decades. In one such gathering of Baptists, there came a moment when the ground shifted: "We immediately discovered that we could describe our theologies of baptism in the polemical language of the past, or we could face up to our common dilemma of the present. Fortunately, the latter option prevailed. . . . We discovered that our practices are not so different as our classical theologies might seem to imply."[27] Ordinary Christians, one might plausibly surmise, had known this all along.

When the preliminary texts were submitted to the churches in the mid-1970s, "the response was overwhelming. . . . In all, 186 official responses were received, but interest went far beyond official bodies. In many churches the texts were discussed in the local congregations." How can this be accounted for? "For many Christians in many churches, the texts were the signal they had been waiting for. The ecumenical movement had created fellowship across confessional boundaries; Christians were meeting one another and sharing more and more of their lives as Christians. As the differences between the churches persisted, however, this fellowship could not develop as they would have wished. Had the moment of 'liberation' come at last?"[28] The texts were not a bolt out of the blue; they gave voice to what Christians had been coming to know in the experience of "fellowship across confessional boundaries."

Clearly, the time was ripe for these basic elements of Christian practice and life—baptism, eucharist, and ministry—to be discussed openly and widely, not just by scholars and religious professionals. But there was a particular feature of *Baptism, Eucharist, and Ministry* that set it apart from nearly all other official ecumenical documents. The text, known also as the Lima Document, from the site of the meeting at which it was endorsed, contains very little theological jargon;

instead it weaves together biblical images that blur lines not by obfuscation but by going deep, to where roots converge. I recall vividly the visceral excitement I felt when I first read the booklet. The words on the page came to life, blazed up in a way that one almost despaired of ever seeing in documents produced by committees. People were not accustomed to having their imaginations ignited by ecumenical prose. Their response revealed just how hungry they were for a way to express what they already knew to be true.

A particular feature of popular ecumenism helps explain the huge impact of this document—the role of biblical study in the coming together of Christians. Different approaches to the Bible have of course been among the most intractable points of contention between churches, and until well into the twentieth century a prediction that the Bible could effectively help to unite Christians would have seemed preposterous. Not many papal encyclicals belong in a chapter on popular ecumenism, but one is unavoidable—*Divino afflante spiritu* (1943) of Pope Pius XII. Earlier popes had prohibited Catholic biblical scholars from making any use of the historical-critical methods or conclusions that had revolutionized Protestant understandings of the Bible. Pius XII not only undid the prohibition but told Catholic scholars that they should actively engage in conversation with their non-Catholic counterparts and learn from them. The consequence was astonishing, and very nearly immediate. The results quickly spilled over into the lives of laypersons.

Once Catholic biblical scholars were free to acknowledge that the Bible was not sealed off from history, with all its probabilities and ambiguities—so that, for instance, you could now argue for the religious meaning of the story of Jonah without having to insist that a man was swallowed by a giant fish and regurgitated alive three days later—the way was open for all sorts of Christians to talk with each other about their own encounters with the Bible. And if engagement with Protestants made Catholics less wary of personal interpretation, Catholics, with their instinctive appreciation for the teaching authority of the church and their sense of tradition, reminded Protestants that no one comes to the Bible in isolation.[29]

A participant in "Ecumenism Among Us" underscored the resonance between biblical understanding and popular ecumenical experience.

The Bible is the model I hold for Christian unity. I read the Bible and see different writers from different centuries, holding different theologies, discoursing on the same problems, stories, events, concepts. I see four gospels that do not agree with each other on who Jesus is, what he said, where he said it, to whom, and why. But I see them standing together, not requiring that the other change, but only that it stand along with it. This is not a war, rather a model of mutual respect and collaboration. I see stories, but not obliterating the story of the other. Embellishing, maybe. Changing the focus, maybe. But not obliterating. Poking fun at, but not dehumanizing the other. Can the church learn from this model?[30]

While I would still argue that the most powerful engine of popular ecumenism is Sister Joan's "cannot," in all its various specific expressions, Christians' recovery of the Bible, *together*, comes in a very close second.

## PEOPLE'S ECUMENISM AND MONASTICISM

In 1982, the same year as *Baptism, Eucharist, and Ministry*, a book called *God on Our Minds* appeared. It grew out of a six-year study project at the Collegeville Institute. Bob Bilheimer had traveled around the United States to ask, "What is the primary ecumenical question?" In a variety of ways he heard this message: the fundamental issue goes much deeper than church divisions, to the basis of theology—what does it mean to confess faith in God today? This question, he came to understand, was the real ecumenical equalizer, since Christians, without respect to denominations, and whether trained theologians or "ordinary" laypersons, were unsure of the answer.

A statement by one participant in the project, quoted early in the book, registers a significant theme of a people's history of ecumenism, and one with which *Baptism, Eucharist, and Ministry*, by its style and tone, resonates: "Theology is too important to be left to the theologians. Theologians need to listen to each other, but they also have to heed the people who make, buy, sell, marry, have children, laugh, cry, sometimes feel forced into situations where they are having to do what they don't want to do, long for the freedom to do all the things they would like to do, and who share one thing in common—that the last thing they will all do is die."[31] (Of course theologians are like this too; the admonition means they should pay more attention not only to others' experience but also to their own.) A participant in "Ecumenism Among Us" made much the same point: "People need to be together as people—talk, eat, spend days, dance, make art and music, consider issues, listen to each other, be silent together, see each other in different moods."[32]

Though popular fashion can easily be dismissed as faddish and ephemeral, there are occasions when what people flock to tells us not about mob behavior but about a precise intuition, almost a homing instinct, for what is profoundly true. The explosion of worldwide lay interest in monasticism as a source of spiritual wisdom is such an occasion, and bears directly on popular ecumenism because of a fact of history. The monastic tradition, in its classic forms, antedates most of the major divisions in the Christian church. Saint Benedict knew nothing of Orthodox and Roman Catholic, much less of Presbyterian and Baptist and Pentecostal. And the form of life he organized has persisted through the rise and fall of empires, discoveries of "new worlds" (though not new to those who were already there), revolutions in thought and technology, and the dizzying splintering of the Christian community.

Among the more delicious ironies of history I would count the huge popularity of a book by Kathleen Norris, *The Cloister Walk*. Her own tradition, Presbyterian, is not historically known for kind thoughts about monks and nuns. The cloister walk—a place where people made the catastrophic mistake of thinking they could earn extra credit with God—had been gladly abandoned. Indeed, for the Protestant reformers, and especially for the former monk Martin Luther, monasticism was the most vivid symptom of the church's having gone off the rails.

Yet in our own time, when in many parts of the world monastic communities are shrinking, Protestants at least as much as Catholics are flocking to monasteries for retreats, and are hungrily buying books by and about monks and nuns because of a well-founded suspicion that monasteries are places where people whose grasp of spiritual truth is as fresh as it is old, where they have tenaciously held on to something of inestimable value that our warring denominations have buried. And the key is in the first word of the Rule of Saint Benedict: "Listen." Popular ecumenism is about listening (as above: "listen," "pay heed"), and as such it is a recovery of an ancient mode of Christian life, prior to the relentless demonizing of those who disagree with you. Of course there was already, in the early centuries, plenty of anathematizing, but there was also the monastic insight, codified by Benedict, that the most you could hope to accomplish was a good beginning, and Christians today who adopt and adapt Benedictine spirituality are finding in its provisions for the journey the resources they need to make sense of their own instinctive ecumenical spirit. As an "Ecumenism Among Us" participant said, "Ignoring is the worst form of violence. We need more of the conversations in which uncertainty, frustration, and pain are freely shared, in which those who speak are not interrupted, corrected, or argued with, and those who listen are not defensive."[33]

A young woman, a college student, wrote about how encountering monastic persons had given focus and direction to her spiritual life: "Of course, Benedictines have a tremendous love for God. However, they have love for many other things. I feel that the Benedictines really are different from the rest of us, sadly because we see the world in black and white. We take many things for granted. The Benedictines see the world in many colors. I really am making an honest attempt to see the world in many colors because of my experiences. I am amazed by the simplest or littlest things."[34] Benedict's admonition that even kitchen utensils are to be treated as vessels of the altar, his instruction to members of his community that they are to keep death daily before their eyes, his insistence that the whole community be called together for counsel and that the youngest be paid special attention to—all these components of Benedictine spirituality make sense to "ordinary" people and cut through denominational obsessions that so often seem the paraphernalia of power games. In their seeking of God, monks and nuns are surprisingly unconcerned about getting all the terminology right. As Kathleen Norris (whose writings both draw on and speak to popular ecumenism) says, in the monastery "doctrine and dogma are effectively submerged; present, but not the point."[35] And a remark at "Ecumenism Among Us" would be instantly recognizable to any Benedictine: "Your doctrines, your view of scripture, might be offensive to me; I may think you narrow-minded, driven by a political agenda. But: how do I choose to respond? Do I choose the offense? Do I respond in unity or division? If your doctrine offends me, there's much about you that doesn't, and I can't be certain it offends God. Ecumenism is the willingness to become family."[36]

## RECONCILING MEMORIES

The offenses that keep Christians apart may seem recent and immediate, but most of them have roots that go back a very long time. One of the ways scholarship instructs popular ecumenism is by demonstrating the degree to which reconciling memories is even more crucial for ecumenism than is dealing with issues.[37]

Popular ecumenism is in fact quite adept at reconciling memories, often better than it knows. Its methods are among its best contributions to the ecumenical gift exchange. Humor is an especially effective solvent of conflict. A book called *Just as We Were: A Nostalgic Look at Growing Up Born Again*, by four evangelical Christians, gently spoofs restrictions they were brought up on while expressing warm appreciation for the good intentions of those who imposed the restrictions. The book not only reconciles the authors to their own memories but also opens their world in an engaging way to those who might have thought it laughable rather than humorous.[38]

While it is true, as noted before, that popular ecumenism doesn't regularly make itself heard in official ecumenical documents, it certainly did in two wonderfully refreshing, witty passages of a recent agreement between the Evangelical Lutheran Church in America and the churches of the Reformed tradition.

- On the issue of the eucharist: "Both Lutheran and Reformed churches affirm that Christ himself is the host at this table. Both churches affirm that Christ himself is truly present and received in the Supper. Neither communion professes to explain how this is so."[39] How many times have we been told, and told others, that the best response to a question when you don't know the answer is "I don't know"? Here, in a church document, memories are reconciled by a simple, honest, and humorous admission: "We don't know."

- On the issue of predestination: "To put the situation sharply: rather than being divided over the doctrine, both sides seem to be united in an equally lukewarm endorsement and an equal embarrassment over any form of predestinarian teaching as part of their theological commitment."[40] "Equal embarrassment"—a fair percentage of church-dividing issues could be resolved by such an admission on both sides, followed by a good laugh. In many of these instances, through the laughter we could hear laypersons saying, with relief, "Finally they've started consulting us in matters of doctrine."

**Fig. 12.2.** *Humor, Holy Conversation, Prayer*, sculpture created by Rosanne Keller at the Ecumenism Among Us conference, 1994. Photo courtesy of Carla M. Durand-Demarais, Collegeville Institute for Ecumenical and Cultural Research.

The basic ecumenical test—do you tell my story in a way that I can recognize?—needs to be modified: once I have heard you tell my story in a way I find acceptable, am I then willing to tell you the parts of my story about which I am embarrassed, about which I would really rather you not know?

We also need to be self-aware and self-critical about why we remember what we remember. Someone at "Ecumenism Among Us" recalled one of the younger participant's saying, "I don't know enough about our past hostilities to want to be apart from you." The fact that ecumenical professionals know a lot about the "past hostilities" does not bestow on them the right to declare open season on those who do not. Moreover, we need to search out memories that don't so much need to be reconciled as to be acknowledged. At an Institute consultation one participant said, commenting on another's paper, "Your feelings about the experience of your church and mine—your anger and my fondness—are probably the most distant from each other in the entire group; but reading what you have written, I sense a kindred spirit." The memories of these two were not in conflict; they had simply never intersected before.

The severest test today of our ability to reconcile memories is signaled in the title of Elisabeth Schüssler Fiorenza's book *In Memory of Her: A Feminist Theological Reconstruction of Christian Origins.* The flowering of scholarship on the history of women in the Christian tradition has begun to redress a huge imbalance. The real question, though, is not whether women have been important in the tradition, but whether the memories will be, can be, reconciled. The future of Christian unity depends on many things; among the most profound is the reconciling of the memories of men and women in the church. And women's memories go back a long way, to times when the divine was mainly female, when patriarchy was not "natural," not "the way things are."

Popular ecumenism, at least as I have witnessed it and taken part in it, is remarkably immune to the virus of caution. When sentiments like "What's the rush?" "What will we lose by taking more time to think through the implications?" get in the way of action, people get irritated, even angry. Of course, there are *always* more reasons not to do something than to do something. The argument was put classically by F. M. Cornford at the beginning of the twentieth century, in what he called "The Principle of the Dangerous Precedent": "Every public action which is not customary, either is wrong, or, if it is right, is a dangerous precedent. It follows that nothing should ever be done for the first time."[41] Reconciling memories means very little, and finally nothing, if we are not prepared to risk, even to risk making mistakes, together. Without such risk taking, we will miss the promise lurking in one of the profoundest of Yogi Berra's koans: "The future ain't what it used to be."

Reconciling memories is not just a device to achieve a goal, nor is ecumenism a method to be jettisoned when the goal is reached. Ecumenism, and reconciling memories, are ways of being in the world; they are human character traits; they are virtues. We reconcile memories not mainly to solve problems, but to become people who reconcile memories.

Because the memories that count, the ones that call powerful emotions into play, have more to do with people than with doctrines, we need a project to be called "Each Other's Saints." We need to know—from the hearts as well as from the heads of our sisters and brothers in other rooms of God's house—whom they revere, treat as exemplars, and why. We need a new, expanded family album. The most compelling example of this I have ever seen followed a meeting in which, on the Feast Day of the Assumption, some Catholics led prayer, and Paul Bassett, a member of the Church of the Nazarene, in the Wesleyan Holiness tradition, felt acutely uncomfortable. But he said to himself, "These are people I know and love, and I owe it to them and myself to learn why this day means so much to them." He went to the library and checked out several autobiographies by Catholics, to learn how their hearts and minds work.

## EXPERIENCE, SERIOUSNESS, REVOLUTION

The popular history of ecumenism—or the history of popular ecumenism—is not easy to sum up, but the conclusion to a chapter on the subject in this unprecedented People's History of Christianity has to try. Popular ecumenism has three features that define its character and make it a source of tenacious hope for the church—and for individual Christians, many of whom have an uneasy suspicion that Christian identity may not be good for people because it seems to require building walls when what the world needs is bridges.

First, *popular ecumenism is experientially based.* In the early church—the first thousand years or so—bishops were more like pastors than they are now, and the bishops were the professors. That is, the shapers of theology were in regular, unremitting contact with ordinary Christians. Augustine, the most formidable of the lot, preached virtually every Sunday for decades to the same people. We do not have much direct access to what those people themselves thought and talked about, but we have every reason to think that Augustine and his ilk knew what those people thought and talked about, and shaped their theology accordingly. Early Christian theology can appear remote and abstract to us, but this is because our imaginations are too cramped. Those early documents are experientially based, and it is not a stretch to say that twentieth-century popular ecumenism is a restoration, a return, a retrieval of the early church's way of expressing "what the church of Jesus Christ believes, teaches, and confesses on the basis of the word of God."[42] "What seems hopeful to me are efforts to minister to persons in their work and living environments: at airports, shopping malls, hospitals, on the street, at vocational training institutions, in support groups."[43]

Second, and following on the first, *popular ecumenism is theologically serious.* More than once I have heard and read dismissals of popular ecumenism by learned scholars who say that it is not rigorous enough, too ready to "compromise" theological principle, a "going along to get along" tolerance. Such high-handedness is called to account by the Bible's frequent reminders that the learned and the self-styled wise are often foolish in God's sight. Popular ecumenism as I have encountered it has an uncanny knack for raising crucial questions about settled answers and proposing answers to convoluted questions. A Pentecostal Christian noted that his tradition originated at the same time as the ecumenical movement, "but we were for the most part found among the disenfranchised of society. While the ecumenical movement drafted documents, we prayed down fire from heaven and experienced wondrous moments of community."[44]

**Fig. 12.3.** Workshop in the Ecumenical Community of Taizé in France, August 14, 2004. Photo © Pascal Deloche /Godong /Corbis. Used by permission.

Third, *popular ecumenism is practically revolutionary.* By this I mean that it generates sparks, it fuels initiatives, and once it is set in motion, it is very hard to stop. Popular ecumenism brings people together and keeps them together. "I'm scared as an individual; but what if all of you come with me?"[45]

I was once invited to speak to a group of laypeople from several denominations who had first gathered in the immediate aftermath of the Second Vatican Council, in one of what were called "living room dialogues." This group had continued to meet once each month for *forty years.* They were living testimony to the conviction that "the boundaries that divide the churches can be approached, and sometimes crossed, only if there is personal contact among credible people of good will committed to the vision of the church's unity." "We need to be affected by the dreams and thoughts of others—to be in constant realignment of our own views. This does not mean that we must all agree, just that we all must be willing to learn. And to learn, we must be willing to accept that we know nothing."[46]

An especially revolutionary instance of popular ecumenism occurred in 1993 to mark the halfway point in a World Council of Churches program called "Ecumenical Decade: Churches in Solidarity with Women." The whole point of the conference, "Re-Imagining," was to re-imagine *the tradition*, not to invent something new or revive old "heresies." Two thousand women and two hundred men affirmed, together, that Christian worship, Christian thought, and Christian community are not a male preserve. Christian imagery, patterns of thought, and rituals can draw deep from the wellspring of women's experience and knowledge.

Many Christians, mostly men but some women, in the aftermath of the conference declared that the people gathered in Minneapolis, Minnesota, had in those four days broken with the Christian tradition. In several denominations that had provided money to support the event, the conference became a flash point. The Presbyterian Church nearly split over the question, "Should we have had anything to do with 'Re-Imagining'?" Jobs were lost, contributions withheld.

To be sure, there was unfamiliar imagery, some from the female body, in the conference worship, but it didn't matter to the detractors that Genesis 1 says male *and female* are made in the image of God. To be sure, Sophia, the Wisdom of God, was often invoked, but it didn't matter to the detractors, who denounced "goddess worship," that Sophia comes straight out of the Bible.

What strikes me as so strange about the virulent church responses to "Re-Imagining" is their failure to see that the people gathered in Minneapolis weren't radicals—they were the conservatives, the ones still willing, in spite of the deplorable record of the churches in the treatment of women, in spite of the patriarchalism of the Bible, to stay with the Christian tradition.[47] In fact, "Re-Imagining" was in continuity with the classic expression of Christian women's ecumenical spirituality, Church Women United:

> Worship, study, celebration, action. . . . When CWU identifies these as its context of involvement, it envisions them not as stages of a linear journey but in a circular configuration. No starting point,

no ending. One grows out of another, leads to another, derives strength from another, gives strength to another, much as the local, state and national units of CWU interact. . . . The style is easy to accept if they see themselves within the larger human sphere and are committed to a circle to which there always is access.[48]

"No starting point, no ending." Revolution continues. A people's history of ecumenism, as it looks forward at the beginning of the twenty-first century, opens onto new vistas of interreligious encounter. The presence of rabbis and imams and yogis and dharma masters at bishops' retirement parties may become as normal as the presence of clergy of other Christian denominations. Some Christians recoil in horror from such a prospect, but as John Henry Cardinal Newman said in the nineteenth century, "To live is to change, and to be perfect is to have changed often."[49] Interreligious dialogue is still in its infancy, but it is likely that people will be ahead of their leaders. One harbinger of things to come was a project of the Collegeville Institute in 1999 and 2000, "Living Faithfully in the United States Today," that involved Buddhists, Christians, Hindus, Jews, Muslims, and Midewiiwin (Ojibwa). The event's report notes in the introduction: "There is another way, in which academic learning or professional expertise is not the most important tool. It is the way of conversation, of story telling, of giving a first person account of one's own life."[50] People become caretakers of one another's stories.

> **Healing the Divisions**
>
> When I look at the divisions among us, I wonder what could possibly bring us together in the oneness for which Jesus prayed—a oneness that would be a witness to the world. Then I recall the fellowship between my mother, raised Dutch Reformed and become Baptist, and Stella, our devout Roman Catholic neighbor. They loved and worshiped the same God. Despite differences in doctrine and practice, they both knew the same forgiveness of sins, the same mercy and grace, the same source of joy and love and hope and peace. The "what" that brings us together is really a "Who." The work of regathering is a work of God.
>
> —Esther Byle Bruland, *Regathering: The Church from "They" to "We"* (Grand Rapids: Eerdmans, 1995), 7.

## UNFINISHED BUSINESS

It remains sadly true, as one of the greatest ecumenists of the twentieth century, Albert C. Outler, lamented shortly before his death, that an aim of ecumenism remains stubbornly unrealized: "I had hoped," he said to me, "to live to see Christians gathered together at the table of the Lord." The circles of eucharistic fellowship have expanded as a result of the ecumenical movement, but they are far from congruent circles. But this is "official" talk. Multitudes of Christians have spoken a different word through their practice—going forward for communion, or taking the elements from the tray, despite the formal prohibitions, whether those in charge say "whoever is not of our flock isn't welcome" or "if you're in our flock, ours is the only table you should come to."

"Jesus ate with everyone. Why can't we?" asked a participant in "Ecumenism Among Us." And another reported, "We have made a

**Figs. 12.4 and 12.5.** Mennonite/Presbyterian Yoked Fellowship in Donnellson, Iowa, which has a very active "Presmonite" Youth Group. The church buildings of Donnellson Presbyterian Church (left) and Zion Mennonite Church (left, below) are shared by a single congregation, who worship and have Sunday School together but maintain separate boards and finances. The congregation alternates every four months between the two church building (changing on February 1st, June 1st, and October 1st every year, which means Easter and Christmas are always alternated). Photos by John Gorham. Courtesy of Zion Mennonite Church and Donnellson Presbyterian Church.

deliberate theological choice to form a house church, because the bottom line is this: the eucharist is so important that we cannot starve to death. We cannot let ourselves go hungry while the churches hold the eucharist hostage." Here at the end of this chapter, as at the beginning is the ecumenical "cannot." "Some issues are resolved by the people long before the institutions resolve them."[51]

On this, more than on any other popular expression of ecumenism, theologians tend to pass critical judgment. Such behavior appears to them grounded in sentimentality, evidence of emotion trumping careful thought and established doctrine. But in a religion that values love over even faith and hope, it is not self-evidently true that doctrine should always win. One of the illuminating moments in church history was Athanasius's recognition that people whom those on his side had been accusing of heresy were saying virtually the same thing he was but using different terms.[52] I suspect there were ordinary Christians in Athanasius's time who figured this out before he did, who knew that their neighbors and friends and wives and husbands, who expressed the faith differently from the way they did, were not enemies of God and were in fact inhabitants of the household of faith—people about whom they would say, "We cannot believe that God hates them." The fourth century was not the first time in the church's history, nor will the twenty-first be the last, when hierarchs and others in authority need to carry a banner saying, "We are their leaders, and we must run to catch up with them."

## FOR FURTHER READING

*Baptism, Eucharist, and Ministry.* Faith and Order Paper 111. Geneva: World Council of Churches, 1982.

Bilheimer, Robert S. *Breakthrough: The Emergence of the Ecumenical Tradition.* Grand Rapids: Eerdmans, 1989.

Lossky, Nicholas, et al., eds. *Dictionary of the Ecumenical Movement,* 2nd edition. Geneva: WCC Publications, 2002.

Kelley, Arleon, ed. *A Tapestry of Justice, Service, and Unity: Local Ecumenism in the United States, 1950–2000.* Tacoma, Wash.: National Association of Ecumenical and Interreligious Staff Press, 2004.

O'Gara, Margaret. *The Ecumenical Gift Exchange.* Collegeville, Minn.: Liturgical, 1998.

# GENDER AND TWENTIETH-CENTURY CHRISTIANITY

## MARGARET BENDROTH

On a cold winter Sunday in 1977, Pauli Murray led Holy Eucharist for the first time, standing in the chapel where her grandmother had once been baptized as a slave. The moment resonated with historical significance. Murray was one of the first women to be ordained by the American Episcopal Church, a veteran of a long and bruising battle for equal rights. That morning she stood behind a lectern engraved with the name of Mary Ruffin Smith, the wealthy white woman who had once owned Murray's grandmother Cornelia and who had built the chapel many years before. The sanctuary overflowed with local and national network media—even Charles Kuralt of the CBS program *On the Road* was on hand to record the event—and a joyous interracial congregation of family, friends, and supporters. At that moment, as Murray recalled in her memoir, *Song in a Weary Throat*, "all the strands of my life had come together. . . . I was empowered to minister the sacrament of One in whom there is no north or south, no black or white, no male or female—only the spirit of love and reconciliation drawing us all toward the goal of human wholeness."[1]

This small but significant moment of transformation is a good place to begin the story of gender and Christianity in the twentieth century. As she stood in that North Carolina chapel, Pauli Murray metaphorically demolished nearly every social category imaginable, breaking down old barriers of race as well as social class, and two millennia of established Christian custom barring women from the priesthood. Moreover, during the course of the late twentieth century, her act of hope and defiance was repeated many times over around the world, as women stepped into new public roles as pastors, theologians, and church leaders. An age-old pattern of predominantly male leadership in Christian churches appeared to be rapidly nearing its end. By the turn of the century, large ecumenical gatherings brought together women from Africa, Asia, and Europe and across the Western Hemisphere to reconsider Christianity's egalitarian message and its influence on the oldest human divide, the one separating male from female.

In many ways, therefore, Pauli Murray's life is emblematic of the much larger story of religion and gender in the twentieth century. There is no denying that a narrative of liberation makes sense for this subject—the past hundred years have seen many vivid accounts of hope and struggle, achievement and success. Pauli Murray's moment of personal triumph encapsulates a whole host of positive changes brought about in the twentieth century.

Of course she does not stand for all. A people's history of the twentieth century, almost by definition, directs our gaze away from solitary achievements, however dramatic, toward the broad range of human experience. Across the dauntingly diverse world of modern Christianity, most women continued to sit in pews and work in kitchens, as their mothers and grandmothers had done for many years before. With limited opportunities for education or leadership, acceptance into ordained ministry was, for many if not most, neither an option nor a dream.

But Pauli Murray's personal battle does open up a useful line of thinking about the complicated dynamics of gender and the larger structures of human experience that historians and anthropologists have documented across time and geography. In that sense, her long trip to the front altar was not just a confrontation with a particular ecclesiastical power structure, but a struggle against deeply rooted social ideologies about women's proper place. What a given culture considers to be "feminine" or "masculine" varies constantly across time and distance; the simple fact of biological difference admits endless nuance in meaning. Moreover, because of their basic interest in family stability and the ordered transmission of belief across generations, religious communities play a central role in shaping gender expectations. They have at their disposal a range of tools—myth and symbol and proscriptive texts—to enforce boundaries between male and female roles, and as we shall see, to critique existing cultural patterns. In the twentieth century, therefore, the intersection of religion and gender was often a deep tangle.

To begin with, there is no simple way to describe twentieth-century Christianity. Clearly, the events of the past hundred years have baffled the expectations of even the most acute observers. With the resurgence of Pentecostal churches and the rise of Catholic lay movements all around the world, the case for secularization seems thin at best. Modern Christianity never slowed down or disappeared, as an earlier generation of sociologists had once predicted; in Latin America, Africa, and Asia, it continued to grow and gather converts, sometimes in unprecedented, almost unimaginable numbers. In Africa, for example, the percentage of Christians grew from about 9 percent in 1900 (around ten million) to over 45 percent by 2000 and should be close to half the continent by 2025, over 633 million. South Korea, a nation closed to the West until the late nineteenth century, could be nearly 80 percent Christian by 2025. Even in thoroughly modernized societies like the United States, religion of every kind continues to flourish. With a religious adherence rate of over 60 percent, the United States is (statistically at least) one of the most religious nations in the world.[2]

It is more accurate to say that over the past hundred years, Christianity has decentered. Once a predominantly Western church, Christianity has become a truly worldwide faith, with the majority of the world's Christians now living outside the United States, Canada, and Europe. By 1980 the "average" Christian was young, brown, female, and living in the Southern Hemisphere. But demographics do not even begin to tell the story. Over the past century, religion of all types has become more contested, more

---

**Feminists Changing the Churches**

Aware of the limitations on the range of options open to women in the past, mainstream Christian feminists—both scholars and ministers—see the church as a significant cultural force in forming the attitudes, self-understandings, and expectations of women—and of men—and of society itself. They are deeply conscious of the damage that the churches have done to women, in the theologies, the language, and the structures that have kept women in a narrowly defined "place." They are determined to change the churches, radically. They refuse to leave. Perhaps they are more revolutionary than those who have given up. They refuse to ignore the liberating, indeed revolutionary, message that the churches bear about the realm of justice, peace, and equality coming in the future but, as the gospel proclaims, even now being born among us.

—Anne E. Carr, *Transforming Grace: Christian Tradition and Women's Experience* (San Francisco: Harper & Row, 1988), 18.

privatized and personal, with an increasingly tenuous hold on the public square. Though the human tendency to doubt is hardly new, public skepticism about religion is no longer checked by social custom or intellectual defense. At the very least, the story of modern Christianity is far more layered and tragic, more triumphant and mysterious than any one-dimensional narrative of progress—or decline—could ever encompass.

Even more daunting is the problem of generalizing about the lives of ordinary believers. Women, for example, form a solid majority of Christian believers: in the United States they have consistently comprised two-thirds of all church members, and in newer areas of Christian expansion their numbers are even higher. In Chinese house churches, Latin American Pentecostal churches, and African indigenous churches, the proportion of women is 70 to 80 percent.[3] Despite the universal themes in Pauli Murray's story, she can hardly speak for the multitude. The average church woman is not behind a pulpit on Sunday morning, but busy in the parish kitchen or in other less visible forms of service. Indeed, in terms of statistical realities, the truth about gender and twentieth-century Christianity is deeply embedded in the regular, often invisible rhythms of local church and parish life.

Generalizations are difficult—but they are not impossible. While there is no single narrative of gender and twentieth-century Christianity, it is not difficult to locate a few common themes. Obviously, for women all over the world the emergence of second-wave feminism in the 1970s and 1980s had a fundamental, permanent effect on church politics; controversies over women's right to ordination have roiled probably every religious body at some point in the last thirty years. In the workplace, home and family life, and countless personal relationships, feminism has deeply altered the expectations of both men and women.

But there are also deeper themes at play, fundamental to second-wave feminism but older and more universal. In a broad sense the history of gender and religion in the twentieth century is about the differential effect of modern individualism. The power to define oneself is, of course, a central motif in the history of Western civilization, easily traceable through the Renaissance and Reformation, the Enlightenment, and the modern era. Even the most overworked undergraduate is probably mercifully unaware of the countless number of books, paintings, and poems that have been devoted to the quest for personal autonomy. In the twentieth-century the discussion became if anything more intense, as scholars and social critics labored to analyze the effects of "expressive individualism," where the old demand for personal freedom is increasingly unhindered by traditional social forms. The debate was much broader than a simple liberal-conservative divide; sometimes it invoked conservative critiques of feminism and warnings about the future of the family, and at others it centered on the future of participatory democracy under the atomizing force of modern technological, political, and economic change.

All too rarely, however, did the debate recognize the added complexities of gender and religion. Certainly most people are aware that even in the most technologically driven societies, women still temper their desire for personal autonomy with the competing demands of home and family, sometimes by choice and sometimes by necessity. And it has become equally clear that, especially for men in modernizing societies, the gift of individual freedom can also be an insupportable burden. The absentee fathers and stressed breadwinners of the late twentieth century signify a growing crisis around the role of men—to the point that popular pundits and social scientists ask, only half in jest, whether men are even "necessary" to the future of the human race.

The Christian tradition has all too seldom addressed these issues in depth. More typically it has followed dominant cultural models, assigning women the obligation of self-sacrifice and men the power to lead, regardless of the strain this might impose on both. But over the course of the twentieth century, genuine Christian critique of modern individualism, recognizing its

> **The Individual in Modern Times**
>
> A half-century ago the family took precedence over the individual; now the individual takes precedence over the family. The individual once was an intrinsic part of his or her family. Private life was secondary, subordinate, and in many cases secret or marginal. Now the relation of individual to family has been reversed. Today, except for maternity, the family is nothing more than a temporary meeting place for its individual members. Each individual lives his or her own life and in so doing expects support from a now informal family. A person who considers his or her family suffocating is free to seek more rewarding contacts elsewhere. Private life used to coincide with family life; now the family is judged by the contribution it makes to the individual private lives of its members.
>
> —Antoine Prost, "The Family and the Individual," in Antoine Prost and Gerard Vincent, eds., *A History of Private Life.* Vol. 5, *Riddles of Identity in Modern Times* (Cambridge: Belknap, 1991), 84.

vastly differential effects on men's and women's lives, slowly began to emerge. Though the specific contours of male and female roles have changed over time, and vary across geographic and cultural contexts, the questions are broadly similar: Does Christianity liberate women? Can—and should—a Christian woman or man operate as a free, autonomous individual? And what kinds of obligations does Christian faith impose on men? Pauli Murray's moment of public triumph demonstrates the hope—and the reality—of reconciliation across many historic divides. But as this chapter suggests, the debate is far from simple and far from over.

## THE FAMILY CLAIM

In the late nineteenth century, the American social reformer Jane Addams coined the term "the family claim" to describe the problem besetting the young women of her generation. Even though opportunities for education and meaningful employment had been growing throughout the post–Civil War era, opting out of marriage and motherhood still took personal courage. "Any attempt that the individual woman formerly made to subordinate or renounce the family claim," Addams observed, "was inevitably construed to mean . . . that she was setting up her own will against that of her family. . . . It was concluded that she could have no larger motive, and her attempt to break away was therefore selfish."[4]

Three-quarters of a century before the emergence of second-wave feminism, the debate over marriage and career was already old and familiar. In the rapidly industrializing, pluralistic world of early twentieth-century American culture, many women were already well-versed in the struggle between personal fulfillment and the demands of family. Enormous cultural tension centered in the fact that though women's domestic responsibilities were lessening, their presence in the home still carried heavy symbolic weight.

If women's role was beset by competing certainties, the role of men seemed disconcertingly vague. The Victorian father was the undisputed head of the family but had no obvious function in the private sphere; by the turn of the century, even his religious obligation to lead in family devotions was falling into disuse. Not surprisingly perhaps, church leaders regularly bemoaned the absence of men at Sunday services and worried about the long hours spent at work away from the arms of wife and children. It hardly seems stretching the point to suggest that a great deal of the social tensions around women's proper place was rooted in deeper anxieties about late nineteenth-century masculinity.

In the late nineteenth century, much of the difficulty stemmed from the widespread cultural assumption that gender differences were fixed, immutable, and primary. Before modern people learned to think of male and female in more physiological terms, as a complex function of genetics, hormones, and social environment, most Western Christians assumed the two categories were fundamentally spiritual, especially in the case of women. A woman was not just someone with a female body or a certain social status but, as one historian has put it, "thoroughly sexed through all the regions of [her] being."[5] Nineteenth-century Victorians read all kinds of psychological, intellectual, and religious implications into the basic fact of biological difference. Indeed, according to influential Protestant theologian Horace Bushnell, men and women were so different in both soul and body "that they are a great deal more like two species, than like two varieties."[6]

As the twentieth century opened, most Western Christians, both Protestant and Catholic, assumed that women's nature was fundamentally domestic and inherently religious. While men's aggressive, dominating temperament pushed them into the public sphere of government, business, and politics, women's gifts of modesty and passivity suited them for the private realm. That division of labor was, to be sure, a middle-class ideal that hardly described the lives of many poor or working-class women; yet it also reflected a significant social reality. By the opening of the twentieth century, opportunities for meaningful, self-supporting employment for women were relatively few, and church work attracted talented, ambitious women in large numbers. Indeed, while male participation lagged, Christian service gradually became the most important means by which women in the industrializing Western world could achieve leadership and expertise, without the appearance of selfish ambition. As Methodist women contemplated forming a missionary society in 1869, one that in just four

## Women and Missions

Men have been the gatekeepers of the institutional church and theories about its relation to mission. Women have rather concerned themselves with the personal and ethical aspects of mission. Put another way women's mission theory focused either on personal witnessing or on working toward the reign of God. Church planting and the subsequent relationship between church and mission was rarely part of women's public missiological agenda. Even if women planted mission churches in practice, suitable men took over the pastoral work as soon as possible....Women were innovators in making personal connections with indigenous people for the sake of sharing the gospel—adopting orphans to teach them about Christianity, initiating house to house friendship evangelism among secluded women in zenanas and harems, living two by two in *pueblos jovenes* among the people they went to serve. From Ann Judson befriending the wives of high Burmese officials to Gertrude Howe setting up house to support her Chinese protégés attending American medical school, the interpersonal side of mission work often wore a female face.

—Dana Robert, *American Women in Mission: A Social History of Their Thought and Practice* (Macon, Ga.: Mercer University Press, 1996), 409–10.

decades would boast a budget of over $800,000, they defended their ambitious dream as "God's voice speaking to us—for who can so well do this work as we? Does it not seem as though the responsibility were thus laid directly on us? And shall we shrink from bearing it?"[7]

In fact, even the ecclesiastical differences between Protestant laywomen and Catholic sisters obscured important similarities in women's roles. At the turn of the century, many a Catholic parish depended on the quiet participation of laywomen in devotional rituals and the religious training of children. And they depended as well on the unstinting labors of many thousands of nuns, who provided the regular unpaid service that made brick-and-mortar Catholicism such a long-term success. Indeed, the model Catholic woman, like the model Protestant one, was a willing servant. Her role was fundamentally domestic, either as a mother at home or as a Sister carrying out an equivalent labor in a school or hospital.

In the decades after the Civil War, many American Protestant women learned to negotiate the demands of the family claim and cement their leading role in Christian service by organizing for foreign missions. Barred from preaching in the mission field or from leading roles in denominational missionary agencies, separate women's groups proved a hugely successful alternative. By the early twentieth century, women from a broad range of Protestant denominations in North America and Europe had established national organizations dedicated to training, funding, and supporting independent female missionaries. They staked their claim to an entirely separate mission field, arguing that only women could reach the heart of non-Christian cultures, through the medium of the home. By the turn of the century, "woman's mission to woman" was all but eclipsing earlier efforts led by men and proving itself a powerful (if not deeply ambiguous) means of exporting both Christianity and Western culture to growing missionary fields in Africa and Asia.

This meant that, for women, Christianity expanded out of its historical Western base as both a conservative force and a modernizing one. Arriving inextricably linked to the aggressive agenda of European and American imperialists, it both affirmed women's traditional, subservient domestic role and inexorably undermined it. Female missionaries insisted that true Christianity was inseparable from a clean, well-maintained home and obedient, well-educated children—yet their own busy, independent lives belied that simple formula. Though often couched in pious phrases, their core message was that Christianity liberated women from "heathen degradation" and subservience to men. Firm believers in the superiority of Western ways, and of the Christian faith, they established schools, clinics, and hospitals that both elevated and undercut women's commitment to the home.

Fig. 13.1. Lecture on "Caring for your Baby," Nanking, China. From *Light and Life* 49 (1919).

Not surprisingly perhaps, Western missionaries enjoyed marked success in gaining female converts—even when they tried not to. To use just one fascinating example, among eastern Africa's Maasai people, a so-called church of women arose in spite of the stated preference of Roman Catholic Spiritan fathers for male converts. Reasoning that male heads of households would provide the quickest and most reliable inroad into Maasai society, the missionaries had begun work in the early twentieth century establishing schools and community centers designed to attract men rather than women.

But their efforts had the opposite effect. "The enthusiasm of Maasai women for the Catholic Church," wrote Dorothy Hodgson, an anthropologist who has studied the Spiritan mission, "was all the more surprising given the erratic and intermittent nature of religious instruction, administration of the sacraments and pastoral care." In a world shaped by the demands of British colonizers, which placed a premium on men's role as property owners and taxpayers, women found church an important compensation. It offered them social space, a place to socialize, share stories, and develop independence from men. "In addition to providing opportunities for women to come together collectively," Hodgson writes, "the church provided formal and informal leadership opportunities for women. Although men were usually elected or appointed to the formal positions such as 'chairperson' and 'secretary' (which required literacy skills and proficiency in Swahili), women seemed to dismiss, ignore, or at best put up with the presumed authority of these men." In effect, Hodgson concludes, the Maasai Catholic Church offered women social breathing room, allowing them to both affirm the family claim and to subtly undermine it.[8]

## SECOND-WAVE FAMILY CLAIM

During the last two decades of the twentieth century, the old question of the family claim reemerged in Christian circles with new urgency and force, spurred in part by the rise of second-wave feminism. Clearly the movement fundamentally shaped the course of the twentieth century. Especially in its broader global context, women's rising aspirations brought about some epic social changes, as charismatic figures like Indira Gandhi, Benazir Bhutto, and Corazon Aquino rose to international leadership, and many lesser local female organizers campaigned for equal rights in marriage, control of sexuality, and access to employment. Though in some quarters changes were slow or nonexistent, they have affected far more than the elite few; in one way or another, women in every modern society have had to grapple with the aspirations the movement unleashed.

But feminism was only one of the new forces affecting the lives of ordinary people. In postindustrial economies like the United

States and Europe, the lines separating work and home—and male and female—had begun to blur and cross each other in complex ways. Technological changes like television, telephones, and computers removed all pretense of home as a sheltered enclave, separate from the secular bustle and flow of the outside world. (As one American fundamentalist noted glumly of television in 1955, "The boast of one network is that it 'brings the world right into your home.' Who wants the world as we know it in our homes?"[9]) The old nineteenth-century divisions of masculine and feminine, public and private, simply made less sense under the fragmenting pressures of modernity.

Economic pressures and rising aspirations also propelled more and more women, including those with school-age children, into the workplace. By the late 1990s, especially in areas of strong economic growth like East and Southeast Asia, over 60 percent of adult women participated in the labor force. Similarly, two-thirds of all mothers in the United States had entered the work force in 1995, a figure that included half of those with children under the age of two.[10] Though conservative churches often decried the erosion of women's domestic responsibilities, they could hardly stem the tide of social change. Studies showed that American evangelical women participated in the work force in almost exactly the same proportion as the population at large; the figure is also basically the same as that of women in more liberal Protestant bodies.[11]

In the midst of such flux, academic theologians and grassroots church leaders struggled to separate the permanent from the transitory. Were women naturally endowed with maternal gifts, and did they imperil both themselves and the wider society by venturing outside the home? Or were the old gendered divisions of labor merely arbitrary social conventions? Social science offered few new certainties; viewed across time and social boundaries, gender categories seemed eminently negotiable, defined more by cultural need than biological necessity. But other scientific research delivered a contradictory word, discovering gender differences deeply fixed in genetics, brain chemistry, and the complex mysteries of prenatal development. What was natural and what was simply imposed by social convention seemed almost impossible to separate.

Within the course of their daily lives, many men and women no doubt experienced the rapid changes of the late twentieth century as both freeing and harrowing, promising much but rarely delivering as anticipated. In Christian circles, of course, the central drama was women's fight for ordination rights. Momentum began building after the first meeting of the World Council of Churches in 1948 and the call for an international forum on "The Life and Work of Women in the Church." Spurred by the ecumenical movement's emphasis on human rights and Christian "essentials," centuries of arbitrary rules against women in the pulpit slowly began to erode. In worldwide Lutheranism, for example, the Slovakian church opened the ministry to women in 1951, and Sweden did so in 1958. During the 1970s, churches in North America, Latin America, and Asia also followed suit, as did African Lutheran churches in the 1980s. By the end of the twentieth century, some 68 percent of the bodies within the Lutheran World Federation ordained women, with those numbers often being matched in other denominations. In 1978, the Lambeth Conference of the worldwide Anglican church allowed women's ordination in principle and within ten years saw the first woman elevated to the office of bishop, when Barbara Harris was elected Suffragan Bishop of Massachusetts. Even among Roman Catholics, where women's ordination was long proscribed by law and custom, the Second Vatican Council opened a range of parish leadership positions to women. As in Protestant churches, women dominated local leadership; in the United States, according to one survey, they accounted for a consistent majority of the laypeople serving in parish councils, eucharistic ministry, and catechism classes.[12]

But timelines and percentages hide as much as they reveal; progress in achieving ordination rights did not necessarily signal changes in the traditional attitudes about gender roles that affected women

**Fig. 13.2.** Barbara Harris at her consecration as bishop in the Episcopal Church in 1989. Photo courtesy of the Office of Women's Ministries, Episcopal Church.

in church pews and kitchens. The overall thrust of papal teaching on women, capsulized by Pope John Paul II's 1988 encyclical "On the Dignity and Vocation of Women," emphasized women's inherent gifts for domesticity and service. "Woman can only find herself," the encyclical declared, "by giving love to others." Ordination had no justification in either church tradition or its understanding of scripture; because Christ himself had called only men to the apostolic succession, Roman Catholic teaching found no warrant for female priests.

And in fact change was slow everywhere. By century's end, even in some of the more liberal American mainline churches, the percentage of female clergy barely climbed above 15 percent, though women routinely numbered more than half of seminary graduates. Overall the proportion of female clergy had risen no higher than that of women in police and fire departments, around 10 percent. Female clergy also found themselves thwarted by a "stained-glass ceiling" and the expectation that women's primary responsibility to the demands of husband and family would necessarily keep them in smaller, less stable or influential parishes—yet another example of the family claim's continuing power. The slow progress of ordination in local churches in fact signaled that the old gender-based division of labor, with men in leadership and women in silent service, was still very much in operation.

In the postcolonial world, the issues were even starker. In many countries, foreign missionaries had left a legacy of commitment to female education and had modeled the power of educated, independent women. But when Europeans and Americans relinquished their mission stations in the decades following World War II, newly independent indigenous churches found themselves in a delicate position. Conservative attitudes toward women persisted where the minority status of Christian leaders made it difficult for them to challenge social norms. But even more to the point, poverty and urbanization patterns in Third World nations wreaked havoc on traditional family life, as the shifting demands for migrant labor forced many men away from their homes for months, even years on end.

During the 1980s and 1990s, perhaps the most concerted wrestling with religion and the family claim came not from Western

Fig. 13.3. Woman evangelist in India. From *Light and Life*, vol. 49 (1919).

feminists but from Christian women in Africa, Asia, and Latin America. Observing the daily struggle of women with poverty, war, and domestic violence, they found it difficult to press for change. The widespread image of Third World women as silent, patient sufferers lionized their tenacity but also perpetuated a deeply ambiguous stereotype. As Indian theologian Ranjini Rebera declared, "Self-sacrifice is a daily reality of Asian women's experience." Whether rich or poor, educated or uneducated, rural or urban, high caste or low caste, professional or unskilled, all women faced the social demand for marriage and passive acts of selflessness.[13]

The Christian tradition often seemed an uncertain ally of change. The conversation at an Asian consultation of Roman Catholic, Eastern Orthodox, and Protestant theologians in 1978 turned quickly to the gendered dimension of traditional caste structures and the exploitation of women through dowry exchanges—and ended with a critique of the missionary legacy. "Even the missions which established Churches in this country . . . handed down to us a tradition of women's inferior role," one of the women present declared. Though, on the one hand, the church had "always proclaimed loudly the freedom and dignity of all human beings," it rarely acknowledged the contradiction in the traditional view "that the subordinate role of women is the order of creation."[14]

But older, pre-Christian ways posed even more complex challenges. Although many women shared the concern of other Third World theologians for an authentic indigenous Christianity, they warned against resurrecting ancient traditions simply for the sake of doing so. Dorothy Ramobide, a South African writer, spoke for many when she declared that an uncritical acceptance of patriarchal African ways "runs the risk of being party to the legitimization of the domination of women."[15] Her hope was that women would not just protest the errors of the past but play a central role in redefining historic Christian tradition. The overriding message of Christian women outside the Western world was the need for a radical new look at the

Bible, taking the inherited tradition down to its original root.

This made for interesting new wrinkles on the old family claim, as articulate women from traditional cultures struggled to speak both *to* and *for* the many others they represented. To use just one telling example, in the late twentieth century the old Christian discussion about polygamy took a new twist. To be sure, the practice had long been condemned by Western missionaries and also by many feminists. But as one African woman theologian pointed out, none of these arguments took women's point of view seriously. Christian missionaries had always been primarily concerned with persuading the male polygamist to choose just one wife and live only with her. But what of the rest? Turning out a woman with children, who had been with one husband for many years, was hardly merciful. "Since each of the wives is married only to one man," this Christian feminist critic wondered, "could they not be considered for baptism if they so desired?" Could not the wives in a polygamous marriage decide along with their husband which of them would stand for Christian baptism?[16] Was it actually possible that Christian polygamy could exist in modern Africa?

> **African Women's Religious Roles**
>
> Religion is an area of life that seems to be able to escape public attention. It is also an area in which individuals may be intimidated to abdicate responsibility for their own lives and to place themselves and everybody else "in God's hands." This should not happen. Christian feminists undertaking "God-talk" must work for the liberation of women from an image of God created for women by men. When examining the role of women in religion in Africa—whether speaking of Christianity, Islam, or African traditional religions—we must face two fundamental questions: what responsibilities do women have in the structures of religion? How does religion serve or obstruct women's development?
>
> —Mercy Amba Oduyoye and Musimbi R. A. Kanyoro, eds., *The Will to Arise: Women, Tradition, and the Church in Africa* (Maryknoll, N.Y.: Orbis Books, 1992), 10–11.

The other rising conundrum of the late twentieth century concerned the role of men. By 1995, at a meeting of the Lutheran World Federation in Geneva, the old pattern of male domination seemed to have thoroughly turned, as the men present found themselves suddenly and unmistakably in the minority. These men responded in time-honored fashion, as many Christian women had a century before, by holding a separate meeting to air their concerns and build solidarity together. Though some of the men were ready to walk out at that point, others urged them to stay and try to influence the proceedings. Most found the experience eye-opening—and deeply frustrating. One Lutheran bishop later confessed to feeling "intimidated" by the women on the podium, and "helpless and powerless because he was not the one setting the agenda." But he worked far enough through his anger to conclude that "if the way he felt was the way women feel when they are in the minority, then there was an urgent need to do something about it."[17]

The deeper problem, however, was that women simply were not a minority in Christian churches—and had not been so for a long time. If anything, the ferment of the late twentieth century had fixed ordinary women more securely in the center of Christian activism and had rendered men more marginal. Around the world and across many communities, the preponderance of women and the general dearth of men began to raise worries about the social, cultural, and theological effects of religious "feminization."

## FUNDAMENTALISM

In the last half of the twentieth century, anxiety about gender found forceful expression in fundamentalism. Especially after the rise of the Taliban in Afghanistan and Islamicist revolutions across the Middle East, the movement became synonymous with conservative views on female sexuality and political rights; yet, in its deepest sense, fundamentalism was not really about Islam, and it was less concerned with proscribing the actions of women than it was with shoring up male authority.

The term "fundamentalism" originated as description of a movement within American Protestantism, joining together conservative, militant voices in response to social and theological changes in the late nineteenth and early twentieth centuries. "Fundamentalists" worried about sliding standards in Christian doctrine and campaigned for a return to basic statements of faith. They decried the loss of biblical authority in an increasingly relativistic moral world, calling for godly separation from the rampant social evils of their age.

But the issues were not just simple matters of correct or incorrect doctrine: fundamentalist protest against secular culture also invoked gender. Many American Protestant fundamentalists were openly critical of women who forsook their appointed moral role, and during the

1920s, they rarely tired of calling down judgments on the "flappers" and "vamps" who smoked and drank in public. They also rejected the popular wisdom that women were more religious than men. Increasingly, fundamentalist diatribes invoked deeply negative portrayals of women as untrustworthy temptresses and, in fact, as symbols of worldly vanity and rebellion against God. The new gender paradigm, emerging out of fundamentalism and exerting a slow but demonstrable influence across other religious communities, turned the old one on its head. No longer the more virtuous sex, and the truest allies of Christianity, women were its bitterest enemies. Godly leadership therefore belonged first and foremost to men.

Recently, scholars and social critics have begun to talk about fundamentalism as a global movement within all of the major world religions. Bruce Lawrence has described it as a "religious ideology of protest" against the forces of modernity: secular nationalism, the rule of technological elites, and the moral relativism of consumer capitalism. But fundamentalists have staged their battle with the best weapons of communication that the latest technology affords, using the resources of the modern world to stake their claim for traditional values. They are, as Lawrence writes, "moderns, but not modernists. . . . at once the consequence of modernity and the antithesis of modernism."[18]

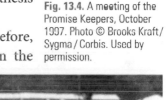

Fig. 13.4. A meeting of the Promise Keepers, October 1997. Photo © Brooks Kraft / Sygma / Corbis. Used by permission.

The fundamentalist reassertion of the family claim, therefore, is both deeply conservative and sharply contemporary. When the Promise Keepers movement emerged in the United States in the 1990s, bringing together thousands of men in huge outdoor stadiums to repent of their sins and confirm their commitment to family, some of its most appreciative admirers were feminists. To be sure, the Promise Keepers rarely missed an opportunity for stereotypical language about

---

**Fundamentalism and the Family Claim**

In the face of . . . frustrations in dealing with external forces beyond their control, fundamentalists have found themselves most able to effect significant change in interpersonal relations, especially within the family. Building upon existing inequalities between women and men, patterns of discrimination against women, and the exclusion of women from positions of power, fundamentalists call for a strengthening of prerogatives for males and elders in the name of a return to "tradition," sanctified as the expression of God's will on earth.

—Helen Hardacre, "The Impact of Fundamentalisms on Women, the Family, and Interpersonal Relations," in Martin Marty and R. Scott Appleby, eds., *Fundamentalisms and Society: Reclaiming the Sciences, the Family, and Education* (Chicago: University of Chicago Press, 1993), 138.

---

female dependency and male leadership, and at times their public rhetoric raised angry protests. But the most astute critics of the movement noticed that a Promise Keeper dad, committed to staying at home nights and sharing in child care and housework, was in many ways a feminist's wish come true.

In poorer parts of the world, where father absence is a matter of survival, conservative evangelical religion also played a somewhat paradoxical role. One study of Pentecostal churches in Colombia, for example, found that both men and women were attracted by their highly traditional teaching on male dominance and feminine submission. Pentecostal preachers insisted that men were to be the head of the household, using language drawn from a culture steeped in male machismo. Yet women recognized in that rhetoric an opportunity for family stability. In the long run it made men relatively immune to the more destructive aspects of male culture and answerable to the needs of their wives and children. Pentecostal women found their standard of living, and their own prospects for success, improving as a result of this gender ideology. Instead of buying alcohol or tobacco, Pentecostal fathers brought home their weekly paycheck; instead of spending evenings in bars and clubs, they were busy at church.[19]

Much has been written on fundamentalism, and there is no doubt much more waiting to be said. Few movements demonstrate so starkly both the adaptability and the rigidity of religion in the modern world. One of the best ways to understand the significance of fundamentalism is to approach it as a parable. The literal meaning is not really the point; who is to say whether fundamentalism is "good" or "bad" for either women or men? The effects of its conservative gender ideology are far too ambiguous to allow for a simple conclusion. What's important is the underlying lesson. Clearly, fundamentalism taps deeply into a classic modern problem, tempering the old masculine prerogative of personal autonomy while pressing anew the old family claim on women. And for that reason it is not likely to disappear any time soon.

## NEW UNDERSTANDINGS OF OLD IDEAS

Almost everything about ordinary life in the twentieth century seems unprecedented: the unimaginable bloodbath of two world wars and a succession of genocides, the constant flow of startling new technologies, the births and deaths of nations, ethnic groups, animal species, and intellectual paradigms. The world of 1900, comfortably Victorian and dominated by Western hegemony, hardly seems real a hundred years later, when so many easy assumptions have been laid bare by violence and technological change.

Yet it is possible to see the "people's story" of the twentieth century, especially as it relates to religion and gender, as somehow familiar. As the material in this essay suggests, the past one hundred years or so have witnessed not simply the end of tradition but its rediscovery. Contrary to our modern propensity for timelines and horizontal charts, history rarely moves in a linear fashion. More often, what appears to be change is actually a long, slow, three-dimensional spiral; the illusion of forward movement is really a constant circling back onto the same scenery, though each time with a slightly different vantage point. Thus, what might look like the tired spectacle of old battles being fought and refought could well be the work of a new set of people on a quest for contemporary understanding.

There is no simple way to sum up such a long and complicated story, especially one that encompasses so many disparate and invisible personal lives. Perhaps it is best to step back finally and acknowledge the obvious: the mysterious success of religion in the modern world owes much to the vitality of our ongoing conversations around gender and the meaning of personhood. Here emerge some of the deepest, most puzzling questions about what it means to be human, to be at once independent and responsive to the needs of others. It raises a myriad of open queries about the family, both its present-day form and its possible futures, refracted through a maze of cultural lenses. It is a conversation almost guaranteed to be constantly new and constantly beyond the reach of easy answers.

## FOR FURTHER READING

Carr, Anne E. *Transforming Grace: Christian Tradition and Women's Experience.* San Francisco: Harper & Row, 1988.

Clark, Elizabeth, and Herbert W. Richardson, eds. *Women and Religion: The Original Sourcebook of Women in Christian Thought.* San Francisco: HarperSanFrancisco, 1996.

Fabella, Virginia, and Mercy Amba Oduyoye, eds. *With Passion and Compassion: Third World Women Doing Theology: Reflections from the Women's Commission of the Ecumenical Association of Third World Theologians.* Maryknoll, N.Y.: Orbis Books, 1988.

Hardacre, Helen. "The Impact of Fundamentalisms on Women, the Family, and Interpersonal Relations." In Martin Marty and R. Scott Appleby, eds., *Fundamentalisms and Society: Reclaiming the Sciences, the Family, and Education,* 129–50. Chicago: University of Chicago Press, 1993.

Melton, J. Gordon, ed. *The Churches Speak On: Women's Ordination.* Detroit: Gale Research, 1991.

Oduyoye, Mercy Amba, and Musimbi R. A. Kanyoro, eds. *The Will to Arise: Women, Tradition, and the Church in Africa.* Maryknoll, N.Y.: Orbis Books, 1992.

Prost, Antoine, and Gerard Vincent, eds. *A History of Private Life.* Vol. 5, *Riddles of Identity in Modern Times.* Cambridge: Belknap, 1991.

Robert, Dana. *American Women in Mission: A Social History of Their Thought and Practice.* Macon, Ga.: Mercer University Press, 1996.

Strawley, John H., ed. *Fundamentalism and Gender.* New York: Oxford University Press, 1993.

# CANADIAN WORKERS AND SOCIAL JUSTICE

## OSCAR COLE-ARNAL

## CHAPTER FOURTEEN

## THE PROTESTANT SOCIAL GOSPEL

### Farm and Factory

On December 18, 1901, angry farmers gathered in the Canadian Pacific Railroad (CPR) town of Indian Head, Northwest Territories (Saskatchewan province by 1905).[1] There in this rail point (population 1,545), they began organizing the Territorial Grain Growers' Association (TGGA), which came to fruition in February of the following year. So began the grassroots upsurge that came to be called the social gospel in Canada. Strain between the independent wheat farmers on one side and the railroad barons, Grain Exchange (Winnipeg), eastern banks, and the international grain market on the other had been growing from harvest to harvest. All too soon, the farmers had come to realize that they were victims of the railroad monopoly, which owned the grain elevators as well. In this situation, grain-loading prices were manipulated by CPR operatives to pay farmers as little as possible in order to extract higher profit levels. Price manipulations and false weights were not uncommon. However, the fiasco around the harvest of 1901 put the torch to the powder keg of farm rage. A massive bumper crop of wheat arrived to be loaded on the trains or stored in the grain elevators. The CPR system at every level failed to provide for this wheat boom. By the end of the year the farmers had half their harvest (thirty billion bushels) spoiling in their own hands.

In this conflict the TGGA came to life, and a local farm leader, W. R. Motherwell, became its leader. From that point until the Depression, farmers organized to fight the economic and political elites via trial-and-error methods in the name of cooperation versus competition. These farmers learned the hard way, moving from one struggle to another until the 1920s, by which time they had created various provincial organizations, press organs, cooperative marketing strategies, and their own grain elevators and companies. Finally, they organized politically, and they helped form governments in Ontario (1919) and Alberta (1921). Indeed, this latter administration was the first in Canada to give a ministry to a woman, the social gospel activist Louise McKinney. Throughout these farm struggles the language that shaped this evolving movement came from an increasingly popular Protestant optimism known as the social gospel.[2]

To be sure, certain Protestant theological liberals in central Canada had already demanded a Christian faith more open to social change, but these voices (Methodist, Presbyterian, and Anglican) reflected British and American borrowings within tight academic circles and the editorial pages of denominational magazines. Initially they were only refined utterances within comfortable discussion circles, until the Protestant call for social change emerged from western grain farmers, workers in urban railway centers, and independent labor unions from the major Prairie cities. Without these massive socioeconomic and political pressure points, the social gospel would have remained an ivory tower phenomenon, but the rapidly expanding prairies, with their increasing class tensions, gave opportunity for the melding of certain religious values with social conflict that brought a unique twist to this Protestant social Christianity in English-speaking Canada.

Until the Canadian Pacific Railway had crossed the vast land mass of Canada in 1885, the national identity lived in the minds of a few visionaries. The new federal government, created through a series of regional deals, came to official birth by a British parliamentary act in 1867. The recently knighted Sir John A. MacDonald became Canada's first prime minister. Part visionary, part pragmatist, MacDonald began a pattern of government-private partnerships with bankers and railroad barons that he and subsequent leaders would use to build a nation. With the government funding railway companies against risk, those same bankers and rail entrepreneurs began to link Canada's vast land mass by ribbons of steel. Of course, the railroads made demands from their government to insure profitability. These included a vast cheap labor force to bring natural resources to rail loading points and urban conglomerations that served as storehouses and manufacturing centers to build and repair railway rolling stock.

The Mercy of His Friends

Fig. 14.1. "The Mercy of His Friends" cartoon by Arch Dale, from *Grain Growers' Guide*, September 22, 1920. Photo courtesy Provincial Archives of Manitoba.

These goals were accomplished in two ways. The federal government, with its new Prairie provincial counterparts, ignited a massive public relations campaign to lure immigrants from eastern Canada and abroad. Clifford Sifton, the minister of Interior for the Liberal Wilfrid Laurier government (1896–1905), persuaded both his colleagues and the eastern economic barons that their future profits lay in selling western railroad land cheaply to desperate eastern farmers and European immigrants, thus populating the West and raising wheat for sale on the international market. Sifton won out on both counts. He got a cheap labor force for the West; by 1901, 8 percent of the national population dwelt in the once sparse prairies. By 1931, that figure had risen to 25 percent. With the end of the war in 1918, wheat had become Canada's most important export, and the Prairies accounted for 90 percent of that production. No wonder wheat became the operative "gold standard" for Canada and received the honorific title of "King Wheat."[3]

This mix of immigration and the rise of railway centers caused an urban boom as well, an expansion underscored by a "self-made man" reflected in the city boosterism. Winnipeg, located in the middle of the nation, became the railway hub of the new Canada. In 1891, the city contained a mere 26,000 people, but by 1916 the number had risen to 163,000, composing approximately one-third of Manitoba's population. As well, this "Chicago of the North" employed 57.3 percent of the Prairie labor force and produced 48.2 percent of the gross value of Prairie manufacturing output. A set of Anglo-Saxon Protestant entrepreneurs came to dominate the political, social, and economic life of the city, and it was they who orchestrated the booster public relations crusade that used the major newspapers to lure further investment into this booming railway center. A combination of arrogance and imperial vision, so common to the successful practitioners of the Protestant work ethic, generated civic leaflets and advertisements, as the following quotation demonstrates so clearly: "The doors of vast opportunity lay wide open and Canada's adventurous sons flocked to Winnipeg to have a part in the great expansion—the building of a new and greater Canadian West. They were big men, come together with big purpose. Their ideas were big, and they fought for the realization of them."[4] Typical and notable among them was James Henry Ashdown, the "Merchant Prince." While making his millions in the hardware industry and real estate speculation, he figured prominently in the city's powerful business organizations, served a term as mayor, directed a city bank, and emerged as the single most powerful influence in the city's Methodist Church institutions, including Wesley College (Prairie Methodism's key seminary).

In spite of the programmatic hype spun by Ashdown and his elite colleagues, the city had its bleak and darker side. Into the northern sector of the city, called alternately "CPR Town" or the "Foreign Quarter," squeezed the hated immigrants and workers who performed hard labor in the city's railroad yards. Shocking conditions of human misery dominated the grim streets of this makeshift ghetto. The Reverend James Shaver Woodsworth, one of the social gospel's most prominent leaders and an early settlement house worker in this neighborhood, was appalled by what he saw. "Let me tell you of one little foreign girl," he penned in a piece he wrote for the *Manitoba Free Press* (March 12, 1909). "She lives in a room in a disreputable old tenement—one of those human warrens which are multiplying with great rapidity in our city. Her father has no work.

---

### The Social Gospel in Canada

The Social Gospel was progressive, optimistic, and driven by a crusading zeal; it was strongest within the Protestant churches that were strongest on the prairies; it provided the support of the churches and the gospel—crucial elements in that age—for campaigns of social reform and regeneration.

—Gerald Friesen, *The Canadian Prairies* (Toronto: University of Toronto Press, 1984), 351.

The men boarders have no work. The place is incredibly filthy. The little girl has been ill for months—all that time living on the bed in which three or four persons must sleep and which also serves the purpose of table and chairs." By this time, the charity-dispensing social gospeler had begun to ask the dangerous question, "Why?" In the same article, he added: "Yes, and many of the well-to-do are drawing large revenues from this same misery. . . . The owners of some of our vilest dens in the city were our 'best' (!) people—our society people, our church people, and that for these houses they obtain in some cases, double the legitimate rentals."[5] In the midst of social misery some adherents of the social gospel began to raise painful issues.

## Birth and Expansion
## (1890s to March 1914)

The social gospel emerged in Canada as part of an international movement of English-speaking Protestants caught up in the liberal optimism of westward expansion and the imperialistic notion of British or American superiority. Along with its antiforeign and racist overtones one found also a broad push for social reform directed toward those who suffered the fallout of such expansionist projects, namely small farmers and workers in the cities. To a person, the public advocates of the early Canadian social gospel were white Anglo-Saxon Protestants, mostly from the Methodist, Presbyterian, and Anglican denominations. Though highly influential by the outbreak of World War I in August 1914, the social gospelers were only a vocal minority within their denominations; their optimism was characterized by expansionist dreams of nation building and the frontier missions that would make this possible. Indeed, Woodsworth's father was Methodism's chief mission official for the Prairie provinces. As the Prairies urbanized in the wake of railway expansion, the three major Protestant denominations replaced an earlier Catholic dominance. With the exception of marginalized immigrant sectors from Central and Eastern Europe, these social gospel churches dominated the Prairie urban scene and most of the grain-farming communities as well. In this overall ecclesiastical context the emerging social gospel found a rather warm welcome within such expansionist dreams. An apparent unity held among social gospelers until Canada was plunged into the European war.

Even so, three tendencies developed gradually. Social gospel historian Richard Allen, in his book *The Social Passion*, describes these as (1) conservative, (2) progressive, and (3) radical. By definition the conservatives represented a largely charitable model supporting the alleviation of social pain as a vital step in the evangelizing process, whereas progressives sought significant social reform largely through official church statements as appeal mechanisms for legislative reform in social and economic matters. The small group of radicals, who emerged as a distinct voice in the latter war years and especially during the Winnipeg General Strike in 1919, promoted a vision, which today would be called democratic socialism, and joined aggressive grassroots movements to give birth to their dreams. In the midst of conflict this handful of radical Protestants was forced to find allies outside of their rejecting denominations. Until the 1920s, the progressives seemed to hold the field, especially in the Presbyterian and Methodist churches.

**Fig. 14.2.** A crowd during the Winnipeg Strike of 1919 outside the Union Bank Building on Main Street. Photo courtesy Library and Archives Canada.

Building on successful alliances in temperance and "Lord's Day" (six-day work week) campaigns with Canada's moderate English-speaking trade union movement, the Methodists and Presbyterians set up official departments charged directly with social gospel concerns under the able leadership of the moderate progressives T. A. Moore and J. G. Shearer respectively. Building upon these early achievements they and others (especially the labor movement) formed the Moral and Social Reform Council (later called the Social Service Council) both to collect vital information in support of social change projects and to lobby governments to promote and produce such measures. Gains in this direction had been accomplished already through the

Woman's Christian Temperance Union (WCTU) under the Canadian leadership of such social gospelers as Sara Rowell Wright and Letitia Youmans. Following the example of its American leader, Frances Willard, the Canadian WCTU moved beyond halting the booze trade into the realm of settlement houses, urban reform, fair labor legislation, Christian socialism, and female suffrage.

As in the United States the WCTU served as a training ground to launch Protestant women into public life. Chief among them was Methodist writer and suffrage activist Nellie McClung, whose long career demonstrates how wide-ranging social gospel issues came to permeate Canadian society. McClung reached the broader public chiefly as a popular writer and speaker, but she engaged also in direct political activism, ran for office in the Liberal Party, served as a Canadian delegate to the League of Nations and became in her elder years the first woman on the Canadian Broadcasting Company's board of directors. The activist McClung claimed that "the meaning of the women's movement" was to "sit down and be resigned" no longer but rather "to rise up and be indignant." She and a band of women managed to do just that when they held a mock parliament of women at Winnipeg's Walker Theater in 1914, which dramatized the silliness of the Manitoba parliament's denial of the vote to women.

> **The Motherhood of God**
> The Church has been dominated by men and so religion has been given a masculine interpretation, and I believe the Protestant religion has lost much when it lost the idea of the motherhood of God.
>
> —Nellie McClung,
> *In Times Like These*
> (New York: Appleton, 1915), 70.

The grand success of these assorted groups of Protestant reformers climaxed on March 3–5, 1914, at the Social Service Congress in Ottawa. Over two hundred delegates gathered there from a wide range of social professions, all dedicated in one way or another to economic and humanitarian reform. Called a "free parliament on social questions," this congress consisted of a "Who's Who" of prominent social gospel leaders in Canada with a sprinkling of American counterparts. A full 50 percent of the presenters at Congress sessions were clergy, mostly coming from the social gospel churches. Although rural issues were voiced, the center of gravity focused on urban concerns such as child welfare, temperance, prison reform, labor unrest, and the role of religion in building the new society. So notable was this conference that Prime Minister Robert Borden and Liberal opposition leader Wilfrid Laurier shared a head table at the opening session. Optimism abounded; a glorious future was at hand. The united social gospel had reached its noontide.[6]

## Conflict and Division

War and labor strife intervened to shatter such dreams. Given the links of social gospel hopes with Anglo-Saxon imperialism, most vocal Presbyterians and Methodists, along with their leadership, viewed the war effort against the German "Huns" as a continuation of social gospel progress. Although the Presbyterian Commission on the War (1917) warned the church and Canadian society that the tyranny of Germany found its parallel in Canadian injustice, almost all social gospel figures called for support in fighting "God's war."

However, two dissidents in Winnipeg among the Methodist clergy proved to be portents of radical activism to come. Woodsworth, the coordinator of the new Bureau of Social Research for the three Prairie provinces, proclaimed a passionate pacifism. Given the fact that this new social work agency, which had emerged from the March 1914 Congress and government funding, stood behind the war effort, Woodsworth was pressured into resigning. Meanwhile a Winnipeg pastor, William Ivens of McDougall Methodist Church, faced a congregation polarized by his stand against the war. Already treading on thin ice with his open labor activism in the community, Ivens had crossed a point of no return when he used his pulpit to cry out against the war. His refusal to back the party line led to several petition campaigns within both church and community to keep him at his post against a growing opposition. However, divisions within the congregation proved too strong and key Methodist elites too powerful to allow him to remain as pastor. The provincial

### A Hymn for the People

We knelt before kings, we bent
before lords;
For theirs were the crowns, and
theirs were the swords;
But the times of the bending and
bowing are past,
And the day of the people is dawning
at last!

—a hymn by the Reverend William Ivens (first labor church pastor) in Dennis L. Butcher, Catherine Macdonald, and Margaret E. McPherson, eds., *Prairie Spirit: Perspectives on the Heritage of the United Church of Canada in the West* (Winnipeg: University of Manitoba Press, 1985), 239.

Methodist Conference gave Ivens a way out. He was granted a year of freedom from stationing at a parish in order to form a popular church sympathetic to labor. This he did on June 30, 1918.[7]

In less than a year the city of Winnipeg had ground to a halt. What began as a manageable labor dispute blossomed immediately into the most famous general strike in Canadian history. From mid-May to June 25, 1919, approximately 35,000 workers in a total city population of 175,000 were out on strike. The Central Strike Committee (with fifteen members) coordinated the running of the community, providing both essential and emergency services. Throughout this brief period the entire nation watched anxiously. Socialist and new more radical labor movements climbed on board, while the local Winnipeg elite enlisted the powerful support of governments, army, and Royal Northwest Mounted Police (the Mounties). In Winnipeg itself local police and sectors of returning veterans supported the strike. Ivens's church found itself at the heart of the work stoppage. Religious services and union rallies blended together effortlessly, and at times Ivens preached his pro-strike sermons to enthusiastic open-air audiences of up to five thousand supporters. The activist pastor wrote radical pro-labor, social gospel hymns for his church and movement, and he edited the strike newspaper the *Western Labor News* during its brief existence.

Meanwhile other social gospel clergy joined this wave of strike enthusiasm. In neighboring Brandon, Manitoba, the prominent Methodist minister A. E. Smith left his divided congregation to create a People's (Labor) Church patterned after the Winnipeg example. He was assisted ably by Beatrice Brigden, an employee of the Methodist Church's Department of Evangelism and Social Service (DESS). After Smith's departure into electoral politics shortly after the strike, Brigden took over the leadership of the Brandon Church. She began as an itinerant teacher at Methodist churches across the land; her mandate involved the training of girls to become appropriate young ladies. But from the beginning Brigden moved beyond this expectation. In preparation she decided to do a stint at Jane Addams's Hull House in Chicago and undertake factory work in Toronto both to meet her economic needs and to understand firsthand the unjust treatment of women workers. Her long-term ties to Woodsworth and her increasing work partnership with Smith helped distance her further from the conservative influence of her direct employer, DESS head T. A. Moore.

William Irvine of Calgary supported the strike through his populist organization, the Alberta Non-Partisan League, and his own newspaper, the *Nutcracker*. In the meantime, Woodsworth had antagonized his parish at Gibson's Landing, British Columbia, over issues of war and working-class justice, and he had received no support from that province's Methodist Conference in these struggles. At this point, he resigned from the ministry, and in order to support his family he undertook dock labor and became a union activist and committed member of his province's Federated Labor Party. Upon hearing of the Winnipeg strike he returned to support this labor activism on his home turf.[8]

These radical individuals, inspired by their visions of a social gospel new day, felt compelled to join farm and radical labor conflicts and thereby uphold the impending new order of God they saw emerging out of such struggles. Their "progressive" comrades, who dominated the ecclesiastical institutions, were frightened and scandalized by such behavior. Content instead to pass high-sounding statements calling for reform, peaking in the detailed social policy paper adopted by the Methodist General Conference in the fall of 1918, they hoped that idealism alone would guide owners and workers together to build God's reign in the midst of social peace. Whether by cynical calculation, naïveté, or a blend of both, they washed their hands of their more radical brothers and sisters, who had endorsed and participated in the Winnipeg general strike. This fear escalated especially when both Ivens and Woodsworth were arrested and jailed as strike leaders. So terrified was Methodism's social gospel bureaucracy that Moore agreed to provide information on the labor churches secretly to the Mounties. Even earlier, in calmer days, signs of a growing division became apparent when the activist church historian at Wesley College, the Reverend Salem Bland, was dropped from the faculty. In spite of appeals from Bland himself and social gospelers

> **On the Labor Church**
>
> The movement [of the Labor Church] is a protest against the present social order. . . . Its aims are social, not merely individualistic, that means it stands for replacing the present selfish scramble for existence by a co-operative commonwealth in which each will have a chance.
>
> —J. S. Woodsworth, *First Story* (1920), 114; reprinted in *Consensus: A Canadian Lutheran Journal of Theology* 19, no. 2 (1993).

in both farm and labor, the "progressive" Methodist establishment turned its back on the popular professor in order not to offend the college's board chair, James Henry Ashdown. It was a sign of things to come.[9]

With the sidelining of social gospel radicals from their churches and with the collapse of the general strike, these activists turned to politics. Initially candidates for independent farm or labor parties, a handful of them won seats in both federal and provincial legislatures. After some successes most farm coalitions were compromised by the old-line Liberals in Ottawa. Only a tiny few remained as radical voices in the federal parliament, where they were called the "Ginger Group." Consisting of such figures as the social gospel veterans Woodsworth and Irvine, they were joined in 1921 by United Farmers of Ontario advocate and social gospeler Agnes Campbell MacPhail, the first woman elected to Canada's federal parliament. The crowning success of this handful of feisty voices came together at Regina, Saskatchewan, in 1933, when, in the midst of the Depression, farm and labor militants from across the country created Canada's enduring social democratic party, the Cooperative Commonwealth Federation (CCF). The CCF and its successor, the New Democratic Party, remain, along with the profession of social work and the justice advocacy of the United Church of Canada, the most enduring concrete legacies of Canada's social gospel.[10]

> **The Beginnings of Canadian Socialism**
> Whether or not the commercial elite of Winnipeg would be overthrown, they had at least met their match [in the Reverend Salem Bland], and an alternative Protestant ethic in Canada was well on its way to becoming the spirit of Canadian socialism.
>
> —Richard Allen, "Salem Bland and the Spirituality of the Social Gospel," in Dennis L. Butcher, Catherine Macdonald, and Margaret E. McPherson, eds., *Prairie Spirit: Perspectives on the Heritage of the United Church of Canada in the West* (Winnipeg: University of Manitoba Press, 1985), 232.

# QUEBEC'S SOCIAL CATHOLICISM

## Setting the Stage

In 1848, all Europe was aflame with revolt. From the western borders of the Russian Empire to the French Atlantic coast, democratic and nationalist radicals marched and fought to overthrow the old monarchical orders on the continent. In Italy Giuseppe Garibaldi led his Red Shirts into Rome, there to hurl out papal rule and install a Roman republic reflecting the dreams of his mentor Giuseppe Mazzini. But 1848 also gave way to counterrevolutionary actions, including the restoration of Rome to the papacy by the French troops of Louis Napoleon Bonaparte. Meanwhile a frightened papacy under Pius IX (1846–1878) retreated behind a wall of medieval dreams that repudiated those democratic ideas born of the Enlightenment and the French and Industrial Revolutions. His successor, the aristocratic Leo XIII, shared his predecessor's fear of modernity, but the new pope adopted strategies to move beyond reaction toward positive solutions. In this context "the social doctrine of the church" (social Catholicism) came to birth in Leo's trail-blazing encyclical *Rerum novarum* (1891). In it the pope railed against the evils of modern industrialization and the socialist firebrands he believed were its diabolical children. Across Western Europe and in North America Catholics responded in various creative ways to their leader's manifesto. Catholic Quebec proved to be no exception.

### Forerunners

Of course, Catholicism's concern for the marginalized did not begin in 1891. In Quebec such a commitment emerged as early as New France in the seventeenth and eighteenth centuries. Here women, both laity and nuns, created unilaterally an entire system of health, education, and welfare often over against male leadership, both clerical and lay. Catholic France had experienced a wave of activist spirituality in the seventeenth century that swept through a number of religious orders while creating others. Given that Europe's Catholic Reformation had forced nuns to live behind cloistered walls, visionary sisters found public ministries increasingly difficult to perform. France's Quebec colony provided an opportunity for these women to exercise creativity through direct action in ways impossible on the Continent. Indeed, in the colonies of Quebec City and Montreal, male leadership concentrated on exploiting the Native population and engaging in sweeping travels in search of the profit maximization promised by the sale of beaver pelts. Consequently both these towns of New France focused upon military protection in service of the fur trade. To be sure, there were timid efforts to provide enduring structures to ensure the sustainability necessary for permanent colonies, but these proved short-lived. Only the religious orders seemed intent upon providing the care necessary both to form covenants with the Natives already on the land and to create systems of education, health care, and social assistance.

After losing her husband, the young widow Marie Guyart, later known as Marie de l'Incarnation, struggled through poverty to raise a young son, all the while feeling called to the religious life. Eventually she entered the revived Ursuline order with the clear notion that God wanted her to serve in the colony of New France. Against much naysaying by male clerical leaders she found a patron in Madame de la Peltrie. Together these women raised the necessary funds to send Marie to Quebec City. There she engineered the construction of a convent house and school through fund-raising and administrative skills. Her attention focused on the education of aboriginal women in Quebec City and environs. Although colored by racist superiority and imperial notions of a civilizing mission, Marie gave her life unsparingly to her Native charges. She learned their languages, taught them to read in their own tongues, defended them against the extremes of colonial oppression, and left a legacy of numerous spiritual writings.

> **The Origins of New France**
> The religious dream was far more powerful than that of the state in the early seventeenth century. Indeed without it there might have been no New France at all.
> —Susan Mann Trofimenkoff,
> *The Dream of Nation:*
> *A Social and Intellectual*
> *History of Quebec*
> (Toronto: Gage, 1983), 3.

In Montreal, then called Ville Marie, a number of women created an entire system of human care from scratch. Jeanne Mance was the traveling patron of this work. She studied medicine in order to create a hospital in the colony as well as enable her to make several trips to and from France to raise money for the colony's hospital system. Joining her in the work of providing schools and housing was Marguerite Bourgeoys, a laywoman who formed a community of women to serve human need at Ville Marie. Women were especially vulnerable in the new colony; they experienced poverty and abandonment and found themselves often forced into prostitution, which led to a large

> **Living in Solidarity with the Poor: Marguerite Bourgeoys**
>
> Our food, our dress, and all the necessities of life ought to appear poor and simple because [with the Blessed Virgin] food, drink, clothing and all the other necessities were always poor.
>
> —Marguerite Bourgeoys, "Document 17: Reaffirmation of the Spirit of Poverty," in Rosemary Radford Ruether and Rosemary Skinner Keller, eds., *Women and Religion in America*, vol. 2 (San Francisco: Harper & Row, 1983), 117.

population of abandoned orphans. Into the breach stepped Marguerite d'Youville and her streetwise Grey Sisters, who provided refuge and safety for these most vulnerable women. Such accomplishments of schools, hospitals, and social assistance, almost exclusively by women, stood against the backdrop of male scorn and opposition not least of all coming from such high-ranking clergy as François de Laval, the powerful bishop of Quebec City. Thus did the reality of New France lay the groundwork for subsequent Quebec Catholic history—namely the prominent role of women meeting immediate grassroots needs and the powerful male authority structure that dominated the church and society in which they operated.[11]

## Clerico-Nationalism

Quebec's status as a thoroughly Catholicized French enclave in North America, combined with its economic tutelage to Anglo-Canadian finance and increasingly American industrial corporations, gave this Canadian province its own unique brand of colonialism. Such an arrangement grew out of the final peace between England and France after the Seven Years War (1756–1763). Because of Britain's continual struggles with France elsewhere and with its colonies to the south, England proposed a deal that permitted the French Catholic culture its autonomy within the larger British Empire. In order for such an arrangement to function, the French-speaking church under its bishops supplied the necessary leadership. So began the powerful independence of Quebec Catholicism, which came to define this sector of Canada so deeply throughout its history.

By the latter nineteenth century, agricultural Quebec was experiencing a population boom. Large families were the norm of rural and pious Quebec, forcing an out migration, first to New England mines and textile factories and then to Quebec cities, especially Montreal, where industrial expansion took advantage of the cheap labor supply pouring into the urban ghettos. This shift from New England back to

Quebec began in earnest at the same time as the emergence of *Rerum novarum*. By the early twentieth century Quebec Catholic elites began to address the social question and bring it into line with the province's French-speaking nationalism. Two male leaders dominated this discourse, and both adopted pro-grassroots tactics upheld by an elitist agenda. Henri Bourassa made his mark by way of journalism and public office. As editor and founder of the daily *Le Devoir* Bourassa trumpeted his vision of Quebec as a Catholic missionary enclave in North America with the God-given mandate of bringing Catholicism, civilization, morality, and social justice to an Anglo-American society characterized by sexual excesses, feminism, secularism, Marxism, and other evils of modern society. Only the paternalism offered by *Rerum novarum* could undermine these barbaric onslaughts on the North American scene.

Father Lionel Groulx offered a more defensive version of the same message. Even more conservative than the optimistic Bourassa, Groulx offered up a dose of survivalism (*survivance*). In his novels and his newspapers and through his fascist-like organization, Action Française, Groulx rallied his troops against perceived invasions of Anglo modernism into Quebec. He pleaded desperately against Anglo business, foreigners, Jews, independent women, socialists, and nonconfessional unions and called for a purely French and Catholic Quebec along mythical lines of a rural piety that never existed except in the minds of its desperate creators. In spite of some clashes with the bishops, largely due to papal changes in Europe, Catholic leaders like Bourassa, Groulx, and others became leading public voices for a system in Quebec that gave its French-speaking Catholic Church control over the social fabric of the province, thus providing the kind of social peace and cheap labor that Anglo-American industrialists found so appealing about Quebec. This socioeconomic situation fed the ambitions of one of the province's most successful politicians, Maurice Duplessis, who served as its premier from 1936 to 1940 and then without interruption from 1944 until his death in 1959.[12]

During this period of harsh economic realities and political repression a tiny grassroots social Catholicism came to fruition and proved to be a forerunner of a modernized Quebec inaugurated by the "Quiet Revolution" of 1960. Even before the Depression fell on Quebec, its industrial workforce suffered under the weight of factory labor and the mines. Not unaware of this and building upon the charitable forms advocated by *Rerum novarum*, church leaders and social reformers began to develop programs to mitigate such injustices. Beginning as top-down efforts, both the passage of time and grassroots membership came to shift, reshape, and redefine the more controlling structures that church figures offered via their charitable motives. Three approaches represented this evolving social Catholicism in Quebec, which moved from a top-down paternalism to popular radicalism from the early 1900s to the explosions growing out of the Quiet Revolution in 1960 into the early 1980s: (1) social Catholic think tanks;

**Fig. 14.3.** Jeunesse Ouvrière Catholique Society, September 1940. Photo by Oscar Chrétien. Johns-Manville Photo Collection: Société d'histoire d'Asbestos. Used by permission.

(2) specialized Catholic Action in the form of the Jeunesse Ouvrière Catholique (JOC; Young Catholic Workers); and (3) Catholic trade unionism.

## Social Catholic Think Tanks

Not surprisingly such think tanks arose from the educated elite in Quebec and included those figures, lay and clergy, who felt a Catholic responsibility to address and mitigate the ravages of the Industrial Revolution in the name of *Rerum novarum* and its 1931 update by Pius XI, *Quadragesimo anno*. A Jesuit team, led by Father Joseph-Papin Archambault, came together with the purpose of taking the principles of *Rerum novarum* and putting them into action. Archambault's École Sociale Populaire (Popular Social School), created in 1911, gathered the leading lay and clergy elites of Quebec's social Catholicism and put them to work creating ideological and practical blue pamphlets that addressed rural and industrial challenges facing the province. These studies sought to inspire projects of social justice under the auspices of the church. Patterned after the continental French Jesuit effort Action Populaire, Archambault borrowed another French model to set up the more broadly based think tank Semaines Sociales du Canada (Canadian Social Weeks), established in June 1920.

For the next four decades once-a-year week-long sessions were held around social justice themes and convened leading Catholic activists, including bishops, priests, nuns, Catholic journalists, Catholic trade union leaders, and even the feminist Catholic organizer Marie-Lacoste Gérin-Lajoie. But even Gérin-Lajoie's progressive credentials did not change the overall antimodern, antileftist character of Archambault's efforts. Tightly connected to Quebec's bishops, both the pamphlets and the Semaines mirrored social policies paralleled by Mussolini's fascist state and its theological dressing in Pius XI's social encyclical *Quadregisimo anno* (1931). Nonetheless, the socially minded Jesuits laid the groundwork upon which others built more progressive models from the latter 1930s into the 1980s.

From the late 1930s through the dark years of the Duplessis regime and up to the outburst of the Quiet Revolution, new leaders emerged who sought to motivate grassroots Quebecers committed to social change, modernization, and social democracy. The Dominican father Georges-Henri Lévesque became the patron of these, being responsible for undermining clergy and top-down models through building nonconfessional cooperatives, training union leaders and militants in study and mobilization tactics, and creating a modern school of sociology at the Université Laval on the outskirts of Quebec City. Lévesque influenced an entire generation of journalists, intellectuals, and union leaders, who formed the vanguard of Catholic resistance to Duplessis's corrupt and authoritarian police state. André Laurandeau used his newspaper, *Le Devoir*, to challenge the old ways, and a cadre of young intellectuals (notably Pierre Trudeau, Gérard Pelletier, and Pierre Vadeboncoeur) published a small periodical *Cité Libre*, which rallied anti-Duplessis forces and inspired alliances with other progressive movements, notably labor. Jean Marchand, one of Catholic labor's firebrands, also felt the guiding hand of Father Lévesque.

After about a decade of this Quiet Revolution, when largely Liberal governments declericalized and modernized Quebec, the think tank model took on a grassroots character among increasing numbers of Catholic laity and progressive priests on the political and social left. In 1970, a Fils de Charité priest, Claude Lefebvre, formed the Centre de Pastorale en Milieu Ouvrier (CPMO; Pastoral Center in a Working-Class Setting) to train priests for work in popular neighborhoods where marginalized workers lived and struggled. Lefebvre insisted on a participatory model in which priests lived in the working ghettos, adopting fully the life conditions they encountered. They were expected to learn from workers rather than teach. Quickly this model led to teams (*équipes*) of priestly activists joining in grassroots movements for neighborhood and factory justice. The next two directors, Raymond Levac and Jean-Guy Cassebon, left the priesthood to assume a lay vocation, and both led the CPMO to help form alliances of study and action with labor and other dissident leftist coalitions.

Building on Latin American liberation theology and its practice, the CPMO used Marxist social analysis to establish popular neighborhood church groups (*églises populaires*), which practiced gender and class equality as matters of principle. Other Catholic think tanks followed suit, notably the Quebec City Carrefour de Pastorale en Monde Ouvrier (Pastoral Crossroad in the Working-Class World) (CAPMO), which used a citizen-oriented town hall model to build a neighborhood CPMO. Easily the most radical of all the think tanks was the ecumenical Politisés Chrétiens (Politicized Christians), which adopted a conscious Marxist-Christian analytical model in support of an egalitarian social revolution in Quebec. A high point of such think tank efforts was the Cap Rouge Conference in 1974, where all elements advocating a grassroots church met to consolidate their efforts. Sadly their visions engendered fear among the bishops, who sought to isolate Catholic socialist radicals from the more moderate progressive groups at the conference.[13]

## Specialized Catholic Action

Other more popularly based groups embracing social Catholicism emerged in interwar Quebec as well. Of these the most notable was the specialized Catholic Action model, initially formed among working-class adolescents in Belgium (1925) and called the Young Christian Workers (Jeunesse Ouvrière Chrétienne). Once again French-speaking Europe provided the model, this time for Quebec's Jeunesse Ouvrière Catholique (JOC). At the same time, the Canadian Oblate priest Henri Roy brought his own inspiration and creativity to the Quebec movement. Though envisioned as a mass movement of Catholic working-class youth led by its chaplain priests as direct representatives of the bishops, the very nature of its working-class base eroded over time this direct control by the priests. Quebec's first official JOC local in Montreal (1931) actually consisted of young women workers (Jeunesse Ouvrière Catholique Féminine). Covering the age range from twelve (when many entered factories) to roughly twenty-five years (unless married), young Catholic workers organized local, sexually segregated cells that banded together into an influential national unit with a peak membership of around forty-two thousand during World War II. For the clergy, including the movement's chaplains and especially the bishops, the JOC/JOCF was their answer to the moral and physical dangers of urban and factory life, which threatened to lure youth away from good Catholic practice. Church officialdom shuddered especially at the notion of women working and living any sort of autonomous life in what the clergy felt to be a sexually charged atmosphere.

Yet even from the 1930s and well into the 1940s, when the church sustained much control over its working-class members, the reality of poverty, factory labor, and struggle shaped youth profoundly. By creating a movement strictly among young industrial workers the church enabled these adolescents to exercise their skills as researchers, organizers, writers, public speakers, lobbyists, and activists. Holding their own study circles, organizing neighborhood programs for social change, joining unions, and publishing their own newspapers generated their own brand of independence in which grassroots youth learned to express their faith beyond the control of the church's religious professionals. Though initially conservative in outlook, these youth witnessed and acted in the midst of their gritty lives without the presence even of those chaplains they most loved and respected. With the arrival of the Quiet Revolution both the JOC and the JOCF, along with their adult counterparts, had begun pressing for more radical changes involving global issues, gender equality, and support of more aggressive union militancy. By the latter 1970s they had adopted elements of liberation theology in both theory and practice.[14]

## Catholic Trade Unions (1921–1980s)

The union movement had entered Quebec well before Catholic trade unionism's appearance. Indeed, Catholic labor organizations emerged as a reaction against more militant, class-oriented, nonsectarian movements that came from the American Knights of Labor followed by the American Federation of Labor. Building upon the visions of *Rerum novarum* a number of compassionate priests gathered together different Catholic unions in Hull (1921) and brought to birth the Confédération des Travailleurs Catholiques du Canada (CTCC; Canadian Catholic Federation of Labor). So conservative was this effort that non-Catholic members had no voting rights; class cooperation and social peace were advocated against the Anglo-American unions; and initially the bishop-appointed chaplain held a veto over all union decisions. Without the bishop's word something as devastating as a strike would not be tolerated. This conservative reality was reflected clearly during the CTCC presidency of Alfred Charpentier (1888–1982) who led his union along cautious traditional social Catholic lines from 1935 to 1946.

Along the same lines as the JOC/JOCF the CTCC proved unable to remain a bastion of clergy control in the midst of the working class. The very reality of harsh working conditions and cheap labor costs alienated Catholic toilers sharply against a rapacious owner class, both Quebecer and American, so much so that the church's authoritarian, class-collaborationist model faced rejection in the midst of such inhumane conditions. A series of strikes—from the conflict of women match workers in Hull (1924) through the shoemakers' walkout (1926) to the especially brutal Sorel shipbuilders strike (1937), where laborers on the picket lines fought police, owners, and the first Duplessis government—hardened the CTCC against official church solutions and mediations that served the corporations more than worker needs.

Radical change came only in the aftermath of World War II. An internal movement toward union democracy saw the beginning of women's inclusion in the leadership ranks of the federation, and Charpentier was turfed out in favor of reformers who repudiated the older, more top-down social Catholic model. With the advent of Gérard Picard as federation president and more militant leaders like Jean Marchand, Michel Chartrand, Yolande Valois, and Madeleine Brosseau, the new CTCC moved beyond internal reform by opening a working dialogue with other union federations and by forging alliances with other Catholic activists fighting the anti-union Duplessis regime. The fact that most of the bishops favored the government alienated the union even further from church officialdom. The test of fire came in the famous Asbestos Strike of 1949. In the mining towns of Quebec's eastern townships CTCC militants walked off their jobs at the asbestos mines in protest against both management's hard line and the notorious anti-union Bill 5 passed by the Duplessis government. Backed by a coalition of other unions, anti-Duplessis political voices, their own grassroots chaplains, and a handful of key bishops, the CTCC strikers stood up to management thugs; an establishment press (save for *Le Devoir*); a Duplessis-inspired, anti-union, provincial police force; and powerful conservative Catholics.

> ### Workers on Strike
> We will not hesitate for an instant to launch a general strike throughout the C.T.C.C. [Catholic trade union federation] if provincial authority will not regulate matters in an equitable manner very soon in this ten-month strike at Louiseville. If Quebec does not act, the workers should defend themselves alone.
> —Gérard Picard, "Si Québec n'agit pas," *Le Travail*, January 2, 1953, 1; translation by the author.

The union's show of solidarity against such odds won over more and more sectors of the church, even to the point of gaining the sympathetic help of the powerful Montreal archbishop Joseph Charbonneau. Although Charbonneau was removed from his post (likely as a result of pressure on the church from Premier Duplessis), Quebec's bishops moved slowly in support of the strikers' claim and arbitrated the dispute. Although immediate gains for asbestos workers were slight, this strike marked a turning point for the CTCC. From that point until the union dropped its Catholic restrictions by the Quiet Revolution of 1960, the Catholic federation provided Quebec's most significant mass force against the province's repressive government and served as a rallying hope for Catholic progressives. It pushed for a unity of trade unions in Quebec, led a number of other militant strikes, and stirred anti-Duplessis forces through the dark years of the 1950s. By the time it became the Confédération des Syndicats Nationaux (CSN; Confederation of National Unions), with emphasis on its French-speaking "national" (Quebec) identity, the federation had moved clearly into a democratic socialist model, which it advocated for the new post-Duplessis Quebec.[15]

## Grassroots Social Catholicism in the New Quebec

In his book *The Church in Quebec* theologian and sociologist Gregory Baum provides a model of how a very conservative, highly clericalized

Catholic Church came to adapt itself without harsh opposition to the newly emerging Quiet Revolution with its secularization and modernization. Beyond the growing influence of Catholic progressives during the Duplessis years, the Quiet Revolution coincided directly with the liberalization of global Catholicism inspired by Pope John XXIII and the Second Vatican Council. The spirit of Vatican II gave Quebec Catholic progressives the opportunity to launch creative ventures that paralleled both earlier developments in France and the emergence of Latin American liberation theology. Newer, more popularly based think tanks like the CPMO became the norm, and specialized working-class Catholic Action (both youth and adult members) pursued more radical and more independent paths toward its growing vision of gender and class equality. The lifelong leadership of Catholic leftist Denyse Gauthier, both provincially and internationally, exemplified such changes.

In the working-class neighborhoods priests and nuns formed small Christian groups that met for worship, reflection, and just social change based on the Latin American model of base Christian communities (*comunidades eclesiais de base*). These popular churches (*églises populaires*) broke with a traditional top-down model, adopting instead the praxis-reflection-praxis model of team sharing and decision making. The priests, nuns, and lay brothers practiced what they preached by living in the same harsh conditions as their neighbors. Following an earlier French and Belgian model, a number of them became worker-priests or worker-nuns by taking up factory labor and thereby earning their own livelihood independent of church financial support. In a number of instances they became union leaders, organizers, and factory militants. Sister Dolorès Léger engaged in union struggles out of the Granby textile plant, where she toiled from 1978 to 1982. After that she worked within the left wing of the separatist Parti Québécois (PQ), where she struggled tirelessly for social justice legislation and feminist causes. In this respect Sister Léger embodied her religious

---

**Living in Solidarity with the Poor: Benoît Fortin**

We must be reborn from among the poor, near to their cries, in solidarity with their struggles. Jesus has embraced the human condition; he has taken the way of the stable. We will recognize nothing of human distress if we do not live in solidarity with the most oppressed through our own flesh.

—Benoît Fortin, worker-priest, "Quand se lève le soleil de justice," 17, from private papers, translated by the author.

order, the Soeurs Notre-Dame du Bon Conseil (Sisters of Our Lady of Wisdom), founded by Marie Gérin-Lajoie, daughter of a famous Catholic suffragist and feminist. Both Father Guy Cousin and Capuchin Benoît Fortin organized union locals against overwhelming odds, bringing them into the CSN. Reflecting upon a Franciscan notion of "spirituality of the feet," Fortin affirmed that a worker-priesthood provided an example of being "reborn from among the poor, near to their cries" and "in solidarity with their struggles."[16] Instead of the old model of church control within the former CTCC, radical and socialist Catholic priests and nuns worked within the newer union movement as part of the rank and file.[17]

Fig. 14.4. People eating in a soup kitchen, Montreal, Quebec, 1931. Photo courtesy Library and Archives Canada.

Even traditional church structures and leadership sought to adapt to changing times. When lay, trained social workers marginalized nuns from their former control of social assistance programs, those religious orders with traditions of hands-on work among the poor (such as Petites Soeurs de Jésus, or the Little Sisters of Jesus) sent nuns to live in hard-pressed working ghettos to help communities organize themselves to pursue just social change. The bishops themselves appointed sociologist and lay Catholic Fernand Dumont to gather research and present a report recommending new models for a church living in the midst of crisis. Broadly based, including progressive Catholic activists, Dumont's group held public hearings throughout the province and published the results in 1971. A new church was called for, more participatory internally and more committed to justice and equality externally. Quebec experienced also its own radical diocese, that of Gatineau-Hull, created in the wake of Vatican II. Its first two bishops formed the new diocese on a Latin American liberationist model. The second bishop, Adolphe Proulx, consulted regularly with his team of community and trade-union activists, both clergy and lay. He supported local protests for justice and gathered into coalition Quebec's most important local Catholic radicals.[18]

In spite of such creative experiments Quebec Catholicism was stumbling by the early 1990s. Church attendance had plummeted from 88 percent in 1960 to around 20 percent in just three decades. The progressive Catholics were an aging phenomenon, and the province had become massively secularized, pushing its major church establishment to the margins. Nonetheless, Quebec's almost century-long social Catholic evolution had laid the groundwork for making the province the most socially progressive region in Canada.

## FOR FURTHER READING

Allen, Richard. *The Social Passion: Religion and Social Reform in Canada*. Toronto: University of Toronto Press, 1973.

Baum, Gregory. *The Church in Quebec*. Ottawa: Novalis, 1991.

Butcher, Dennis L., Catherine Macdonald, and Margaret E. McPherson, eds. *Prairie Spirit: Perspectives on the Heritage of the United Church of Canada in the West*. Winnipeg: University of Manitoba Press, 1985.

Fay, Terence J. *A History of Canadian Catholics*. Montreal: McGill-Queen's University Press, 2002.

Gutkin, Harry, and Mildred Gutkin. *Profiles in Dissent: The Shaping of Radical Thought in the Canadian West*. Edmonton: NeWest, 1997.

Linteau, Paul-André, René Durocher, Jean-Claude Robert, and François Ricard. *Quebec since 1930*. Trans. Robert Chodos and Ellen Garmaise. Toronto: James Lorimer, 1991.

Stebner, Eleanor. "More Than Maternal Feminists and Good Samaritans: Women and the Social Gospel in Canada." In Wendy J. Deichmann Edwards and Carolyn De Swarte Gifford, eds., *Gender and the Social Gospel*, 53–67. Urbana: University of Illinois Press, 2003.

Trofimenkoff, Susan Mann. *The Dream of Nation: A Social and Intellectual History of Quebec*. Toronto: Gage, 1983.

# POPULAR CATHOLIC SEXUAL ETHICS

## CRISTINA L. H. TRAINA

Do not endeavor to excuse [sexual thoughts] on any pretense whatever. Do not say they are natural; do not think of such things on the idea that you will marry by and by, but simply put them all out and keep them out. When you have closed the door of your heart the enemy cannot find any entrance for evil.

—From a *Guide for Young Catholic Women*, 1871[1]

Creative abstinence is best understood as the conscious effort a couple makes to enflame their desire for one another and enhance their intimacy by taking short breaks (about a week or so) from genital intercourse while at the same time intensifying the amount of nongenital physical contact . . . and other expressions of affection.

On the tenth day while you were cuddling, you might tell each other all the pleasures that you have in store for each other the following evening.

—From *The Exceptional Seven Percent: Nine Secrets of the World's Happiest Couples*, 2000[2]

At the turn of the twenty-first century as at the turn of the twentieth, Roman Catholic popular manuals on sex and marriage agreed that genital sexuality was a power to be foregone outside marriage and to be employed with restraint within it.[3] But this formal similarity masks a sea change in American Catholic views of sex. At the beginning of the period, the American Catholic popular press bombarded its readers with incessant warnings against the dangers of enjoying pesky but inevitable impure thoughts (let alone acting on them) and urged Catholics to exercise constant vigilance against sexual desire. A hundred years later, Catholic popular writings extolled the pleasures of marital sex, recommending periodic abstinence not as a way to quench desire but as a way to increase it, and even to encourage exactly those fantasies that were so deeply feared a century earlier.

The story of this transformation includes the evolution of official Roman Catholic teaching on sexuality, but it reflects just as strongly ethnic Catholic assimilation and coming-of-age in American culture. It is also an effect of Roman Catholics' traditional approach to cultural common wisdom, both scholarly and popular: because there is only one truth, church teaching, cultural sexual "best practices" confirmed by sociology, and biological-psychological discoveries about human sexuality could not in the end be contradictory. However loudly and forcefully American Roman Catholic guides on sex might resist some elements of popular sexuality, they were destined to embrace still others with breathtaking enthusiasm. Here I will focus on three periods with very distinctive characters: the minority, "fortress" writings of the early twentieth century; the psychologically sophisticated postwar literature produced before 1968; and the snappy self-help literature of the late 1990s.

## PURE THOUGHTS AND GUARDED EYES

Nowadays everybody "knows" that early and even mid-twentieth-century popular Roman Catholicism was sexually repressed, and it is implied that of course it must have been more repressed than the surrounding culture. Leslie Woodcock Tentler's *Catholics and Contraception* gives the lie to this assumption. Early twentieth-century Protestants do not in fact seem to have been significantly less anxious about sex than Catholics or to have endorsed birth control or abortion with any greater regularity. Protestants, like Catholics, participated in a culture of abstinence and believed that the best way to contain the growth of subversive sexual forces was to ignore them as much as possible in public speaking and writing. Roman Catholics, like Protestants, probably continued in a combination of ignorance and defiance of Christian prohibitions of abortion and birth control, although abortion may have dropped slightly in the early twentieth century.[4]

But if Roman Catholics' anxiety over sex was roughly equal in degree to Protestant anxiety, it had a distinctive quality. Most obviously, Tentler notes, Roman Catholics heard clerical tirades against abortion and family limitation and were taught that sex's only moral redemption lay in procreation and payment of the "marital debt," a euphemism for providing a licit outlet for one's spouse's sexual desire, which might otherwise find relief in affairs or masturbation.[5] This skepticism was magnified by a tradition nearly unknown to Protestants: the self-conscious culture of celibacy, obedience, and self-denial for priests and for the women religious who constituted the corps of parochial school teachers. These celibate men and women were also the authoritative interpreters of the Catholic moral sexual tradition.

In addition, in 1900 most American Roman Catholics were in some sense part of a subculture: in American culture but not of it. The Roman Catholic Church in the Unites States was still officially a mission church, despite its longevity on both the West and the East coasts. More highly educated and assimilated Roman Catholics were integrated into the culture economically, but they were acutely aware of Rome's skepticism about intellectual freedom, democracy, and association with members of other religious communities, and they feared running afoul of American antipapist anxiety. Among recent immigrants, illiteracy, language barriers between laity and clergy, and the clergy's penchant for allusions and euphemisms made it unlikely that many immigrants had a clear understanding of church teaching. And immigrants were mostly concerned with survival, not sex. They were often isolated physically from native-born Americans—whether in New York ghettos or on California farms—and found that their languages, dialects, and cultural practices cut them off from fellow immigrant Catholics. They were victims of anti-Catholic invective and even violence. For these and other reasons—like culture, language, race, Protestant indoctrination in public schools—Catholics tended to be educated in Roman Catholic schools at all levels, which reinforced their separation from American popular culture and their development of an alternative, parallel route to Americanization.

Catholic life guidebooks of this period, mostly aimed at literate English speakers, agreed on two strategies that perfectly reflected Catholic ambivalence toward American culture. On one hand they reinforced the divide between Catholics and other Americans generally by appealing to Catholic virtue-centered piety and warning of the spiritual dangers of reading popular novels, associating with non-Catholics, and above all marrying outside the faith. On the other, like Protestant guides, they both demurred to mention sexuality directly[6] (preferring the more circumspect term "purity") and paradoxically often made impurity the central example of sin or even implied that it lay at the root of all other vices.

An excellent exemplar of this double strategy is George Deshon, a West Point graduate, Catholic convert, and priest who was one of the founding members of the Paulist order. His *Guide for Young Catholic Women* in domestic service went through thirty-two editions in the late nineteenth century. Deshon warned that "impurity" was a vice that destroyed "all goodness, all virtue, all love of God, all faith, hope, or charity." He lectured too on evil thoughts and roving eyes, sexual sins that a penitent might have neglected to confess unless her confes-

**Fig. 15.1.** Father George Deshon, author of the *Guide for Young Catholic Women.* Photo courtesy of the Missionary Society of St. Paul the Apostle

sor was forthright or salacious enough to inquire about them. Still, his practical concerns about "the loss of that good name without which life is a burden" and about the possibility that physical attraction could induce a girl to marry an alcoholic and become the "bloated, coarse-looking woman" "who has not, apparently, combed her hair for a week, with a lot of ragged children bawling, and fighting, and cursing around her in her miserable, dirty hovel"[7] could easily be found in any girls' advice book of the period. They reveal important underlying cultural assumptions about sex: in order to preserve her reputation, a woman must guard not only her purity but her appearance of purity, and frequent sex (symbolized by the "lot of ragged children," in comparison with the few, well-mannered children of a well-to-do, presumably more continent couple) correlates to the vices of drunkenness and irresponsibility.

The psychology of Roman Catholic writings of this period is complex. They combined rigorous, hyper self-critical vigilance in every imaginable dimension of thought and comportment with a comparatively benevolent pastoral realism. Early twentieth-century Catholic vigilance against bodily temptation is the stuff of which satires and bitter memoirs have been made. The body was the enemy. Tentler writes that in the popular literature of this period, sexuality (along with the body, its exclusive residence) was seen as "external to the moral self and powerfully subversive of it."[8]

Madame Cecilia is typical. She was an author of scripture commentaries; her *More Short Spiritual Readings for Mary's Children* was inspired by a vision of the Gospels that equated holiness with purity from contamination. The person was a house with three stories: the body at ground level, the intellect above that, and the soul at the top. The holy girl was to occupy only the top floor, but she must keep constant guard at the front door of the lower floor: "Temptations against the angelic virtue of purity come in through the doors of the senses. Consequently, we must avoid all looks, words, or actions which would compromise the purity of our souls." Because "the soul imprisoned in the body looks out on the world by the windows of the eyes,"[9] one must especially train one's eyes to look at only what was chaste and uplifting—and also avoid glances that might suggest flirtation. This constant vigilance was a matter of salvation. For Deshon, impurity was "a monster with jaws wide open to destroy us. It is the very pit of hell which yawns wide at our feet, ready to swallow up those who do not watch their steps with the utmost precaution."[10]

Not surprisingly, early twentieth-century Catholic clergy were so anxious to protect the eyes and ears from sights and sounds that might inspire lust that they barely alluded to sex in mixed-company Sunday sermons. Tentler relates that they often aimed their mission (or "revival") preaching and writing on sex to single-sex audiences, separating the single women from single men and from the married—and sometimes even husbands from wives—when they preached missions.[11] This habit may have implied to their hearers that sex was properly a matter of private morality (even though it was not only interpersonal but also had grave social consequences), and more importantly that open discussion of it risked arousing morally dangerous levels of sexual interest. It would certainly have been inappropriate for clergy to invite laypeople to events that were occasions of sin! The same anxiety may also explain why manuals for married couples appear to have been rare.

The overriding concern was to avoid sin by trying to avoid all that might produce it: knowingly visiting places, associating with people, reading books, engaging in flirtations and intimacies, and even welcoming daydreams that might arouse desire were all strictly forbidden. In his short chapter "Custody of the Eyes," Deshon warns that "your mind will become filled with the images and pictures of what your eyes behold. So, if you look on any impure sight *to notice it*, it will be sure to create evil thoughts in your mind"[12] (emphasis mine). But because their second purpose was to prepare readers for the sacrament of penance—which mental events needed to be confessed, and which did not?—he and Madame Cecilia were also fascinatingly realistic, and even lenient, on the question of unintentional acts. Consistent with Catholic moral theology and penitential practice, a person who happened to see an impure sight and quickly diverted her attention and thoughts was neither culpable nor contaminated. Similarly, Deshon said, "our imaginations and our fancies are not always in our power."[13] Impure thoughts happen even to the saints. Consequently, added Madame Cecilia, one should not waste time feeling guilty about them: "these thoughts are powerless to stain the soul unless they are *deliberately accepted and welcomed*."[14]

This important distinction between independently arising thoughts and their intentional cultivation creates space for later engagement with psychology. What divides these early twentieth-century thinkers from their successors is the formers' assumption that spontaneously arising sexual thoughts are not benign or natural but are the devil's means of tempting the holy, and they must be resisted by calling upon God and the Virgin Mary. In addition, they found it easy to enumerate the dangers of illicit or frequent sexual relations, masturbation, onanism, and other transgressions but difficult to list any benefits of "fulfilling the marital debt" other than procreation and avoidance of adultery. Even "good sex" was morally fraught and preferably infrequent. Catholics who read and heeded this literature were likely to be tied in knots of scrupulous self-examination: Did I invite that impure thought by dressing too warmly or eating rich food? Did I desire my wife too ardently? But it is likely—at this stage, at least—that an equal or greater number remained blissfully ignorant of these worries.

## THE DISCOVERY OF PSYCHOLOGY

By the end of the Second World War Catholic culture had undergone almost unimaginable change. Buoyed by national prosperity, literacy, higher education funded by the GI Bill, assimilation, proof of good citizenship through support for two world wars, and the cultural exposure that war travel had brought their young men, American Catholics were now eager participants in American economic and popular culture. The cumulative effect of all these changes on the Catholic lay culture of sexuality should not be underestimated. Although some postwar Catholics—particularly some clergy and women religious—continued to fear that all discussion and exhibition of sexuality were equally morally dangerous, other Catholics began to make distinctions between constructive and purely salacious presentations.

This transformation was evident even at the popular level. For instance, in his 1960 film *La Dolce Vita*, Federico Fellini gambled that sex could function legitimately as a social critique rather than necessarily and solely as an illicit turn-on. And he won. The Catholic film censor board, the Legion of Decency, awarded the film a "separate classification" rather than a "disapproved for all" rating.

In addition, two important developments had cleared the way for tentative affirmation of marital sex as a good beyond procreation. First, Pius XI's 1930 encyclical *Casti connubii* (On Christian Marriage) declared that sex also has important "secondary ends, such as mutual aid, the cultivating of mutual love, and the quieting of concupiscence" (para. 59). These secondary ends would later be picked up under the label "unitive ends of marriage" and elevated to a level equal with procreation in Pope Paul VI's 1968 encyclical *Humanae vitae* (On the Regulation of Birth). Second, by the mid-1930s knowledge of the rhythm method, which allowed couples to discourage or encourage conception by restricting intercourse to limited periods in the wife's fertility cycle, was fairly widespread. Although critics charged that rhythm was morally inferior to the more challenging practice of complete abstinence, much of the informational literature produced for laypeople emphasized intercourse's value as an expression of love and communion.[15] The idea of intercourse as a positive force in marriage had not taken over, but it had taken root.

Finally, development of an assimilated, educated Catholic middle class produced a sizable elite of Catholic families who were highly informed about church teaching, attempted to live it as much as possible in daily life, and openly discussed the challenges of doing so. One telling indicator was British author David Lodge's 1965 comic novel *The British Museum Is Falling Down*,[16] which meditated hilariously and painfully on the fraughtness of life under the rhythm method. That Lodge could expect the average American reader of his light novel to follow discussions of medieval moral theology, references to papal documents,

> ## Sex and Romanticism
> "Not very romantic," Virginia seemed indistinctly to say. "Sex isn't," he snapped back.
> —David Lodge, *The British Museum Is Falling Down* (New York: Penguin, 1981 [1965], 156.

and even a dream that parodied members of the Roman curia indicates that the Catholic middle class (and maybe the whole middle class) was rather well-informed in matters of Catholic moral theology of sexuality, its justifications, and its frustrations. Appreciative readers might well have been members of the Christian Family Movement, a postwar, mostly lay-led organization of primarily well-educated, suburban, white Catholic families. Although they focused on liturgical and social issues too, uppity "CFMers" discussed responsible procreation and the difficulties of the rhythm method at length; Pat and Patty Crowley, long at the center of the organization, were two of the few laypeople called to Rome to reexamine the question of contraception before Paul VI's publication of *Humanae vitae*.

Not surprisingly, Catholic life guides in this transitional period were extremely varied. Priests and religious continued to produce daily meditation guides for single women that echoed the turn-of-the-century vision of sex, procreation, and the body. Jesuit author Raoul Plus, whose 1927 *Facing Life: Meditations for Young Women* continued to be published through 1960, railed against scantily clad girls who become occasions of sin for others; he praised holy women who insisted on covering themselves modestly even while on the scaffold or being gored by bulls.[17] He also condemned contraception. Edging perilously close to heresy, he argued, "One might *almost* say that there are souls which God has not been able to create, because selfishness has reared a barrier between these souls and the will of God"[18] (emphasis mine). Father Camillo Zamboni, whose 1961 book

*Jesus Speaks to You* thankfully seems to have had only one printing, recalls medieval spirituality.[19] In chapters with titles like "Do Not Offend Me Again" and "I Await You, My Beloved," Zamboni idiosyncratically merges two streams of traditional Catholic devotionalism in the same voice: a Father God who attends minutely to every sin of vanity and impurity and a Lover God who satisfies all longing. Both authors' clerical authority is backed by ecclesiastical approvals (an imprimatur for both, and a *nihil obstat* for Plus) guaranteeing orthodoxy.

> **On Chastity**
>
> Chastity . . . is not a precept that is distinctively Catholic or distinctively Christian or Jewish, but it is distinctively *human*. According to Catholic teaching, it binds every human being, regardless of race or creed.
>
> —Gerald Kelly, S.J., in collaboration with B. R. Fulkerson, S.J., and C. F. Whitford, S.J., *Modern Youth and Chastity* (St. Louis: Queen's Work, 1941), 62.

Two other volumes by priests (bending under the weight of the *nihil obstat*, imprimatur, and *imprimi potest*) echo this earlier tradition but hint at important changes. Gerald Kelly's *Modern Youth and Chastity*, first published in 1941, also saw service well into the postwar period and formed a whole generation of American Catholics. Like his predecessors, the Jesuit Kelly laid out the dangers of stimulating the sexual appetite. Yet by naming and matching particular sexual activities with degrees and kinds of sin he demystified the sections of moral theology manuals (often still published in Latin) that guided priests in hearing confessions of sexual sin, transferring both the power for and the anxiety of cataloguing sexual sins from priest to penitent: "A wholesome frankness [on the part of the penitent] relieves the confessor of the burden of asking many questions that are distasteful to him and embarrassing to the penitent."[20] The booklet was a cheerful, somewhat chatty publication aimed at middle- and upper-class college students of both sexes, referring briefly to the appropriate joys of married sex and openly exploring what it called "the psychology of sex attraction." In the same vein, Joseph Haley's *Accent on Purity* (1948) extolled modesty, mortification (self-denial), and the grand design of God, who creates sexual desire and marriage to ensure procreation; it assailed reductionistic "scientific"

> **On Attractiveness**
>
> Men . . . are especially attracted by the grace, the emotional susceptibility, the beauty, the tenderness of women. Women are attracted by the strength, the courage, the energy, the calm deliberation of men."
>
> —Gerald Kelly, S.J., in collaboration with B. R. Fulkerson, S.J., and C. F. Whitford, S.J., *Modern Youth and Chastity* (St. Louis: Queen's Work, 1941), 13.

descriptions of human sexuality. Still, its audience and purpose were radically new: it provided priests, nuns, and lay religious educators with models for comprehensive "purity education" curricula, reminding them that sex is a good that deserves to be discussed and condemning the "puritanic attitude" that treats sexuality generally as an unmentionable.[21] It signaled a change of perspective that resulted in a veritable cascade of new books on sexuality for both educators and the general laity.

Implicit in these shifts were two important, related changes. First, the question of authority—who had the knowledge and the authorization to teach about sexuality?—shaped the whole period. In a refreshing departure from early twentieth-century silence, Haley insisted that students learn the physiology of sexuality from medical professionals outside the religious education classroom and the theology and morals of sexuality within it. Implicit in this position is a doctrine of dual but complementary authority: doctors and nurses had authority over the physical dimension of sexuality, and (celibate) priests and nuns had authority over its moral and spiritual dimensions. In one Christian Brothers high school in the mid-1960s, students received separate presentations on sex and marriage from both medical doctors and an elderly—and presumably pastorally experienced—brother. It was assumed that the three authorities—that of the elderly brother, his safely orthodox interpretation of ordinary sexual experience, and scientific wisdom—complemented rather than contradicted each other.

But this facile division of labor and authority was already eroding in the face of developmental psychology. Psychology was the most powerful intellectual and scientific development of the mid-twentieth century. Developmental psychology in particular was friendly to highly educated Catholics interested in reviving religious education, pastoral care, and the sacrament of penance, three of the practices in the life of the church that most profoundly shaped lay visions of sexuality.[22]

Psychology's role in mid-century sex guides was complex. For centuries Roman Catholic theology had steadfastly assumed that good science and revelation could not conflict. Thus, where psychological studies agreed with church teaching, they were summoned in support, and where they did not, they were dismissed as bad science.

For example, Alphonse Clemens encouraged couples to make use of Albert Kinsey's research into male and female arousal patterns, but he rejected Kinsey's correlation between women's marital orgasm and their marital satisfaction as antithetical to Catholic teaching on marriage. Still, theological credibility benefited from scientific confirmation, so Clemens cited an earlier psychological study in support of his claim that women's marital happiness did not depend on high rates of orgasm. And he offered wives a scientifically certified consolation prize: the theory that women's absorption of semen promotes their psychological well-being, even without orgasm.[23] Later, psychology's contradictory findings would not be so easily dismissed.

Another important theme sounded consistently in later literature of this period was that psychology and sociobiology confirmed divine design. Male-female complementarity was generic and comprehensive, psycho-spiritual as well as physical, and was directed toward procreation, parenting, and disparate roles within family and society: "man" naturally and inherently turned outward to the world and "woman" inward to the household and to motherhood. Women's roles were usually more narrowly described than men's: François Dantec opined, "Motherhood is a woman's natural function, a function she is meant to fulfill both by her physical nature and by every faculty of her mind and heart."[24] Haley added ominously but typically, "it is the law of nature that women are to set the ideal of purity in society."[25]

Fig. 15.2. Photo of a large British Catholic family, four of whose sons (in cameo shots in each corner) became Redemptorist priests. Photo © Transalpine Redemptorists.

Not surprisingly, any other sort of attraction or any other view of sex was believed to subvert the natural order of things revealed by God and confirmed by psychology and sociobiology. In Clemens, the "Divine Plan for sex," including male-female attraction, was intended "to keep the human race alive"[26]—a modern version of a traditional theological move, but also oddly deterministic. Couples wanting sex but not children would therefore not be just selfish or sinful but also psychologically maladjusted and biologically obstructionist. Not surprisingly, Clemens declared sex not prompted by love animalistic, called sex "diverted from its natural goal of generation" subanimalistic—for not even animals perverted sex in this way[27]—and did not mention homosexuality at all.

The themes of psychological and lay authority met tellingly in the work of lay authors—including women—with advanced degrees in psychology. Clemens's 1957 book *Marriage and the Family: An Integrated Approach for Catholics* beautifully illustrates the careful blending of this new authority with the clerical traditionalism of earlier periods. To begin with, although the "Alphonse" conjured visions of a priest or vowed brother, it was followed only by the initials "Ph.D."; likewise, the title page declared that Clemens was director of the Marriage Counseling Center (psychological connection) at Catholic University (church connection). By dedicating the work to "Our Lady, my wife, and my mother," Clemens proclaimed himself both an adherent of traditional devotionalism and a man experienced in marriage and sexual relations. The pages were sprinkled liberally with notes to Catholic teaching and the works of psychologists. Even the book's production planted its feet firmly in two intellectual communities: it was published by a trade press, but it bore both the *nihil obstat* and the imprimatur. And from the very first page, Clemens paid homage to two authorities: "At this time both religion and science agree that the chief reason for failing marriages is the absence of proper and adequate preparation"[28]—preparation that presumably should be informed by good psychology but guided by Catholic values. The church "baptized" the "good" science of Kelly and others, lay and clerical, by awarding imprimaturs and *nihil obstats* to their burgeoning literature on sexuality and marriage (most frequently, sexuality *in* marriage).

These psychologically informed guides on marriage, sexuality, and sex education differed markedly from their predecessors. In early guides, the important distinction was between the unmarried state (in which sex was forbidden and all temptations to it were to be avoided) and the married state (in which sex was permissible "to pay the debt" and produce children but was still a site of moral danger). In postwar guides, although intercourse was still confined to marriage, the important pedagogical distinction was not state but stage: they emphasized the developmental progress of intellect, emotions, and sexuality in each person and even in each marriage.

In addition, many aimed at a more sophisticated audience with clear pedagogical purpose—in Clemens's case, Catholic priests, but also the lay counselors, educators, and parents who had begun to replace priests and nuns as the mediators of ecclesiastical teaching. Appropriately, their tone was more often collegial than condescending. Dr. Audrey Kelly, who with Gerald Kelly also symbolizes the arrival of assimilated Irish Catholicism, personifies this trend. Catholic adults raised in an era of hyper vigilance and awkward silence about sex needed expert, sympathetic support for their new role as sex educators. Kelly's *A Catholic Parent's Guide to Sex Education* offered these anxious parents a no-nonsense tour of basic anatomy and physiology, followed by chapters on sexual development and education at each of several crisply delineated developmental stages, capped off by frank discussions of homosexuality, venereal disease, masochism, and sadism—and a word of encouragement urging "late starters" to open the subject with their children as soon as possible.[29]

Oddly, even these more modern authors eschewed candid discussion of the mechanics of sex and the challenges of birth regulation. They no longer feared that sex education would arouse lust, but with Clemens they harbored a paternalistic worry that any discussion of technique would encourage laypeople to view sex mechanically, rather than holistically, placing too much weight on sexual prowess and too little on dimensions of marriage that were far more essential to marital success.[30] This worry seems to have persisted among Catholics to the end of the century, despite the notable proliferation of explicit, liberally illustrated sex guides among equally conservative Protestants. In addition, most later postwar guides played down the challenges of "the safe method" and played up the potential of periodic abstinence (and of raising children) to develop virtues of self-restraint and selflessness in married couples. Lurking in the background was anxiety over rising divorce rates: Could Catholics harness the wisdom of the new psychology to strengthen marriage without ceding their beliefs about marriage as an indissoluble sacrament and marital sex as a pathway to parenthood?

Two final, related characteristics point toward the manuals of the late twentieth century. Both are grounded in a curious optimism. The first is an absence: the postwar manuals seemed to assume that although a couple might be misdirected or selfish, both partners were usually of one mind and of equally good will. They shied away from questions like "What if I have medical reasons to prevent pregnancy, but my husband forces himself on me?" or "How may I protect myself if I suspect my spouse has contracted a sexually transmitted disease elsewhere?" Sexual sin was assumed to be pesky and spiritually but not physically dangerous.

Second, the authors went out of their way to extol the blessings of marital sex, in an effort both to elevate marriage (the Cana marriage movement was in full swing) and to overcome earlier fears of desire's dangerous power. Guides praising marriage and married sex proliferated at an astounding rate. The earlier focus on squelching sexual feelings *outside* marriage gave way to a focus on encouraging sexual affection *inside* marriage. Formerly the door to sin and temptation, the body was now the route to graced marital union. This was the beginning of the inkling that a good marriage ideally involves good sex. François Dantec, whose 1952 marriage guide *Love Is Life* was adapted for the American market in 1963, devoted well over a third of its pages to questions of sexual relations and family planning. T. W. Burke's *The Gold Ring* intoned that God intended sex to be "an act of intense pleasure" for both partners.[31] And Clemens agreed that "though sex is a minor portion of the totality of married life, it is an extremely important one."[32] It might in some sense be even more important than bearing children. In *The Meaning of Marriage* Herbert Doms—writing in 1939 but anticipating the postwar approach—waxed rhapsodic without loss of his imprimatur by allowing a nineteenth-century author to speak for him: in "marital chastity" the partners were "united not only by love and sensual pleasure, but by delight and moral joy in a community which fully satisfies the natural instincts to which it conforms. From the *subjective* point of view the child is, [*sic*] only a secondary purpose of marriage."[33]

Indeed, marriage manuals of the period praised the goodness of married, sexual love so highly that it seemed a prerequisite for human spiritual and emotional development. Clemens argued that "the entire human personality, even in its supernatural aspects, is prospered by sex since the act of marital love also merits grace"; "the deeper love generated by it generates overflows in charity toward neighbors; the very incompleteness of it causes the soul to yearn for perfect union with God."[34] True to his trademark double-barreled approach, he also cited statistics showing that marriage is good for health, lowering mortality rates across the board.[35] Flamand believed that physical love helped to accomplish interior, mysterious transformations, producing a "kind of human fulfillment . . . possible only in married love."[36] These claims hint that married sex might be developmentally necessary to emotional maturity and spiritual fulfillment, challenging the long-standing Catholic culture of celibacy as the spiritual high road and marriage as the way of compromise.

Equally unexpectedly, freedom to enjoy married sex sometimes became a command to do so. Burke demanded that mere human beings accomplish a union as pure and high-minded as the eucharist: "Bodily union is the 'sacrament' of human marriage, while the Eucharist is that of the marriage between Christ and his Church"—or at least "this is the ideal to be sought *and achieved*" by married couples.[37] It also signals that the carefully distilled "psychological self" cautiously embraced by postwar sex manual writers might have contained more of Protestant popular culture's belief in the necessity of pairing and sexual pleasure than intended. Two things are clear. First, if the authors of the new books exited the postwar period in a state of euphoria over the blessings of married sexuality, this level of comfort with sex had not yet filtered down to the general laity, who still struggled with scrupulous consciences. Second, the new canonization of married sexuality was of little comfort to those whose desire took a different shape.

## SACRED PLEASURE

Pope Paul VI's 1968 encyclical *Humanae vitae* (On the Regulation of Birth) capped off the postwar explosion of books on sexuality and marriage. Preceded by unprecedented consultation with a few married laypeople (who presented often-anguished written testimonies from thousands more), the document was widely expected to embrace sexual pleasure as a true marital good and to pronounce the church's blessing on limited marital contraceptive use. It emphatically agreed to the first, raising sex's emotional/spiritual or "unitive" purpose to an equal level with its procreative purpose and even embracing the idea of family limitation, but it rejected the second, declaring that each and every act of intercourse must be free from both physical and pharmaceutical barriers to the union of sperm and ovum.

Much has been written on the effect of this event on American Catholic consciousness. Many faithful Catholics—including the majority of well-educated, self-organized Christian Family Movement members—were shocked and disappointed. Over two decades priests, bishops, theologians, and knowledgeable laypeople had collaborated in a tentative but increasingly open, critical process of describing the spiritual and "human" meanings of marital sex. The logical conclusion, according to these Catholics, was that marriages would be less anxious, and unexpected children rarer, if couples could use contraception judiciously (Tentler notes that 78 percent of married American Catholic women between twenty and twenty-four were using some forbidden method of birth regulation in 1970, shortly after the encyclical was issued[38]). *Humanae vitae* signaled the church hierarchy's rejection of this new, collaborative, multidisciplinary approach to truth, and thus the end of what these Catholics had come to regard as Catholicism.

For others, *Humanae vitae* confirmed that lay-clerical collaboration could only interpret traditional teaching in the new language of psychology. The *nihil obstats* and imprimaturs on the mid-century manuals had been meant to say "this far, but no farther": psychology helps us understand how *from a subjective, experiential viewpoint* sex might be about emotional union, and mutual pleasure might be indispensable in marriage, but unless sex was at least open to conception it put pleasure before marriage's main *objective, natural, and canonical* goal: birthing and nurturing children. For these Catholics, *Humanae vitae* pulled the church back from the brink of ceding its authority to secular scientific reason, reminding everyone that the one truth was revealed and changeless and that the pope was its interpreter.

The immediate consequence was a deep split that skewed the Catholic sex-and-marriage advice literature. Dismayed progressives put pen to paper to denounce the encyclical's vision of authority and sexuality, but their audience was more scholarly than popular. Progressive lay Catholics seem to have turned to Protestant and secular sexuality guides rather than producing their own.

Thus by the last decade of the twentieth century, rounding the cusp of the twenty-first, self-consciously Catholic guides made a point of strictly and wholeheartedly embracing church teaching. Only a few decades separated them from their mid-century predecessors, but their position in American culture was completely different. First, as most Protestants now favored birth control, *Humanae vitae* made opposition to contraception the hallmark of American Catholicism. Thenceforth, orthodox Catholic identity would be defined and declared primarily in writing on marriage and sexuality. In addition, whereas the burden of the mid-century guides was to argue for the goodness of pleasurable marital sex, the later guides took this as a given. Sometimes trading on their authors' own bad experiences of casual sex, and nearly always on their clients', they sought instead to demonstrate why nonmarital and contracepted sex of all sorts were great evils.

Consequently these guides championed church teachings rather than challenged them. Trading ecclesiastical authority for the authority of a trusted commercial brand, they tended to be published by Catholic presses with a reputation for orthodoxy—like Our Sunday Visitor or Ignatius Press—often dispensing with ecclesiastical certifications. They courted the "great sex" generation by offering readers a carrot: although there's more to life than sex, God wants them to have great sex, and they will have superlative sex only if they do it the orthodox Catholic way; liberal, contracepted, nonmarital sex is mediocre by comparison.

The books' style was as much a part of this effort as their content. Their authors—typically lay—often worked the motivational speaking and relationship workshop circuit. Witty and engaging, they enticed the reader with amusing asymmetries and allusions (Gregory Popcak titled a chapter "'Holy Sex, Batman!' [or Why Catholics Do It . . . Infallibly]").[39] Their chatty style, conventional wisdom, and question-and-answer format echoed two familiar contemporary genres: "self-help" books and Protestant evangelical apologetics.

---

**The Key to Sexual Satisfaction**

The most sexually satisfied people in America . . . are . . . *highly religious married people who have saved sex for marriage.*

—Mary Beth Bonacci, *Real Love: Mary Beth Bonacci Answers Your Questions on Dating, Marriage and the Real Meaning of Sex* (San Francisco: Ignatius Press, 1996), 36.

---

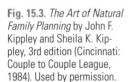

Fig. 15.3. *The Art of Natural Family Planning* by John F. Kippley and Sheila K. Kippley, 3rd edition (Cincinnati: Couple to Couple League, 1984). Used by permission.

The best-known representatives of this movement are Mary Beth Bonacci's *Real Love,* Christopher West's *Good News about Sex and Marriage,* and Gregory Popcak's many manuals on marriage and parenting.[40] Like the mid-century authors, they began with God's intention. According to Mary Beth Bonacci, "Not only is sex good, but it is *amazingly* good, for more reasons than you may think. Why did God create the world? To fill it up with individual, irreplaceable, unrepeatable people—each one of whom He is madly in love with and wants to share eternity with. . . . This is where sex enters the picture. God needed to design a system to get us all here."[41] When human beings adhered to this logical system, they reaped spiritual and physical rewards. Popcak argued, "sacred lovemaking . . . *helps the spouses experience, in a physical way, how passionately they are loved by God*"[42]

All authors—drawing on *Humanae vitae* and Pope John Paul II's extensive theology of the body—argued that when a couple was completely vulnerable and self-giving, actively welcoming a possible new child in every act of sex by refusing to impede pregnancy, they also partook in both God's original creative ecstasy and the promise of heaven. Popcak puts it this way: "To experience sacred sex is to experience the cataclysmic eruption of love that was the cosmological orgasm we call the 'Big Bang.'"[43] Christopher West agreed: "The joy of sex—in all its orgasmic grandeur—is meant to be the joy of loving as God loves. The joy of sex—in all its orgasmic grandeur—is meant to be a foretaste of the joys of heaven: the eternal consummation of the marriage between Christ and the Church."[44] Regular self-denial only magnified this ecstasy. Popcak claimed, "Men and women who practice periodic abstinence have reported more intense and frequent orgasms than other couples. God always rewards his faithful."[45]

All three authors embraced a physico-psychospiritual determinism that traded on both the idea of act as language (a newer idea) and sociobiology (carried forward from mid-century). Acts were words with single meanings. According to Popcak, "every time a married couple [makes] love, they [are] physically restating their wedding vows to each other—in fact, they [are] celebrating the sacrament of marriage."[46] For Bonacci, "Sex speaks one language and one language alone": "Sex has an inherent meaning. It means 'forever.'"[47] West agreed: "Sexual intercourse speaks. . . . the language of the marriage bond, the language of wedding vows. Anything less is a cheap counterfeit for what our hearts truly desire."[48] Sex in any other context, or contracepted sex, was literally a lie,[49] because it contradicted the meaning that God assigned to the word-act of sex.[50]

Fig. 15.4. For Better . . . Forever! A Catholic Guide to Lifelong Marriage by Gregory K. Popcak (Huntington, Ind.: Our Sunday Visitor, 1999). Photo courtesy of Our Sunday Visitor Publishing.

Although West preferred to remain on the symbolic plane, Popcak and Bonacci reinforced their point through a new version of the sociobiological argument. God wired the sacramental permanence and meaning of sexual language into our bodies through the hormone oxytocin. Bonacci called the hormone, which is released (among other times) during sexual arousal, the "superglue of the heart."[51] Its true purpose was to bond married couples emotionally. But, like superglue, once out of the bottle it created a permanent bond, even where none was desired. Thus, one should "glue" oneself only to one's carefully chosen, permanent partner. Bonacci argued, "Once a bond forms, the brain is no longer in charge. Feelings take over, drowning out logic."[52] Popcak likened it to an addictive drug: when people were "'hopped up' on oxytocin," "drugged by their own biochemistry," they trapped themselves in bad relationships.[53] Lest we miss the point, Bonacci reiterated, "This bond isn't something you can consciously control."[54]

The same idea underlies West's opinion that people who do not adhere to God's plan for sex will "forfeit true joy, true happiness"—not as a punishment, but simply as a logical consequence of "miss[ing] the meaning of [their] existence altogether."[55] Bonacci concurred: "Morality is just an instruction manual for your body. Sex speaks a language—a language of permanent love. . . . You are free to take it out of that context if you choose to, but there will be physical, emotional and spiritual consequences. Abusing that language can hurt you—badly."[56] Why? Breaking a premature bond inevitably damaged both partners and made it more difficult for them to adhere to spouses later. Like overused duct tape, promiscuous people's "hearts lose their adhesiveness, their ability to bond in sexual activity."[57] These spiritual and psychological wounds, West believed, had enormous social consequences: "It's difficult to find even one social evil, one element of societal chaos, that is not in some way related to the breakdown of marriage and the misuse of sex."[58] In sum, a person is an emotional, spiritual, physical whole. This whole is set up so that when the body is used in certain ways, it creates an emotional and spiritual bond between people, the foundation and condition for long and happy life together. The sin is not in giving into the body (the body is meant to be given into), but in doing so prematurely.

> ## Catholics and Sex
>
> The non-Catholic mind cannot even begin to imagine how much real Catholics honor, esteem, and *enjoy* sex. Sex to the true Catholic is like what relativity was to Einstein, the vaccination was to Pasteur, or the electric light was to Edison.
>
> —Gregory K. Popcak,
> *For Better . . . Forever!*
> *A Catholic Guide to Lifelong Marriage*
> (Huntington, Ind.: Our Sunday Visitor, 1999), 201.

To this point it would seem that sexual bonding and permanent commitment could occur between any two people. But according to this group of authors men and women were created to attract and complement each other physically, emotionally, and spiritually. On the physical level, Bonacci explains, they were intended to procreate in marriage: "If you know anything about biology, you know that the parts are designed to work together. . . . His body is designed to manufacture sperm. Her body is designed to receive it and possibly to lead it to a waiting egg."[59] Popcak mapped complementary emotional and intellectual roles to these physical differences: "At the dawn of creation . . . while both Adam and Eve were given the responsibility to nurture, emote, communicate, etc., God created Eve's body to *emphasize* such qualities in her life, and this emphasis was what God called 'femininity.' Likewise, while both Adam and Eve were given the responsibility to make plans, set goals, provide for their needs, solve problems, etc., God created Adam's body to *emphasize* such qualities in his life, and this emphasis is what the Lord called 'masculinity.'"[60]

West's embrace of gender complementarity was the most comprehensive. For West, marriage was the "primordial sacrament" because it

symbolizes Christ's self-gift to the church: "Christ, our heavenly Bride-
groom, shows us what sexual union means by making an everlasting
gift of his body to us (his Bride) on the cross,
which we receive sacramentally in the Eucharist.
The sexual union of husband and wife participates
in Christ's eucharistic self-giving," a sacrifice also
fraught with pain and risk.[61] Baptism, usually
considered the foundational Christian expression of God's love and mercy, took a back seat.[62]
Consequently, for West, altering the order of
sacramental male-female procreative union did
not merely tinker with ethics; it threatened the
very core of the Christian doctrine of salvation.
Couples who contracepted committed sacrilege against Christ and
the church, whom their marriage symbolized.[63] Here gender becomes
icon, without reference to either psychological or social reality.[64]

> **The Superiority of Christian Sex**
> What passes for secular, pagan 'sexu-
> ality' is merely a shabby, tacky imita-
> tion of what sex really is. They don't
> have the real thing; *we do.*
> —Gregory K. Popcak, *Beyond the
> Birds and the Bees* (Huntington, Ind.:
> Our Sunday Visitor, 2001), 59.

One of the chief differences between mid- and late-century works
was a decline in serious engagement with psychology. Although
Popcak has degrees in licensed clinical social work and a master's in
social work, for the most part these recent works eschewed the extensive footnotes and doctoral degrees that certified the scholarliness of
mid-century guides. The coherence between science and theology was
assumed rather than proved. For instance, Bonacci simply said that she
was "certain" that men experience involuntary bonding in sexual relationships; related that "a doctor once told me that female sexual satisfaction is in part tied to her body receiving and absorbing semen and
that her body is even designed to come to recognize and accept one
man's sperm and to tend to reject other sperm"; and confused artificial
insemination with in vitro fertilization.[65] West felt no need to back up
his suggestion that sexual disorder (rather than greed, for instance) was
the common root of all social ills. Theological citations were equally
spotty. The outlines of church teaching provided the superstructure,
but the detailed contents seemed to come primarily from the authors'
reflections on their own and their clients' experiences.

In addition, these guides' astonishing degree of agreement
masked an unacknowledged tension. On one hand, Popcak was so
confident that revelation accords with reason that he wrote a secular

marriage guide recommending the same practices he touted in his self-consciously Catholic books, even prescribing scheduled monthly "abstinence breaks" to impassion sexual relations.[66] Catholic teaching on sex was just right reason; no theology was necessary. Here he had support from another sort of manual, the Couple to Couple League's *The Art of Natural Family Planning*, which promoted the sympto-thermal method of natural family planning (NFP) over "non-natural" contraceptive methods.[67] The authors not only embraced science by relying on extensive research into the precise indicators of women's fertility but also hinted that this method—because it necessarily engaged both husband and wife—made decisions about sexual intercourse more egalitarian than they might have been if every day were "safe." Popcak picked up on NFP's implications for male involvement and restraint, even recommending that boys take charge of their teenaged sisters' temperature charts in order to get early training in understanding and record-keeping (although one assumes he would disapprove of a boy telling his sister that tonight would be a safe night for sex with her boyfriend!).[68]

At the other extreme, West insisted that Catholic sexual mores cannot be understood without faith: "Sex in God's plan is more awesome than any human being could possibly dream. It's quite literally *in-credible*—that is, unbelievable. Only faith is able to believe 'the great mystery.'"[69] Bonacci hovered in the middle; Catholic sexual teaching is a commonsense "owner's manual" for the body, but some features of sexual relations remain mysterious.[70] Are Catholic sexual ethics a matter of solid reasoning about universal human nature, or a matter of authoritative church interpretation of sacred revelation? In these books, the jury is still out.

One lesser known genre of the late twentieth century—predating the 1990s but certainly following Vatican Council II—traced the path some Catholic writing on marriage might have taken had *Humanae vitae* not intervened. These were psychologically smart guides on managing celibacy without unhealthy repression or crushing degrees of guilt. They melded the psychological and the theological in a more sophisticated way than most marriage and dating guides that followed them, perhaps because the debates over gender, contraception, and nonmarital sex were irrelevant to an audience already committed to celibacy. Their premise was that *being sexual* was part of being human, but *not being genitally active* was a challenge in service of a vocation that had rewards and privileges: as Patrick Carroll's "Becoming a Celibate Lover" put it, "loving, or even trying to love, as God loves us: Freely, deeply, broadly, unpossessively."[71] In chapters with titles like "Chastity and Tactility" and "The Sexual Life of a Celibate Person," Donald Georgen's *The Sexual Celibate* declared that the path to healthy celibacy was lined with intimate friendships in which sexual desire was not denied or repressed; it must be accepted, examined for its meaning with the help of a counselor or spiritual director, and sometimes even discussed with the people toward whom it was directed.[72] Mary Anne Huddleston's collection *Celibate Loving: Encounter in Three Dimensions* was even more explicit about these claims. The subtitle was a tantalizing pun. It introduced the "three dimensions" of celibacy that organized the book (psychological, spiritual, and social), but the immediate image of "three dimensions" was embodied relationship. In one essay William Kraft struck a note that united all of the late-century writings, for both married and single people: "A person, celibate or married, can refuse the call of integration and focus exclusively on the physical nature of genitality"; instead, the goal was "to come to feel wholly at one with genitality and to experience the spirituality of sexuality."[73]

These guides also point to the familiar unresolved tensions: Is station or development the best yardstick for measuring sexual behavior? How is the authority of ecclesiastical moral theology related to the authority of developmental psychology? West's nuptial theology and Bonacci's emphasis on waiting until marriage echoed early twentieth-century visions of marriage and celibacy as ecclesiastical vocations, states with static rules, not dynamic processes with evolving standards. Popcak's response to the question was "both/and." He embraced developmental views of both single sexuality and marriage. Yet he believed that both processes could and must be navigated within Catholic moral guidelines. Georgen, who envisioned life as an unending journey toward perfection, embraced a developmental vision of chastity that was only slightly more permissive than the gradualist description of chastity in the most recent *Catechism of the Catholic Church*: "Chastity is a process, an unfinished one, life-long. It is something we long for; it is something we pray for. Celibate chastity, as an ideal, is seldom perfectly realized in the concrete. Yet it must be continually sought and held up as an ideal." On the path to the goal, desire might, and probably would, burst forth occasionally in masturbation. Hardly Deshon's yawning pit of hell, masturbation merely "points to the unfinishedness of the process of spiritualization. To be unfinished is not to be immoral nor irresponsible. It is, however, to be challenged toward further growth. We must accept unfinishedness but not choose to remain there."[74] Georgen explicitly accepted a fact some others ignore: psychology had not just interpreted moral theology but subtly altered it, bringing former mortal sins under the less-threatening heading of growing pains.

We leave the twentieth century with these three apparently very different expressions of the moral life: to adhere strictly to the rules inscribed in biology and theology, to strive toward maturity within the limits of these rules, to strive toward psycho-spiritual maturity so as perhaps to adhere to the ecclesiastical ideal eventually. Yet all concurred in one belief: if you are single, God wants you to have intimate, nongenital friendships; if you are married, God wants you to have the most passionate, exciting sex life you can possibly imagine. To the surprise of disappointed Vatican II progressives, who found the later manuals rigid and restrictive and who pointed to high rates of contraceptive use among married Catholics (estimates run to 95 percent), this consensus generated great excitement among some young adult and college-age Catholics disillusioned by a culture of "hooking up." These youthful enthusiasts felt freed by their embrace of newfound reverence, sacramentality, and self-denial and felt respected by authors who responded to their hunger for meaning with frank, experiential reasoning.

## FULL CIRCLE

By the turn of the twenty-first century, both traditionalist and progressive Catholic writings on sexuality had sold out to culture, if differently. Their common belief in the agreement of faith and reason led them to give slightly different advice: on the one hand, follow church teaching, and your sex life will top the secular charts; on the other, use the best of psychologically informed contemporary sexual culture to transform church teaching. But all the dating and marriage manuals sold hot sex for straight couples. Deaf to the warnings of Protestant guides (like Lauren Winner's *Real Sex*[75]) about the "fun" of illicit liaisons and the comforting ordinariness of much married lovemaking, they argued that fidelity to church teaching was the pathway to phenomenal sex—and they implied that if you were not having phenomenal sex, you were not trying hard enough to be a good spouse. Celibacy guides indicated that desire was no longer considered too arousing to discuss. Rather, sexual feelings were too arousing *not* to discuss—they must be named and dealt with openly if they were not to lead to disastrous consequences. The homosexual desires that flustered the marriage-manual authors found comfortable treatment here. For heterosexual and homosexual celibates, repression was passé.

Still, this is not the end of the story. The American Roman Catholic church was surprisingly similar at the turn of the twentieth century and at the turn of the twenty-first. All recent guides on sex target an acculturated, relatively well-educated population. Yet in 2005 over 12 percent of Americans were foreign-born, and some sources placed the Catholic proportion of this immigrant population at over 40 percent. Other sources estimated the immigrant Latino Catholic population at thirteen million, which amounts to approximately 17 percent of American Catholics.[76] During both periods the American Catholic Church was composed of two populations with very different pastoral needs: assimilated, fairly well-educated Catholics who were formed as much by American civic, mostly Protestant, culture as by their own religious tradition, and poor and less-educated recent immigrants for whom simple survival—often in isolation from familiar traditions and from family—was the most immediate concern. There are important differences, of course: the virulent anti-Catholicism of the early twentieth century had abated by the end, removing one barrier to comfortable identification with American culture; the proportions had shifted from an immigrant majority to an immigrant minority within Catholicism; and the cultural norm had shifted from studied reticence about sex to open and almost constant conversation. All of these changes profoundly affected the literature on sexuality produced for American lay consumption. But the continuing tension between immigration and assimilation reminds us that Catholic views on sexuality had not yet reached equilibrium, and Catholic literature on sexuality was not reaching everyone.

## FOR FURTHER READING

Burns, Jeffrey M. *Disturbing the Peace: A History of the Christian Family Movement 1949–1974.* Notre Dame, Ind.: University of Notre Dame Press, 1999

Gillespie, C. Kevin, S.J. *Psychology and American Catholicism: From Confession to Therapy?* New York: Crossroad, 2001.

John Paul II [Karol Wojtyla]. *Love and Responsibility.* Revised edition. Trans. H. T. Willetts. San Francisco: Ignatius, 1993.

John Paul II. *Man and Woman He Created Them: A Theology of the Body.* Trans. Michael Waldstein. Boston: Pauline Books and Media, 2006.

Lodge, David. *The British Museum Is Falling Down.* New York: Penguin, 1980 [1965].

McClory, Robert. *Turning Point: The Inside Story of the Papal Birth Control Commission, and How Humanae Vitae Changed the Life of Patty Crowley and the Future of the Church.* New York: Crossroad, 1995.

Paul VI. *Humanae vitae.* 1968.

Pius XI. *Casti connubii.* 1930.

Skinner, James M. *The Cross and the Cinema: The Legion of Decency and the National Catholic Office for Motion Pictures, 1933–1970.* Westport, Conn.: Praeger, 1993.

Tentler, Leslie Woodcock. *Catholics and Contraception: An American History.* Ithaca: Cornell University Press, 2004.

# LIFE AND DEATH
# IN MIDDLE AMERICA

## ANN M. PEDERSON

It was society who told these stories—we ourselves. The stories are our ways of contextualizing technology. . . . Are there better and worse, more or less adequate, ways of creating and telling stories? Are there criteria governing our stories? What makes a dream true? These questions are urgent when we reflect on technology.

—Philip Hefner[1]

## SETTING THE STAGE

What may seem like an ending can become complicated by a beginning.* Let me explain.[2] A health care professional in Sioux Falls, South Dakota, shared a story with me that illustrates how decisions about beginnings and endings of life and the nature of human personhood might be more complicated than we can imagine.[3] A young man was rushed to the emergency room at a local hospital after being involved in a serious car accident. He suffered major traumas including neck and head injuries, and it became apparent that he would probably not live very long. His family and his long-time girlfriend rushed to the ER and stayed by his bedside over the course of a few days.

When it became apparent that he might not live, the family struggled with whether or not to withdraw the respirator. Over the minutes and hours, the family argued and struggled with this difficult decision. The medical team indicated clearly that he would not survive very long, and decisions were urgent. And then his girlfriend of many years requested that the parents allow the sperm of her boyfriend to

*Portions of this chapter were originally published as "South Dakota and Abortion: A Local Story about How Religion, Medican Science, and Culture Meet" by Ann Milliken Pederson from *Zygon*, vol. 42, no. 1 (March 2007). Copyright © 2007 by the Joint Publication Board of Zygon. Used by permission.

be given to her so that she could become pregnant with his child. A beginning of new life for her would become possible even while his would end. The parents and girlfriend could barely cope with the present grief, and yet they were being asked to think about the possibility of creating new life.

Questions followed for all—the parents, the girlfriend, the health care providers. They asked about life and death, endings and beginnings, what it means to be a person, and where God was in all of this. To withdraw the respirator would most likely bring a quick death, but it would also hasten the intensity of grief for their young son. Was the family using him as a means to deal with their grief? Did they want to prolong his life for his own sake or for theirs or for both? To whom did the sperm belong? In the midst of such an urgent crisis, how would the family and girlfriend make these decisions? In that moment the questions were transfigured. Decisions needed to be made in haste. And the possibilities of making a new life from the end of another one just didn't make sense.

> ### Death and the Family
> It is her restlessness that weighs on me now. Her anguish over us—the living watching the dying—the dying watching the living. She is still the peacemaker trying to create a calm in the midst of her death. And there is nothing she can do to ameliorate the situation. . . . An individual doesn't get cancer, a family does.
> —Terry Tempest Williams,
> *Refuge: An Unnatural History
> of Family and Place*
> (New York: Vintage, 1992), 214.

The need to make profound ethical and spiritual decisions with such great urgency insures that the decisions will feel ambiguous, because they are usually made in a state of bewilderment. John Lantos, a Chicago pediatrician, writes from his experience as a physician in the neonatal intensive care unit about this ambiguity of decisions that crises create:

> Our practices respond to the inextricably tangled web of moral obligations within families and among family members and to the complex negotiations that take place between doctors, patients, and family members. Perhaps because these areas of human experience are so complex and difficult to describe in general terms or to regulate in rational ways, neither law nor bioethics has done a particularly good job in exploring them. Instead, they might be better understood through a domain of inquiry that focuses on the complexity of the family decision making.[4]

Where can people turn as they have to make decisions about beginnings and endings of life? What kinds of perspectives and wisdom, irrespective of what the "authorities" have to say, are ordinary people starting to figure out and articulate for themselves? As Lantos indicates, whether it is the family facing the decision, or the health care provider working with the family, no clear answers appear in the moment of urgency.[5] Medicine and technology don't solve the questions, but more likely complicate the answers. The same might be said about religion. The Sioux Falls hospital scenario would not have even been possible a few decades before. *Beginnings and endings are not discrete simple moments but are processes moving through an entire life story.*

> **Being Dead**
>
> The way I see it, being dead is not terribly far off from being on a cruise ship. Most of your time is spent lying on your back. The brain has shut down. The flesh begins to soften. Nothing much new happens, and nothing is expected of you.
>
> —Mary Roach, *Stiff: The Curious Lives of Human Cadavers* (New York: Norton, 2003), 9.

To be human is to seek meaning, to ask questions, and to tell stories. At the end of the twentieth century, stories shaped by all of the scientific and technological innovations radically altered people's lives. This story from Sioux Falls, while particular in its local context, illustrates the universal human search for meaning amid the crises raised by medical science and technology. This family realized that they were confronting questions that, finally, were spiritual or theological in nature. In the intensity of the moment, what once seemed familiar and secure became blurred and unfamiliar. Even the familiar spiritual foundations upon which so many Christians rely can seem to falter. This ragged edge of life is where medical science and religious beliefs intersect with profound consequences.

## SETTING THE LOCAL SCENE IN SOUTH DAKOTA

A brief history of South Dakota will help to set the local scene and the concurrent reflections about the relationship between religion and medicine. South Dakota was the last state in the United States to get a Starbucks and the first to pass legislation outlawing all abortions with no exceptions other than to save the life of the mother—no exceptions for rape or incest, or for the health of the mother. At first glance, the media tells stories about a seemingly conservative, mostly rural state that is at war over a cultural, religious, and even scientific issue. But to assume that this is all there is to the narrative is to not see the whole picture.

While the state has a relatively small population of 754,844 (according to the 2000 U.S. Census), South Dakota is comparably larger in its physical size (seventeenth in the country). Many South Dakotans travel great distances for services such as health care. The racial makeup is predominantly white (88 percent) with approximately 8.5 percent of the population being Native American (third highest in the continental United States).[6] South Dakota has some of the poorest counties in the United States, and approximately 20.2 percent of children younger than six live at or below the federal poverty level.[7] Poverty creates urgent public health care needs in South Dakota, particularly among the Native American population and populations in other isolated, rural areas. Approximately 65 percent of the people are Protestant, and 25 percent are Roman Catholic. Lutherans make up approximately 28 percent of the Christian population.[8]

At the end of the twentieth century three large hospital systems spanned the state of South Dakota from Rapid City to Sioux Falls. Avera Health, a Roman Catholic health care system, employs approximately 3,100 people and has about a hundred locations in South Dakota and neighboring states.[9] In recent years, tensions have developed in the state regarding access to women's reproductive health options, like abortion and contraception. Most of the religious perspectives expressed in the media are from those who consider abortion a sin, except possibly to save the life of the mother. Because of the large Roman Catholic population in South Dakota, the popular press often cites papal authority and church doctrine on the issue of abortion. And yet other denominations have much different stances, including the Evangelical Lutheran Church in America (ELCA), of which South Dakota has a large population. Recently, newspaper columns by Methodists, United Church of Christ (UCC) clergy, and Lutherans (ELCA) have been offering other perspectives and noting that they are Christian as well.

The other major health care system, Sioux Valley Health System, has 24 hospitals and about 150 health care facilities in South Dakota.[10] For those who live near the five major cities in South Dakota, access to health care is not particularly problematic. But that leaves thousands of folks in rural communities, where getting to hospitals or even clinics can mean traveling long distances. These local statistics indicate the importance of location—in all of its cultural, religious, economic, and geographic specificities, for understanding the relationship between religion and medical science.

The religion and scientific narratives need to be told within the larger sociopolitical economic realities of the current culture. And the way science(s) and religion(s) are practiced in South Dakota raises issues in the broader political and cultural landscape.

## THE LARGER HISTORICAL-CULTURAL CONTEXT

At the twilight of the twentieth century, stories appeared in the news that changed the way people understood beginnings and endings of life. Medical technology was transforming and challenging traditional notions of what it meant to be a human person. In 1978, Louise Joy Brown was born to a British couple through the process of in vitro (Latin for "in glass") fertilization. Unable to conceive because of blocked fallopian tubes, Lesley Brown underwent this radically novel technological procedure that created a new life in her. By the very end of the twentieth century, in vitro fertilization, once considered very new, was nearly passé. In the 1990s, Dolly, a cloned sheep from Scotland, was born, and people struggled with questions about cloning and embryonic stem cell research. The news seemed to reach every corner of the planet. All of a sudden, people realized that the potential of technology to change the human being far exceeded their ability to cope with those changes. The plotline of the human story was moving faster than the species had expected.

At the other end of life, technology once used to save a life was withdrawn in order to end a life. Two famous stories of young women, Karen Ann Quinlan and Nancy Cruzan, brought the issues about the end of life and the right to die to the public's attention. Karen Ann Quinlan and her parent's story sharpened the culture's awareness of how technology, medicine, religion, and politics are woven together into one complex narrative web of living and dying. After collapsing

**Fig. 16.1.** Parents of Karen Ann Quinlan with magazine bearing her photo, September 24, 1977. Photo © Bettmann/Corbis. Used by permission.

in April 1975 from a drug and alcohol overdose, Karen remained hospitalized in a "persistent vegetative state." At the request of her parents, her breathing tube was removed. She continued to breathe on her own and died in 1985, two years after Nancy Cruzan's car accident resulted in a similar situation. At the site of the accident, Nancy was pronounced dead by the local patrolman. And yet, "he could have no idea just how widely society would debate exactly the same question that he had answered so simply, perhaps prophetically—whether this accident victim was dead. Nor could he know that the accident would indeed claim other victims. But none lay at the scene that night."[11] Nancy Cruzan, a young woman whose story gripped the nation, told the public about a patient's rights to die and the struggles of her family.

The story of Nancy Cruzan, while it is clearly about her living and dying, is also about her family and others who found their lives tied to this ongoing saga. Beginnings and endings ran concurrently through the legal courts—to begin what had ended, to end what had begun. The toll on her family was unimaginable, and several years after Nancy Cruzan died, her father committed suicide.[12] Death is not a solitary event. Unnecessary suffering was caused by the polarized positions of the media, by the polarized positions of religious denominations, and by reactions of popular media figures like Peter Singer and Dr. Kevorkian.

In a recent survey, 70 percent of Americans said that they wanted to die at home, surrounded by their loved ones. And yet in South Dakota, about 19 percent of people died at home in 1997, and the rest died in hospitals or nursing homes.[13] These figures are not atypical for the rest of American culture. While many people at the moment of crisis want "everything to be done," they don't recognize the implications of how far technology can prolong life. A few decades ago,

Nancy Cruzan would have been pronounced dead at the scene of her automobile accident, and she would have remained dead. Because of technological enhancements, she was able to be revived; she then stayed in a persistent vegetative state for years. While the statistics go up for preserving life, so also do the chances of staying in a persistent vegetative state. Taught to preserve life at all costs, most health care providers fight against giving up on life. This is reinforced by the public attitude that technology and medicine can "fix" everything. However, as right-to-die cases became more prominent in the news, the general public became more educated on end-of-life issues. *Beginnings and endings are not discrete simple moments but are processes moving through the entire human story.*

From the incubator developed in the 1880s to the latest technologies in the NICU (neonatal intensive care unit), premature babies have a much greater chance of surviving. John Lantos relates the "narrative of progress" that has been at the heart of neonatal medicine. He notes that it became the fastest growing field in pediatrics and that this success story is linked to its financial gains. The infant mortality rate between "1900 and 1960 . . . dropped from 122 per 1,000 to 26 per 1,000."[14] Those statistics were cut in half again as the life expectancy in the NICU increased. Technologies developed for decreasing infancy mortality came with a price, however. New moral dilemmas were raised as the technologies advanced. The courts and lawyers could barely keep up with the new dilemmas. An unprecedented interest in "medicine, neonatology, and the moral dilemmas of medicine and technology" came to the fore.[15]

Each human being has a story, a narrative that is connected in, with, and under the stories of others. As folks hear the stories of Louise Brown and Nancy Cruzan, they can't help but wonder about their own story and what it means in the larger scheme of the cosmos. These larger cultural narratives of technology, human persons, medicine,

> **The Drama of Life and Death**
> Over the last twenty years in America, both doctors and patients have tried to tell certain stories about end-of-life care in the language of bioethics and in the language of legal rights. Other stories have been told in the languages of clinical epidemiology and health services research. None of these stories captures the complexity of the drama that the people who are living their lives or dying from their deaths in the same way that fiction or poetry does.
> —John Lantos, *The Lazarus Case: Life and Death Issues in Neonatal Intensive Care* (Baltimore: Johns Hopkins University Press, 2001), 104.

and religion sharpen the questions about the world and what it means to be a part of it. To pursue these questions is to pursue a quest for meaning. Does human personhood begin at conception? At birth? If sperm are donated, the eggs donated, and a surrogate mother utilized, who are the parents? What does it mean to be part of a family? If someone is in a persistent vegetative state, does our culture consider him or her to be a person? Is it ethical to "do everything" in order to keep someone alive? Beginnings lead to questions about endings.

Many people imagine a fairly clear, simple, straightforward story about what it means to be human. Lines between death and life, science and religion, humans and nature have appeared to be separate, distinct, and clear. The stories of beginnings and endings of life at the end of the twentieth century, however, tell about a much more complex web of technology and nature, humans and machines, religion and science, nature and culture, than could have been imagined. The boundaries that were once unambiguous (or so some hoped) were revealed as fuzzy and permeable. What folks once thought was "true" and "right" shifted faster than they could manage. Religious people, caught in these cultural stories of life and death, floundered to make sense of their faith's convictions and the concomitant realities of technology and science. And so the stories of who humans thought they were no longer had simple plots and characters, with clear beginnings and endings. Making sense of the human story is more akin to jumping into the middle of the story, where beginnings and endings collapse into one another and the characters move through the plot as if it were an endless maze. Beginnings and endings will cross one another, move through each other, and define where the path leads. While many Christians will desire clarity and direction, the ambiguous and messy may be the only guide. Ordinary Christians are caught in the midst of dramas of life and death for which no clear directions are given, no map is provided. How they find their way is of utmost importance to the ongoing story.

Birth and death: no other events in human lives are more mysterious or have created more spiritual and ethical questions. Medical science and biotechnological advances have drastically altered the way life and death are defined and understood, and about what it means to be human in relationship to technology. Human beings are tethered in, with, and under technologies that shape and define human nature.

People become who they are amid and in these new technologies, and not apart from them. Lives are extended by respirators, premature babies are kept alive in the NICU, computers take vital signs, and pacemakers are implanted. And in the middle of it, people try to make sense of it all, asking questions along the way. And these questions are at the heart of what it means to be human, to be related to God and creation.

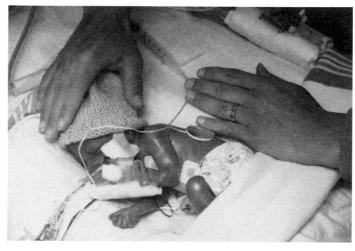

Fig. 16.2. Premature baby in neonatal intensive care unit. Photo © Ken Glaser/Corbis. Used by permission.

How do Christians struggle with these spiritual questions in light of recent discoveries in medical science and biotechnology? To answer this question requires telling yet more stories, reflecting on the questions, and thinking about the quest for meaning. If people truly become who they are *in, with, and under* technology, then coping with technology and their relationship to it is a spiritual struggle. Human beings can no longer afford to think that they are separate from nature, the apex of God's creation. New boundaries and new stories define the human person. The ways people struggle with these difficult questions are shaped by larger cultural narratives that include, of course, religious and scientific stories.

## TECHNOLOGY, THE MARKET, AND MEDICAL SCIENCE

Nothing can reveal more about human beings than what they see and hear on their televisions at night as they flip through the channels. Commercials advertise that medicine and doctors can provide some sort of eschatological salvation; they can save people from their humanness. Local hospitals advertise the *wonders* of medicine and the advances of technology for problems ranging from infertility to heart disease. The business of health care delivery reaches out to consumers with messages of hope and promise of relief from their illnesses. And

---

### Religion and Technology

I will pose two questions for reflection and then elaborate one theological interpretation of technology. The two questions: Where does religion take place? What shapes does religion take? My answer: If we speak about technology at its deepest levels, we are at the same time speaking about its religious dimension, even if we do not use conventional religious terminology.

—Philip Hefner, *Technology and Human Becoming*, Theology and the Sciences (Minneapolis: Fortress Press, 2003), 73.

---

consumers expect these results, even demand them. As soon as a new technological advance is promoted or a new pill advertised, American consumers expect that it is their right to have access to it. People have faced not only the wonders of technology, but also its limitations and horrors. Television seems to ignore these realities except through occasional sound bites on the evening news. The future seems up for grabs; what once seemed safe and secure is not the case anymore (or never really ever has been). Ironically, while some of the technological innovations have led to "bigger and better" ways of living, the public has become more restless, more uneasy than ever. The world changes so fast that folks can't keep up. And they expect a quick fix for this spiritual malaise.

The questions about technology and medicine are just a tip of this age of anxiety. The late twentieth century shared both the hopeful and the fearful attitudes that the Enlightenment twilight produced. As members of a do-it-yourself, future-looking culture, Americans expect that the limits of the human condition can be overcome or escaped. Much like their cultural expectations about life and death, their religious expectations reflect the culture. People don't really want to think seriously about death, illness, and human frailties. Many people shop for church the way they do for food—they want something to provide immediate comfort. Ironically, the price they ultimately pay for such comfort foods and quick fixes is denial of and postponement of their pain. The questions will always be there; they don't go away.

## DIFFERENT CHRISTIAN RESPONSES TO TOUGH QUESTIONS

The many faces of the Christian tradition approach these spiritual questions in different ways. Some avoid addressing the questions directly and simply quote from the Bible. Others leave the meaning up to each individual believer. Some denominations write position papers, while others have authorities issue statements. These statements of the various denominations illustrate approaches that are often so divisive that ordinary people are bombarded with confusing messages about what *the Christian* response should be. Sometimes the messages come in sermons, or are played on tape to a congregation at the request of a bishop, or are studied in groups. How religious traditions wrestle with these difficult and often ambiguous questions will reveal much about the stories of the relationship between religion and science at the end of the twentieth century.

Some Christian denominations, usually Protestant, elevate the written text of the Bible above all other authorities. Other bodies, like the Orthodox and Roman Catholic Churches, also include the role of tradition, experience, and reason. And most parishioners struggle with questions of authority, despite their denominational affiliation. No wonder people have a difficult time working how to discern a path through these difficult questions when the official guides are so diverse. This is not necessarily a hazard, however. The diversity among Christians can produce angst and fear, or it can be seized as an opportunity to expand the question for truth through incorporating many voices. Whether the ultimate authority is the written text, a papal writing, or one's individual inner voice, the way people come to spiritual discernment mirrors not only their religious background but also their cultural values.

The following three traditions span some of the variety of Christian responses to ethical and spiritual dilemmas about the beginnings of life. Their written documents embody the cultural and religious themes that shape the way religion was practiced in the late twentieth century. They are a part of the story, but not its totality by any means. They reflect a diversity of their respective Enlightenment and Reformation inheritances. The three positions are: The ELCA statement on abortion, the UCC statement on reproductive rights, and the Roman Catholic 1987 document "Respect for Human Life."[16] The statements were created in different ways, indicating how the direction of laypeople's perspectives are gathered, evaluated, and formulated. Of course it must be said that within each denomination great variety exists. Often, liberal Roman Catholics will have more in common with liberal Lutherans than conservative Roman Catholics. This variation in part exists because of the culture wars that occur in the political and religious arenas. In a time in which warfare seems to pervade these difficult issues, rhetoric escalates, and political lines are drawn.

All three denominations seek counsel from a number of sources, including scientists, ethicists, and theologians, to formulate their statements. How the statements are considered authoritative and what role they play in parishioners' lives vary among the denominations. For example, the ELCA's statement came after much deliberation with laypeople, holding regional hearings in various synods, and taking a final vote of the national body of laypeople and clergy. The process is somewhat similar in the General Synods of the UCC. Both statements leave more room for moral ambiguity, and while they give counsel, the final decision about an abortion is left to the individual. The Congregation for the Doctrine of the Faith issued the 1987 statement "Respect for Human Life" from the magisterium and reflects previous authoritative teachings and traditions. No votes were taken by laypeople. The statement is much less ambiguous than the Protestant ones and does not leave the same room for individual decisions. This examination of how the statements are constructed by denominational bodies provides insights into the web of narratives that shape laity when they confront difficult moral issues like abortion or end-of-life decisions.

All three statements begin with a theological affirmation that life is a gift from God and is good. Not inconsequentially, all three acknowledge that the issues raised by technology at the beginning of life are morally freighted and require careful discernment. The ELCA document on abortion acknowledges the differences that people have and the life circumstances that shape these differences. This was an important statement to include because the ambiguous conclusions of the position paper itself created differing receptions among laypeople. Some Lutherans would like to have seen a more definitive statement that clearly condemned abortion. For others, the strength of the Lutheran tradition is precisely in its ability to relate the texts of its tradition (scripture and the confessions) to the particular contemporary context. Lutherans have understood themselves to be a part of a church always undergoing reformation. This is exactly what the ELCA document on abortion reiterates—the context and text as an interactive process of interpretation.

Both the UCC and ELCA acknowledge that women often face difficult and even dire circumstances that shape their individual reproductive needs and decisions. Such circumstances might include a forced pregnancy, poverty, violence, and abuse. The ELCA states that neither the pregnant woman nor the "developing life in the womb" has a *right*. In fact, the language of rights is not helpful because this implies an absolute for either the woman or the fetus.[17] To quote at length from the statement on abortion of the ELCA:

> The language used in discussing abortion should ignore neither the value of unborn life nor the value of the woman and her other relationships. It should neither obscure the moral seriousness of the decision faced by the woman nor hide the moral value of the newly conceived life. Nor is it helpful to use the language of "rights" in absolute ways that imply that no other significant moral claims intrude. A developing life in the womb does not have an absolute right to be born, nor does a pregnant woman have an absolute right to terminate a pregnancy. The concern for both the life of the woman and the developing life in her womb expresses a common commitment to life. This requires that we move beyond the usual "pro-life" versus "pro-choice" language in discussing abortion.[18]

These different views on abortion and reproduction are related to both denominations' understandings of authority, which are very different from that of the Roman Catholic Church. Theology is after all a practice.

The UCC statement indicates that it has affirmed and "reaffirmed since 1971 that access to safe and legal abortion is consistent with a woman's right to follow the dictates of her own faith and beliefs in determining when and if she should have children, and has supported comprehensive sexuality education as one measure to prevent unwanted or unplanned pregnancies."[19] The UCC's statements are clearer than the ELCA's about affirming that women have access to safe and legal abortions. The UCC takes very seriously the context of the moral dilemma and makes this a priority in the statement. The decision clearly resides within the woman's autonomous prerogative.

Finally, the Roman Catholic statement on "Respect for Human Life," claims that from the moment of fertilization a human being is created and that this life is sacred. The focus is clearly on the sacred nature of human life and that the proper context for creating human life should be within marriage. Abortion and other reproductive issues are considered from these priorities. The statement reminds people that society often commodifies and commercializes human life and that this is problematic from a Christian perspective that declares life as sacred, created by God. The Roman Catholic document also cautions that the biological and reproductive sciences have powers that may have reached beyond what should and could be done. The language of individual rights should not be the first concern, but instead the goal of the common good comes first—preserving and honoring the sacred nature of all life. The Roman Catholic Church continues to and constantly "reaffirms the moral condemnation of any kind of procured abortion. This teaching has not changed and is unchangeable."[20]

In many ways, the issues and dilemmas around the end of life are similar in the three perspectives. And laypeople are caught somewhere between their own operating theology and the statements and beliefs of their religious denomination and tradition. For some, personal beliefs are consonant with denominational beliefs, while for many others, personal beliefs are at odds with those of the religious body. Then the beliefs become more complicated because life is more complex. Stories are also complicated because neither the sciences nor religious traditions are monolithic. And the relationship between them is multilayered.

## SPECIFIC STORIES

One way to see what is happening on a college campus is to read what's posted on the walls. A few years ago many of us couldn't miss a poster on the wall sponsored by two campus groups asking people to pray for a woman who was going to have an abortion (selective embryo reduction). Her name was not given, but the details of her situation were apparent. The poster claimed that the woman's husband had asked for the prayers from groups and was pleading with his wife not to have the abortion. Furthermore, the poster claimed that if she went through with the abortion she would be murdering her own child. Even though the poster's information was supposedly anonymous, the gossip began to spread around campus, creating a heated debate on campus about abortion. Were the campus bulletin boards the right place to display such information? Was this woman's right to privacy being violated? Somewhere in South Dakota a woman's life and her relationship with her physician and her husband became fodder for public warfare. Other campus groups and religious communities felt that they needed to respond. And since the rhetoric had escalated, the exchanges between both sides was not helpful for anyone in creating a safe place for discussion.

This example, while localized, symbolizes the incredible emotional tension that an issue like abortion can elicit. People line up to take figurative and real shots at each other. Soon, protective gear is needed! Battlegrounds include school classrooms, church sanctuaries, medical clinics where abortions are performed, political campaign advertisements, and personal friendships. In all cases, rhetoric heats up, and both sides want to claim their way is the only way, and even God's way. Both claim to have the god's-eye view of life. If one is trying to discern one's way through this minefield, battle wounds often seem the only reward.

In the 1980s and 1990s, both medical sciences and religious traditions faced new questions of what it means to be human in light of such rapid technological and scientific transitions. One way to face such change is to answer the question in different ways by viewing science and religion as independent spheres that offer different answers. Religious or theological language is supposedly subjective, answers the why questions, and belongs in church or in one's own private life. Scientific language is public, answers the how questions, and is objective. When I have listened to medical faculty give lectures to residents, I have heard an occasional doctor say that all religious, political, emotional, and cultural biases should be checked at the door on the part of the physician or health care worker. Their hope is that some kind of objectivity and distance can be maintained from the patient so that the treatment is not compromised.

The church is hardly exempt from such a worldview about the relationship between religion and science. The realm of faith is reduced to a privatized world in which the purpose of Christianity is for the individual alone. While an occasional adult forum might address complicated issues around the end of life, how often does one hear a thoughtful sermon or prayers or other liturgical forms address these difficult moments in one's life—and actually addresses them in such a way that the worshiper doesn't feel "told" what to believe? Catechetical materials don't adequately prepare young adults to face questions about life and death, at least not in ways that prepare them for the pain and difficulty of such questions. Seminary curricula have just begun to address the questions involving what it means to be human in an age of technology and science in meaningful and thoughtful ways.

When the reproductive embryologist comes to church, she leaves her scientific hat at the door. And the same happens at work with her religious beliefs. College students are educated this way. A student once remarked to me, as he saw me wandering through the Gilbert Science Center, that science is in this building or hallway and religion is in the other building or hallway and rarely shall they meet. I was notably out of place. And while it may seem convenient to separate religion and science, it is also rarely the case in matters of life and death that it is possible or desirable to do so.

What happens if the reproductive endocrinologist or palliative care physician is facing a difficult issue about the morality of her or his work? In South Dakota, multiple attempts have been made to either severely restrict or eliminate abortions. What if at the local level a legislative bill that eliminates all abortions and that defines human personhood from the moment of conception is passed and becomes law? Legislative bills have been introduced that would force artificial nutrition and hydration in cases in which it is not wanted by a patient. In many of these cases, religious views of the human person are at work in the legislature's production of the bills. Many of these legislative changes could have a profound effect on the work of scientists, the practice of physicians, and the health care of patients. All of a sudden the personal becomes public. Physicians have to decide how to work in a context that doesn't easily separate public from private, religion from science. Consequently, some physicians and scientists have begun to lobby legislatures and inform the public about the consequences of such legislation. Here the relationship between religion and science intersects in profoundly personal and political ways.

In South Dakota (and other states whose primary economic base is agricultural), human reproductive issues cannot be separated from other sciences like veterinary medicine. What ends up at the in vitro lab in the city probably began in the barns of the university veterinary school. At Augustana College in Sioux Falls, South Dakota, biology students under the tutelage of Dr. Maureen Diggins do research on body fat and fertility, by using the lethal yellow mouse mutant.[21] Their research is used by the faculty at the University of South Dakota Sanford School of Medicine for work on reproductive medicine. At the medical school, other faculty do research on in vitro fertilization and other biomedical issues related to reproduction. The relationship is fertile and has yielded multiple articles and grants.

On the other side of Sioux Falls is Hematech, which "is developing a novel system for production of human polyclonal antibodies."[22] Transgenic cows are "created" or reproduced to treat human diseases. "Human polyclonal antibodies can be used for a wide variety of therapeutic applications, including treatment of antibiotic-resistant infections, biodefense, immune deficiencies, cancer and various auto-immune diseases."[23] Boundaries between human animals and nonhuman animals collapse and implode to regenerate life—to create transgenic species. Humans sacrifice the lives of mice and cows in order to understand and improve their own species. And yet these incredible and powerful scientific and biotechnological innovations are never linked to the politics of abortion and other human reproductive concerns. Abortion of human embryos and fetuses is only one small layer of a much more complicated relationship between human and nonhuman, science and religion.

Scientific evidence is utilized by both sides of the debate in South Dakota. The intersection of

> **Bioethical Complexities**
>
> Bearing all this in mind, I find myself supporting stem cell research. This does not by any means indicate that I am persuaded by ethical arguments that depend on distinctions between totipotent and pluripotent cells. In fact, I am not finally persuaded at all. I find myself in an interim state, struggling to weigh the complex factors. My theological excursis into dignity is illuminating, but it does not make answering the central ethical question clear enough to be decisive. This may be disappointing to some readers.
>
> —Ted Peters, quoted in *The Human Embryonic Stem Cell Debate*, Suzanne Holland, Karen Lebacqz, Laurie Zoloth, eds. (Cambridge: MIT Press, 2002), 137.

personal and medical opinions gives way to more division. "Determining scientific fact on abortion is difficult, medical experts say. Even within the state's medical community, the abortion debate has been divisive."[24] The South Dakota State Medical Association issued a policy statement declaring that the matter of abortion is personal in nature and that the SDSMA should not attempt to change personal beliefs. Whether an abortion should be performed is also a matter of personal conscience, but the patient's health should not be compromised.[25]

Dr. Maria Bell, a Sioux Falls gynecologist and member of the faculty of the University of South Dakota Sanford School of Medicine, has found herself in the crossfire of the debate around science, medical practice, and ethics. She said that "she wasn't looking to become involved in politics but has felt compelled to become a public face in what might become the most bitter and divisive battle in South Dakota election history."[26] In hotly debated concern about abortion, Bell spoke publicly about her pro-choice position. Speaking out on this divisive issue can result in hate mail, death threats, and compromise in one's medical practice. "Bell said she's received many harassing e-mails—and a few that she considered to be threatening to herself and her family. She said she removed her children from Catholic school after they were taunted by other students. But like her counterparts on the opposite side of the debate, Bell is not deterred."[27] Maria Bell has found herself in the midst of a situation in which she cannot be expert in all of its dimensions—legal, spiritual, ethical, and scientific. In the ongoing story of abortion politics in South Dakota, the relationship between medical science and religious beliefs unfolds in people's lives that change the very way they practice both their science and their religion. This issue becomes more complicated in a state like South Dakota, where boundaries of geography, landscape, economics, and race further divide a small population.

In other stories told to me, some nurses, pharmacists, and physicians who firmly believe that personhood is established from the moment of conception find it very difficult to work with patients who demand health care procedures or protocols that go against this view. What about the nurse who works on the floor in a local hospital where an embryo reduction might take place? Should the nurse be required to participate in the procedure against his religious beliefs, against his will? Some hospitals allow nurses not to participate in the procedure for reasons of conscience. But think about this a bit further. I have participated in lively discussions with medical residents and pre-medicine undergraduates about how physicians should handle situations in which they might have to go against their conscience. For example, many physicians have refused to participate in or administer lethal injections to prisoners on death row. The situation can become more complicated when individual patients come to their physicians looking for help.

What happens when a young woman comes to her physician seeking a prescription for birth control and the physician's religious beliefs are opposed to prescribing birth control? Should the physician refuse the patient's request, or refer the patient to another doctor? If, for example, the physician believes that birth control is a form of abortion, then is the physician complicit in what he or she calls sin? What happens to the young woman? Or on another occasion, the physician might refer the patient, and then she receives the prescription only to find that the local pharmacist refuses to fill it for reasons of conscience. How do health care providers provide adequate health care without either being paternalistic or compromising the patient's care?

In a geographically isolated area like South Dakota, health care providers have unique responsibilities to their patients. For example, when pharmacists with certain religious views object to filling an order that is prescribed by the physician, women living in rurally isolated areas may not have access to referral to other pharmacies. This pits the needs of the patient against the views of the pharmacist. Some states include a "conscience clause" that exempts pharmacists from filling certain prescriptions because of their religious or philosophical beliefs. If the pharmacist believes that contraceptives destroy unborn children, even the fertilized eggs not yet implanted in the uterus, then the pharmacist need not fill the order requested by the patient and the physician. With increasing political attempts backed by religious groups to limit or prohibit abortion, medical and health care providers will find themselves in ongoing religious struggles as well as medical ones. Clearly the conservative religious climate in South Dakota (a partnership between Roman Catholicism and Protestant fundamentalist and evangelical denominations like Southern Baptists) shapes the way technology and access to reproductive health care is being delivered.

Educating health care professionals about reproductive technologies and reproductive health care issues becomes increasingly complex in a culture like South Dakota. South Dakota was the first state to require pregnant women who abuse alcohol or drugs to be rehabilitated. Women can be incarcerated for using alcohol when pregnant, and using drugs during pregnancy is defined as child abuse. While not directly religious issues, the implications for the status of both the women and the fetus have religious implications for some health care providers. Given the more conservative religious climate and geographical isolation of our region, physicians, for example, have difficulty in getting medical training about abortion procedures. In a state where only one community offers abortion services, many women must travel up to 350 miles for such services and then must return to their own communities for follow-up care. Will the follow up care be adequate for the patient if the physician has refused to learn about abortion or if he or she refuses to help the patient on moral grounds? If medical students are opposed to learning about contraception and/or abortion procedures, whose burden is it to offer an exemption from the requirement? Should the pressure be on the student to "opt out" and possibly face criticism from faculty and other students? Or in other cases, some students have felt criticism and ostracism from faculty and other students for requesting such education. In their stories, religious and cultural issues have shaped how their education is delivered.

To complicate the situation even more in South Dakota, access to good reproductive health care can seem a luxury for the poor, and particularly for American Indian women. Many Native women writing about reproductive health care and freedom argue that the Christian religion had a deleterious affect on Native women and their needs. "With the imposition of colonization and Christianity, foreign values, belief systems, and practices were forced upon our communities. Within those foreign systems, decisions pertaining to reproductive health were made by the Church with little regard to individual rights. Traditionally, reproductive health issues were decisions made by the individuals, and was not pushed into the political arena for close examination. The core of decision-making for Indigenous women is between her and the Great Spirit."[28] From forced sterilizations to policies of incarceration for pregnant women using alcohol, Native women must overcome many barriers to trust that adequate health care can be provided by a predominantly white culture. Steven Charleston, a citizen of the Choctaw Nation and president of the Episcopal Divinity School, underlines the point that racism formed the relationship between Christian missionaries and Native communities. "Exploitation, even genocide, was permissible under the cover of a racist mentality that allowed Europeans, including European Christians, to believe that they were racially superior to all others with whom they came into contact. . . . American colonizers could hang hundreds of 'Indians' because 'Indians' were only savages, not real people."[29] When American Indians were classified as savages, as not fully human, policies could be justified that allowed horrific atrocities like genocide.

Such cultural and religious arrogance is still a problem in areas like South Dakota. Charleston claims that, when it comes to missionary outreach, "transformation is the goal, not conversion."[30] Ironically, the same goal might be applied to the exchange between Native and white medical practices. The institutions of religion and medicine still suffer from the problem of racism. Is there openness on the part of Western medicine to learn from and be transformed by Native medicine? The same question must be asked of the respective religious traditions. The transformation can begin at the level of the personal, with sharing stories.

At various points in teaching undergraduates, I have offered courses on beginnings and endings of life and learned how incredibly painful, personal, and political these issues are. From a course entitled "Reproduction and the Family" to one on end-of-life issues entitled "Living Until We Die, Dying until We Live," I have watched students leave their academic façade and enter personal and often painful discussions about loved ones, family members, and friends.[31] For example, as part of his final presentation, a student named John told the story about his grandmother's dying by using powerful black-and-white pictures of her life and those around her. While a local physician would have diagnosed her as a relatively healthy elderly woman, she felt she was dying. John's pictures told the story of her life: most of her friends had died, the small rural South Dakota town in which she lived was losing population, she still lived alone in her small house, and her local church was losing members. Her self-diagnosis was one in which she experienced profound loss—all that was familiar to her was dying, and so was she.

I have listened to students talk about how painful it was to watch a grandparent be diagnosed with Alzheimer's disease and slowly become a different person from the one they knew. Jane, a senior in the class, spoke about how she watched her parents struggle with the care of her grandmother. The family coped with loss at several levels: of the person they once knew, of a hope that didn't seem to exist, and of the family that had changed drastically.

For other students a close friend might be diagnosed with cancer, and all of a sudden their world changes. Priorities shift, and the friendship can no longer remain the same. For some students who marry and decide to have a family, infertility becomes a problem. I met several times with a young woman to sort out the spiritual dilemmas about the couple's discovery of infertility. Sarah and Rich tried over and over to conceive only to find themselves at their local reproductive endocrinologist's office facing decisions about in vitro fertilization. All of a sudden in these situations, what once seemed distant, even abstract, becomes intense, personal, and urgent. Sarah wondered if God was punishing them, and Rich struggled to even find a way to talk about the situation. They learned that *beginnings and endings are not discrete simple moments but are processes moving through an entire life story.*

One of the more amazing discussions I had with a student centered on the theme of "playing God." Inevitably, when discussions turn to technology

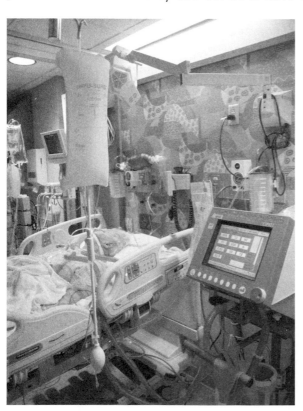

Fig. 16.3. This elderly woman in an intensive care unit appears lost among the machines that are monitoring and, most likely, sustaining her life functions. Photo © Mediscan/Corbis. Used by permission.

and what it means to be human, Christians in turn ask what it means to be divine. The concern seems to be that when technology runs amok, humans have exceeded their capacities to benefit others and have begun to trust in technology to do more than God intended. Christians often assume that playing God implies that God is an intervening, interfering, all-powerful know-it-all. "Divine" is the exact opposite of "human." How ironic when Erin, a junior premedical student in my class, suggested that the discussion might be framed differently. She said, "If indeed God becomes human, and takes on the suffering of humans for humans, isn't that what it means to 'play' [God] or be divine? What if playing God was fulfilling what it means to be human—that is, caring for the neighbor?" Then using technology to heal and help would be part of God's intention for humankind. Erin's words changed the way the class thought about what it means to be divine and human.

Students in this course on theology and medicine often pointed out that God calls people to use what God has given them and to use it for the benefit of others. Humans, according to Christian tradition, are created in the image of God—they are to imagine who they are from within the reflection of divine creativity. What better way to become and be a human person than to employ technology for the benefit of humanity and the created order. Christians begin to think differently about who they are and what their vocation is.

Theology emerges through the stories that are told, stories about what it means to be a human person created in the image of God. These stories from South Dakota are not unique; they represent the broader conversations that occur among ordinary Christians. And as people think about the beginnings and endings of their own lives, they can't help but wonder where they have come from and what they are here for. Such a quest requires that Christians reflect on their place in the universe, in all of its interlocking pieces and relationships. The larger narratives about what it means to be human don't begin or end in South Dakota! When Christians listen and learn from the particulars of their own stories they discover deeper and more meaningful connections that matter to the lives of all people. Christians learn about what it means to be a human person when they are willing to share in the stories of all people. As a people born of the Incarnate

One, Christians are part of the story of flesh and blood, broken and shared. Living and dying is what humans were created to do. And there is no simple beginning or ending, but each day is a beginning and ending, a dying and rising rooted in the hope of God, a baptismal faith of death and resurrection. Christians are learning that *beginnings and endings are not discrete, simple moments but are processes moving through an entire life story, one that was begun in baptism and ends in resurrection.*

## FOR FURTHER READING

Barbour, Ian G. *When Science Meets Religion: Enemies, Strangers, or Partners?* San Francisco: HarperSanFrancisco, 2000.

Colby, William H. *Long Goodbye: The Deaths of Nancy Cruzan.* Carlsbad, Calif.: Hay House, 2002.

Haraway, Donna. *The Haraway Reader.* New York: Routledge, 2004.

Hefner, Philip. *Technology and Human Becoming.* Theology and the Sciences. Minneapolis: Fortress Press, 2003.

Holland, Suzanne, Karen Lebacqz, and Laurie Zoloth, eds. *The Human Embryonic Stem Cell Debate.* Cambridge: MIT Press, 2002.

Lantos, John. *The Lazarus Case: Life-and-Death Issues in Neonatal Intensive Care.* Baltimore: Johns Hopkins University Press, 2001.

Maguire, Daniel, ed. *Sacred Rights: The Case for Contraception and Abortion in World Religions.* Oxford: Oxford University Press, 2003.

Roach, Mary. *Stiff: The Curious Lives of Human Cadavers.* New York: Norton, 2003.

Waters Brent, and Ronald Cole-Turner, eds. *God and the Embryo: Religious Voices on Stem Cells and Cloning.* Georgetown: Georgetown University Press, 2003.

Williams, Terry Tempest. *Refuge: An Unnatural History of Family and Place.* New York: Vintage, 1992.

# NOTES

## Introduction. Multiplicity and Ambiguity

1. Conversation with Cesar del Rio, November 1, 2006.

2. "The Key to the Churches in the Diocese of Visby" (Church of Sweden, 2001).

3. Jim Forest, *The Resurrection of the Church in Albania: Voices of Orthodox Christians* (Geneva: WCC Publications, 2002), 37.

4. Masao Takenaka, *God Is Rice: Asian Culture and Christian Faith* (Geneva: WCC Publications, 1986), 6–7. The quote from Watanabe comes from Masao Takenaka, "Sadao Watanabe—The Man and His Work," in *Biblical Prints by Sadao Watanabe*, Sadao Watanabe and Masao Takenaka (Tokyo: Shinkyo Shuppansha [Protestant Publishing Co.], 1986).

5. Joseph Healey and Donald Sybertz, *Towards an African Narrative Theology* (Maryknoll, N.Y.: Orbis, 1996), 123–24. The authors are Maryknoll missionaries.

6. *New St. Joseph's People's Prayer Book* (New York: Catholic Book, 1980, 1993), 442.

7. One of the most recent and complete is volume 9 of the Cambridge History of Christianity Series, *World Christianities c. 1914–c. 2000*, ed. Hugh McLeod (Cambridge: Cambridge University Press, 2006).

8. In *Icons of American Protestantism: The Art of Warner Sallman, 1892–1968* (New Haven: Yale University Press, 1994), the editor, David Morgan, cites an estimate by Sallman's publisher, Kriebel and Bates, Inc., that *Head of Christ* has been reproduced more than 500 million times and has been distributed around the world (210n1).

9. Kwok Pui-lan has creative things to say about this process in "Discovering the Bible in the Non-Biblical World," in *Lift Every Voice: Constructing Christian Theologies from the Underside*, ed. Susan Brooks Thistlethwaite and Mary Potter Engel, revised and expanded edition (Maryknoll, N.Y.: Orbis Books, 1998), 276–88.

10. Estimates of the numbers of Christians in the world and in various parts of the world tend to be just that—estimates. One of the most frequently cited sources is David B. Barrett, George T. Kurian, and Todd M. Johnson, eds., *World Christian Encyclopedia*,

2 vols. (Oxford: Oxford University Press, 2001), 1:4, 12. Scholars like Philip Jenkins in *The Next Christendom: The Coming of Global Christianity* (Oxford: Oxford University Press, 2002) advise caution in using statistics about how many Christians there are in the world and where they are, and points to discrepancies in various sources. In "Counting Christians in China: A Cautionary Report," *International Bulletin of Missionary Research* 27, no. 1 (January 2003): 6–10, Tony Lambert relates that "the last two decades have seen no resolution to the problem posed by the yawning gulf between statistics issued by the Chinese government or state-approved church representatives, and those figures published by some Christian agencies elsewhere" (6). One place to keep track of numbers of Christians and the percentage of the population they comprise in a given continent or country is on the website of the World Christian Database: http://www .worldchristiandatabase.org/wcd/esweb.asp.

11. Rodney Stark and William Sims Bainbridge, *The Future of Religion: Secularization, Revival and Cult Formation* (Berkeley: University of California Press, 1985), 2.

12. Kenneth R. Ross, "'Blessed Reflex': Mission as God's Spiral of Renewal," *International Bulletin of Missionary Research* 27, no. 4 (October 2003): 162–68. Another instructive article related to this phenomenon is by William B. Frazier, "Nine Breakthroughs in Catholic Missiology, 1965–2000," *International Bulletin of Missionary Research* 25, no. 1 (January 2001): 9–14. Among some of the changes he chronicles are "from unrefined to unmistakable articulation of the universal availability of salvation" and "from exclusion to inclusion of the local church in full missionary responsibility."

13. Roberta Bondi, *Memories of God: Theological Reflections on a Life* (Nashville: Abingdon Press, 1995).

14. Nancy Ammerman, *Pillars of Faith: American Congregations and Their Partners* (Berkeley: University of California Press, 2005), 1.

15. Dana L. Robert, "World Christianity as a Women's Movement," *International Bulletin of Missionary Research* 30, no. 4 (October 2006): 180–88. In her article Robert acknowledges the premise of Ann Braude's well-known essay, "American Religious History *Is* Women's History," in *Retelling U.S. Religious History,* ed. Thomas A. Tweed (Berkeley: University of California Press, 1997), 87–107. Braude argues that American religious history would look very different if women were the focus.

16. See Nancy Eiseland, *The Disabled God: Toward a Liberatory Theology of Disability* (Nashville: Abingdon, 1994).

17. Mark Noll, *History of Christianity in the United States and Canada* (Grand Rapids: Eerdmans, 1992), 428.

18. David Chidester, *Christianity: A Global History* (San Francisco: HarperSanFrancisco, 2000), 8.

19. William A. Dyrness, *Learning about Theology from the Third World* (Grand Rapids: Zondervan, 1990), 84–85.

20. In his lecture "The Ecclesiology of Vatican II," given in 2001 to open a pastoral congress in Italy dedicated to a rereading of the documents of the Second Vatican Council, then Cardinal Joseph Ratzinger, now Pope Benedict XVI, gave a sophisticated interpretation of the church as the Body of Christ as "a living organism," and of the concept of the church as "the people of God" as an ecumenical bridge. He lamented, however, that "commentators very soon completely handed the term 'people' in the concept

'People of God' to a general political interpretation." "Marxist" or "popular sovereignty" were two of the negative examples given. The lecture can be found at http://www.ewtn.com/library/curia/cdfeccv2.htm.

21. Charles Taylor, for example, in *A Secular Age* (Cambridge: Harvard University Press, 2007), argues for an understanding of secularity that is not simply the "subtraction" of belief in God from society but rather that belief in God is "understood to be one option among others and frequently not the easiest to embrace" (3).

22. Margaret O'Gara, *The Ecumenical Gift Exchange* (Collegeville, Minn.: Liturgical, 1998).

23. Lamin Saneh, *Whose Religion Is Christianity? The Gospel beyond the West* (Grand Rapids: Eerdmans, 2003).

24. Joy Harjo, "Perhaps the World Ends Here," in *The Woman Who Fell From the Sky* (New York: Norton, 1994), 68.

## Chapter One. Filipino Popular Christianity

1. Salvador Martinez, "Jesus Christ and Popular Piety in the Philippines," in *Asian Faces of Jesus*, ed. R. S. Sugirtharajah (Maryknoll, N.Y.: Orbis, 1993), 247.

2. Orlando Espín, "Tradition and Popular Religion: An Understanding of the Sensus Fidelium," in *Frontiers of Hispanic Theology in the United States,* ed. Allan Figueroa Deck (Maryknoll, N.Y.: Orbis, 1992), 62.

3. Ibid., 63.

4. David Bosch, *Transforming Mission: Paradigm Shifts in Theology of Mission* (Maryknoll, N.Y.: Orbis, 1991), 302–3.

5. Martinez, "Jesus Christ in Popular Piety in the Philippines," 248. For various accounts of the origin of Santo Niño, see Manolo Vaño, *Christianity, Folk Religion, and Revolution* (Quezon City, Philippines: Giraffe Books, 2002).

6. See Fernando Segovia, "Aliens in the Promised Land: The Manifest Destiny of U.S. Hispanic Theology," in Ada María Isasi-Díaz and Fernando Segovia, eds., *Hispanic/Latino Theology: Challenges and Promise* (Minneapolis: Fortress Press, 1996), 16.

7. John Leddy Phelan, *The Hispanization of the Philippines* (Madison: University of Wisconsin, 1959), viii.

8. Aloysius Pieris, *Asian Theology of Liberation* (Maryknoll, N.Y.: Orbis, 1988), 69–86.

9. Steffi San Buenaventura, "Filipino Religion at Home and Abroad: Historical Roots and Immigrant Transformations," in Pyong Gap Min and Jung Ha Kim, eds., *Religions in Asian America: Building Faith Communities* (Walnut Creek, Calif.: Altamira, 2002), 147.

10. James Alexander Robertson, "Catholicism in the Philippines," *Catholic Historical Review* 3 (1918): 382–83, cited in ibid., 148.

11. Buenaventura, "Filipino Religion." See also Steffi San Buenaventura, "Filipino Folk Spirituality and Immigration: From Mutual Aid to Religion," in *New Spiritual Homes: Religion and Asian Americans*, ed. David K. Yoo (Hawaii: University of Hawaii Press, 1999), 52–86.

12.  Douglas Elwood and Patricia Magdamo, *Christ in Philippine Context* (Quezon City, Philippines: New Day, 1971), 18. See also F. Landa Jocano, *Folk Christianity: A Preliminary Study of Conversion and Patterning of Christian Experience in the Philippines*, Monograph Series No. 1 (Quezon City: Trinity Research Institute, 1981).

13.  Jocano, *Folk Christianity*.

14.  Buenaventura, "Filipino Religion," 149.

15.  Benigno Beltran, *The Christology of the Inarticulate: An Inquiry into the Filipino Understanding of Jesus the Christ* (Manila, Philippines: Divine Word, 1987), 97.

16.  Martinez, "Jesus Christ in Popular Piety in the Philippines," 249.

17.  Jimmy Belita, "Filipino Popular Catholicism: The Struggle against Cultural Gods," *Dialogue and Alliance* 5, no. 4 (Winter 1991/1992): 53.

18.  What C. Gilbert Romero says about Hispanic popular Christianity finds resonance with Filipinos. See his essay "Tradition and Symbol as Biblical Keys for a United States Hispanic Theology," in Deck, *Frontiers of Hispanic Theology in the United States*, 47.

19.  Thomas Andres, *Understanding Filipino Values: A Management Approach* (Quezon City, Philippines: New Day, 1981), 66.

20.  Jocano, *Folk Christianity*, 5.

21.  Andres, *Understanding Filipino Values*, 161.

22.  Beltran, *Christology of the Inarticulate*, 123.

23.  Ibid., 115.

24.  This happened in Laguna de Bay, Philippines. The students who were with me when this insightful moment happened were Karen Aitkens, Sally Mann, and Daniel Narr. See Eleazar S. Fernandez, *Reimagining the Human: Theological Anthropology in Response to Systemic Evil* (St. Louis: Chalice, 2004), 195.

25.  This is a revised telling of Juan Flavier's story in *Doctor to the Barrios* (Quezon City, Philippines: New Day, 1970), 28–29.

26.  Ligaya San Francisco, a Filipina student at United Theological Seminary of the Twin Cities (2005–2006), was a helpful resource for some of the Filipino sayings.

27.  Melanio Aoanan, "Teolohiya ng Bituka at Pagkain: Tungo sa Teolohiyang Pumipiglas," *Explorations in Theology: Journal of the Union Theological Seminary* 1, no. 1 (November 1996): 23–44.

28.  Beltran, *The Christology of the Inarticulate*, 247.

29.  José M. de Mesa, *In Solidarity with the Culture: Studies in Theological Rerooting*, Maryhill Studies 4 (Quezon City, Philippines: Maryhill School of Theology, 1987), 147–77; José M. de Mesa, *And God Said, "Bahala Na!": The Theme of Providence in the Lowland Filipino Context* (Quezon City, Philippines: José M. de Mesa, 1979), 81–161; see also Theresa Dagdag, "Emerging Theology in the Philippines Today," *Kalinangan* 3. no. 3a (September 1983): 7.

30.  Joseph Frary, "The Philippines: February 1986 in Retrospect," *Asian Journal of Theology* 1, no. 2 (1987); Allan J. Delotavo, "A Reflection on the Images of Christ in Filipino Culture," *Asian Journal of Theology*, 3, no. 2 (1989): 524–31.

31.  Reynaldo Ileto, *Pasyon and Revolution: Popular Movements in the Philippines, 1840–1910* (Quezon City, Philippines: Ateneo de Manila University Press, 1979).

32.  Bishop Teordoro Bacani, *Mary and the Filipino* (Makati, Philippines: St. Paul Publications, 1985), 86–88.

33. *People's Participation for Total Human Liberation* (Pasay City, Philippines: Alay Kapwa, 1982), 36.

34. Ed Gerlock, "The Living and the Dead," in *Signs of Hope: Stories of Hope in the Philippines* (Quezon City, Philippines: Claretian, 1990), 75.

35. Beltran, *The Christology of the Inarticulate*, 196.

36. Ibid., 241.

## Chapter Two. Rural Southern Black Women in the United States

1. Interview with Victoria Way DeLee, July 4, 1988, Ridgeville, South Carolina.

2. Fannie Lou Hamer, "Fannie Lou Hamer Speaks Out," *Essence* 1, no. 6 (October 1971): 53.

3. For example, the U.S. Department of Agriculture reports that black farmers were less than 14 percent of farm owners in 1925 and less than 12 percent in 1945. But among African American farm workers more than 80 percent in 1925 and more than 75 percent in 1945 related to farms other than as full owners. See Bruce J. Reynolds, *Black Farmers in America, 1865 to 2000: The Pursuit of Independent Farming and the Role of Cooperatives*, RBS Research Report 194 (Washington, D.C.: United States Department of Agriculture, 2002, 2003).

4. Rosetta E. Ross, *Witnessing and Testifying: Black Women, Religion, and Civil Rights* (Minneapolis: Fortress Press, 2003), 119.

5. Ibid., 98.

6. J. H. O'Dell, "Life in Mississippi: An Interview with Fannie Lou Hamer," *Freedomways* 5 (1965): 232; ibid., 92.

7. See, for example, discussions in Paula Giddings, *When and Where I Enter: The Impact of Black Women on Race and Class in America* (New York: William Morrow, 1984); Deborah Gray White, *Ar'n't I a Woman?: Female Slaves in the Plantation South*, rev. ed. (New York: Norton, 1999); Deborah Gray White, *Too Heavy a Load: Black Women in Defense of Themselves, 1894–1994* (New York: Norton, 2000).

8. Ross, *Witnessing*, 121.

9. From Stewart E. Tolnay and E. M. Beck, *A Festival of Violence: An Analysis of Southern Lynchings, 1882–1930* (Urbana: University of Illinois Press, 1992). They write that there were "2805 victims of lynch mobs killed between 1882 and 1930 in ten southern states. Although mobs murdered almost 300 white men and women, the vast majority . . . of lynch victims were African-American. Of these black victims, 94 percent died in the hands of white lynch mobs. The scale of this carnage means that, on the average, a black man, woman, or child was murdered nearly once a week, every week, between 1882 and 1930 by a hate-driven white mob" (ix).

10. O'Dell, "Life in Mississippi," 233–34.

11. Ross, *Witnessing*, 120.

12. O'Dell, "Life in Mississippi," 233–34; interview with DeLee; interview with Thomas H. Ross, Dorchester, South Carolina, March 11, 1994; ibid.

13. Interview with DeLee; Calvin Trillin, "U.S. Journal: Dorchester County, S.C.-Victoria DeLee in Her Own Words," *New Yorker* 47 (March 27, 1971): 86; Ross, *Witnessing*, 121.

14. Phyl Garland, "Builders of a New South," *Ebony* 21 (August 1966): 29.

15. Ross, *Witnessing*, 119.

16. O'Dell, "Life in Mississippi," 232; Garland, "Builders of a New South," 28.

17. Ross, *Witnessing*, 131.

18. Howell Raines, *My Soul Is Rested: Movement Days in the Deep South Remembered* (New York: Penguin, 1983), 252; Fannie Lou Hamer, "To Praise Our Bridges," in *Mississippi Writers: Reflections of Childhood and Youth, Volume 2: Nonfiction,* ed. Dorothy Abbott (Jackson: University of Mississippi, 1986), 325.

19. Ross, *Witnessing*, 104.

20. Hamer, "Fannie Lou Hamer," 53, 54; O'Dell, "Life in Mississippi," 231–32, emphasis added.

21. Rayford Whittingham Logan, *The Betrayal of the Negro: From Rutherford Hayes to Woodrow Wilson* (New York: Da Capo, 1954).

22. Laughlin MacDonald, "An Aristocracy of Voters: The Disfranchisement of Blacks in South Carolina," *South Carolina Law Review* 37 (Summer 1986): 570–71.

23. Hamer, "To Praise Our Bridges," 324; Garland, "Builders of a New South," 29; Chana Kai Lee, *For Freedom's Sake: The Life of Fannie Lou Hamer* (Urbana: University of Illinois, 1999), 18.

24. Interview with DeLee; Trillin, "Victoria DeLee," 86.

25. See Peter J. Paris, *The Social Teaching of the Black Churches* (Philadelphia: Fortress Press, 1985), and Latta R. Thomas, *Biblical Faith and the Black American* (Philadelphia: Judson, 1976).

26. See Riggins Earl Jr., *Dark Symbols, Obscure Signs: God, Self, and Community in the Slave Mind* (Knoxville: University of Tennessee Press, 2003); Eugene D. Genovese, *Roll, Jordan, Roll: The World the Slaves Made* (New York: Vintage, 1976).

27. Charles Marsh, *God's Long Summer* (Princeton: Princeton University Press, 1999).

28. Ross, *Witnessing*, 118–19.

29. Ibid., 119.

30. See, for example, William Jones, *Is God a White Racist? A Preamble to Black Theology* (Boston: Beacon, 1997), and Anthony Pinn, *Why Lord? Suffering and Evil in Black Theology* (New York: Continuum, 1995).

31. Ross, *Witnessing*, 97.

32. Ibid., 111.

33. Interview with DeLee.

34. Ross, *Witnessing*, 135.

35. Barbara S. Williams, "Victoria DeLee Denies Charges Lodged by Police," *Charleston News and Courier*, May 8, 1971, B1; see also ibid., 134.

36. Ross, *Witnessing*, 134.

37. Raines, *My Soul Is Rested,* 252, and Hamer, "To Praise Our Bridges," 325.

38. Fannie Lou Hamer, foreword, in Tracy Sugarman, *Stranger at the Gates: A Summer in Mississippi* (New York: Hill and Wang, 1967).

39. Taylor Branch, *Pillar of Fire: America in the King Years 1963–1965* (New York: Dutton, 1993), 470.

40. William Julius Wilson, *The Declining Significance of Race: Blacks and Changing American Institutions* (Chicago: University of Chicago Press, 1980), 144.

## Chapter Three. African Women Theologians

1. A term that covers several ethnic groups in Ghana whose languages are dialects of one language. Akan society is matrilineal.

2. Mercy Amba Oduyoye, *Daughters of Anowa: African Women and Patriarchy* (Maryknoll, N.Y.: Orbis, 1995), 12–13.

3. Oduyoye, *Daughters of Anowa*, 1–2.

4. Mercy Amba Oduyoye and Musimbi Kanyoro, Talitha, Qumi! Proceedings of the Convocation of African Women Theologians, Trinity College, Legon-Accra, September 24–October 2, 1989 (Ibadan, Nigeria: Daystar, 1990), 4. These goals have been repeated at several local meetings and continue to guide the Circle, as it seeks to remain relevant to the changing context. Cf. Rosemary N. Edet and Meg A. Umeagudosu, *Life, Women and Culture*, Proceedings of the National Conference of the Circle of Concerned African Women Theologians (Lagos, Nigeria: African Heritage Research and Publications, 1990), 2.

5. Isabel Apawo Phiri, "Doing Theology in Community: The Case of African Women Theologians in the 1990s," *Journal of Theology for Southern Africa* 99 (November 1997): 69–70.

6. In addition to Njoroge from Kenya, the Cartigny group included Elizabeth Amoah (Ghana), Brigalia Bam (South Africa), Toyin Isaacs (Nigeria), Nzeba Kalenda (Zaire—Democratic Republic of the Congo), Charity Majizah (South Africa), Daisy Obi (Nigeria), Mercy Amba Oduyoye (Ghana, and Amal Tawfik (Egypt).

7. Musimbi Kanyoro, *Introducing Feminist Cultural Hermeneutics: An African Perspective* (New York: Sheffield Academic, 2002), 28–29.

8. Virginia Fabella, *Beyond Bonding: A Third World Women's Theological Journey* (Manila: EATWOT and Institute of Women's Studies, 1993), 49.

9. I personally have roots in the World Student Christian Federation, the World Council of Churches, the Oxford Institute of Wesleyan Studies, and the Ecumenical Association of Third World Theologians. I studied dogmatics at Cambridge University after earning a degree in the study of religion from the University of Ghana, Legon. At that time, 1959–1963, it was a program of London University's bachelor of divinity degree. Before going to Legon, I had been a schoolteacher with a Cambridge school certificate taken through Achimota School, followed by two years of pedagogy. After Tripos Part III Cambridge, I was again a schoolteacher, then an ecumenical youth worker, first for the World Council of Churches and then for All Africa Conference of Churches (AACC). Then I was once more a schoolteacher, this time in a boys' school, before I was invited to apply for a position in the Religious Studies Department at the University of Ibadan, Nigeria.

10. This lecture was published in two parts in *African Notes* 18, nos. 1 and 2 (1979). *African Notes* is the bulletin of the Institute of African Studies, University of Ibadan, Nigeria.

11. Oduyoye and Kanyoro, *Talitha, Qumi!* 19.

12. Walter Davis subsequently went on to the faculty of San Francisco Theological Seminary and became key to its doctor of ministry program in feminist theology. Three members of the Circle have graduated from this program.

13. Fabella, *Beyond Bonding*, 46.

14. Oduyoye and Kanyoro, *Talitha, Qumi!*

15. Kanyoro, *Feminist Cultural Hermeneutics*, 28.

16. Ibid., 29.

17. Edet and Umeagudosu, *Life, Women and Culture*, 5–6.

18. Mercy Amba Oduyoye, "The Asante Woman: Socialization through Proverbs," *African Notes* 8, nos. 1 and 2 (1979).

19. Fabella, *Beyond Bonding*, ix.

20. Kanyoro, *Feminist Cultural Hermeneutics*, 27.

21. Ibid.

22. Edet and Umeagudosu, *Life, Women and Culture*, 1.

23. Kanyoro, *Feminist Cultural Hermeneutics*, 29.

## Chapter Four. Hispanic Women: Being Church in the U.S.A.

1. People from the Spanish-speaking Caribbean and Central and South American nations who live in the U.S.A. are referred to as Hispanics or Latinos. Here I will use "Hispanics" since this is the term used more often in the Catholic Church and among those of us from Caribbean nations.

2. National parishes are Catholic parishes that serve particular ethnic communities instead of serving a geographic area as territorial parishes do. National parishes have existed in the U.S.A. since the mid-nineteenth century, when they were established to meet the needs of immigrants who did not speak the language of the majority population. For a history of national parishes and chapels in the archdiocese of New York, see Jaime R. Vidal, "Citizens Yet Strangers: The Puerto Rican Experience," in Jay P. Dolan and Jaime R. Vidal, eds., *Puerto Rican and Cuban Catholics in the U.S., 1900–1965*, Notre Dame History of Hispanic Catholics in the U.S. 2 (Notre Dame, Ind.: University of Notre Dame Press, 1994), 11–143.

3. Ibid, 25.

4. Ana María Díaz Stevens, *Oxcart Catholicism on Fifth Avenue: The Impact of the Puerto Rican Migration upon the Diocese of New York* (Notre Dame, Ind.: University of Notre Dame Press, 1993), 128.

5. Many Hispanics consider arrogant the appropriation by the U.S.A. of the name "United States," the same being true of the way "America" is used often to refer to the U.S.A. There are other countries that have "United States" as part of their official name, and the U.S.A. is not the only country in America. Many Hispanics when talking in English use "U.S.A." also because it can be said as a word that we find easy to pronounce, "usa."

6. Díaz Stevens, *Oxcart Catholicism*, 128.

7. This is why Ivan Illich, then a monsignor in the Catholic Church, insisted that the priests had to know not only the people's language but also their history and that the priests had to understand the challenges of intercultural communication. Ibid, 140.

8. I live in Washington Heights, in New York City, an area with the largest concentration of people from the Dominican Republic except for the capital of that Caribbean country. Different candidates running for president in the Dominican Republic

campaign in my neighborhood (not personally), and many of my neighbors vote in the presidential election of their country. In the very important 2007 plebiscite of Venezuela in which Hugo Chávez attempt to change the constitution of that country to continue to be president beyond the two terms allowed, Venezuelans in the U.S.A. voted. These are just two examples of how Hispanics in the U.S.A. are transnationals.

9. For a fascinating account of the history of unknown or ignored Hispanics in the U.S.A. see Juan Gonzalez, *Harvest of Empire: A History of Latinos in America* (New York: Viking, 2000).

10. Saskia Sassen, *Globalization and Its Discontents: Essays on the New Mobility of People and Money* (New York: New Press, 1998).

11. David Rieff, "Nuevo Catholics," *New York Times Sunday Magazine,* December 24, 2006.

12. Ibid. Also at http://www.nccbuscc.org/hispanicaffairs/demo.html and http://www.catholic.com/thisrock/2005/0509fea3.asp. Accessed January 14, 2008.

13. I am here disagreeing with the conclusion drawn by Rieff in "Nuevo Catholics."

14. For a fuller discussion of this perspective, see Ada María Isasi-Díaz, *En La Lucha—In the Struggle: Elaborating a Mujerista Theology*, 2nd ed. (Minneapolis: Fortress Press, 2004), chapter 5.

15. Ada María Isasi-Díaz and Yolanda Tarango, *Hispanic Women: Prophetic Voice in the Church/Mujer hispana—voz profética en la iglesia* (San Francisco: Harper & Row, 1988; repr.: Scranton, Pa.: University of Scranton Press, 2006), 52.

16. Ibid, 53.

17. Ibid.

18. I was part of the group meeting with the bishops and personally witnessed what happened.

19. Arturo Perez, Consuelo Covarrubias, and Edward Foley, eds., *Así Es: Historias de Espiritualidad Hispana* (Collegeville, Minn.: Liturgical, 1994), 67. This quote is from a Latina who is a nun.

20. Isasi-Díaz and Tarango, *Hispanic Women*, 14–19.

21. Ibid, 32–38.

22. Rafael de Andrés, lyrics, Juan A. Espinosa, music, "Dolorosa," in *Flor y Canto*, 2nd ed. (Portland, Ore.: OCP Publications, 2001), H389.

23. This is in line with the concept of *theosis* prevalent in Eastern Christianity. See Mark O'Keefe, O.S.B., *Becoming Good, Becoming Holy* (New York: Paulist, 1995).

24. Robert D. McFadden and Colin Moynihan, "Protest Vigil Begins at Church Set to Be Closed by Archdiocese," *New York Times,* February 12, 2007.

25. James Barron, Jennifer Lee, and Rebecca Cathcart, "After Vigil to Protest Church Closing, Six Women Are Arrested," *New York Times,* February 13, 2007.

26. Colin Moynihan, "Locked Doors Don't Stop Prayers at East Harlem Church," *New York Times,* February 19, 2007.

27. James Barron, "A Church Protest Ends Quickly, but the Anger Is Likely to Endure," *New York Times,* February 14, 2007.

28. Private conversation of author with Carmen Villegas.

29. "Dogmatic Constitution on the Church," in *Lumen Gentium*, chapter 2.

## Chapter Five. Orthodoxy under Communism

1. There is no instrumental music in the Orthodox Church. Instead there are sometimes as many as three choirs located in various places in the sanctuary singing harmonious responses to the priestly chants or hymns.

2. Eastern Orthodox Churches are those churches that have accepted dogmatic Christological formulas of the Council of Chalcedon (451 c.e.) on the two natures of Christ. Among them are the Greek, Russian, Bulgarian, Serbian, Albanian, Georgian, Ukrainian, the Orthodox Church of America, and related churches. Oriental churches are sometimes called non-Chalcedonian as they accept only the decisions of the first four ecumenical councils and initially were divided into Monophysite and Nestorian Churches. Among the Oriental Christian Churches are the Armenian, Coptic, Ethiopian, Syriac, Indian, Malankara Jacobite Syriac Orthodox, and the Assyrian Church of the East.

3. Paul Mojzes, *Religious Liberty in Eastern Europe and the USSR* (Boulder: East European Monographs, 1992), 66–67.

4. Ibid., 125. This lasted until the collapse of Communism in Albania in 1990.

5. In all of Russia there was for a long time only the *Journal of the Moscow Patriarchate*, mostly a bulletin of events and announcements, and the annual of the Saint Petersburg Theological Academy, which published a few arcane theological articles. It was almost the same in Bulgaria, and only a little better in the Serbian Orthodox Church. None were published in Albania.

## Chapter Six. Evangelicalism in North America

1. Examples include David Edwin Harrell, *Oral Roberts: An American Life* (Bloomington: Indiana University Press, 1985); James Hunter, *Culture Wars: The Struggle to Define America* (New York: Basic Books, 1991); and Michael Cromartie, ed., *A Public Faith: Evangelicals and Civic Engagement* (Lanham, Md.: Rowman & Littlefield, 2003).

2. See, as examples, R. Stephen Warner, *New Wine in Old Wineskins: Evangelicals and Liberals in a Small-Town Church* (Berkeley: University of California Press, 1988); James M. Ault, *Spirit and Flesh: Life in a Fundamentalist Baptist Church* (New York: Knopf, 2004); and Randall Balmer, *Mine Eyes Have Seen the Glory: A Journey into the Evangelical Subculture in America*, 4th ed. (New York: Oxford University Press, 2006).

3. Examples include Robert Wuthnow, *Acts of Compassion: Caring for Others and Helping Ourselves* (Princeton: Princeton University Press, 1991); Christian Smith, *Christian America? What Evangelicals Really Want* (Berkeley: University of California Press, 2000); Michael O. Emerson and Christian Smith, *Divided by Faith: Evangelical Religion and the Problem of Race in America* (New York: Oxford University Press, 2000); and Nancy Tatom Ammerman, *Pillars of Faith: American Congregations and Their Partners* (Berkeley: University of California Press, 2005).

4. Leigh Eric Schmidt, "Mixed Blessings: Christianization and Secularization," *Reviews in American History* 26 (December 1998): 640.

5. The references are to Clifford Geertz, *The Interpretation of Culture* (New York: Basic Books, 1973); and Robert A. Orsi, *The Madonna of 115th Street: Faith and Community in Italian Harlem, 1880–1950* (New Haven: Yale University Press, 1985).

6. This summary is taken from David W. Bebbington, *Evangelicalism in Modern Britain* (London: Unwin Hyman, 1989), 2–17.

7. Angus Reid Group, "God and Society in North America: A Survey of Religion, Politics and Social Involvement in Canada and the United States." For permission to use this poll, we are grateful to Angus Reid and Andrew Grenville.

8. Rick Ostrander, *The Life of Prayer in a World of Science: Protestants, Prayer, and American Culture, 1870–1930* (New York: Oxford University Press, 2000); and George A. Rawlyk, *Is Jesus Your Personal Saviour? In Search of Canadian Evangelicalism in the 1990s* (Montreal: McGill-Queen's University Press, 1996).

9. William Patton, *Prayer and Its Remarkable Answers*, cited in Ostrander, *Life of Prayer*, 51.

10. Rawlyk, *Canadian Evangelicalism*, 103, 127–28.

11. Ibid., 129–31.

12. Marsha Witten, *All Is Forgiven: The Secular Message in American Protestantism* (Princeton: Princeton University Press, 1993).

13. For a report on the worship wars in contemporary American churches, see John D. Witvliet, *Worship Seeking Understanding: Windows into Christian Practice* (Grand Rapids: Baker Academic, 2003).

14. Larry Eskridge, "Slain by the Music," *Christian Century*, March 7, 2006, 18, which draws on Larry Eskridge, "God's Forever Family: The Jesus People Movement in America, 1966–1977" (Ph.D. diss., Stirling University, Scotland, 2005). Eskridge's dissertation forms the basis for much that follows.

15. For orientation to the history sketched here, see Stephen A. Marini, *Sacred Song in America: Religion, Music, and Popular Culture* (Urbana: University of Illinois Press, 2003); David W. Stowe, *How Sweet the Sound: Music in the Spiritual Lives of Americans* (Cambridge: Harvard University Press, 2004); and Richard J. Mouw and Mark A. Noll, *Wonderful Words of Life: Hymns in American Protestant History and Theology* (Grand Rapids: Eerdmans, 2004).

16. See especially S. Sizer (= Tamar Frankiel), *Gospel Hymns and Social Religion in the Rhetoric of Nineteenth-Century Revivalism*, American Civilization (Philadelphia: Temple University Press, 1978); and for a revision of her arguments, Richard J. Mouw, "'Some Poor Sailor, Tempest Tossed': Nautical Rescue Themes in Evangelical Hymnody," in Mouw and Noll, eds., *Wonderful Words of Life*, 234–50.

17. For illuminating exposition on Crossley and Hunter, as well as their predecessors and successors, see Kevin B. Kee, *Revivalists: Marketing the Gospel in English Canada, 1884–1957* (Montreal: McGill-Queen's University Press, 2006).

18. For full treatment of her important achievement, see Edith Waldvogel Blumhofer, *Her Heart Can See: The Life and Hymns of Fanny Crosby* (Grand Rapids: Eerdmans, 2005).

19. See especially Edward H. McKinley, *Marching to Glory: The History of the Salvation Army in the United States, 1880–1992*, 2nd ed. (Grand Rapids: Eerdmans, 1995).

20. For background, see James R. Goff, *Close Harmony: A History of Southern Gospel* (Chapel Hill: University of North Carolina Press, 2002).

21. Thomas Bergler, "'I Found My Thrill': The Youth for Christ Movement and

American Congregational Singing, 1940–1970," in Mouw and Noll, *Wonderful Words of Life*, 123–49.

22. See especially David Edwin Harrell, *All Things Are Possible: The Healing and Charismatic Revival in Modern America* (Bloomington: Indiana University Press, 1975).

23. Eskridge, "Slain by the Music," 19.

24. A fine book dealing mostly with the Calvary Chapel and Vineyard movement is Donald E. Miller's *Reinventing American Protestantism: Christianity in the New Millennium* (Berkeley: University of California Press, 1997).

25. See http://www.willowcreek.org.

26. See G. A. Pritchard, *Willow Creek Seeker Services: Evaluating a New Way of Doing Church* (Grand Rapids: Baker Books, 1996).

27. For different approaches, see Marva J. Dawn, *Reaching Out without Dumbing Down: A Theology of Worship for the Turn-of-the-Century Culture* (Grand Rapids: Eerdmans, 1986); and D. G. Hart, *Deconstructing Evangelicalism: Conservative Protestantism in the Age of Billy Graham* (Grand Rapids: Baker Academic, 2004).

28. This datum is from Colleen McDannell, *Material Christianity: Religion and Popular Culture in America* (New Haven: Yale University Press, 1995), 246. McDannell's volume and the participant-observations of Ethan Sanders are the main sources for this section.

29. See http://www.mardel.com.

30. McDannell, *Material Christianity*, 1.

31. See the earlier work by McDannell, *The Christian Home in Victorian America, 1840–1900* (Bloomington: Indiana University Press, 1986).

32. The key work, with splendid illustrations, is Paul C. Gutjahr, *An American Bible: A History of the Good Book in the United States, 1777–1880* (Stanford: Stanford University Press, 1999).

33. See David Morgan, *Icons of American Protestantism: The Art of Warner Sallman* (New Haven: Yale University Press, 1996).

34. Various aspects of that earlier history are treated superbly in R. Laurence Moore, *Selling God: American Religion in the Marketplace of Culture* (New York: Oxford University Press, 1994); David Paul Nord, *Faith in Reading: Religious Publishing and the Birth of Mass Media in America* (New York: Oxford University Press, 2004); and Candy Gunther Brown, *The Word in the World: Evangelical Writing, Publishing, and Reading in America, 1789–1880* (Chapel Hill: University of North Carolina Press, 2004).

35. Examples include David F. Wells, *Losing Our Virtue: Why the Church Must Recover Its Moral Vision* (Grand Rapids: Eerdmans, 1998); and Craig M. Gay, *Cash Values: Money and the Erosion of Meaning in Today's Society* (Grand Rapids: Eerdmans, 2003).

36. McDannell, *Material Christianity*, 223; emphasis in original.

37. See especially Tona J. Hangen, *Redeeming the Dial: Radio, Religion, and Popular Culture in America* (Chapel Hill: University of North Carolina Press, 2002).

38. On this matter, we are following Benton Johnson, "On Dropping the Subject: Presbyterians and Sabbath Observance in the Twentieth Century," in Milton J. Coalter, John M. Mulder, and Louis B. Weeks, eds., *The Presbyterian Predicament: Six Perspec-*

tives (Louisville, Ky.: Westminster John Knox, 1990), 90–108; and Paul Laverdure, *Sunday in Canada* (Yorkton, Sask.: Gravelbooks, 2004).

39. The question has been asked in important historical studies like Harry S. Stout, *The Divine Dramatist: George Whitefield and the Rise of Modern Evangelicalism* (Grand Rapids: Eerdmans, 1991); Nathan O. Hatch, *The Democratization of American Christianity* (New Haven: Yale University Press, 1989); and Douglas Frank, *Less Than Conquerors: How Evangelicals Entered the Twenty-first Century* (Grand Rapids: Eerdmans, 1986).

## Chapter Seven. Pentecostal Transformation in Latin America

1. David Martin is one of the few scholars who has noticed the importance of the conversion of Taso Zayas to Pentecostalism in Mintz's text. See David Martin, *Tongues of Fire: The Explosion of Protestantism in Latin America* (Cambridge, Mass.: Blackwell, 1990), 191–97.

2. On Pentecostalism, see the useful essays in Allan H. Anderson and Walter Hollenweger, eds., *Pentecostals after a Century: Global Perspectives on a Movement in Transition* (Sheffield: Sheffield Academic, 1999). Harvey Cox, *Fire from Heaven: The Rise of Pentecostal Spirituality and the Reshaping of Religion in the Twenty-First Century* (Reading, Mass.: Addison-Wesley, 1995), is an informative text in which the former "secular city" theologian becomes an advocate of the "spiritual city." For a sociological analysis of global Pentecostalism, see David Martin, *Pentecostalism: The World Their Parish* (Oxford: Blackwell, 2002). Martin is another theoretician of secularization now bewildered by the new Pentecostal religious revival. Stanley M. Burgess, Gary B. McGee, and Patrick H. Alexander, eds., *Dictionary of Pentecostal and Charismatic Movements* (Grand Rapids: Zondervan, 1988), is a useful reference text.

3. See the splendid study of the cultural consequences of the sugarcane plantation for the Caribbean by Antonio Benítez-Rojo, *The Repeating Island: The Caribbean and the Postmodern Perspective* (Durham, N.C.: Duke University Press, 1992 [1989]). Sidney Mintz has written an elegant and intelligent text on the development of the sugarcane plantations in the British Caribbean. Sidney Mintz, *Sweetness and Power: The Place of Sugar in Modern History* (New York: Penguin Books, 1986).

4. See Elizabeth Brusco, "The Reformation of Machismo: Ascetism and Masculinity among Colombian Evangelicals," in Virginia Garrard-Burnett and David Stoll, eds., *Rethinking Protestantism in Latin America* (Philadelphia: Temple University Press, 1993).

5. Tommy Lee Osborn (sometimes spelled Osborne) was a self-appointed American evangelist who conducted healing crusades through the Caribbean (Jamaica, Puerto Rico, and Cuba). His book *Healing the Sick* (Tulsa, Okla.: Harrison House, 1986 [1951]) has sold over one million copies. It contains a short summary and photos of the healing campaign (February 1950) in which Taso Zayas alleges to be healed (Osborn, *Healing the Sick*, 416–21).

6. Sidney W. Mintz, *Worker in the Cane: A Puerto Rican Life History* (New York: Norton, 1974 [1960]), 211–12.

7. D. A. Brading, *Mexican Phoenix: Our Lady of Guadalupe: Image and Tradition across Five Centuries* (Cambridge: Cambridge University Press, 2001).

8. See Jacques Lafaye, *Quetzalcóatl and Guadalupe: The Formation of Mexican National Consciousness, 1531–1813* (Chicago: University of Chicago Press, 1976). According to Octavio Paz, the Virgin of Guadalupe has been the main source of the Mexican sense of nationhood, more influential in its shaping than the official nationalist myths of the several republican and revolutionary governments of the last two centuries. Octavio Paz, *Sor Juana, or, The Traps of Faith* (Cambridge: Harvard University Press, 1988), 478.

9. Miraculous healings have not been restricted to the first wave of Pentecostal evangelization in Latin America. The phenomenon has also been one of the keys for the exceptional growth of the Brazilian Universal Church of the Kingdom of God, considered by some scholars as a Neo-Pentecostal church that promises social and economic prosperity and not only spiritual benefits. See Leonildo Silveira Campos, *Teatro, Templo e Mercado: Organização e marketing de um empreendimento neopentecostal* (Petrópolis: Editora Vozes, 1997). See the theological conversation about "healing and deliverance" between the Pentecostal Cheryl Bridge Johns, the Roman Catholic Virgil Elizondo, and the Reformed feminist Elisabeth Moltmann-Wendel in Jürgen Moltmann and Karl-Josef Kuschel, eds., *Pentecostal Movements as an Ecumenical Challenge* (Maryknoll, N.Y.: Orbis, 1996), 45–62.

10. Mintz, *Worker in the Cane*, 220–21.

11. Ibid., 223.

12. Ibid., 216.

13. Ibid., 241–44.

14. Ibid., 231.

15. It would be interesting to compare the ecstatic experiences of Taso and Elizabeth with that of John, a rather skeptical young man and the protagonist of James Baldwin's novel *Go Tell It on the Mountain* (first published in 1953). John's possession by the Holy Spirit takes place in the early '50s, in a storefront Harlem Pentecostal church with the significant name, the Temple of the Fire Baptized.

16. Mintz, *Worker in the Cane*, 217.

17. Ibid., 276.

18. Ibid., 277.

19. Ibid., 225.

20. See Christian Lalive d'Epinay, *The Haven of the Masses* (London: Lutterworth, 1969); and Paul E. Sigmund, ed. *Religious Freedom and Evangelization in Latin America: The Challenge of Religious Pluralism* (Maryknoll, N.Y.: Orbis, 1999).

21. See Raymond Carr, *Puerto Rico: A Colonial Experiment* (New York: Vintage Books, 1984); José Trías Monge, *Puerto Rico: The Trials of the Oldest Colony in the World* (New Haven: Yale University Press, 1997); and Efrén Rivera Ramos, *The Legal Construction of Identity: The Judicial and Social Legacy of American Colonialism in Puerto Rico* (Washington, D.C.: American Psychological Association, 2001).

22. Mintz, *Worker in the Cane*, 276.

23. For the Iberian royal patronage in Latin America, and the debates it engendered, see William Eugene Shiels, S.J., *King and Church: The Rise and Fall of the Patronato Real* (Chicago: Loyola University Press, 1961), and Luis N. Rivera-Pagán, "Formation of a Hispanic American Theology: The Capitulations of Burgos," in Daniel

Rodríguez-Díaz and David Cortés-Fuentes, eds., *Hidden Stories: Unveiling the History of the Latino Church* (Decatur, Ga.: Asociación para la Educación Teológica Hispana, 1994), 67–97. For the history before and after the independence of the Latin American nations, see Hans-Jürgen Prien, *La historia del cristianismo en América Latina* (Salamanca: Ediciones Sígueme, 1985).

24. See Luis N. Rivera-Pagán, "Violence of the Conquistadores and Prophetic Indignation," in Kenneth R. Chase and Alan Jacobs, eds., *Must Christianity Be Violent? Reflections on History, Practice, and Theology* (Grand Rapids: Brazos, 2003), 37–49, 239–43; Luis N. Rivera-Pagán, "A Prophetic Challenge to the Church: The Last Word of Bartolomé de las Casas," *Princeton Seminary Bulletin* 24, no. 2, new series (July 2003): 216–40; and Luis N. Rivera-Pagán, "Freedom and Servitude: Indigenous Slavery in the Spanish Conquest of the Caribbean," in Jalil Sued-Badillo, ed., *General History of the Caribbean*, vol. 1, *Autochthonous Societies* (London: UNESCO and Macmillan, 2003), 316–62.

25. See, for example, the intelligent discussion of the history of the juridical bonds between the state and the Roman Catholic Church in Argentina by José Míguez Bonino, in his article "Church, State, and Religious Freedom in Argentina," in Sigmund, *Religious Freedom*, 187–203. Samuel Silva Gotay has made an important recent contribution to the study of the relations between the Roman Catholic Church and the state in Puerto Rico, first in the nineteenth century, when the island was a colonial possession of Spain, and then during the first decades of the twentieth century, when it became a territory of the United States. Samuel Silva Gotay, *Catolicismo y política en Puerto Rico bajo España y Estados Unidos: Siglos XIX y XX* (San Juan: Editorial de la Universidad de Puerto Rico, 2005). The classic text about the whole region is that of J. Lloyd Mecham, *Church and State in Latin America: A History of Politicoecclesiastical Relations* (Chapel Hill: University of North Carolina Press, 1966).

26. David Stoll, *Is Latin America Turning Protestant? The Politics of Evangelical Growth* (Berkeley: University of California Press, 1990).

27. For the spread of Pentecostalism in Latin America, see the variety of perspectives in Benjamin Gutiérrez and Dennis Smith, eds., *In the Power of the Spirit: The Pentecostal Challenge to Historic Churches in Latin America* (Arkansas City: Asociación de Iglesias Presbiterianas y Reformadas en América Latina; Centro Evangélico Latinoamericano de Estudios Pastorales; Presbyterian Church [U.S.A.], Worldwide Ministries Division, 1996); and Edward L. Cleary and Hannah W. Stewart-Gambino, eds., *Power, Politics, and Pentecostals in Latin America* (Boulder: Westview, 1997).

28. See, for example, Michael Dodson, "Pentecostals, Politics, and Public Space in Latin America," in Cleary and Stewart-Gambino, *Power*, 25–40.

29. See Carmelo Álvarez, *Pentecostalismo y liberación* (San José, Costa Rica: DEI, 1992); Richard Shaull and Waldo Cesar, *Pentecostalism and the Future of the Christian Churches: Promises, Limitations, Challenges* (Grand Rapids: Eerdmans, 2000); Douglas Petersen, *Not by Might Nor by Power: A Pentecostal Theology of Social Concern in Latin America* (Oxford: Regnum Books, 1996); and Eldin Villafañe, *The Liberating Spirit: Toward an Hispanic American Social Ethic* (Grand Rapids: Eerdmans, 1993).

30. See the doctoral dissertation of the Chilean Pentecostal theologian Juan Sepúlveda, *Gospel and Culture in Latin American Protestantism: Toward a New Theological Appreciation of Syncretism* (Ph.D. diss., University of Birmingham, 1996).

31. Andrew Walls, *The Missionary Movement in Christian History: Studies in the Transmission of Faith* (Maryknoll, N.Y.: Orbis, 1996); Lamin Sanneh, *Whose Religion Is Christianity? The Gospel beyond the West* (Grand Rapids: Eerdmans, 2003); Philip Jenkins, *The Next Christendom: The Coming of Global Christianity* (Oxford: Oxford University Press, 2002).

32. Bernardo Campos, *De la Reforma Protestante a la Pentecostalidad de la Iglesia: Debate sobre el Pentecostalismo en América Latina* (Quito: Ediciones CLAI, 1997).

33. John Locke, *An Essay Concerning Human Understanding* (New York: Dover, 1959 [1690]), vol. 2, bk. 4, chap. 19, par. 13, 438.

34. A note of gratitude to Susan Richardson, who reviewed the draft of this chapter, saved the author from many linguistic infelicities, and enabled him to write a more readable and elegant text. The author also wants to acknowledge the collaboration of Luiz Nascimento, a Brazilian doctoral student at Princeton Theological Seminary, for the selection of the chapter illustrations.

## Chapter Eight. Apocalypticism in the United States

1. Larry Eskridge, "And, the Most Influential American Evangelical of the Last 25 Years Is . . ." *Evangelical Studies Bulletin* (Winter 2001): 3. Eskridge would name Billy Graham as the most influential American evangelical overall in the twentieth century, but much of Graham's influence came earlier.

2. Billy Graham, *Just As I Am: The Autobiography of Billy Graham* (San Francisco: HarperSanFrancisco, 1997).

3. "Different Groups Follow Harry Potter, Left Behind, and Jabez," October 22, 2001, Barna Research Online, http://www.barna.org.

4. Ibid.

5. Eugen Weber, *Apocalypses: Prophecies, Cults, and Millennial Beliefs through the Ages* (Cambridge: Harvard University Press, 1999), 2.

6. Christopher Columbus, *Memorials of Columbus: A Collection of Authentic Documents of That Celebrated Navigator*, comp. Giovanni Battista Sopotorno (London: Treuttel and Wurz, Treuttel jun. and Richter, 1823), 224, cited in Jeanne Halgren Kilde, "How Did Left Behind's Particular Vision of the End Times Develop? A Historical Look at Millenarian Thought," in Bruce David Forbes and Jeanne Halgren Kilde, eds., *Rapture, Revelation, and the End Times: Exploring the Left Behind Series* (New York: Palgrave Macmillan, 2004), 46.

7. "History of Opinions Respecting the Millennium," *American Theological Review* 1 (1859): 655. Much of this discussion of postmillennialism, premillennialism, and amillennialism is drawn from chapters by Jeanne Halgren Kilde and Stanley J. Grenz (chapters 2 and 4) in Forbes and Kilde, *Rapture*.

8. Kilde, "Left Behind's Particular Vision," 49–50.

9. Grenz, "When Do Christians Think the End Times Will Happen? A Comparative Theologies Discussion of the Second Coming," in Forbes and Kilde, *Rapture*, 120. Grenz's chapter is based upon Stanley J. Grenz, *The Millennial Maze: Sorting Out Evangelical Options* (Downer's Grove, Ill.: InterVarsity, 1992).

10. Hal Lindsey with Carole C. Carlson, *The Late Great Planet Earth* (Grand Rapids: Zondervan, 1970). For *A Thief in the Night*, see Randall Balmer, *Mine Eyes Have*

*Seen the Glory: A Journey into the Evangelical Subculture in America* (New York: Oxford University Press, 1993), chap. 3.

11. Carl Olson, *Will Catholics Be Left Behind? A Critique of the Rapture and Today's Prophecy Preachers* (Fort Collins, Colo.: Ignatius, 2003); Paul Thigpen, *The Rapture Trap: A Catholic Response to "End Times" Fever* (West Chester, Pa.: Ascension, 2001); Barbara Rossing, *The Rapture Exposed: The Message of Hope in the Book of Revelation* (Boulder: Westview, 2004); Gary DeMar, *End Times Fiction: A Biblical Consideration of the Left Behind Theology* (Nashville: Thomas Nelson, 2001).

12. Paul S. Boyer, "John Darby Meets Saddam Hussein: Foreign Policy and Bible Prophecy," *Chronicle of Higher Education*, February 14, 2003.

13. Robert N. Bellah, "Civil Religion in America," *Daedalus: Journal of the American Academy of Arts and Sciences* 96, no. 1 (1967): 1–21.

14. John Wiley Nelson, *Your God Is Alive and Well and Appearing in Popular Culture* (Philadelphia: Westminster, 1976), 19–21. Several paragraphs in this section on popular theology are revised and adapted from Bruce David Forbes, "Battling the Dark Side: *Star Wars* and Popular Understandings of Evil," *Word & World* 19, no. 4 (Fall 1999): 352–56.

15. Joseph Campbell, *The Hero with a Thousand Faces* (New York: Meridian, 1956), 30. Also quoted in Robert Jewett and John Shelton Lawrence, *The American Monomyth*, (Garden City, N.Y.: Anchor, 1977), xix.

16. Jewett and Lawrence, *American Monomyth*, xx.

17. Ibid.

18. Nelson, *Your God Is Alive*, 31–32. Much of Nelson's analysis of the western genre is based upon John G. Cawelti, *The Six-Gun Mystique* (Bowling Green, Ohio: Bowling Green State University Popular Press, 1970).

19. Nelson, *Your God Is Alive*, 32.

20. Les Daniels, *Comix: A History of Comic Books in America* (New York: Bonanza Books, 1971), 11, quoted in John Shelton Lawrence and Robert Jewett, *The Myth of the American Superhero* (Grand Rapids: Eerdmans, 2002), 42.

21. See also Bruce David Forbes, "Batman Crucified: Religion and Modern Comic Book Superheroes," *Media Development* 4 (1997): 10–12.

22. Quoted by Les Daniels in *DC Comics: Sixty Years of the World's Favorite Comic Book Heroes* (Boston: Little, Brown, 1995), 58. Marston wrote an article about his involvement with comic books for the *American Scholar*, a Phi Beta Kappa publication.

23. This summary is slightly revised from Bruce David Forbes, "How Popular Are the Left Behind Books . . . and Why? A Discussion of Popular Culture," in Forbes and Kilde, *Rapture*, 24, and influenced by the writings of Jewett and Lawrence.

24. See Amy Johnson Frykholm, "The Gender Dynamics of the Left Behind Series," in Bruce David Forbes and Jeffrey H. Mahan, eds., *Religion and Popular Culture in America*, rev. ed. (Berkeley: University of California Press, 2005), 270–87.

## Chapter Nine. Catholics in China

1. On this issue, see the excellent article by Geoffrey King, "A Schismatic Church? A Canonical Evaluation," in Edmond Tang and Jean-Paul Wiest, eds., *The Catholic Church in Modern China: Perspectives* (Maryknoll, N.Y.: Orbis, 1993), 80–102. An explicit decree of excommunication was issued to the vicar general of Nanjing,

Li Weiguang, for publishing a declaration promoting the Communist interpretation of the three autonomies and accusing the pope and his nuncio of collusion with the imperialists. This excommunication, however, took place before Li's ordination as a bishop without Rome's approval.

2. For more on this question, see Kim-Kwong Chan, *Towards a Contextual Ecclesiology: The Catholic Church in the People's Republic of China (1979–1983), Its Life and Theological Implications* (Hong Kong: Chinese Church Research Center, 1987), 81–82, 443–48. Chan also points out that leaders of the so-called patriotic church were careful in their use of expressions. They "usually employed terms like 'Roman Curia' and 'the Vatican' instead of terms like 'the Holy See' or 'the Apostolic See.' The former denotes political status whereas the latter terms signify the religious and ecclesiastical dimension" (79).

3. Pope John Paul II in Manila, 1995.

4. See statement on the website for the Embassy of the People's Republic of China in the Republic of Zimbabwe: http://zw.china-embassy.org/eng/xwdt/t148718.htm.

5. Letter of the Holy Father Pope Benedict XVI to the Bishops, Priests, Consecrated Persons and Lay Faithful of the Catholic Church in the People's Republic of China is available on the Vatican site at www.vatican.va/holy_father/benedict_xvi /letters/2007/documents/hf_ben_xvi_let_20070527_china.

## Chapter Ten. Existential Ritualizing in Postmodern Sweden

1. This quote comes from a pilot study of how medical professionals in Sweden, especially in psychiatry, are identifying and understanding the kinds of existential challenges that exist in ordinary people's lives in contemporary Sweden. Initial mention of the study and more of the clinical analysis concerning existential function and dysfunction can be found in Valerie DeMarinis, "Existential Dysfunction as a Public Mental Health Issue for Post-Modern Sweden: A Cultural Challenge and a Challenge to Culture," in *Tro på teatret: Essays om religion og teater*, ed. Bent Holm (Copenhagen: Copenhagen University Press, 2006), 240–41.

2. All of these terms are discussed in Valerie DeMarinis, *Pastoral Care, Existential Health and Existential Epidemiology: A Swedish Postmodern Case Study* (Stockholm: Verbum, 2003).

3. Ronald Inglehart, "Mapping Global Values," in Yilmaz Esmer and Thorleif Pettersson, eds., *Measuring and Mapping Cultures: 25 Years of Comparative Value Surveys* (Leiden: Brill, 2007), 16.

4. Ibid.

5. Thorleif Pettersson, "Religion in Contemporary Society: Eroded by Human Well-being, Supported by Cultural Diversity," in Esmer and Pettersson, *Measuring*, 146.

6. The following books provide excellent overviews of the Church of Sweden's history, its changes at the end of the twentieth century, and its transition period: Sören Ekström, *Svenska kyrkan i förändring* [The Church of Sweden in Transition] (Stockholm: Verbum, 1999); Anders Bäckström, *Svenska kyrkan som välfärdsaktör I en global kultur: En studie av religion och omsorg* [The Church of Sweden as a Welfare Actor in a Global Culture: A Study of Religion and Social Care] (Stockholm, Verbum, 2001).

7. Pippa Norris and Ronald Inglehart, *Sacred and Secular: Religion and Politics Worldwide* (Cambridge: Cambridge University Press, 2004), 75.

8. See Önver Cetrez, *Meaning-Making Variations in Acculturation and Ritualization: A Multi-Generational Study of Suroyo Migrants in Sweden* (Uppsala: Uppsala University Press, 2005).

9. See, for example, Arthur Kleinman, *Patients and Healers in the Context of Culture* (Berkeley: University of California Press, 1980).

10. DeMarinis, *Pastoral Care*, 126. This young man's situation represents one type of existential worldview existing in Sweden at the current time. For more information on existential worldviews in Sweden, see DeMarinis, *Pastoral Care*, which was part of a nationally funded research study on changing patterns of religiosity, spirituality, and the welfare state in Sweden at the beginning of the twenty-first century.

11. A thorough presentation of the Sann Människa group can be found in the following theoretically and contextually rich doctoral dissertation in psychology of religion and ritual studies: Maria Liljas, *Ritual Invention: A Play Perspective on Existential Ritual and Mental Health in Late Modern Sweden* (Uppsala: Uppsala University Press, 2005).

12. A thorough presentation of feminist liturgies in Sweden is found in this well-documented and multidisciplinary doctoral dissertation in church history: Ninna Edgardh Beckman, *Feminism och liturgi: En ecklesiologisk studie* [Feminist Liturgy: An Ecclesiological Study] (Uppsala: Uppsala University Press, 2000). Three related articles in English by the same author on this topic are "The Theology of Gathering and Sending: A Challenge from Feminist Liturgy," *International Journal for the Study of the Christian Church* 6, no. 2 (2006): 144–65; "Lady Wisdom as Hostess for the Lord's Supper: Sofia-Mässor in Stockholm, Sweden," in *Dissident Daughters: Feminist Liturgies in Global Context*, ed. Teresa Berger (Louisville, Ky.: Westminster John Knox, 2001); and, "The Relevance of Gender in Rites of Ordination," in *Rites of Ordination and Commitment in the Churches of the Nordic Countries: Theology and Terminology*, ed. Hans Raun Iversen (Copenhagen: University of Copenhagen, Museum Tusculanum Press, 2006).

13. An important multigenerational study of this population is found in Cetrez, *Meaning-Making Variations*, a doctoral dissertation in psychology of religion, cultural psychology, and acculturation studies.

14. See F. Deniz, *En minoritets odyssey: Upprätthållande och transformation av etnisk identitet I förhållande till moderniseringsprocessor: Det assyriska exemplet* [An Odyssey of a Minority: Maintenance and Transformation of Ethnic Identity in Relation to the Processes of Modernization: The Assyrian Example] (Uppsala: Uppsala University Press, 1999); ibid.

15. Deniz, *En minoritets odyssey*.

16. Cetrez, *Meaning-Making Variations*, 29.

17. Ibid., 30.

18. A. Bredström, "Gendered Racism and the Production of Cultural Difference: Media Representations and Identity Work among 'Immigrant Youth' in Contemporary Sweden," *NORA* 11 (2003): 82.

19. Cetrez, *Meaning-Making Variations*, 311–12.

20. DeMarinis, *Pastoral Care*, 126.

21. See I. Kickbush, "The Contribution of the World Health Organization to a New Public Health and Health Promotion," *American Journal of Public Health* 93, no. 3 (2003): 383. For a discussion of an application in the Swedish context see DeMarinis, "Existential Dysfunction."

## Chapter Eleven. Ordinary Christians and the Holocaust

1. Marlies Flesch-Thebesius, *Zu den Aussenseitern gestellt: Die Geschichte der Gertrud Staewen 1894–1987* (Berlin: Wichern, 2004), 209.

2. Susannah Heschel, "When Jesus Was an Aryan," in Robert P. Ericksen and Susannah Heschel, eds., *Betrayal: German Churches and the Holocaust* (Minneapolis: Fortress Press, 1999), 70–71.

3. Dietrich Bonhoeffer, *Letters and Papers from Prison*, enl. ed. (New York: Macmillan Collier Books, 1971), 300; translation revised.

4. Several works that explore this are Christopher Browning, *Ordinary Men: Reserve Police Battalion 101 and the Final Solution in Poland* (New York: HarperCollins, 1992); Robert Gellately, *The Gestapo and German Society: Enforcing Racial Policy, 1933–1945* (New York: Oxford University Press, 1990); and Peter Haas, *Morality after Auschwitz: The Radical Challenge of the Nazi Ethic* (Philadelphia: Fortress Press, 1988).

5. Peter Fritsche, *Germans into Nazis* (Cambridge: Harvard University Press, 1998), 8.

6. See Victoria J. Barnett, *Bystanders: Conscience and Complicity during the Holocaust* (Westport, Conn.: Greenwood, 1999), esp. chap. 1. For how this was experienced by German Jews, see Marion Kaplan, *Between Dignity and Despair: Jewish Life in Nazi Germany* (New York: Oxford University Press, 1998).

7. Matthew Hockenos, *A Church Divided: German Protestants Confront the Nazi Past* (Bloomington: Indiana University Press), 187.

8. Works that cover this research include Ericksen and Heschel, *Betrayal*; Wolfgang Gerlach, *And the Witnesses Were Silent: The Confessing Church and the Jews* (Lincoln: University of Nebraska Press, 2000); Doris Bergen, *Twisted Cross: The German Christian Movement in the Third Reich* (Chapel Hill: University of North Carolina Press, 1996); and Kevin Spicer, ed., *Anti-Semitism, Christian Ambivalence, and the Holocaust* (Bloomington: Indiana University Press, 2007).

9. Claudia Koonz, *The Nazi Conscience* (Cambridge: Belknap, 2003), 13.

10. Cited in Victoria Barnett, *For the Soul of the People: Protestant Protest against Hitler* (New York: Oxford University Press, 1992), 32.

11. Ibid., 128.

12. See Bergen, *Twisted Cross*, esp. chap. 4.

13. An English translation of the Barmen Declaration is in Hockenos, *A Church Divided*, 179–81.

14. Barnett, *For the Soul of the People*, 142.

15. Ibid., 129.

16. For Catholic Church examples, see Michael Phayer, *The Catholic Church and the Holocaust, 1930–1965* (Bloomington: Indiana University Press, 2000), esp. chap. 7. For Protestant examples, see Barnett, *For the Soul of the People*, esp. chaps. 6 and 7.

17. See Barnett, *For the Soul of the People*, chap. 7; and Flesch-Thebesius, *Zu den Aussenseitern gestellt*.

18. See John Conway, "Between Pacifism and Patriotism—A Protestant Dilemma: the Case of Friedrich Siegmund-Schultze," in Francis Nicosia and Lawrence Stokes, eds., *Germans against Nazism: Nonconformity, Opposition and Resistance in the Third Reich* (New York: Berg, 1990), 87–114.

19. See Ute Gerdes, *Ökumenische Solidarität mit christlichen und jüdischen Verfolgten: Die CIMADE in Vichy-Frankreich, 1940–1944* (Göttingen: Vandenhoeck & Ruprecht, 2005); Klemens von Klemperer, *German Resistance against Hitler: The Search for Allies Abroad* (New York: Oxford University Press, 1992); and John J. Michalszyk, ed. *Resisters, Rescuers and Refugees: Historical and Ethical Issues* (Kansas City: Sheed and Ward, 1996).

20. Samuel and Pearl Oliner, *The Altruistic Personality* (New York: Free Press, 1988), 155.

21. Ibid., 249.

22. Carol Rittner, Stephen D. Smith, and Irena Steinfeldt, eds., *The Holocaust and the Christian World* (London: Kuperard, 2000), 113.

23. Ibid., 109.

24. Jan Gross, *Fear: Anti-Semitism in Poland after Auschwitz* (New York: Random House, 2006).

25. The most famous cases were Gerhard Kittel, Paul Althaus, and Emanuel Hirsch. See Robert P. Ericksen, *Theologians under Hitler* (New Haven: Yale University Press, 1985).

26. The text of the Seelisberg document can be found on the website of the International Council of Christians and Jews, http://www.jcrelations.net/en/?item=983.

27. Two articles on the Seelisberg meeting can be found in the winter 2008 edition of the online journal *Studies in Christian-Jewish Relations*, http://escholarship.bc.edu /scjr/.

## Chapter Twelve. Ecumenism of the People

1. From William Temple's sermon at his enthronement as archbishop, cited in F. A. Iremonger, *William Temple, Archbishop of Canterbury: His Life and Letters* (London: Oxford University Press, 1948), 387.

2. Joan Chittister, *In Search of Belief* (Liguori, Mo.: Liguori/Triumph, 1999), 12.

3. Chilstrom has reported this story to me personally.

4 For comprehensive and succinct information, and for guidance to other literature, see Nicholas Lossky, José Miguez Bonino, John Pobee, Tom F. Stransky, Geoffrey Wainwright, and Pauline Webb, *Dictionary of the Ecumenical Movement*, 2nd ed. (Geneva: World Council of Churches, 2003).

5. Robert S. Bilheimer, *Breakthrough: The Emergence of the Ecumenical Tradition* (Grand Rapids: Eerdmans, 1989), 4.

6. The *Reader's Digest* attacks were published in October 1971, August 1982, and February 1993.

7. Robert S. Bilheimer, quoted (anonymously) in Patrick Henry and Thomas F. Stransky, C.S.P., *God on Our Minds* (Philadelphia: Fortress Press; Collegeville, Minn.: Liturgical, 1982), 21.

8. Quoted in Esther Byle Bruland, *Regathering: The Church from "They" to "We"* (Grand Rapids: Eerdmans, 1995), 100.

9. Margaret O'Gara, *The Ecumenical Gift Exchange* (Collegeville, Minn.: Liturgical, 1998), x.

10. *Ecumenism Among Us: Report of a Cross-Generational Conversation about the Unity of the Church and the Renewal of Human Community*, June 4–8, 1994, Saint John's University, Collegeville, Minnesota (Collegeville, Minn.: Institute for Ecumenical and Cultural Research, 1994), 1.3; see also http://www.collegevilleinstitute.org. The report weaves together things that were said and written by participants, and it is to first-person statements that reference is here made. The report itself includes permission for quotation and even reproduction.

11. Patrick Henry, "The Singapore Faith and Order Consultation, November 1986," *Mid-Stream* 26, no. 2 (April 1987): 248–53

12. *Ecumenism Among Us*, 1.3.

13. Ibid., 1.2.

14. Ibid.

15. Ibid., 1.3.

16. Ibid., 2.1

17. Ibid., 2.2.

18. Ibid.

19. Ibid., 2.4.

20. Ibid., 3.1.

21. Ibid., 3.2

22. Ibid., 3.5.

23. Ibid., 4.5, 4.4.

24. *Baptism, Eucharist, and Ministry*, Faith and Order Paper No. 111 (Geneva: World Council of Churches, 1982).

25. Lukas Vischer, "The Convergence Texts on Baptism, Eucharist and Ministry: How Did They Take Shape? What Have They Achieved?" *Ecumenical Review* 54, no. 4 (October 2002): 431–54, quotation at 434.

26. *Ecumenism Among Us*, 4.6.

27. Vischer, "Convergence Texts," 442–43, citing "Louisville Consultation on Baptism," Faith and Order paper No. 97, *Review and Expositor: A Baptist Theological Journal* 72, no. 1 (1980): 6.

28. Vischer, "Convergence Texts," 445–46.

29. For a more extensive discussion of the significance of *Divino afflante spiritu*, see Patrick Henry, *New Directions in New Testament Study* (Philadelphia: Westminster, 1979), chap. 10, "The Apostolic Book and the Apostolic See," 225–40.

30. *Ecumenism Among Us*, 3.3.

31. Henry and Stransky, *God on Our Minds*, 6.

32. *Ecumenism Among Us*, 4.2.

33. Ibid., 2.6.

34. Cited in the foreword to Imogene Blatz, O.S.B., and Alard Zimmer, O.S.B., *Threads from Our Tapestry: Benedictine Women in Central Minnesota* (St. Cloud, Minn.: North Star, 1994), xi.

35. Kathleen Norris, *The Cloister Walk* (New York: Riverhead Books, 1996), xv.

36. *Ecumenism Among Us*, 5.3.

37. This section draws on Patrick Henry, "Reconciling Memories: Building an Ecumenical Future," *Ecumenical Trends*, 26, no. 4 (April 1997): 1–8.

38. Edited by Patricia Klein, Evelyn Bence, Jane Campbell, and David Wimbish (Grand Rapids: Revell, 2003).

39. Keith F. Nickle and Timothy F. Lull, eds., *A Common Calling: The Witness of Our Reformation Churches in North America Today* (Minneapolis: Augsburg Fortress Press, 1993), 49–50.

40. Ibid., 54.

41. F. M. Cornford, *Microcosmographia Academica: Being a Guide for the Young Academic Politician* (Cambridge: Bowes & Bowes, 1908), 15.

42. Jaroslav Pelikan, *The Christian Tradition: A History of the Development of Doctrine*, vol. 1, *The Emergence of the Catholic Tradition (100–600)*(Chicago: University of Chicago Press, 1971), 1.

43. *Ecumenism Among Us*, 5.2.

44. Ibid., 1.2.

45. Ibid., 5.2.

46. Ibid., 1.3, 4.4.

47. On "Re-Imagining" see Nancy J. Berneking and Pamela Carter Joern, eds., *Re-Membering and Re-Imagining* (Cleveland: Pilgrim, 1995); and Patrick Henry, *The Ironic Christian's Companion: Finding the Marks of God's Grace in the World* (New York: Riverhead Books, 1999), 160–63.

48. Roberta Grimm and Kathleen S. Hurty, "Prayer, Power, and Action: Church Women United," in *A Tapestry of Justice, Service, and Unity: Local Ecumenism in the United States, 1950–2000*, ed. Arleon L. Kelley (Tacoma, Wash.: National Association of Ecumenical and Interreligious Staff, 2004), 79, citing Margaret M. Schiffert, "Church Women United: On the Dynamic Diagonal," *Ecumenical Trends* 14, no. 4 (April 1985). 55–57.

49. *An Essay on the Development of Christian Doctrine*, 1.1.7 (New York: Image Books, 1960 [1845]), 63.

50. This report, like that of *Ecumenism Among Us*, is available at the Institute's website, http://www.collegevilleinstitute.org.

51. *Ecumenism Among Us*, 2.6, 3.4, 4.5.

52. Henry Chadwick, *The Early Church* (New York: Penguin Books, 1967), 144.

## Chapter Thirteen. Gender and Twentieth-Century Christianity

1. Pauli Murray, *Song in a Weary Throat: An American Pilgrimage* (New York: HarperCollins, 1987), 435.

2. See David Barrett, George Kurian, and Todd M. Johnson, eds., *World Christian Encyclopedia*, vol. 1, *The World by Countries, Religionists, Churches, Ministries*, 2nd ed. (New York: Oxford University Press, 2001), 4, 682–85; Roger Finke and Rodney Stark, *The Churching of America, 1776–2005: Winners and Losers in Our Religious Economy*, 2nd ed. (New Brunswick, N.J.: Rutgers University Press, 2005), 23.

3. Figures cited in Wendy Murray Zoba, "A Woman's Place," *Christianity Today* 44, August 7, 2000, 4.

4. Jane Addams, "The College Woman and the Family Claim," *Commons* 29 (September 1898): 6.

5. Anthony Fletcher, "Beyond the Church: Women's Spiritual Experience at Home and in the Community, 1600–1900," in *Gender and Christian Religion,* ed. R. N. Swanson (Woodbridge, U.K.: Published for the Ecclesiastical Society by Boydell, 1998), 190.

6. Horace Bushnell, *Woman Suffrage: The Reform Against Nature* (New York: Charles Scribner, 1869), 51, 83.

7. "Appeal to the Ladies of the Methodist Episcopal Church," *Heathen Woman's Friend* 1 (1869): 1.

8. Dorothy Hodgson, *The Church of Women: Gendered Encounters between Maasai and Missionaries* (Bloomington: University of Indiana Press, 2005), 180–81, 184.

9. R. W. Battles, "What about Television?" *Sunday School Times*, November 26, 1955, 942.

10. Estelle B. Freedman, *No Turning Back: A History of Feminism and the Future of Women* (New York: Ballantine Books, 2002), 151.

11. Sally Gallagher, *Evangelical Identity and Gendered Family Life* (New Brunswick, N.J.: Rutgers University Press, 2003), 134.

12. See Gary L. Ward, "Introductory Essay: A Survey of the Women's Ordination Issue," in *The Churches Speak On: Women's Ordination*, ed. J. Gordon Melton (Detroit: Gale Research, 1991), xvi–xvii.

13. Ranjini Rebera, "Introduction: Difference and Identity," in *Affirming Difference, Celebrating Wholeness: A Partnership of Equals,* ed. Ranjini Rebera (Hong Kong: Clear-Cut, 1995), 12.

14. Quoted in Constance F. Parvey, "Third World Women and Men: Effects of Cultural Change on Interpretation of Scripture," in John C. B. Webster and Ellen Low Webster, eds., *The Church and Women in the Third World* (Philadelphia: Westminster, 1985), 110.

15. Dorothy Ramobide, "Women and Men Building Together the Church in Africa," in Virginia Fabella, and Mercy Amba Oduyoye, eds., *With Passion and Compassion: Third World Women Doing Theology: Reflections from the Women's Commission of the Ecumenical Association of Third World Theologians* (Maryknoll, N.Y.: Orbis, 1988), 15.

16. Lloyda Fanusie, "Sexuality and Women in African Culture," in Mercy Amba Oduyoye and Musimbi R. A. Kanyoro, eds., *The Will to Arise: Women, Tradition, and the Church in Africa* (Maryknoll, N.Y.: Orbis, 1992), 114.

17. Musimbi R. A. Kanyoro, "Introduction: Background and Genesis," in *In Search of a Round Table: Gender, Theology, and Church Leadership*, ed. Rachel Kanyoro (Geneva: World Council of Churches, 1997), ix–x.

18. Bruce Lawrence, *Defenders of God: The Fundamentalist Revolt against the Modern Age* (San Francisco: Harper & Row, 1989), 2.

19. Elizabeth Brusco, *The Reformation of Machismo: Evangelical Conversion and Gender in Colombia* (Austin: University of Texas Press, 1995).

## Chapter Fourteen. Canadian Workers and Social Justice

1. The author wishes to thank the Social Sciences and Humanities Research Council of Canada for the three-year research grant and one additional summer grant that provided the extensive primary material that shaped this chapter.

2. Gerald Friesen, *The Canadian Prairies* (Toronto: University of Toronto Press, 1984), 327–38; Seymour Martin Lipset, *Agrarian Socialism* (Berkeley: University of California Press, 1971 [1968]), 39–50, 57–94.

3. Alvin Finkel and Margaret Conrad, *History of the Canadian Peoples*, vol. 2, *1867 to the Present* (Toronto: Copp Clark, 1998), 58–60, 72–75, 101–3; Friesen, *Canadian Prairies*, 201–3, 218; Lipset, *Agrarian Socialism*, 39–40; Pierre Berton, *The Promised Land* (Toronto: Penguin Books, 1984), 264, 375–81.

4. Quoted in Alan F. Artibise, *Winnipeg: A Social History of Urban Growth, 1874–1914* (Montreal: McGill-Queens University Press, 1975), 22.

5. Quoted in Kenneth McNaught, *A Prophet in Politics: A Biography of J. S. Woodsworth* (Toronto: University of Toronto Press, 1967 [1959]), 56–57.

6. Richard Allen, *The Social Passion* (Toronto: University of Toronto Press, 1973), 3–34; McClung quoted in Candace Savage, *Our Nell* (Halifax: Formac, 1979), 81–82.

7. Allen, *Social Passion*, 35–54.

8. Kenneth McNaught and David J. Bercuson, *The Winnipeg Strike: 1919* (Don Mills, Ont.: Longman Canada, 1974), 44–100; Norman Penner, ed., *Winnipeg 1919* (Toronto: James Lorimer, 1975), 175; Allen, *Social Passion*, 45–54, 83–103, 159–74; Joan Sangster, "The Making of a Socialist Feminist," *Atlantis* 13, no. 1 (1987): 13–28; Vera Fast, "The Labor Church in Winnipeg," in Dennis Butcher, Catherine Macdonald, and Margaret E. McPherson, eds., *Prairie Spirit: Perspectives on the Heritage of the United Church of Canada in the West* (Winnipeg: University of Manitoba Press, 1985), 233–49.

9. Allen, *Social Passion*, 54–80, 104–47, 170–73; Richard Allen, "Salem Bland and the Spirituality of the Social Gospel," in Butcher, Macdonald, and McPherson, *Prairie Spirit*, 217–32.

10. Lipset, *Agrarian Socialism*, 81, 99–117; Terry Crowley, *Agnes MacPhail* (Toronto: James Lorimer, 1990), 24–127.

11. Terence J. Fay, *A History of Canadian Catholics* (Montreal: McGill-Queens University Press, 2002), 8–13, 15–19, 26.

12. Susan Mann Trofimenkoff, *The Dream of Nation: A Social and Intellectual History of Quebec* (Toronto: Gage Publishing, 1983), 169–75, 198–99, 218–32; Paul-André Linteau, René Durocher, and Jean-Claude Robert, *Quebec, a History, 1867–1929*, trans. Robert Chodos (Toronto: James Lorimer, 1983), 489–95, 535–39, 552; Paul-André Linteau, René Durocher, Jean-Claude Robert, and François Ricard, *Quebec since 1930*, trans. Robert Chodos and Ellen Garmaise (Toronto: James Lorimer, 1991), 1–12, 24, 33–38, 145–50.

13. Fay, *Canadian Catholics*, 206–7, 247–48, 252, 304; Linteau, *Quebec since 1930*, 62; Jean Hamelin and Nicole Gagnon, *Histoire du catholicisme québécois*, vol. 1, *1898–1940* (Montreal: Boréal, 1984), 227–29, 417–19; Jean Hamelin, *Histoire du catholicisme québécois*, vol. 2, *De 1940 à nos jours* (Montreal: Boréal, 1984), 187–88, 359–60; Gregory Baum, *The Church in Quebec* (Ottawa: Novalis, 1991), 67–89.

14. Oscar Cole-Arnal, "Shaping Young Proletarians into Militant Christians: The Pioneer Phase of the JOC in France and Quebec," *Journal of Contemporary History* 32, no. 4 (1992): 509–26; Fay, *Canadian Catholics*, 206, 279; Baum, *The Church*, 70–71; Hamelin and Gagnon, *1898–1940*, 420–25, 431–32; Hamelin, *De 1940*, 64, 68, 72–82, 324–28, 359–61, 374–75.

15. Fay, *Canadian Catholics*, 224, 249–54, 304; Baum, *The Church in Quebec*, 31–32; Trofimenkoff, *The Dream of a Nation*, 197, 228–29, 288–91, 295; Linteau, *1867–1929*, 408–15, 455–56; Linteau, *Quebec Since 1930*, 224–26; Hamelin and Gagnon, *1898–1940*, 215–19, 285–89; Hamelin, *De 1940*, 82–102, 158–60, 243–45.

16. Benoît Fortin, "Quand se lève le soleil de justice," 14–19, in private papers granted to the author for use in research, translated by the author.

17. By far, most of the material described above came from primary sources in French used by the author during research in Quebec, but for a brief sampling, note Hamelin, *De 1940*, 359–62; Baum, *The Church in Quebec*, 44–46, 71–89; Oscar Cole-Arnal, *To Set the Captives Free* (Toronto: Between the Lines, 1998), 140–41, 146–49, 161–62, 176–78.

18. Baum, *The Church in Quebec*, 45, 49–65; Cole-Arnal, *To Set the Captives Free*, 156–58.

## Chapter Fifteen. Popular Catholic Sexual Ethics

1. George Deshon, *Guide for Young Catholic Women, Especially Those Who Earn Their Own Living*, 5th ed. (New York: Catholic Publication House, 1871), 246. The thirty-first edition, published in 1897, appears virtually unchanged except for a few elisions. The last (32nd) edition according to WorldCat is 1899.

2. Gregory K. Popcak, "Exceptional Sex: Your Master Sex," in *The Exceptional Seven Percent: Nine Secrets of the World's Happiest Couples* (New York: Kensington, 2000), 194, 195.

3. Without the inspiration and advice of the following people, this chapter would have been poorer: Mary Bednarowski, Rebecca Davis, Amy Derogatis, R. Marie Griffith, Karla Jo Grimmett, Richard Kieckhefer, Patricia Beattie Jung, Evyatar Marienberg, Susan Ross, Julie Hanlon Rubio. Without Meghan Courtney, my research assistant, it would not have been at all; I only wish I had room to include half of what she found! As always, my family has graciously borne the burden of construction.

4. Leslie Woodcock Tentler, *Catholics and Contraception: An American History* (Ithaca: Cornell University Press, 2004), 5–8, 16–20. Periodic continence was not a popular method of birth control before the 1930s. In the early part of the century the infertile period was thought to fall at the middle of the menstrual cycle; not until the late 1920s was it discovered that this is the most fertile period.

5. Ibid., 31–38, 20–21.

6. This reticence extended to parish preaching and the confessional; priests who preached parish missions (the Catholic equivalent of revivals) faced audiences only once and were more willing to address sexual topics. See Tentler, *Catholics and Contraception*, 23–41.

7. Deshon, *Guide for Young Catholic Women*, 241–42, 243, 295.

8. Tentler, *Catholics and Contraception*, 20.

9. Madame Cecilia, *More Short Spiritual Readings for Mary's Children* (New York: Benziger Brothers, 1910), 33.

10. Deshon, *Guide for Young Catholic Women*, 241.

11. Tentler, *Catholics and Contraception*, 23.

12. Deshon, *Guide for Young Catholic Women*, 247.

13. Ibid., 245.

14. Cecelia, *Spiritual Readings*, 31.

15. Tentler, *Catholics and Contraception*, 106–22. For an admittedly rare example of contemporary opposition to natural family planning, rhythm's still more precise successor, see Michael Dimond, O.S.B., and Peter Dimond, O.S.B., "Natural Family Planning Is Evil," http://www.mostholyfamilymonastery.com/Natural_Family_Planning.html.

16. David Lodge, *The British Museum Is Falling Down* (New York: Penguin, 1981 [1965]).

17. Raoul Plus, S.J., *Facing Life: Meditations for Young Women* (n.p. [Maryland]: The Newman Press, 1960), 52.

18. Ibid., 135.

19. Camillo Zamboni, *Jesus Speaks to You* (Boston: Daughters of St. Paul, 1961).

20. Gerald Kelly, S.J., *Modern Youth and Chastity* (St. Louis: The Queen's Work, 1941), 82.

21. Joseph E. Haley, C.S.C., *Accent on Purity: Guide for Sex Education* (Chicago: Fides, 1957), 35–36; editions seem to range from 1948 to 1960.

22. C. Kevin Gillespie, S.J., *Psychology and American Catholicism: From Confession to Therapy?* (New York: Crossroad, 2001), 102–3.

23. Alphonse Clemens, *Marriage and the Family: An Integrated Approach for Catholics* (Englewood Cliffs, N.J.: Prentice-Hall, 1957), 196–98, 190. Clemens's source, R. De Guchteneere, cited multiple sources from the late nineteenth and early twentieth centuries who warned that the substances women absorb from semen are essential to their physical and psychological health; both remained silent on the psychological dangers this theory implies for celibate women (see R. De Guchteneere, *Judgement on Birth Control* [New York: Macmillan, 1931], 155–60).

24. François Dantec, *Love Is Life: A Catholic Marriage Handbook* (Notre Dame, Ind.: University of Notre Dame Press, 1963), 4.

25. Haley, *Accent on Purity*, 24.

26. Clemens, *Marriage and the Family*, 199.

27. Ibid., 189.

28. Ibid., 1.

29. Audrey Kelly, *A Catholic Parent's Guide to Sex Education* (New York: Hawthorn, 1962).

30. Ibid., 190–98.

31. T. W. Burke, *The Gold Ring: God's Pattern for Perfect Marriage* (New York: David McKay, 1963), 72.

32. Clemens, *Marriage and the Family*, 189.

33. Herbert Doms, *The Meaning of Marriage*, trans. George Sayer (New York: Sheed & Ward, 1939), xix, quoting Linsermann (1878).

34. Clemens, *Marriage and the Family*, 189–90.

35. Ibid., 185.

36. G. Flamand, "The Scope of Marriage," in *Marriage Is Holy*, ed. H. Caffarel, trans. Bernard Murchland (Notre Dame, Ind.: Fides, 1963 [1957], 21–33, quotation at 25.

37. Burke, *Gold Ring*, 71–72.

38. Tentler, *Catholics and Contraception*, 266.

39. Gregory K. Popcak, *For Better . . . Forever! A Catholic Guide to Lifelong Marriage* (Huntington, Ind.: Our Sunday Visitor, 1999), 199.

40. Mary Beth Bonacci, *Real Love: Mary Beth Bonacci Answers Your Questions on Dating, Marriage, and the Real Meaning of Sex* (San Francisco: Ignatius, 1996); Christopher West, *Good News about Sex and Marriage: Answers to Your Honest Questions about Catholic Teaching* (Cincinnati: Servant Books, 2000); Gregory K. Popcak, *Beyond the Birds and the Bees* (Huntington, Ind.: Our Sunday Visitor, 2001); Gregory K. Popcak, *The Exceptional Seven Percent: Nine Secrets of the World's Happiest Couples* (New York: Kensington, 2000); Popcak, *For Better*.

41. Bonacci, *Real Love*, 26–27.

42. Popcak, *For Better*, 212, emphasis in original.

43. Ibid., 203.

44. West, *Good News*, 40.

45. Popcak, *For Better*, 31.

46. Popcak, *Beyond the Birds and the Bees*, 24.

47. Bonacci, *Real Love*, 81, 36.

48. West, *Good News*, 67.

49. Ibid., 112.

50. Bonacci, *Real Love*, 147.

51. Ibid., 33.

52. Ibid., 77.

53. Popcak, *Beyond the Birds and the Bees*, 54.

54. Bonacci, *Real Love*, 74.

55. West, *Good News*, 17.

56. Bonacci, *Real Love*, 38.

57. Ibid., 85.

58. Ibid., 35.

59. Bonacci, *Real Love*, 126.

60. Popcak, *Beyond the Birds and the Bees*, 22.

61. West, *Good News*, 20–21, 60.

62. In Popcak (*For Better*), the eucharist is a profound (and for him, unacknowledged homoerotic) experience of orgasmic union with Christ: "Having won his prize, our salvation, [Jesus] gives himself to us completely, body and blood, soul and divinity, through the Most Blessed Sacrament. We draw him close. He enters us. His flesh becomes one with our flesh. His blood courses through our veins. Fearful and eager at once to be completely vulnerable to him, we fall prey to his all-consuming love. Inspired by his passion, nourished by his loving embrace, and propelled by the power of his Holy Spirit alive within us, we enter the world again, refreshed, to do the great work of bringing new children to him through the waters of baptism" (203).

63. West, *Good News*, 109, 114.

64. See Susan A. Ross, "Can God Be a Bride?" *America* 191, no. 13 (November 1, 2004): http://www.americamagazine.org.

65. Bonacci, *Real Love*, 74–75, 126, 116–17.

66. Popcak, *Exceptional*, 194–96, 203.

67. John and Sheila Kippley, *The Art of Natural Family Planning*, 3rd ed. (Cincinnati: Couple to Couple League, 1984 [repr. 1994]), 9–28.

68. Popcak, *Beyond the Birds and the Bees*, 142–43.

69. West, *Good News*, 18.

70. Bonacci, *Real Love*, 32.

71. L. Patrick Carroll, S.J., "Becoming a Celibate Lover," in Mary Anne Huddleston, IHM, ed., *Celibate Loving: Encounter in Three Dimensions* (New York: Paulist, 1984), 111–18, quotation at 112.

72. Donald Georgen, *The Sexual Celibate* (New York: Seabury, 1974).

73. William Kraft, "Celibate Genitality," in Huddleston, *Celibate Loving*, 69–90, quotation at 89.

74. Georgen, *The Sexual Celibate*, 202–3.

75. Lauren F. Winner, *Real Sex: The Naked Truth about Chastity* (Grand Rapids: Brazos, 2005).

76. United States Census Bureau American Fact Finder, see http://factfinder .census.gov; Donald Kerwin, "Immigration Reform and the Catholic Church," *Migration Information Source*, May 2006, see http://www.migrationinformation.org/Feature /display.cfm?id=395; Bruce Murray, "Latino Religion in the U.S.: Demographic Shifts and Trends," FACSNET, January 5, 2006, http://www.facsnet.org/issues/faith/espinosa. php. These figures are based on a population of roughly seventy-five million Catholics (nearly 25 percent of the U.S. population). American Religious Identity Survey (2001), the Graduate Center (CUNY), http://www.gc.cuny.edu/faculty/research_briefs/aris /key_findings.htm. The survey queried adults age eighteen and older; the calculation above assumes that roughly the same percentages hold for children under eighteen.

## Chapter Sixteen. Life and Death in Middle America

1. Philip Hefner, *Technology and Human Becoming*, Theology and the Sciences (Minneapolis: Fortress Press, 2003), 63.

2. I teach theology at a small liberal arts college in Sioux Falls, South Dakota. I'm also privileged to be part of the Section for Ethics and Humanities at the University of South Dakota School of Medicine. What I have learned from living at this intersection of medicine and religion is that the challenges raised by medical science and technology raise profound questions about what it means to be a human person. These questions are fundamental to the human story. And people tell stories to make sense of their lives. The following reflections on these questions about human personhood are told from local anecdotes and experiences, but I hope that their universal application will become apparent as this chapter unfolds.

3. This story was shared with me by a health care administrator. The retrieval of gametes after death has become a controversial issue for both the families of the patients and health care providers.

4. John D. Lantos, *The Lazarus Case: Life-and-Death Issues in Neonatal Intensive Care* (Baltimore: John Hopkins University Press, 2001), 98.

5. "For better or worse, decisions at the end of life seem to be made as communal decisions rather than individual ones, with the patient's voice among many. The goal

in these discussions for both doctors and patients seems to be a little different from the goal initially imagined by lawyers and bioethicists. It is not simply to empower the dying patient against the doctor. Instead, it is to achieve some semblance of family moral harmony, some course of action that violates neither the values of the dying patient nor the values of the survivors, who must live with the memory of the action." Lantos, *The Lazarus Case*, 97.

6. See U.S. Census information at http://quickfacts.census.gov/qfd/states/46000 .html.

7. See http://www.state.sd.us/factpage.htm.

8. Ibid.

9. Ibid.

10. http://www.siouxvalley.org; http://www.avera.org.

11. William Colby, *Long Goodbye: The Deaths of Nancy Cruzan* (Carlsbad, Calif.: Hay House, 2002), 9.

12. Ibid.

13. Steve Young. "Group's Goal: Dying Better, " in "A Time to Die," *Argus Leader*, December 22, 2002.

14. Lantos, *The Lazarus Case*, 15–17.

15. Ibid., 17.

16. "Respect for Human Life" can be found on the Vatican's website, http://www .vatican.va; (the UCC's statement can be found at http://www.ucc.org/justice/choice; the ELCA's statement can be found at http://www.elca.org/dcs.abortion.htm.

17. See http://www.elca.org/dcs./abortion/html.

18. Ibid.

19. See http://www.ucc.org/justice/choice.

20. See http://www.vatican.va.

21. See http://www.augie.edu/dept/biology/Web/faculty/diggins/diggins.html.

22. See http//www.hematech.com.

23. Ibid.

24. Megan Myers, "Doctors Take Sides on Abortion Ban," *Argus Leader*, July 16, 2006.

25. South Dakota State Medical Association Policy Statement, adopted by the Council of Physicians, June 7, 2006.

26. Myers, "Doctors Take Sides."

27. Ibid.

28. See http://www.nativeshop.org/pro-choice.html.

29. Steven Charleston, "The Good, the Bad, and the New: The Native American Missionary Experience," *Dialog* 40, no. 2 (Summer 2001): 103.

30. Ibid.

31. All the names of the students have been changed to maintain anonymity.

# INDEX

*Page numbers in italics indicate images.*